CLOSE-UP

CLOSE-UP

THE COMPLETE GUIDE TO
MACRO PHOTOGRAPHY

MATT DOOGUE
FOREWORD BY CHRIS PACKHAM

ilex

Contents

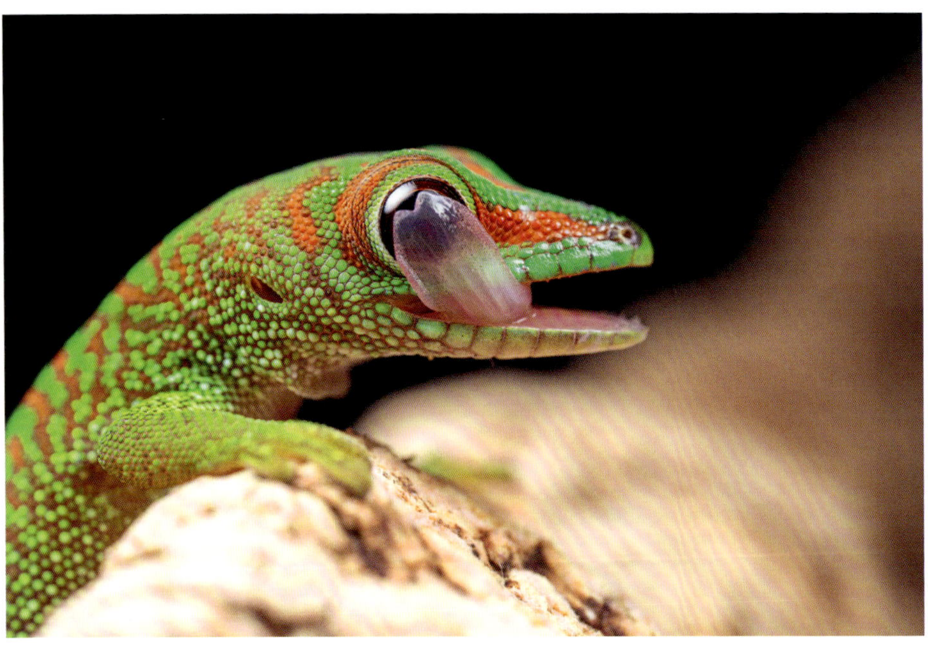

Left A baby giant day gecko gives its eyes a quick wash.

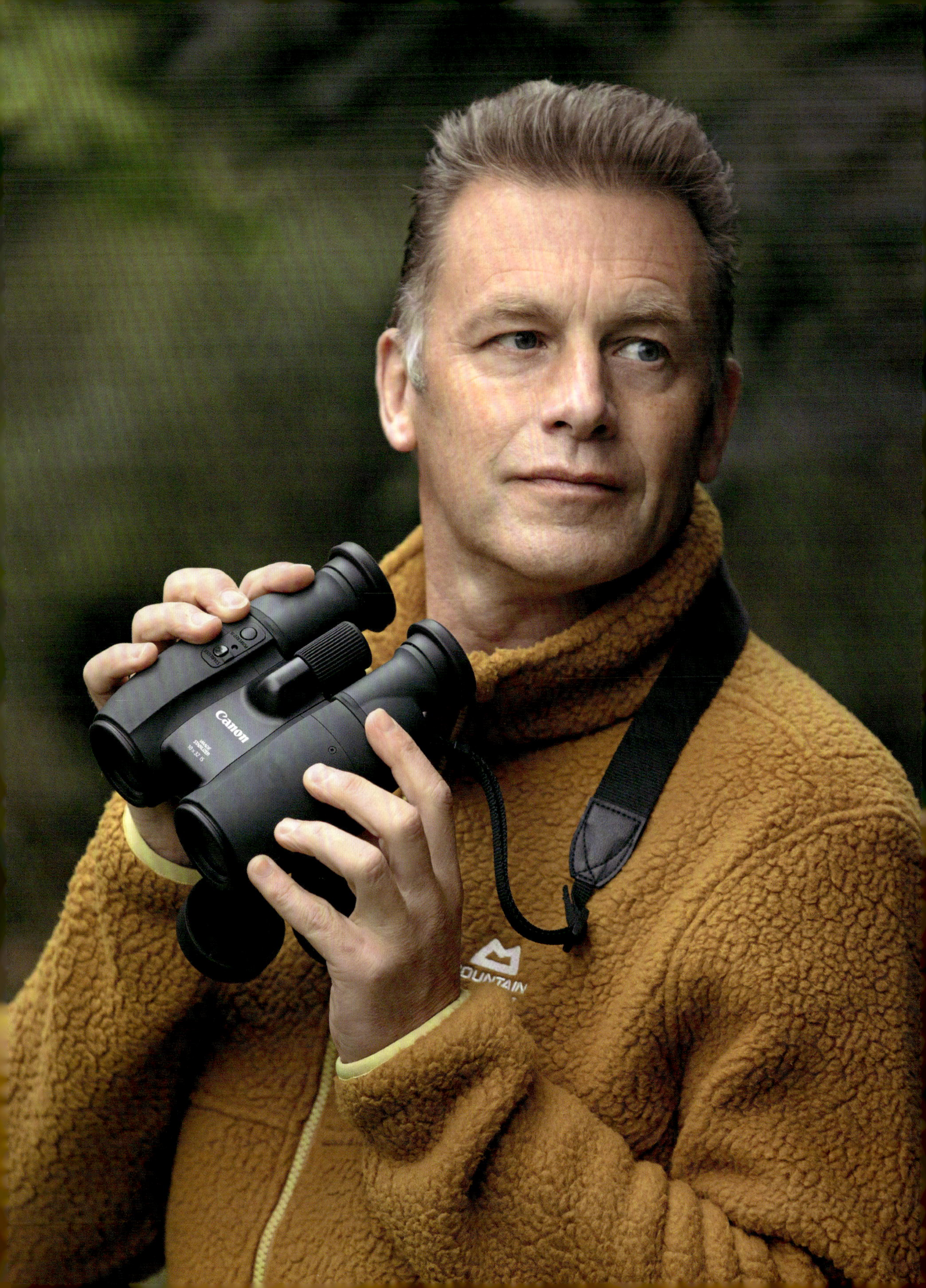
Canon
IMAGE STABILIZER
10 × 32 IS
MOUNTAIN

Foreword by Chris Packham

Brilliant. Complete. Concise. There are few guides that offer such precise and accessible advice when it comes to macro photography. And let's be honest, recent technological developments have radically changed how and what we can do in our living rooms, gardens and local parks. Digital photography and post-capture processing have revolutionized how we can see the natural world. But as Matt's remarkable images show, it's not all about silicon chips and sensors: imagination and creativity remain the fundamental keys to making beautiful photographs.

The human eye is, unfortunately, limited, especially when it comes to seeing things in extreme close-up. This physical limitation also becomes a handicap when it comes to understanding and appreciating the miniature organisms that truly make our world go round. Little creatures are sadly still referred to as 'creepy crawlies' or collectively as 'bugs' and such negative stereotyping is harmful – considering the next word in this outdated vernacular would be 'pest'. Ecologically speaking, however, the multitudes of these tiny species are essential to the maintenance and survival of all life on earth. So it is important that we learn to love the little things.

To achieve that, we must learn to engage with them – and there is no better way than photography. When you see the 'wow' factor; the striking, sometimes almost unbelievable physical appearance; the character and personality of these species captured in close-up, it can draw us into that alien and otherwise inaccessible world. Matt's innovative and imaginative approach makes celebrities and heroes out of the everyday, the downtrodden and the overlooked. From lichens to spiders, and from ants to snowflakes, his captivating imagery introduces us to another world within our own – and he generously explains how he does it, too! Superb.

– Chris Packham
New Forest, England, 2024

Introduction

Macro photography is a unique genre of photography that reveals a hidden world full of colour, texture and the minute details of subjects up close. This genre allows us to explore our surroundings in a new way and reveal things that normally escape the naked eye. Whether it's the details of a frog's eye, the delicate petals of a flower or even the textures and patterns of an insect's wing, macro photography grants us a special window into this incredible world.

But what is macro photography? It is all about capturing stunning details up close, often starting at a magnification ratio of 1:1 and progressing to 5:1 and beyond. To achieve this, specialist equipment is needed, such as macro lenses, converters, extension tubes and close-up attachments. Extra lighting equipment may also be needed, depending on what techniques you use, how modern your camera is and how creative you want to be.

Macro photography creates a new world of possibilities and allows you to view the world in a way that most people will never see. It is not just confined to living subjects such as arthropods and reptiles, as macro photography can be used to reveal the intricate details of household objects, jewellery and fruit. Some dentists even use macro lenses to capture photos of our teeth, making it a very versatile form of photography.

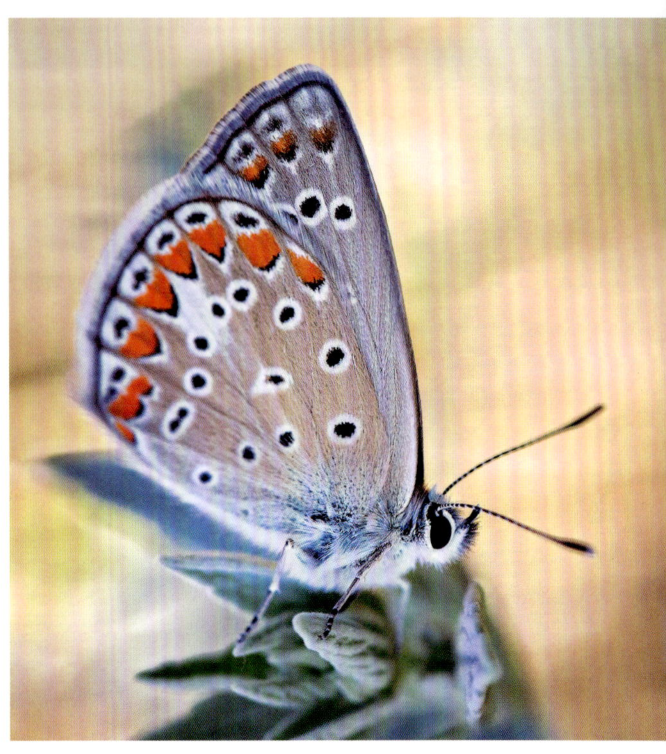

All Macro photography is all about capturing that detail; showcasing amazing and unseen creatures, and patterns that can be found in the most ordinary of places. It's about composition, lighting and exploring a tiny world that often goes unseen.

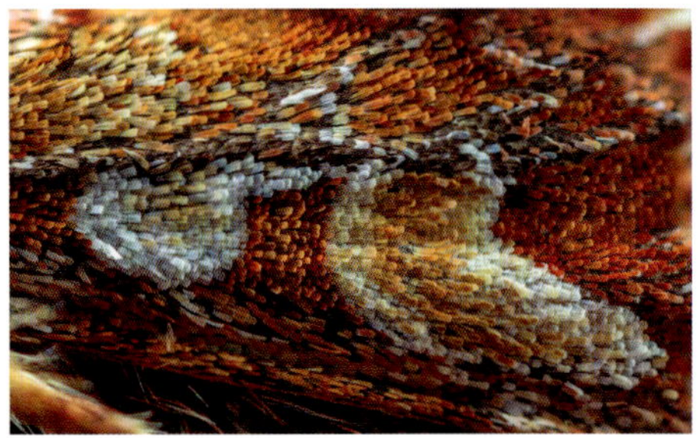

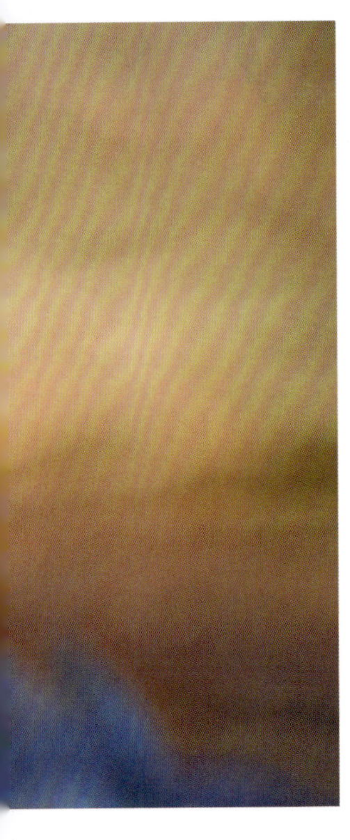

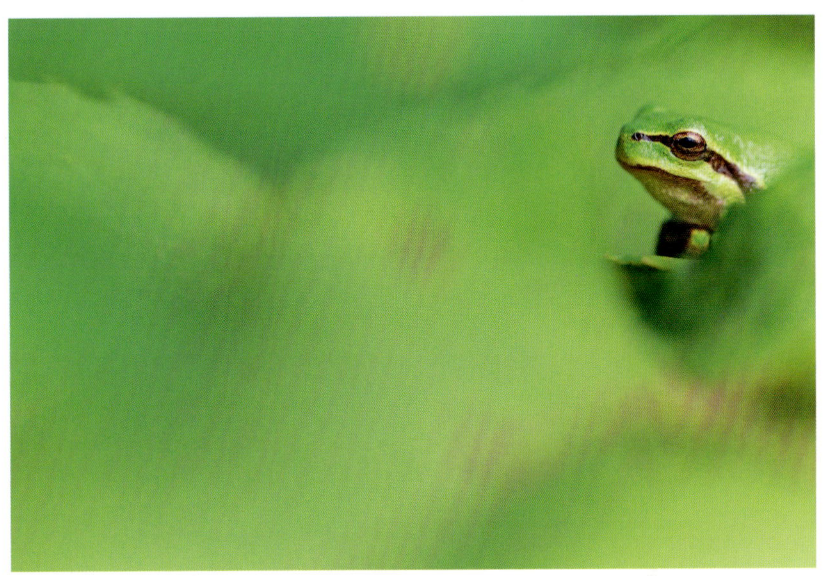

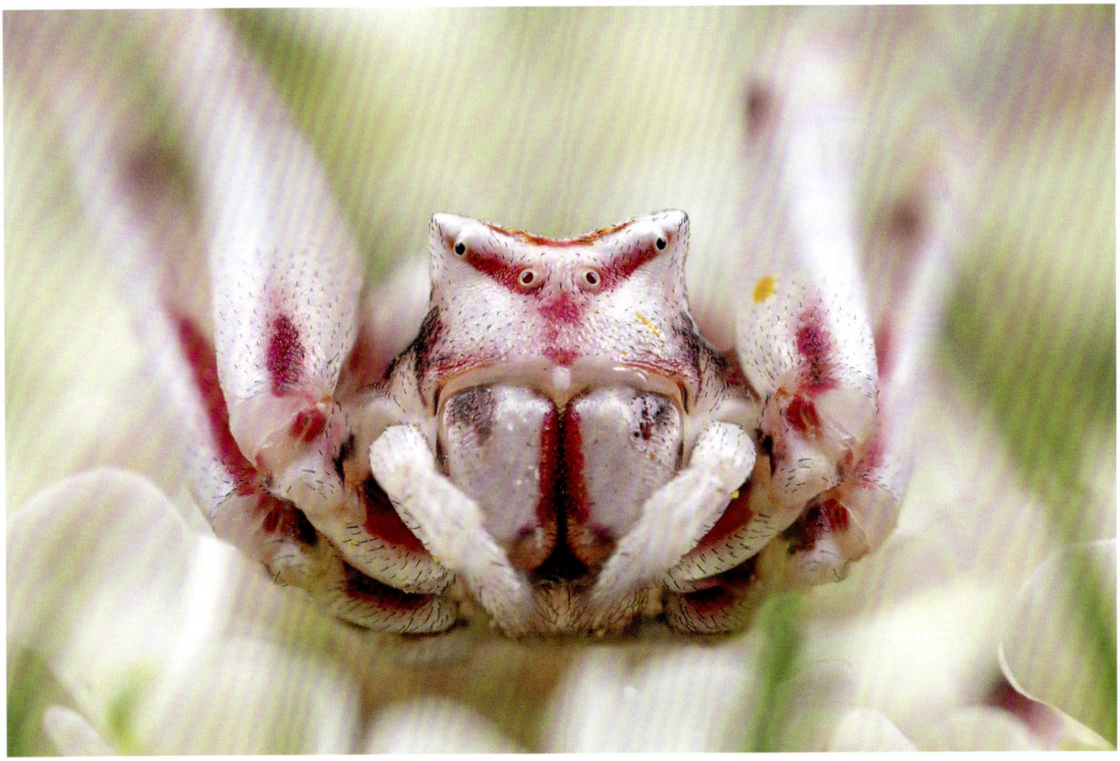

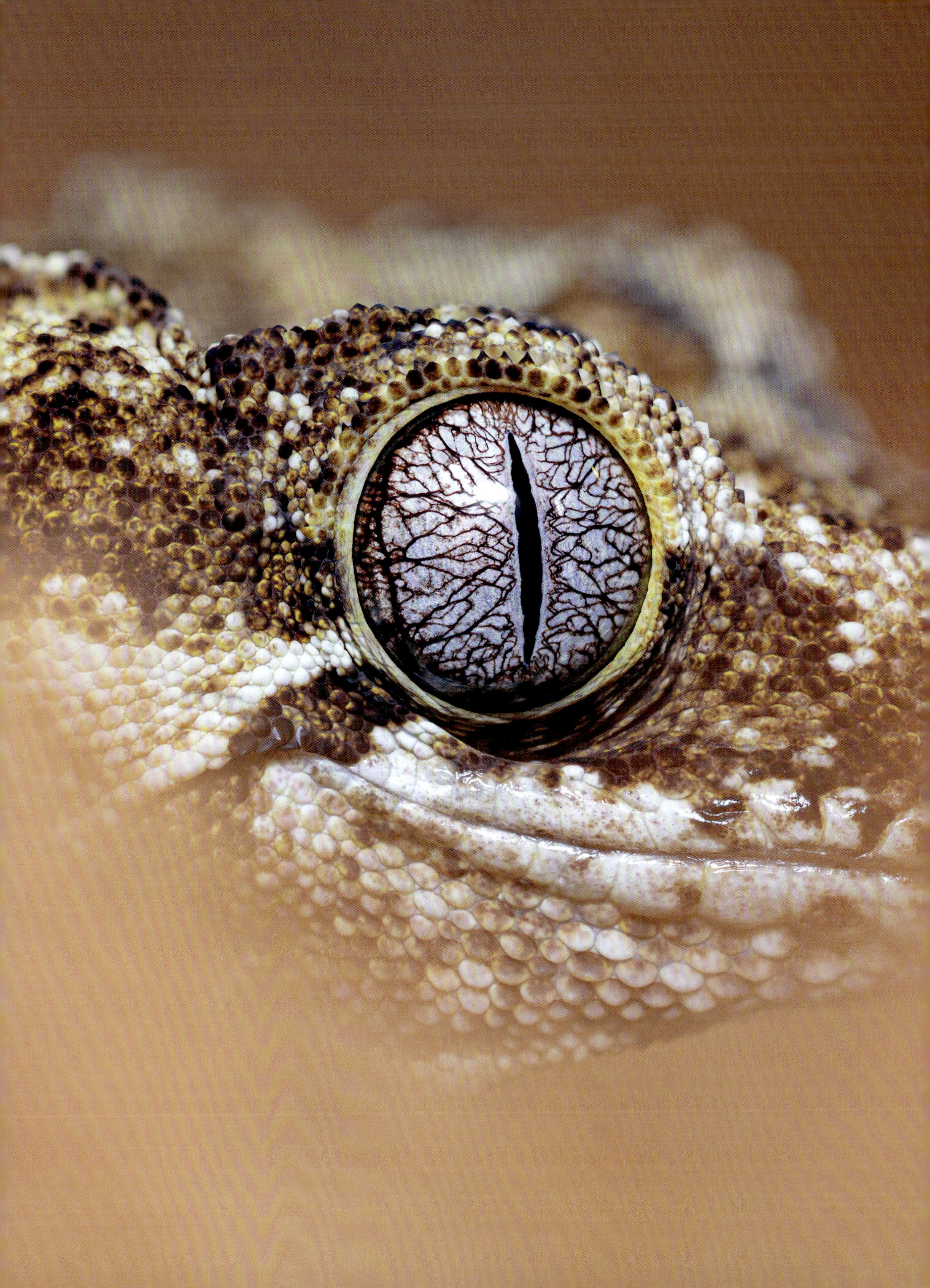

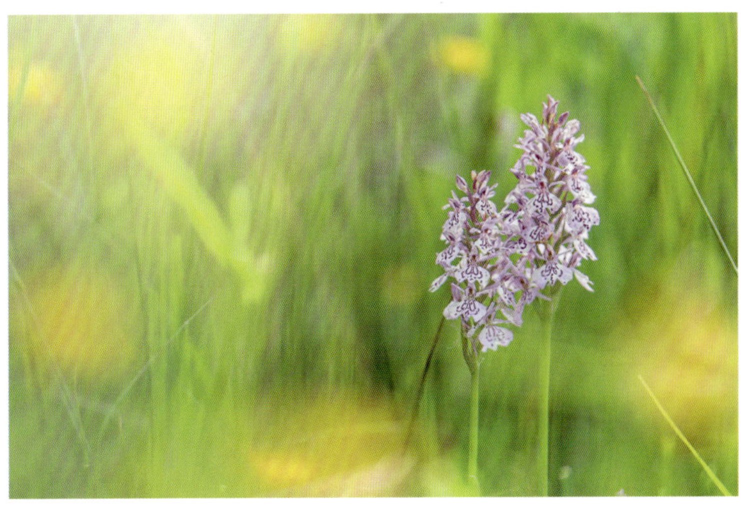

Over the years, the popularity of macro photography has boomed due to social media and online communities. With platforms such as Instagram and Flickr, it's never been easier to share your macro photographs with the rest of the world.

I have been a macro photographer for almost 15 years, and in that time I have learned and practised various techniques. My photography journey didn't start at school or college, but out of a need to occupy my mind and time after a tough mental health breakdown in my early twenties. I started with a cheap DSLR camera, purchased from my uncle, and would take it on hikes in the Peak District National Park. I didn't have a macro lens at the time, just a small kit lens that I would use to photograph the landscape. This is when I began to learn about lighting, composition and various other techniques. Over the years, I developed my understanding of photography and in doing so I opened myself up to trying new genres of photography such as portraiture, architecture, street and wildlife. As I explored these new genres, I found macro.

As a young boy, I was fascinated with the natural world and smaller creatures such as ants and spiders, and now I knew exactly how camera operators got so close on all those natural history documentaries I would watch. It was macro, and I instantly knew this was the genre for me.

Macro is a specialist form of photography and can be quite challenging for beginners. It requires dedicated equipment, patience and persistence but with a little time, practice and this book to guide you, you will be on your way to becoming a skilled macro photographer in no time. Whether you are a complete beginner looking to try macro photography for the first time or a seasoned professional looking to add or learn about new techniques, I hope you will find this book of benefit as you progress in your photographic journey. It will cover the basics of macro photography, as well as advanced techniques such as focus stacking and creative lighting.

Most importantly, this book will guide you not just on technique, but also on wildlife photography ethics and the benefits that nature photography has on our mental wellbeing.

Despite its challenges, this can be an incredibly rewarding form of photography, so remember to have fun and stay curious as you dive into the world of macro. Happy shooting!

What makes macro special?

Macro photography challenges us to see the world we know in a different way. In everyday life we tend to walk past many subjects and take them for granted. In our busy world, rushing from A to B, we rarely stop and take it all in. As a result, we miss so much beauty and wonder, and we forget it's even there.

Think back to when we were children. We didn't have the pressures of life on our shoulders. There were no mobile devices to distract us and no job or family demanding our time. We were free to explore with a rapid desire to discover and with it came a natural curiosity for the world around us. This curiosity can be rekindled at any age and macro photography is perfectly suited to do that.

Macro encourages us to explore all that is around us in new and exciting ways. When we view the world through a macro lens, it's like being offered a free pass into this magical and secret world; we are forced to slow down and appreciate the beauty and complexity of the smallest things. This can be a transformative experience, allowing us to reconnect to the natural world, to rediscover and learn to not only appreciate the life around us, but to also understand it. We begin to realize that a small creature perched on the edge of a flower may have previously seemed insignificant, but through macro photography we can capture its beauty, and realize how crucial these creatures are to our survival. As macro photographers we can begin to highlight the importance of preserving and protecting this incredible flora and fauna through our photographs.

Macro photography teaches us to be patient and observant, qualities you will need in abundance, especially when working with living subjects. This genre requires extreme precision and attention to detail, and you must be willing to take the time to prepare your equipment and wait for the right moment to take your shots. Patience and observation are valuable skills not just for macro photography, but in everyday life as well. As you progress your skills and fieldcraft, you will notice that your woodland walks begin to change as you start to spot macro opportunities along the paths, in the bushes and on the trees.

With so many subjects to explore and a variety of techniques to learn and experiment with, macro photography offers endless creative possibilities, and it can be done pretty much anywhere. Whether you're exploring a local meadow or sitting inside on a rainy day, there are always new opportunities to capture stunning macro shots. From a butterfly's wing to the details of a ballpoint pen, macro photography can capture it all.

Above A springtail on a penny really puts the scale we're working at into perspective.

Right Robber flies are fast-flying predators. Using a longer focal length macro lens helps you get up close from a distance.

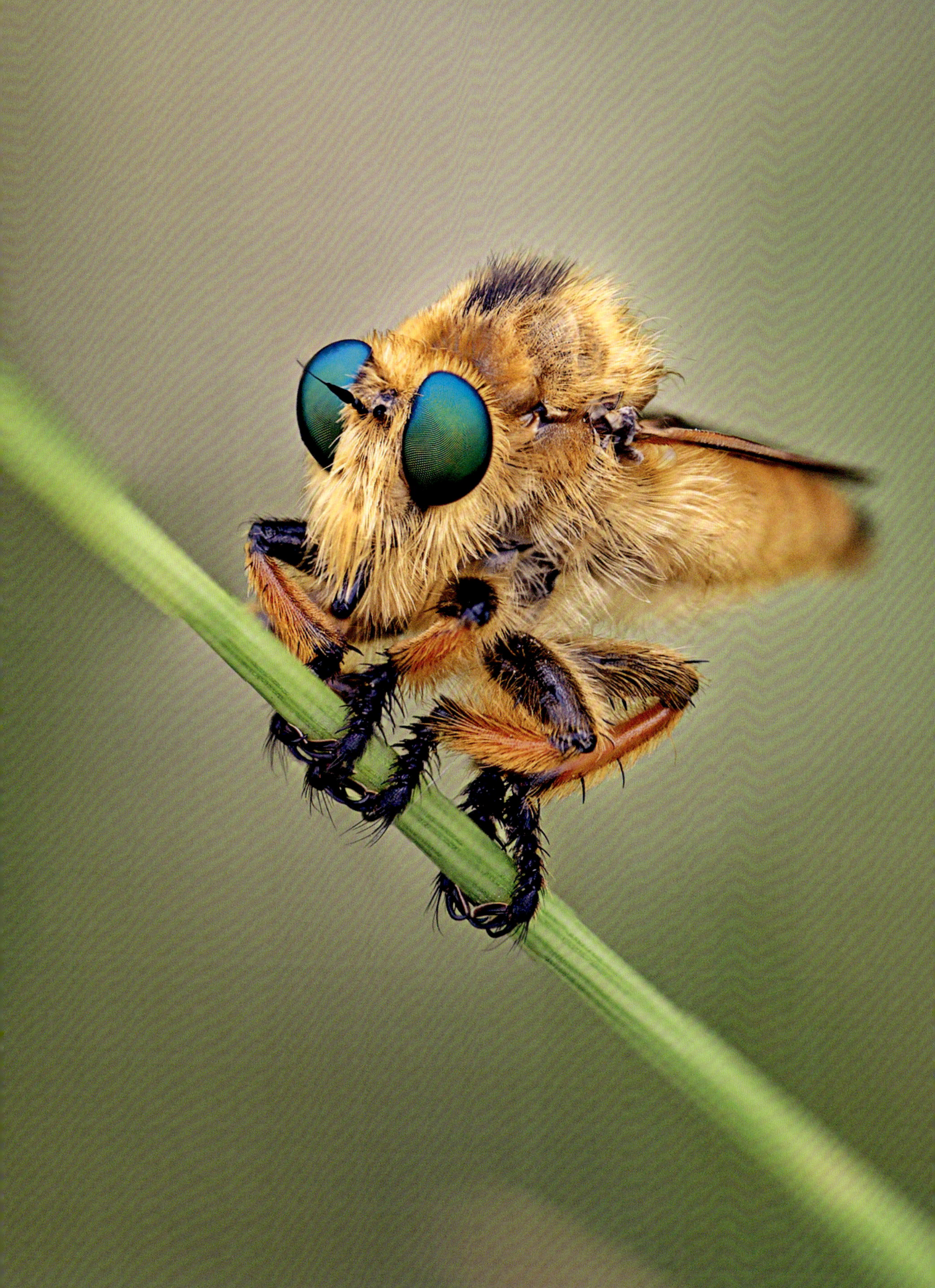

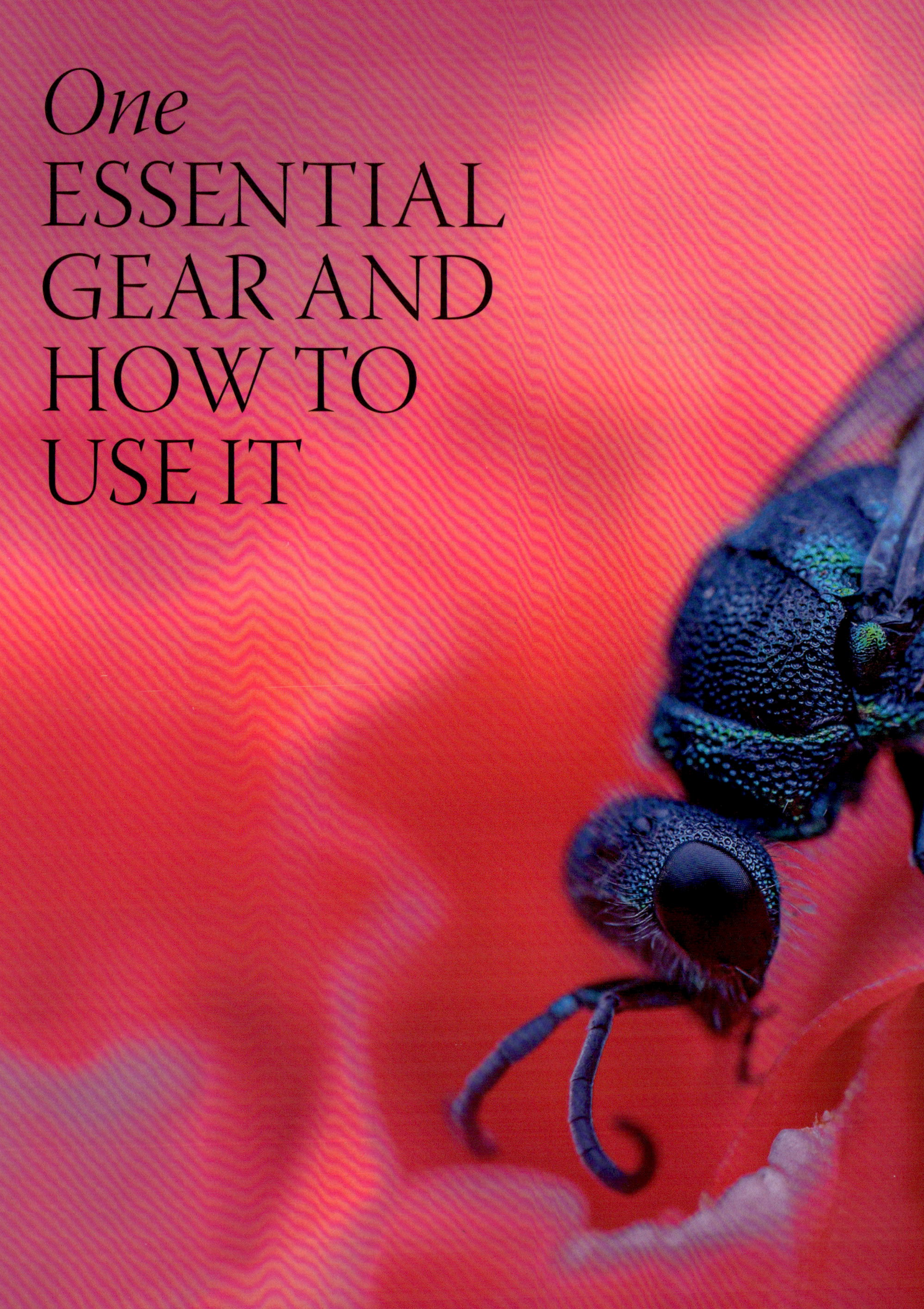
One
ESSENTIAL
GEAR AND
HOW TO
USE IT

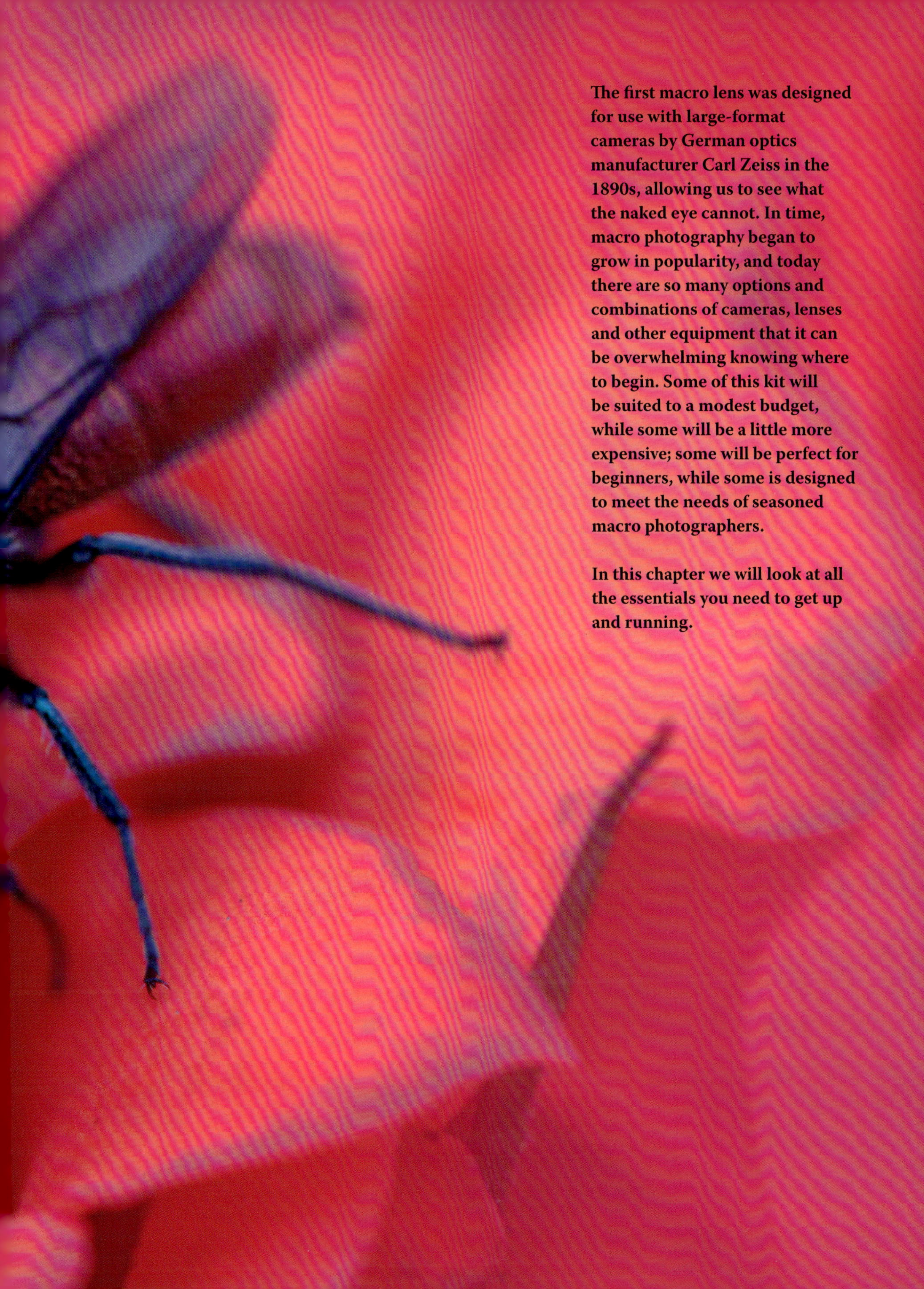

The first macro lens was designed for use with large-format cameras by German optics manufacturer Carl Zeiss in the 1890s, allowing us to see what the naked eye cannot. In time, macro photography began to grow in popularity, and today there are so many options and combinations of cameras, lenses and other equipment that it can be overwhelming knowing where to begin. Some of this kit will be suited to a modest budget, while some will be a little more expensive; some will be perfect for beginners, while some is designed to meet the needs of seasoned macro photographers.

In this chapter we will look at all the essentials you need to get up and running.

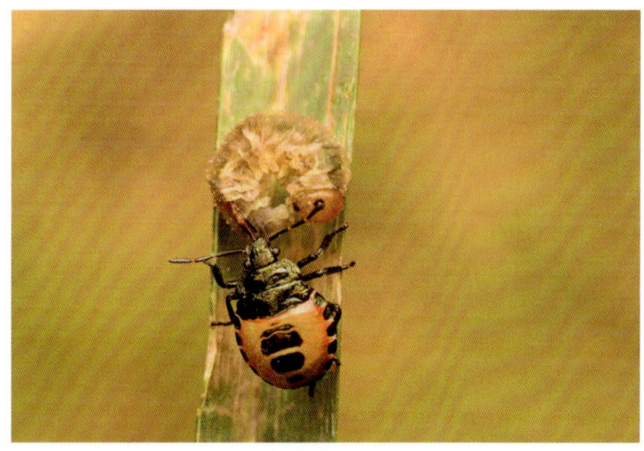

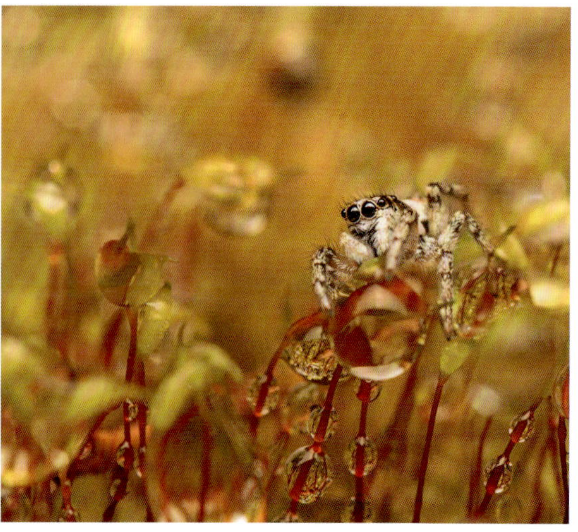

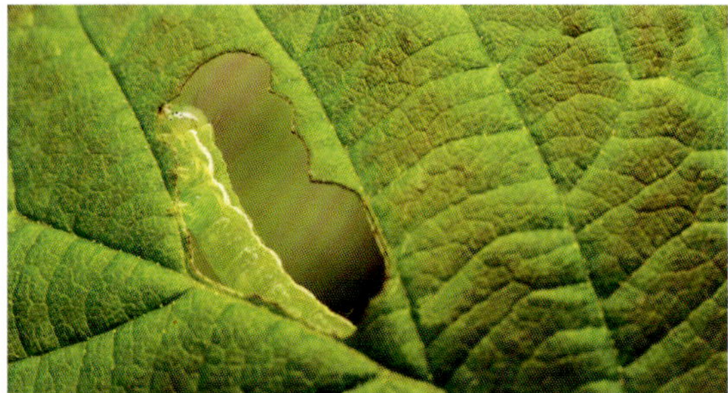

This page The best macro equipment can be expensive, but you don't need expensive gear to get a good shot. All the images on this page were taken using basic equipment.

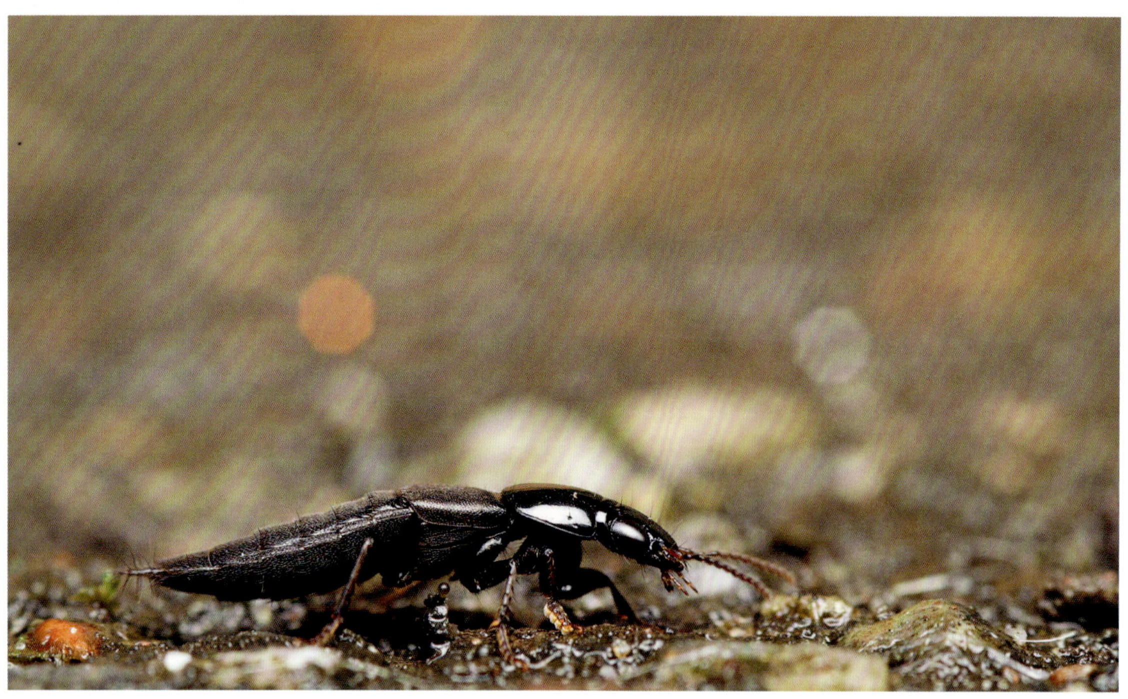

Getting started

Getting started with macro photography doesn't have to break the bank. I started out with second-hand equipment: a Sony Alpha 100 camera body, a Sigma 105mm macro lens and a flash head that cost approximately £300–400 ($380–500) in total. Times have moved on and so has the technology, but there are still bargains to be found on resale websites and photography forums. One of my most successful years as a photographer came from using this second-hand kit. I photographed species in my garden over 100 days and the resulting photographs garnered the attention of BBC's *Springwatch*, which resulted in my television debut.

A lot of the time, the kit you already have will be sufficient to get you started – even if it's basic. As you will see, there are a few accessories you can use to give your gear a helping hand. Macro photography can be difficult to master, so the last thing you want to do is invest thousands into photography equipment and not enjoy the genre!

Lenses

Your lens choice determines how close you need to get to your subject and how much magnification you can achieve. Weight and stability are both factors to consider – heavier or longer lenses may require using a tripod to get the best result. I would always recommend investing in a dedicated macro lens if you can.

Camera body

Camera bodies can vary in price and quality. It goes without saying that the more expensive camera systems, such as the new mirrorless systems, offer higher resolution, improved internal features (for example, in-camera stacking) and compatibility with the latest cutting-edge lenses, but great results can still be achieved with a 15-year-old, second-hand DSLR. Whatever your camera choice is, make sure that the lenses and accessories you buy are compatible.

Flash

Flash heads are a great addition to the macro kit bag, and there's a range of options, including single flash heads, dual flash and more. I would always suggest starting out with a single flash head before venturing into more creative (and expensive) set-ups, adding in extra lights.

Tripods

Tripods can be hit and miss: while you don't want to spend a fortune on one, if you buy too cheap, you'll end up with a flimsy tripod that may break easily. I prefer to shoot by hand – maybe five percent of my work uses a tripod – but they do have their uses. When it comes to buying a tripod, consider how you want to use it and whether the tripod will be able to perform the tasks you need it for. For example, some tripods open up and allow you to get very low to the ground, while others may not offer this feature.

DSLR and mirrorless cameras

Macro photography is all about capturing beautiful details and intricate patterns, and equipping yourself with the right camera can make a real difference. While most of the work is done by the macro lens, the camera body determines how far you can push its functionality.

The two most common camera types used by macro photographers are DSLRs and mirrorless cameras. Here, we'll get into what those terms mean, and what the pros and cons of each are.

DSLR (Digital single-lens reflex)

DSLRs are very popular among photographers for the high-quality images they produce, their fast autofocus systems and their noise-handling capabilities (see page 60). These cameras feature a reflex mirror that allows you to see through the viewfinder and capture your imagery with precision, composing your shots effortlessly and nailing the focus, which is crucial for macro photography. When you press the shutter button, the mirror flips up, allowing light to pass through the lens to the camera's sensor, where the image is recorded. When the shutter button is half-pressed, the camera's autofocusing system can use various sensors to determine the distance to the subject and adjusts focus accordingly.

Most modern DSLRs are equipped with a large LCD screen to the rear, which is a huge benefit for reviewing images and live focusing. Some screens can be pulled out to the side of the camera and rotated, making them a great tool when working at tricky angles.

Importantly, DSLRs support interchangeable lenses, enabling photographers to employ a range of optics for various genres of photography – including macro lenses. This makes the DSLR a great choice over any standard point-and-shoot or bridge camera.

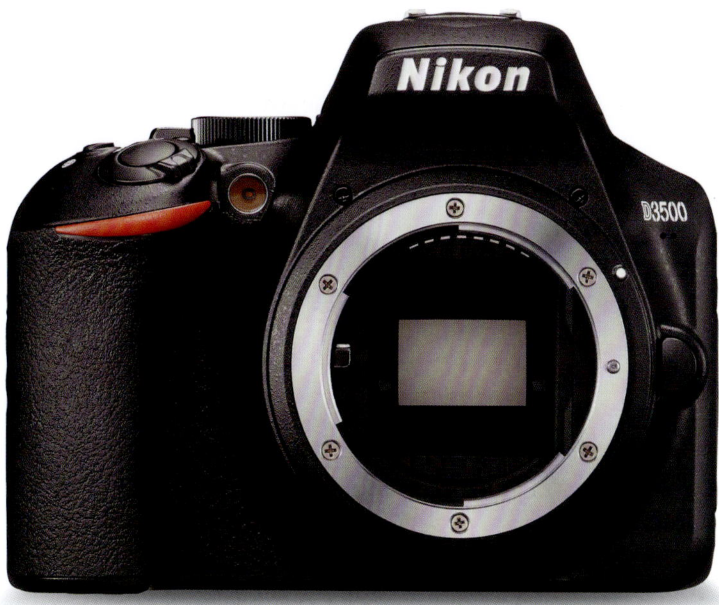

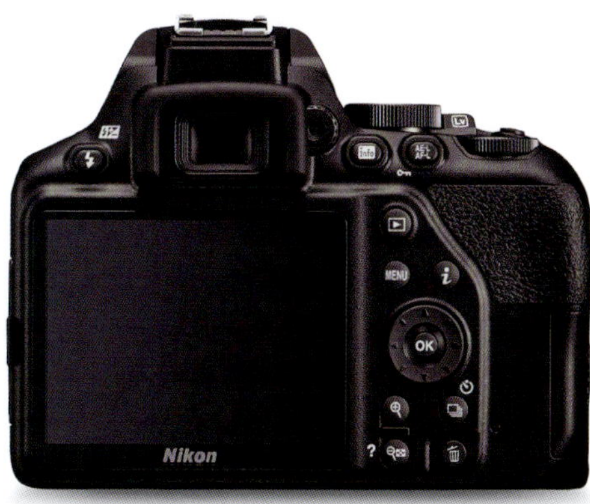

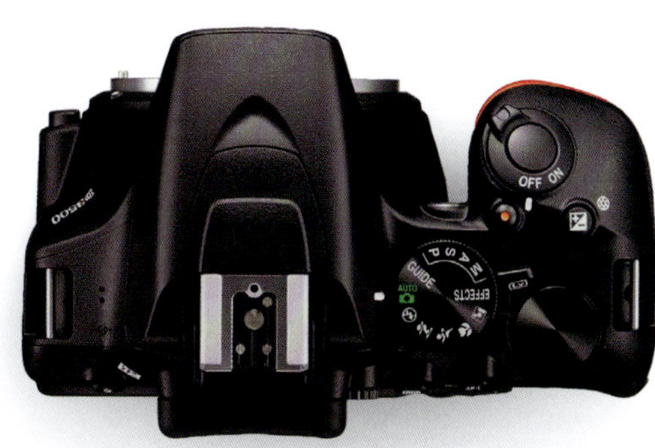

Above The Nikon D3500 is a great choice for amateurs interested in macro photography. With its 24.2-megapixel sensor, it captures detailed images of close-up subjects. Its user-friendly interface and guide mode make it easy for beginners to operate. Additionally, it offers compatibility with a range of lenses, including macro lenses, for capturing intricate details.

Mirrorless

Mirrorless camera systems have grown in popularity in recent years, as they offer photographers even more flexibility and creative options than DSLRs. Unlike DSLRs, mirrorless cameras don't contain a reflex mirror. Instead, they have an electronic viewfinder, often referred to as an EVF, and a rear LCD screen to preview your shot.

This system transfers the data captured by the camera's sensors to the viewfinder as real-time imagery. This means that what you see in the EVF is exactly what your final photograph will look like, including exposure and white balance. For example, when you adjust your aperture setting, you will see in real time how it affects the depth of field, and therefore how much of your subject is in focus. Similarly, as you adjust ISO, you will immediately see how it affects the other exposure variables. What this amounts to is more accurate results straight out of the camera.

The LCD is essentially a larger version of the EVF and, providing you with the same real-time data. Some LCD screens can flip out at various angles, which can be very useful for composing

This page The Canon EOS R5 is a beginner-friendly mirrorless camera with a compact design. It has a full-frame sensor for high-quality photos, and the electronic viewfinder and LCD screen make it easy to frame your shots. The autofocus system ensures sharp images, and it supports interchangeable lenses for versatility. Overall, it's a great camera for beginners looking to capture impressive photos effortlessly.

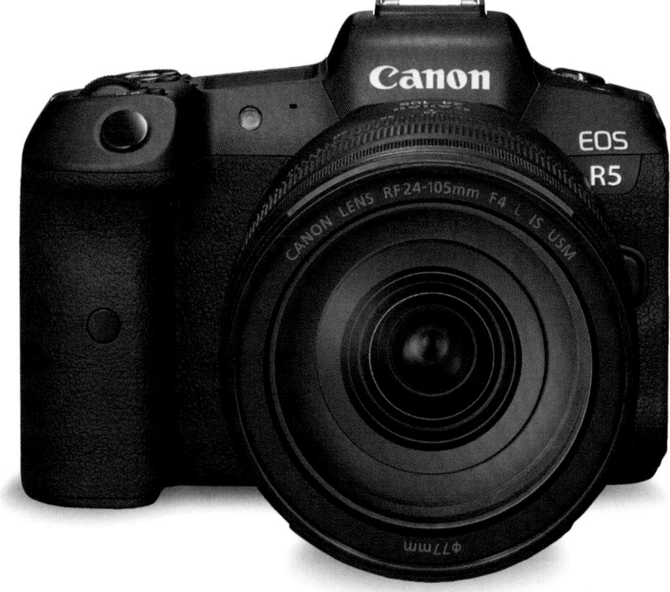

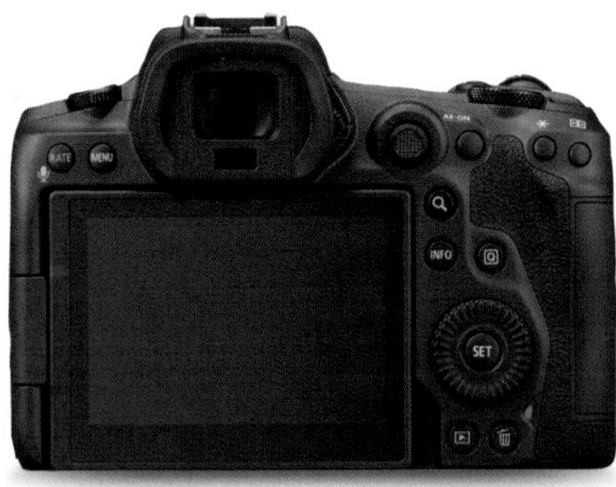

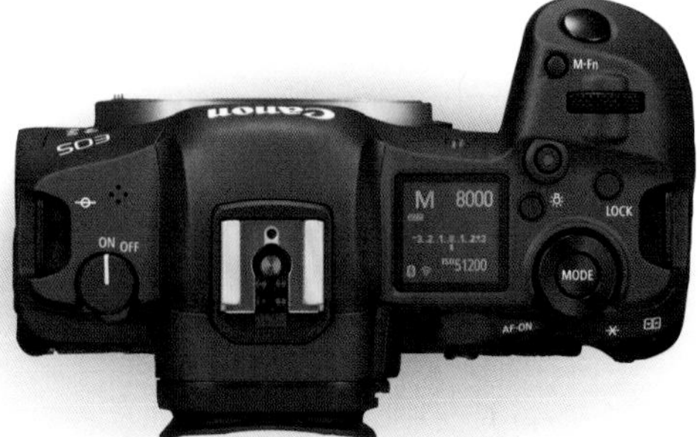

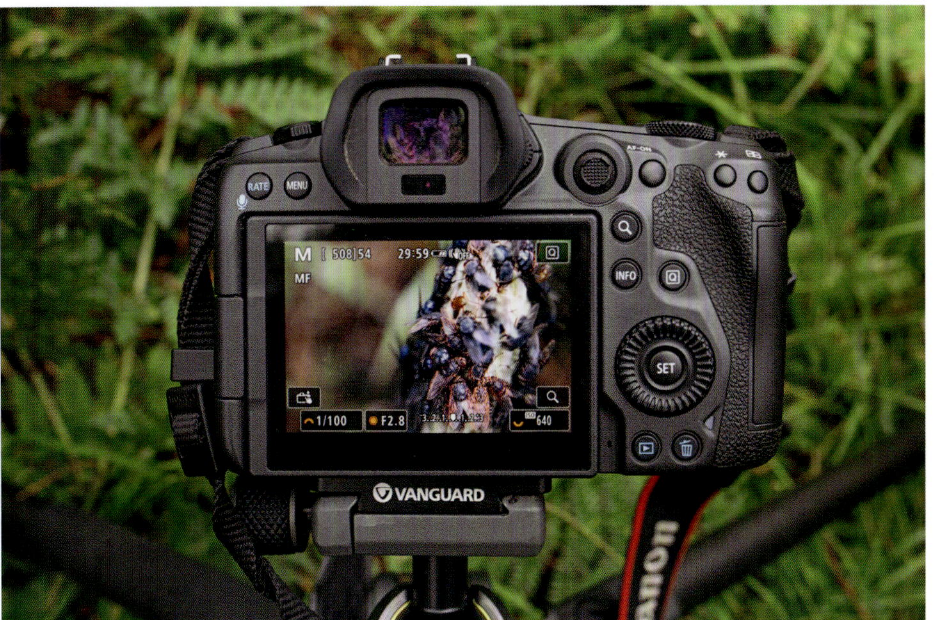

shots in tricky situations. What's more, some LCD screens have touchscreen functionality, allowing you to select a point of focus and even take a photograph with one tap of the screen. These two features give the mirrorless system a big advantage over a DSLR, plus, the absence of a reflex mirror reduces vibrations, allowing for clearer and sharper images.

Mirrorless cameras excel in areas such as autofocusing, and when you don't want to use autofocus, the EVF has a function called 'focus peaking', which allows you to see (with an on-screen mark-up), exactly which parts of your subject are in focus. AF can be particularly useful for macro photography when shooting larger subjects such as dragonflies and butterflies.

A final benefit to mirrorless cameras is that they tend to be more lightweight and compact than DSLRs, making them a great choice for photographers who want to travel light and shoot handheld. Like DSLRs, mirrorless cameras support interchangeable lenses, including dedicated macro lenses that are designed to fit the mirrorless system. It's worth noting that most lenses designed for DSLRs can also be used on mirrorless systems with the addition of an adapter.

Sensor types

One of the many confusing aspects of choosing a camera is what kind of sensor you need. The choice of sensor size comes down to your individual preferences, shooting requirements and budget. Full-frame sensors provide excellent image quality, especially in low light. APS-C and Micro Four Thirds sensors are more compact and cost-effective, but still deliver good image quality, making them suitable for absolute beginners and seasoned enthusiasts.

Full-frame sensor

A full-frame sensor typically measures 36x24mm, which is the size of a traditional 35mm film frame. Commonly found in high-end camera systems, they offer more surface area for collecting available light, providing excellent noise-handling performance.

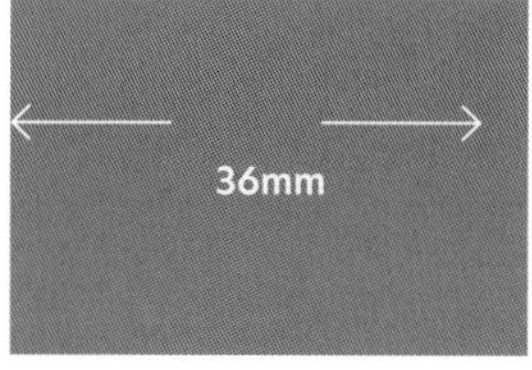

Full-frame sensor

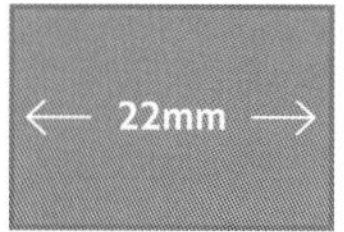

APS-C or 'crop' sensor

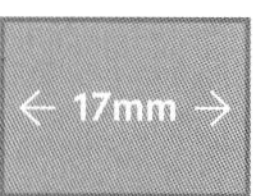

Micro Four Thirds sensor

APS-C sensor

APS-C sensors are commonly found in entry-level to mid-range camera systems. They are sometimes referred to as 'crop' sensors because they are smaller than full-frame sensors and therefore capture a smaller section or 'crop' of the scene compared to a full-frame sensor. Due to this, APS-C sensors give the perception of getting closer or multiplying the focal length of the lens being used. For instance, a 100mm lens or focal length on an APS-C sensor would provide a field of view that is 1.5x the focal length, effectively turning 100mm into 150mm.

Micro Four Thirds sensor

Micro Four Thirds (MFT or 4:3) sensors are even smaller than APS-C sensors and have a crop factor of 2x. The diagonal measurement is approximately half the size of a full-frame sensor. The smaller size of Micro Four Thirds sensors results in a deeper depth of field and a narrower field of view, meaning that the same lens used on an APS-C camera will have a wider field of view compared to a Micro Four Thirds camera. Cameras with MFT sensors are often favoured by photographers who prioritize mobility and versatility while still desiring good image quality.

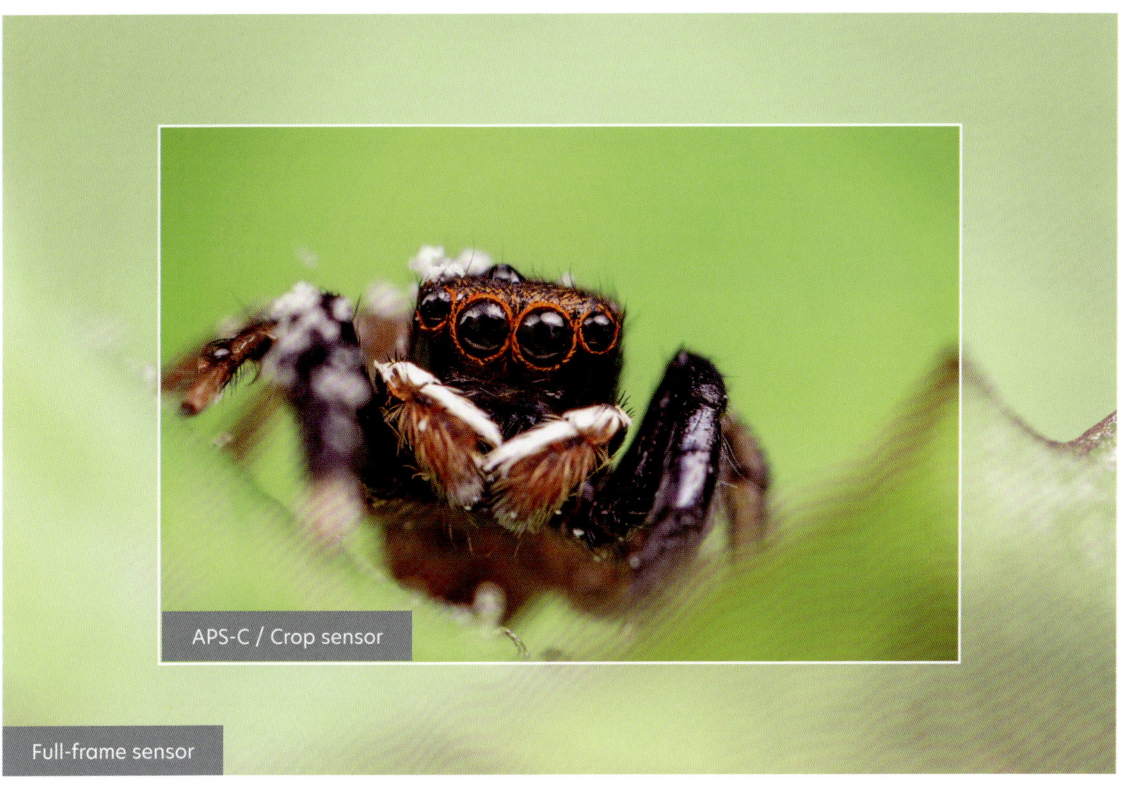

Above The field of view of an APS-C sensor versus
a full-frame sensor. The Micro Four Thirds sensor
would give an even narrower field of view.

Macro lenses

Entering the world of macro lenses can be daunting. Which length to choose? Will I need filters? To add to the confusion, many standard lenses that have the word 'macro' printed on them (or in some cases even in the title) are not true macro lenses. So, first things first, what constitutes a 'true' macro lens? Simply put, a true macro lens is a lens that is capable of achieving a 1:1 magnification ratio, which means that the subject you photograph will be reproduced at life-size on the camera's image sensor. Lenses labelled 'macro' are typically able to focus a little bit closer to the subject than a standard lens, helping you capture all the details. Dedicated macro lenses also come in various focal lengths, from 35mm to 200mm, each one with advantages and disadvantages out in the field.

Short focal length lenses

Shorter focal length macro lenses typically range between 35mm and 65mm. These lenses are designed to be compact and, in most cases, lightweight, making them ideal for handheld macro photography and manoeuvrability. Some also offer a wider field of view, which is excellent for incorporating more of the natural environment into a shot.

This type of macro lens has a close focusing distance, meaning you will be extremely close to your subject when attempting to photograph them. This can pose a problem when working with more skittish subjects such as insects, reptiles and amphibians. That's not to say they can't be used for these animals – the more you hone your technique and fieldcraft (see page 110), the better you will become at approaching your subjects with stealth and patience.

Shorter focal length macro lenses are ideal for photographing flowers and still life subjects, which is a great place to start with macro photography. What's more, these lenses are in most cases cheaper than their longer focal length counterparts.

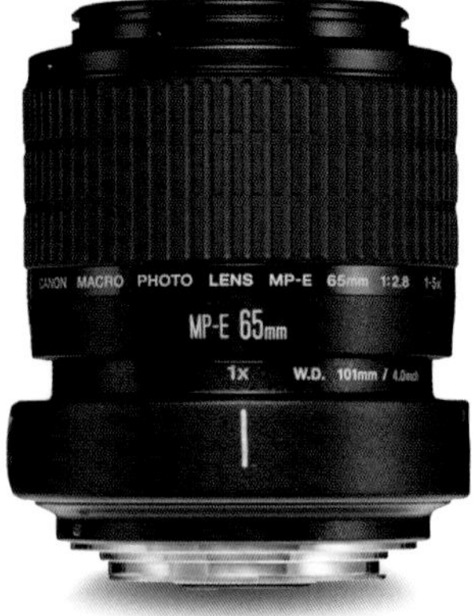

Left The Canon MP-E 65mm f/2.8 1-5X Macro is a specialized macro lens that allows you to capture the minute details of your subjects at high magnification. This unique lens offers a magnification range of 1x to 5x, meaning you can capture your subjects at life-size (1:1) all the way up to five times life-size (5:1) This lens is for the more advanced macro photographer or those looking for a challenge.

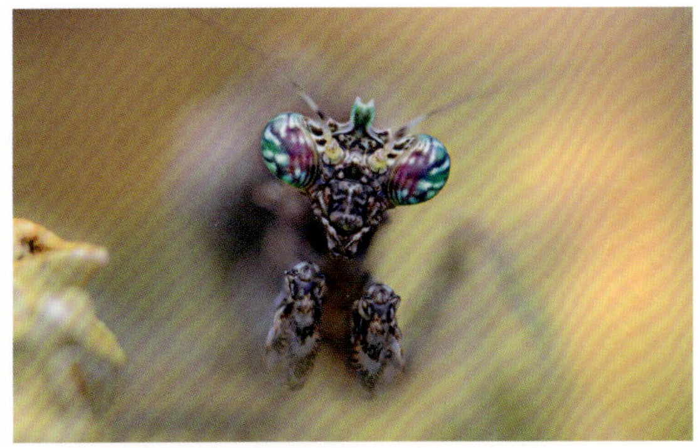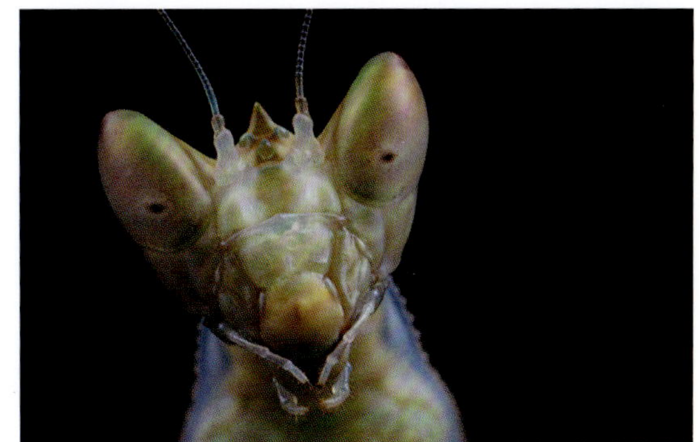

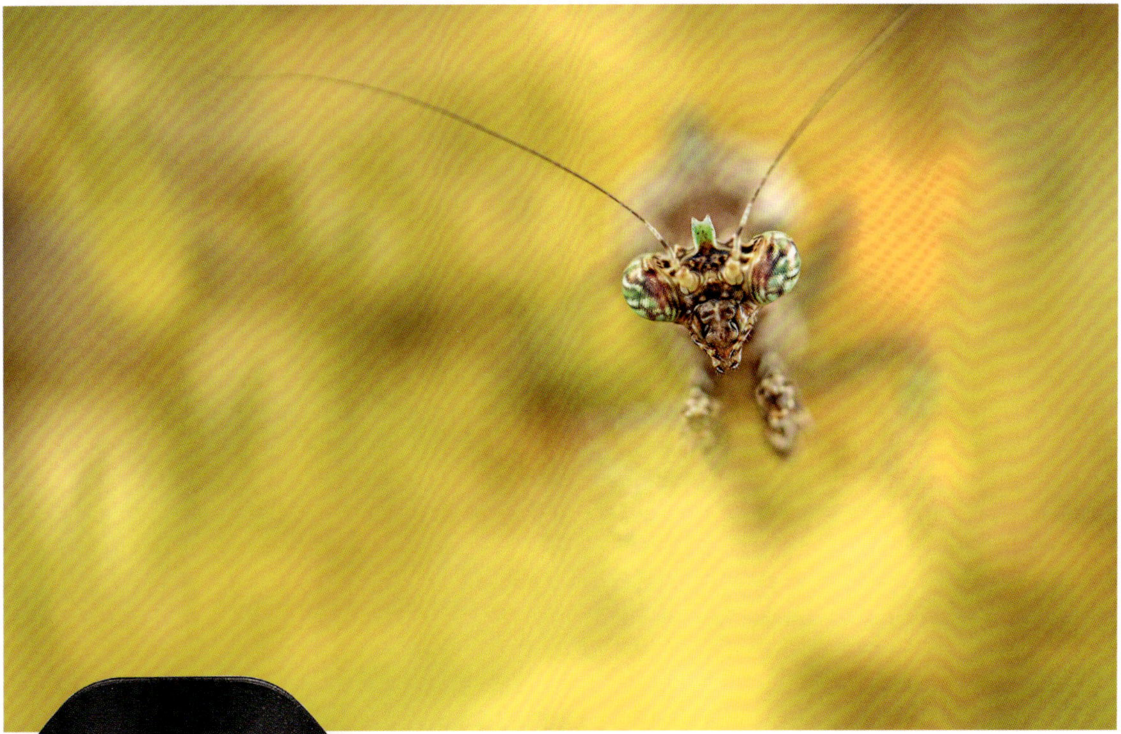

Above Shorter focal length lenses will let you get extremely close to your subject.

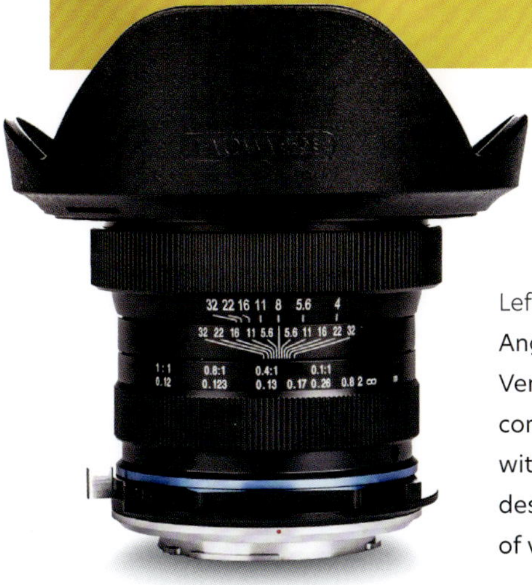

Left The Laowa 15mm f/4 Wide Angle Macro, manufactured by Venus Optics, is a unique lens that combines a wide-angle perspective with macro capabilities. It is designed to provide a wide field of view while allowing close-up focusing on subjects for macro photography. It also features a unique +/- 6mm shift feature, which makes this lens the ultimate creative tool for landscape, macro and architectural shooting. This lens is fully manual.

Medium focal length lenses

Medium focal length macro lenses typically range from 90mm to 105mm and are the most popular type among macro photographers. They provide a moderate telephoto effect, which allows you to maintain a comfortable distance from your subject while still achieving a 1:1 magnification ratio. This can be helpful when photographing flighty butterflies and other skittish insects. The working distance also allows for more available light between your lens and subject, whether that's an external flash or natural light. These lenses are crafted with high-quality optics and lens elements that help to reduce optical aberrations such as distortion and chromatic aberrations, resulting in higher image quality and overall sharpness.

This type of macro lens often has a wide maximum aperture, typically in the range of f/2.8–f/4, which allows a shallow depth of field and pleasing background blur (bokeh). This enables you to isolate your subject from the background, creating a sense of depth and drawing attention to the main subject. Medium focal length macro lenses offer a good balance between size and performance, allowing for handheld shooting and easy transportation. This portability is advantageous, especially for outdoor or on-location macro photography.

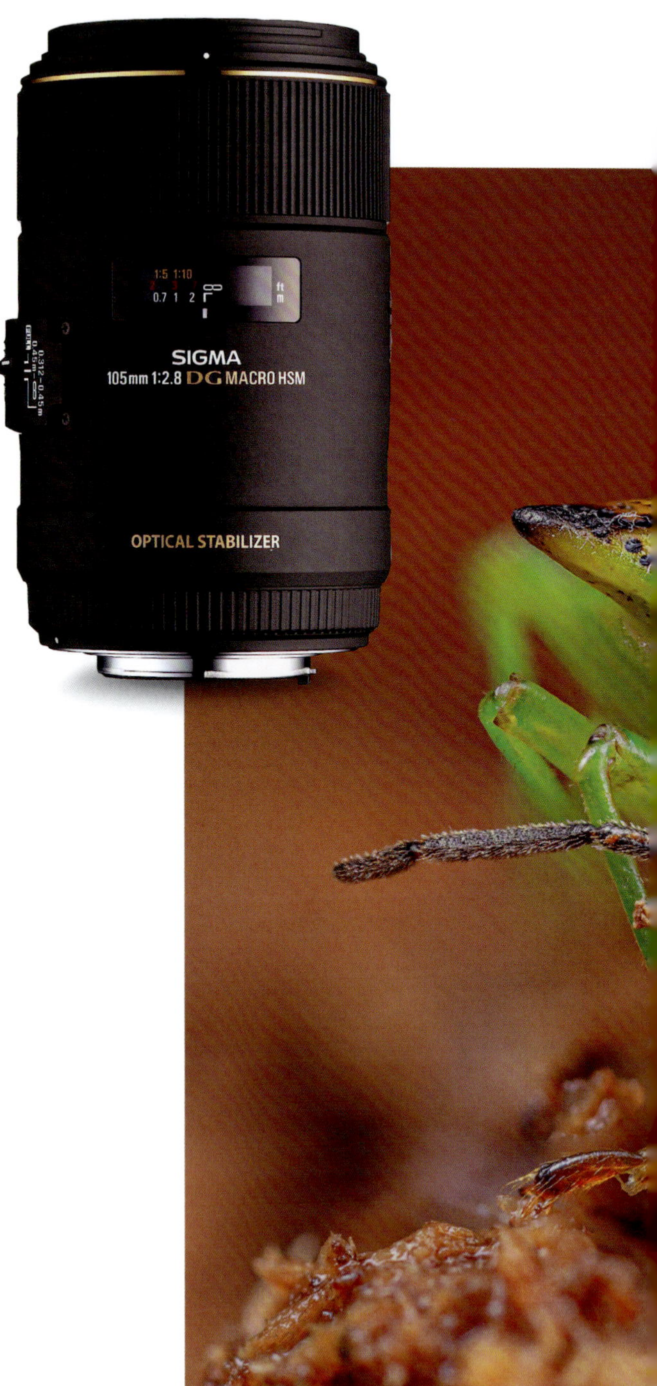

Left The Sigma 105mm f/2.8 EX DG OS HSM is a medium focal length macro lens that offers some telephoto perspective and 1:1 magnification. It offers great image quality and optical stabilization, which comes in handy when shooting handheld. As this impressive lens is manufactured by a third-party company, it is available for most camera systems.

Below A beautiful background blur is a benefit of working with a wide aperture, contrasting all the amazing foreground details.

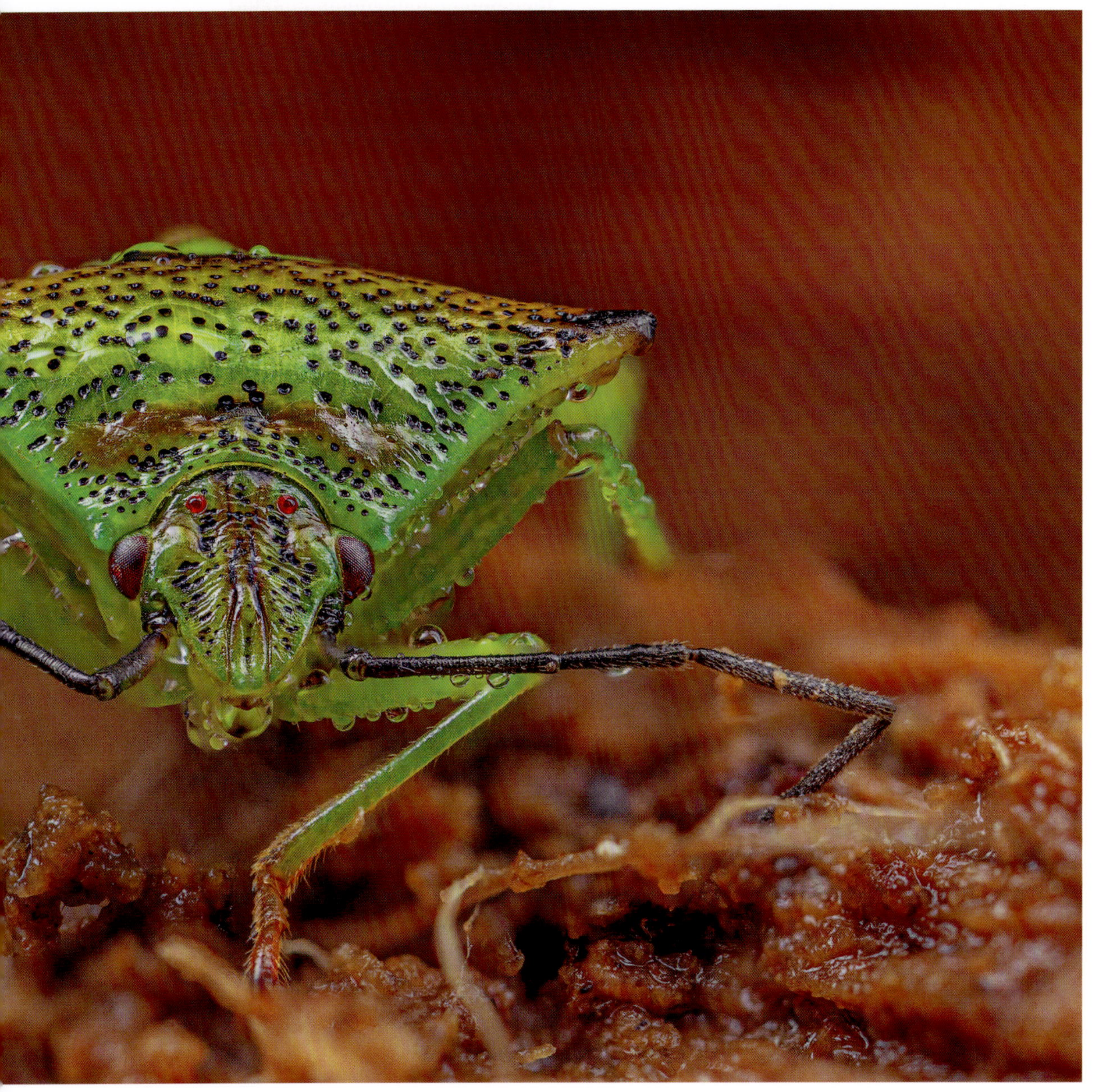

Long focal length lenses

Longer focal length macro lenses typically range from 150mm to 200mm and tend to be larger and heavier than their shorter focal length counterparts due to their extended optical designs and additional elements. This may impact portability and handling, especially for extended shooting sessions or when travelling. It's important to consider the balance between performance and practicality based on your specific needs.

These lenses allow you to capture macro shots from a greater distance while still maintaining the desired magnification. This feature is particularly useful when photographing skittish or delicate subjects that require a greater working distance to avoid disturbing them. It also provides a safer working distance when photographing potentially dangerous subjects such as snakes.

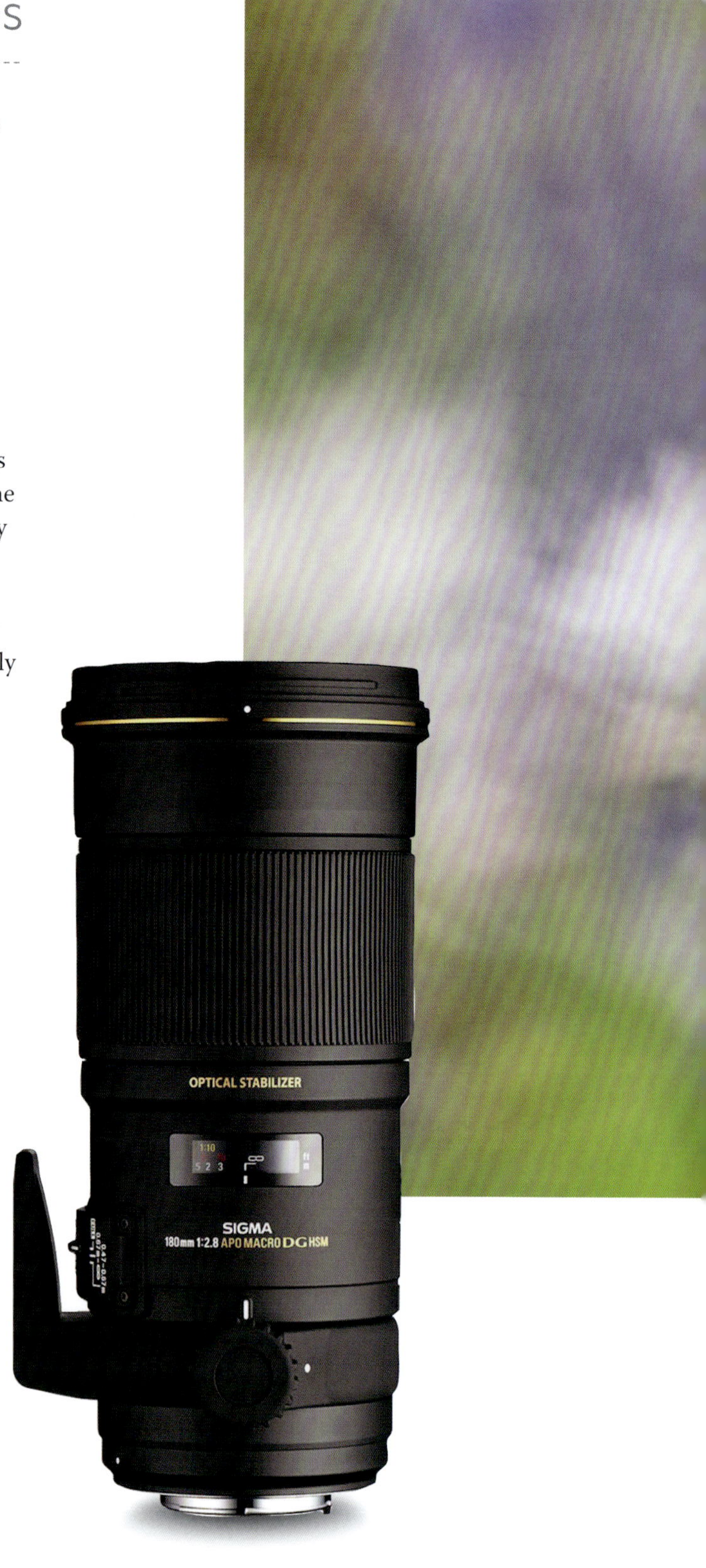

Right Lenses such as the Sigma APO Macro 180mm f/2.8 EX DG OS HSM provide better background compression due to their narrower field of view. This compression results in a more visually pleasing separation between the subject and the background, creating a smooth bokeh. It helps to emphasize the subject by blurring out distractions and drawing attention to the main subject.

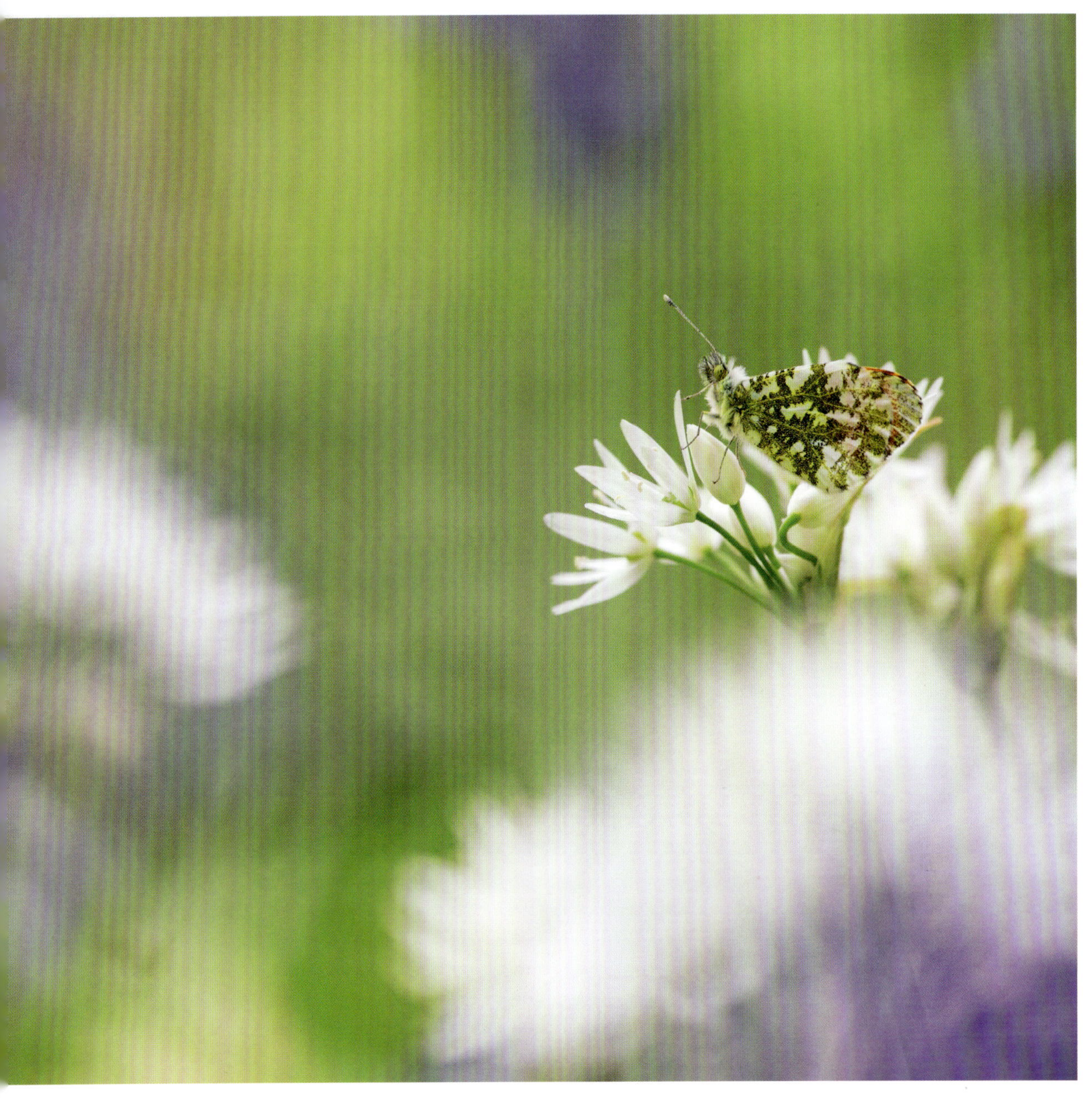

Above A green-veined white butterfly rests while I photograph from a distance using a Sigma 180mm macro lens.

Optical accessories and lens attachments

While a dedicated macro lens will always be preferred for its optimal quality and performance, there are other ways to achieve magnification on a budget. These alternatives will allow you to get close-up captures of your subjects, but they may have some limitations in terms of overall quality, magnification and performance.

Close-up lenses

Supplementary close-up lenses (often referred to as dioptres or, incorrectly, 'filters'), are similar in appearance to a clear UV filter and screw directly onto the front of a standard lens. These lenses were my first venture into macro photography and are affordable, accessible and very easy to use. But how do they work?

Close-up lenses contain convex lens elements that act like a magnifying glass. When screwed onto a regular camera lens they increase its refractive power, magnifying the image onto the sensor, and reduce the minimum focusing distance, allowing you to focus more closely.

Close-up lenses are normally labelled with dioptre values such as +1, +2, +4 and +10, indicating their optical power, and are available in various thread sizes. You can stack close-up lenses on top of each other to increase magnification; for example, adding a +1 and +2 lens will give you a +3 optical power. However, as you add more layers of glass you risk introducing chromatic aberration, lens distortion and discolouration. Some close-up lenses are designed with better optics, such as multi-coated glass, which can help reduce these undesirable effects.

Supplementary close-up lenses have limitations compared to a dedicated macro lens and their performance will vary depending on the lens you attach them to; image quality will be influenced by factors such as a lens's optical design and maximum aperture. However, close-up lenses provide a convenient and cost-effective way to explore macro photography with your existing lenses.

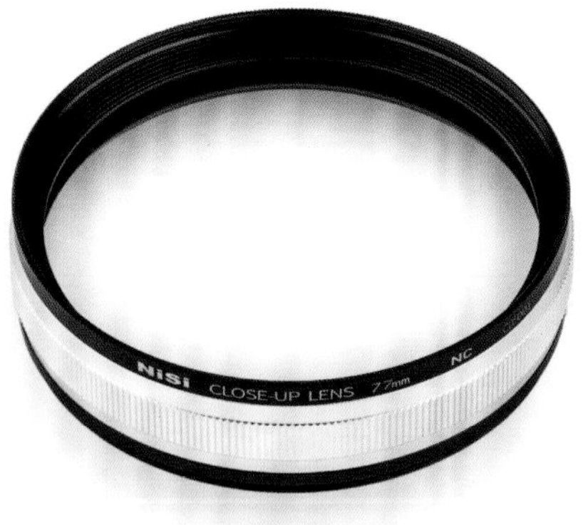

Left A close-up lens is a cheap and easy way to add magnification power to a standard lens.

Auto extension tubes

Auto extension tubes are ideal for beginners eager to explore the intriguing world of close-up photography. These hollow tubes, which are inserted between the camera body and lens, extend the lens-to-sensor distance, essentially acting as magnifiers for your lens. The ability of auto extension tubes to retain electronic connection between your camera and lens is one of their key benefits. This guarantees a seamless and uncomplicated shooting experience by ensuring that crucial functionality such as autofocus, image stabilization and aperture control remain fully operational.

The length of the extension tubes is important when it comes to magnification. The most common sizes are 12mm, 25mm and 36mm. To calculate the approximate magnification, you can use the following formula:

The magnification gained increases with the length of the tube. You may alter the extension tube arrangement to get the required level of magnification by mixing different tube lengths or by employing many tubes at once. However, be aware that using extension tubes can result in less light reaching your camera's sensor, which could have an impact on how well your photographs are exposed. To counteract this, you could increase the ISO, set a bigger aperture (lower f-number), use a slower shutter speed and/or introduce additional lighting, such as flash or a continuous light source.

$$\textit{Effective magnification} = \frac{\textit{Extension tube length (mm)}}{\textit{Focal length of the lens (mm)}}$$

So, in the case of a 12mm extension tube on a 35mm lens, the equation would be:

$$\textit{Effective magnification} = \frac{\textit{12mm}}{\textit{35mm}} \approx \textit{0.34x}$$

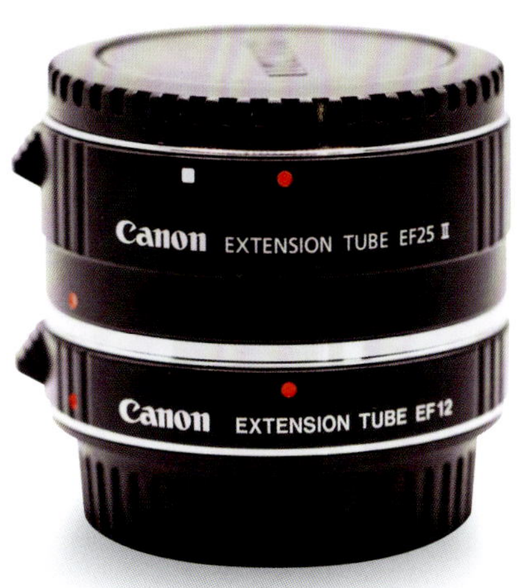

Above Extension tubes can be stacked together to further increase magnification.

Raynox adapters

Raynox adapters are small, supplementary lenses that attach to the front of your lens via a snap-on universal mount that's compatible with filter thread sizes from 57mm to 67mm. The main purpose of Raynox adapters is to provide additional magnification or widen the angle of view.

Macro conversion adapters such as the Raynox DCR-150 and DCR-250 enable you to achieve greater magnification without the need for a dedicated macro lens, allowing you to focus much closer than you can with a traditional lens. The Raynox DCR-150 offers 1.5x magnification while the DCR-250 offers 2.5x magnification. These versatile adapters can also offer greater-quality optics compared to supplementary close-up lenses, but this is dependent on the quality of the lens they are attached to. They can also be used on dedicated macro lenses, allowing you to go beyond 1:1 magnification.

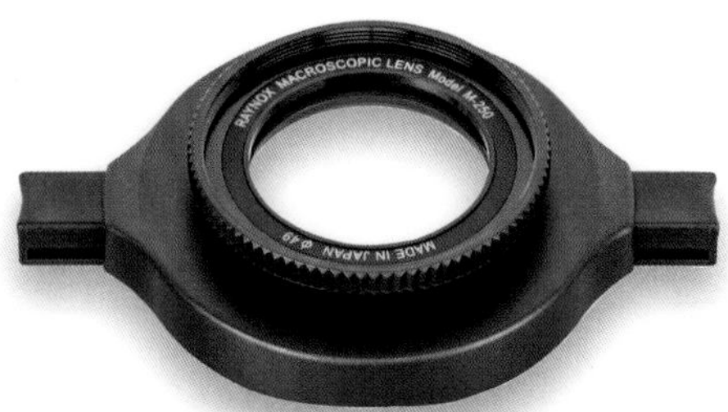

Above & right By pairing a Raynox DCR-250 with my Canon 100mm f/2.8 lens, I unlocked an exceptional level of magnification. The DCR-250 acted as a powerful supplement, allowing me to get even closer and reveal mesmerizing details that might have otherwise gone unnoticed. This combination of lens and adapter offers an affordable and versatile solution for expanding the macro capabilities of your photography gear.

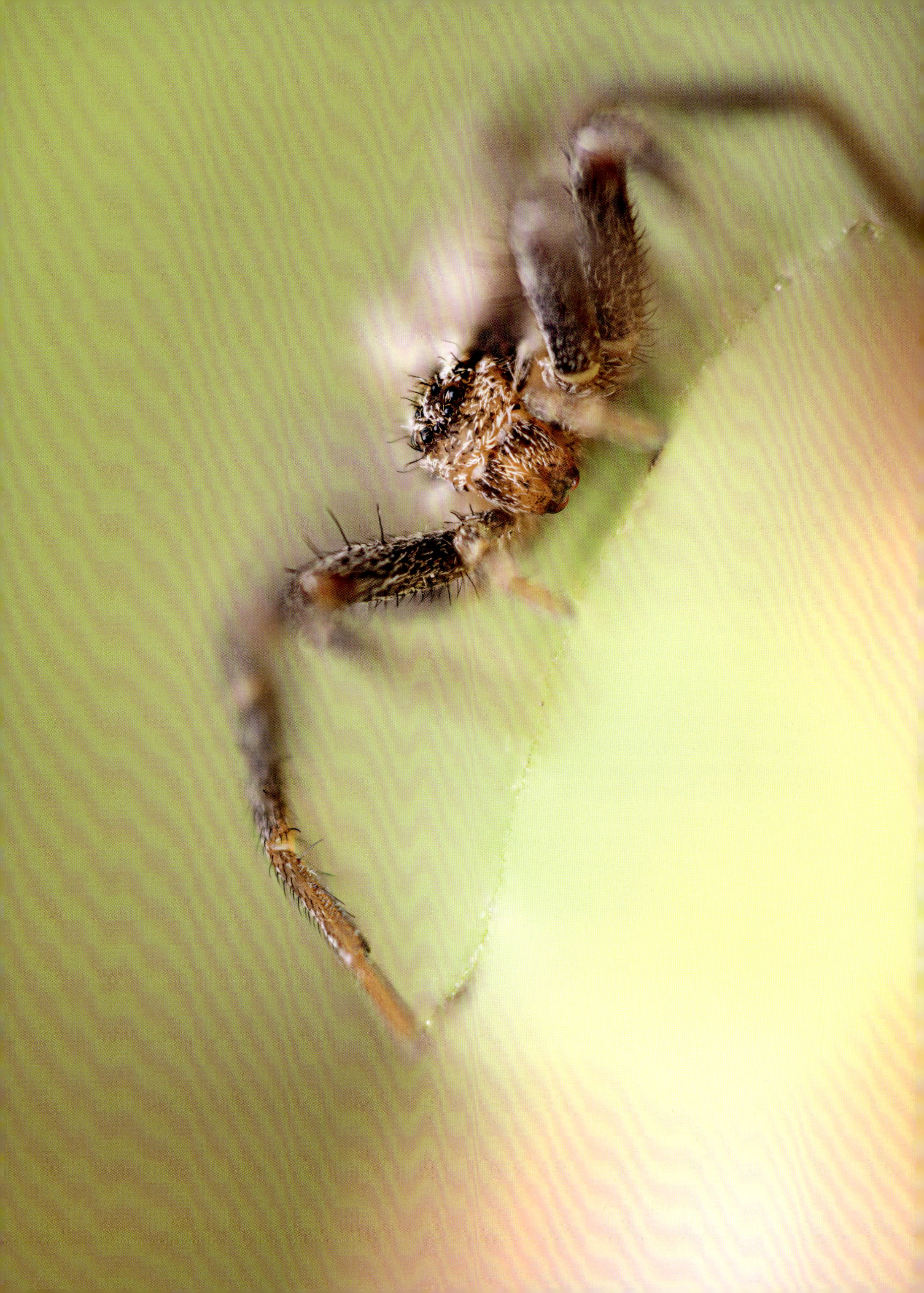

Lighting accessories

Macro photography requires you to be very close to your subject with a dedicated macro lens, which restricts light levels. Add to this the fact you may be shooting with small apertures such as f/9, and light quickly becomes in short supply. Adding a flash to your set-up can provide much-needed illumination when there's not enough ambient light. A flash will, in most cases, allow quick-enough captures to freeze movement, allowing you to handhold your camera and not be restricted to a tripod. This is a real benefit when working with live subjects in the field.

Flash can be daunting and tricky to use for those photographers who have never used it before, but when mastered it can result in beautifully lit, sharp and correctly exposed macro images. There are many options to choose from when selecting a flash unit for your camera, so let's break them down.

Flash units

Built-in flash

A built-in pop-up flash can be found on many digital cameras. Despite not having the same flexibility or power as an external speedlight, a pop-up flash can still be useful for fill flash, adding to the ambient light and illuminating some close-up subjects. The flash's fixed position on the camera body increases the likelihood that it will either miss the subject or only partially illuminate it. To avoid this, simple diffusers can be employed to not only soften the harsh light, but also spread it more evenly so that it illuminates your subjects.

Right A built-in flash typically comes with the kit and pops out of the top of the camera.

External flash/speedlight

Adding an external flash to your camera system will provide you with greater flexibility. These devices can be positioned vertically or horizontally, allowing you to create interesting lighting effects. External speedlights slot into your camera's hotshoe (the mounting point at the top of your camera) and sit higher than a conventional built-in flash, allowing for a larger, softer spread of light.

External flashes also allow you to adjust their power and focal length (how wide or narrow the field of illumination will be). That extra bit of control can be very beneficial in low-light situations and night-time macro adventures. These flash units can also sync with your camera allowing for high-speed flash and TTL (through-the-lens) control, meaning it will be automatically set according to the available light. Not only that, they can be mounted off camera using brackets, tripods and other accessories, and triggered using remote devices and, in some cases, other flash units.

As with built-in flash, external flash works best when combined with a level of diffusion (see page 38). It is good practice to experiment with your external flash, adjusting the power settings, switching from automatic (TTL) and manual adjustments, and adding various diffusers to see what works best for you before going out into the field.

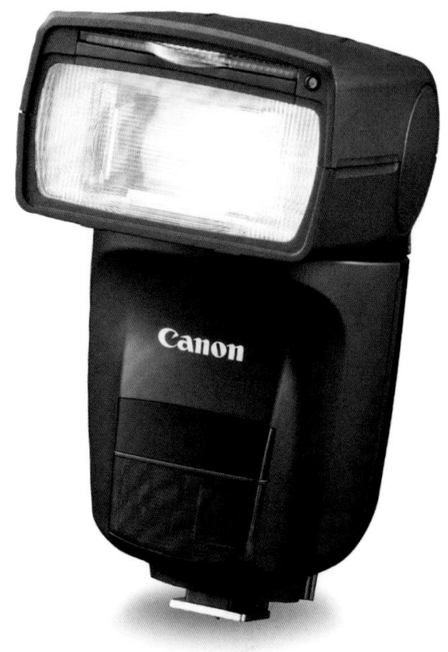

Above A speedlight is the ultimate lighting tool for photographers. These powerful flash units enhance your creativity with precise lighting control, high-speed sync and versatile wireless capabilities.

Ring flash

Ring flash is often used in portrait photography, but it also has its uses for macro photography. The flash system unit slots into the camera's hotshoe while the ring light attaches to the end of your lens. A ring flash emits an even cast of circular light and, because the light unit is situated at the end of your lens, the shadows cast are minimal, so the lighting can be quite flat. Some systems allow you to dial in adjustments to the ratio of circular light, allowing for more power from one side or the other. This creates a more three-dimensional look by adding shadow and contrast to a scene.

It's worth noting that a ring flash is bulky and often restricts movement at ground level, which becomes even more apparent as you extend your magnification beyond the standard 1:1 ratio.

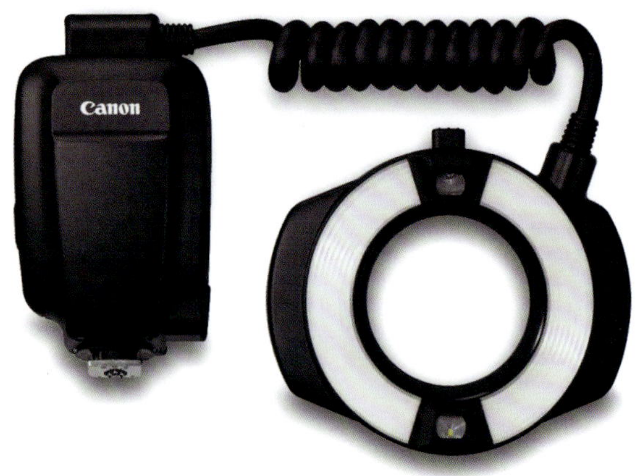

Above A ring flash can add even illumination to your scene. However, they can be bulky and tricky to use.

Portable constant light

Along with flash units, a constant light source such as the Lume Cube can prove extremely useful when the need for more subtle light is required. These small, portable units can be mounted onto small tripods, rested on the ground and even mounted on your camera. Considering the small unit size, they produce a huge amount of light.

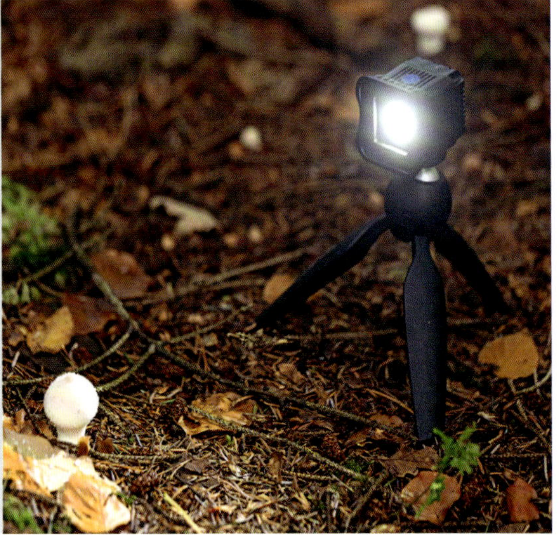

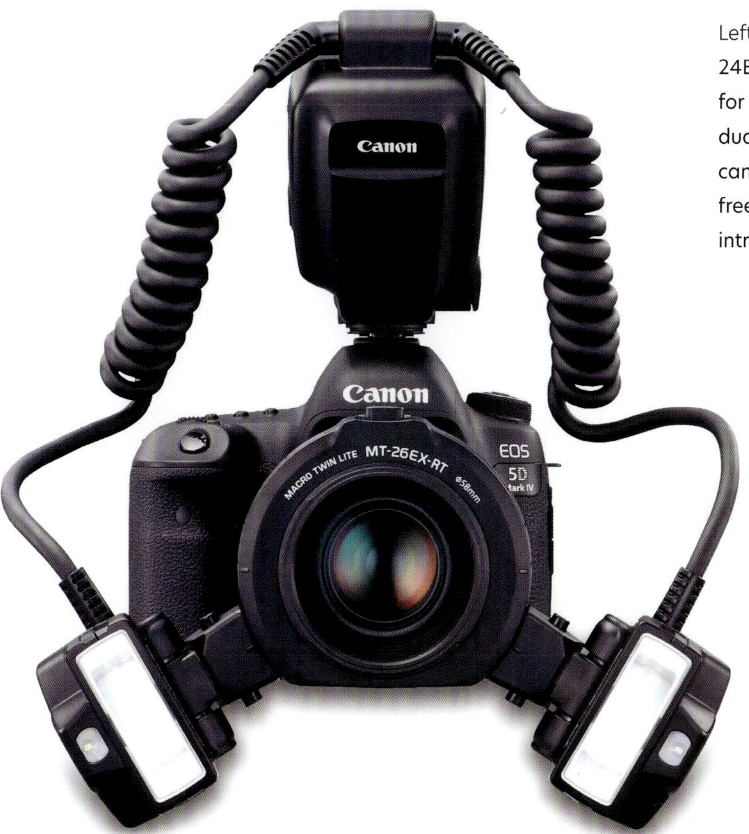

Left The Canon Macro Twin Lite MT-24EX offers creative lighting options for macro photography. With its dual flash heads, photographers can achieve precise and shadow-free illumination, bringing out the intricate details of small subjects.

Dual flash

A dual flash system works in a similar way to a ring flash (opposite). The main control unit slots into the camera's hotshoe and the two small flash units are mounted onto a small ring adapter at the end of the lens. The flash units are adjustable both horizontally and vertically. What's more, the ring adapter they're mounted on can be rotated independently around the end of the lens. Dual flash is designed to provide more controlled and balanced lighting, with the flash units working together to illuminate a larger surface area.

Each flash unit can have its power levels adjusted via the main control unit, offering more versatility and creativity when it comes to lighting your subjects. You can use one flash at full power as the main light, and the second one set at a lower power and different angle for some nice side or rim lighting (see page 65).

Additionally, you can add hotshoe adapters to the ring mount to give both flash units extra elevation. Both flash units can be diffused relatively easily and can add much-needed illumination for 1:1 macro photography and above. In most cases these units aren't too heavy, but they can be bulky and intrusive when photographing subjects in the field.

Again, it is best to practise with this system on household subjects or flowers before going out into the field.

Flash diffusers

Using a flash can really help you achieve sharp, well-exposed macro images, but if the light produced from the flash isn't diffused, your subjects will typically be illuminated with harsh light, resulting in deep shadows and overexposed highlights or hotspots, particularly if your subject has an extremely shiny and reflective body. Not only can adding diffusion help create beautifully soft light, some diffusers can also help to channel the light to the end of your lens. Here are some of things to consider when looking for a diffuser:

Size and shape
Is the diffuser designed for your flash unit? Will the diffuser become an obstruction in dense foliage? Might it scare away your subjects?

Quality of light
The surface area of the diffuser panel and the material it is made of determine how much and how effectively diffusion occurs. Additionally, it is important to remember that the diffusion material may add a slight colour cast.

Efficiency
How much light reaches our subject versus how much is lost? With the best possible diffusion, we want as much light as we can get. Some diffusers are concave or domed, and lined with a reflective foil that helps to bounce the light while keeping it contained. Other diffusers are simply sheets of material held in front of your flash unit, which results in a huge loss of light.

Portability and convenience
Some diffusers fold away flat, while some are made from hard, durable plastic. It's important to consider how your diffuser fits into your camera bag and how quickly it can be assembled and dissembled when working out in the field.

Homemade diffusion vs. professional
Most macro photographers have at some point opted to make homemade diffusers. They can be as simple as placing packing foam or kitchen paper over your flash unit, creating a lighting tube from a Pringles can or even making small softboxes out of milk cartons.

Experimenting with homemade diffusers is a great way to learn about diffusion and how it affects your overall image. However, as the market for macro photography advances, various ready-made diffusers have become available to purchase.

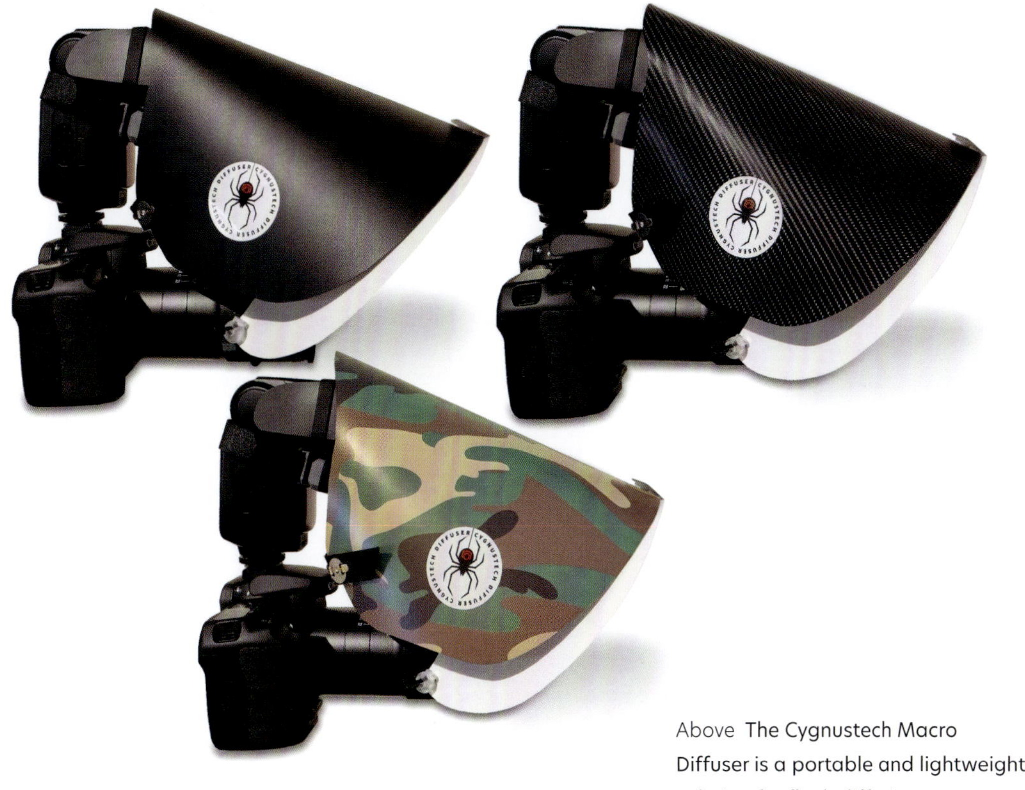

Above The Cygnustech Macro Diffuser is a portable and lightweight solution for flash diffusion.

Cygnustech Macro Diffuser

The Cygnustech Macro Diffuser is one of the most popular external flash diffusers on the market. This diffuser was designed by Brendan James, a professional macro photographer from Australia, who began to make DIY diffusers on his quest to find beautiful light diffusion.

The Cygnustech is made from durable plastic and folds down completely flat, making it ideal for packing into your camera bag. It is easily assembled and keeps the light well contained. It is also adjustable and comes in various sizes. This flash diffuser is designed to work with external flashes mounted in your hotshoe.

Tripods and supports

Tripods can prove useful for macro photography, especially when working with a still life, flowers or roosting insects such as butterflies and dragonflies. When working at high magnification, camera shake and movement are amplified and become very noticeable. Using a tripod can help to eliminate this movement, resulting in sharper, more detailed images. Tripods can help keep a consistent composition, which is crucial for advanced macro photography techniques such as focus stacking (see page 114), and also allow you to use longer exposure times to bring in more available light.

For most of my photography I shoot handheld, even when focus stacking. Tripods can become restrictive when working out in the field with live subjects, as we want to be able to react quickly and switch up our compositions, move in and out of foliage and get low to the ground or in a tight crevice of some rocks. A tripod can really slow this process down.

However, there are times when a tripod can prove useful, so it's worth having one in your kit. There are several factors to take into account when choosing a tripod:

Stability

This is the primary purpose of a tripod, so you want to make sure it is sturdy and able to support your camera and equipment such as a macro focusing rail (see page 42). The material is also something to consider – you want a tripod made of aluminium or carbon fibre rather than cheap plastic. Look at how the legs work. Can they open so you can get to ground level? Can they be adjusted individually? Does the tripod have a centre column that can be removed and repositioned?

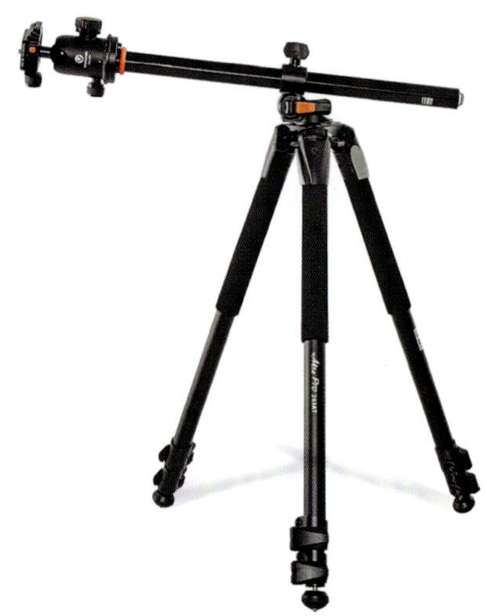

Above An articulated centre column that can be moved into a horizontal position can be a useful tripod feature for macro photography.

Load capacity

Double-check the load capacity of the tripod. How much weight can it handle? You don't want to load up a tripod with an expensive camera body and lens only for it to give way and fall to the floor.

Height and size

Make sure the tripod is suitable for the heights you want to work at. This includes how low to the ground it will go, as well as how high. Size also matters. You ideally want a tripod with legs that collapse, making it more portable.

Additional features

Built-in spirit levels and quick-release plates can all be a benefit when shooting macro.

Tripod head types

A tripod head is a small mechanical component that fits to the top of a tripod's legs and plays a vital role in providing flexibility and control for your camera. There are various head types to choose from, but no real 'perfect' one for macro photography. When I use a tripod, the type of head I opt for is a ball head. Ball heads act like a ball-and-socket joint and provide 360-degree tilting and panning with smooth and fluid movement.

Below Ball heads such as this Vanguard VEO BP-120T are widely used by amateur photographers for their easy-to-use mechanics and 360-degree pan and tilting options.

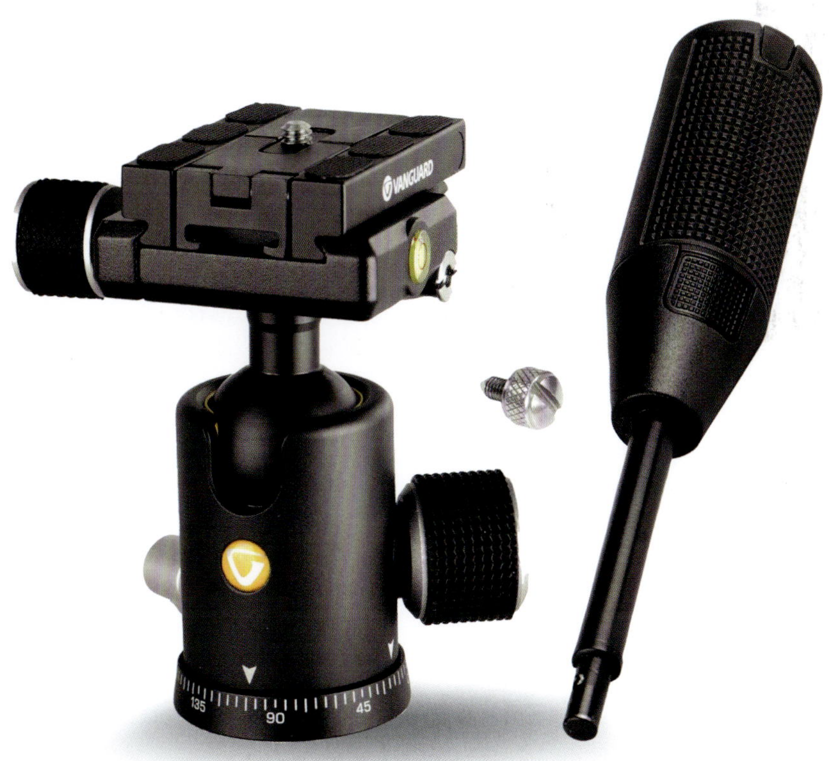

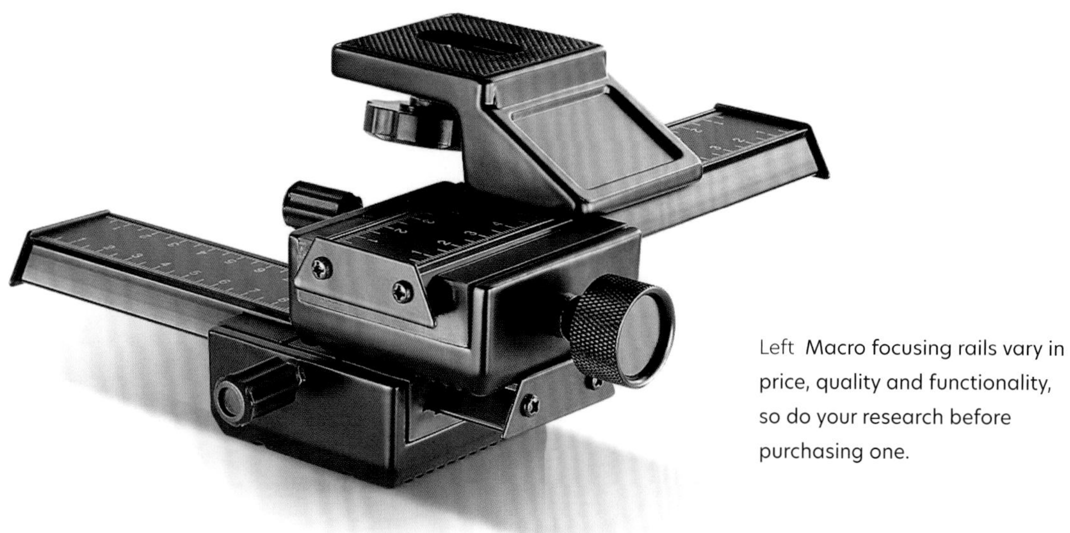

Left **Macro focusing rails vary in price, quality and functionality, so do your research before purchasing one.**

Macro focusing rail

A macro focusing rail is a dedicated accessory designed to help you fine-tune the camera and lens position. Typically, there are two adjustable plates or sliders mounted on top of the rails that allow you to move the camera and lens forwards, backwards or side to side. This enables you to take several pictures while gradually moving the focus plane around the subject. This is a huge benefit when focus stacking, which requires multiple shots at varying focal points (see page 114).

Focus-stacked images can be taken more successfully and methodically thanks to the focusing rail's controlled and smooth movement. Repeating the same movement and increment between shots produces consistent results and reduces the possibility of focus overlap or missing a point. The number of adjustments needed will depend on your overall depth of field and the size of your subject.

The rail sits on top of your tripod, usually via a locking plate or screw, and your camera and lens are mounted on top of that the rail. It can become quite bulky and heavy. There are two types of focusing rails: manual and automatic. A manual rail requires you to turn the small dials in whichever direction is needed to make the small adjustments. An automatic rail syncs directly with your camera and/or computer. You tell the rail how far and which direction you would like it to move, along with how many shots you want to take at each step, making the whole thing automatic.

It's important to remember that different models and brands of automatic focusing rails can have different features and functions. For comprehensive details on how a specific focus rail functions, consult the manufacturer's instructions and specifications.

Camera bag essentials

Memory cards and backing up

If you don't want to run out of space midway through a shooting session, it's worth buying extra memory cards. These cards vary in terms of maximum storage, speed and, of course, cost, so do some research to choose the best option to suit your needs. If you plan on stacking your images, then a memory card with a fast writing speed is essential, as this will allow the camera to keep firing while sending images to the memory card, without overloading the camera's internal buffer. The writing speed of my cards is 200MB/s, which is usually sufficient for my stacking needs.

Memory cards should be formatted for your camera before use (check your manual to see how), and they can be delicate, so don't leave them loose in your camera bag or pocket, but buy a dedicated case. Some brands such as SanDisk will provide a small clear plastic case for your cards.

You absolutely must back up your photos – ideally in three places, with one of them being either the cloud or a physically different location to your other two. I learned this the hard way and lost a full spring and summer's worth of photos in 2016. Get into the habit of importing your photos, backing them up and formatting your memory cards ready for re-use.

Camera batteries

Camera batteries have a tendency to run out of juice right at the worst possible moment. Cold weather only makes this worse, so having a fully charged spare battery (or two!) is a good idea. Try and avoid the lure of cheaper third-party batteries, the cheaper costs often reflect the cheaper quality and you may find they don't hold charge for as long.

File formats: Raw vs. JPEG

The file format you choose to save your photographs in will make a big difference to how large the file is and what you can do with it in post-processing.

A Raw file is an unprocessed, uncompressed file that includes all the 'raw' information the camera's sensor has recorded about that exposure. This gives you a huge amount of creative options when it comes editing, and most professional photographers choose this option. However, the images can appear a little flat and dull straight out of the camera, and the files are inevitably a lot bigger than JPEGs. Raw files will need to be processed in post-production software such as Adobe Lightroom or Photoshop. It is worth noting that some cameras' LCD screens may display a brighter, more saturated version of your Raw file on the screen and if, like me, you shoot simultaneously Raw and JPEG, the image displayed on the rear of the camera will be the JPEG.

A JPEG is a compressed file that has already been somewhat processed by your camera, and each camera will have its own 'profile' as to what 'good' looks like, so keep this in mind when using different camera systems. A JPEG is a standard format that is easy to save and share. However, as always when your camera is making some of the decisions for you, your own creativity is limited.

Finally, it is always good habit to pack a lens cloth, a lens cleaning pen, a small soft bristled brush, a rainproof cover for shooting in the rain, a torch and most importantly supplies such as a reusable water bottle, snacks (the best part) and of course a first aid kit.

In the world of macro photography, there is
very rarely a time where a 'one size fits all'
setting can be deployed. Each scenario is
unique and factors such as lighting, subject
size, shape and appearance, plus your artistic
intent, mean that various settings will be used.
By learning how your camera's settings affect
how to expose an image correctly, you will
be able to capture beautifully lit and detailed
macro imagery.

Two BASIC TECHNIQUES

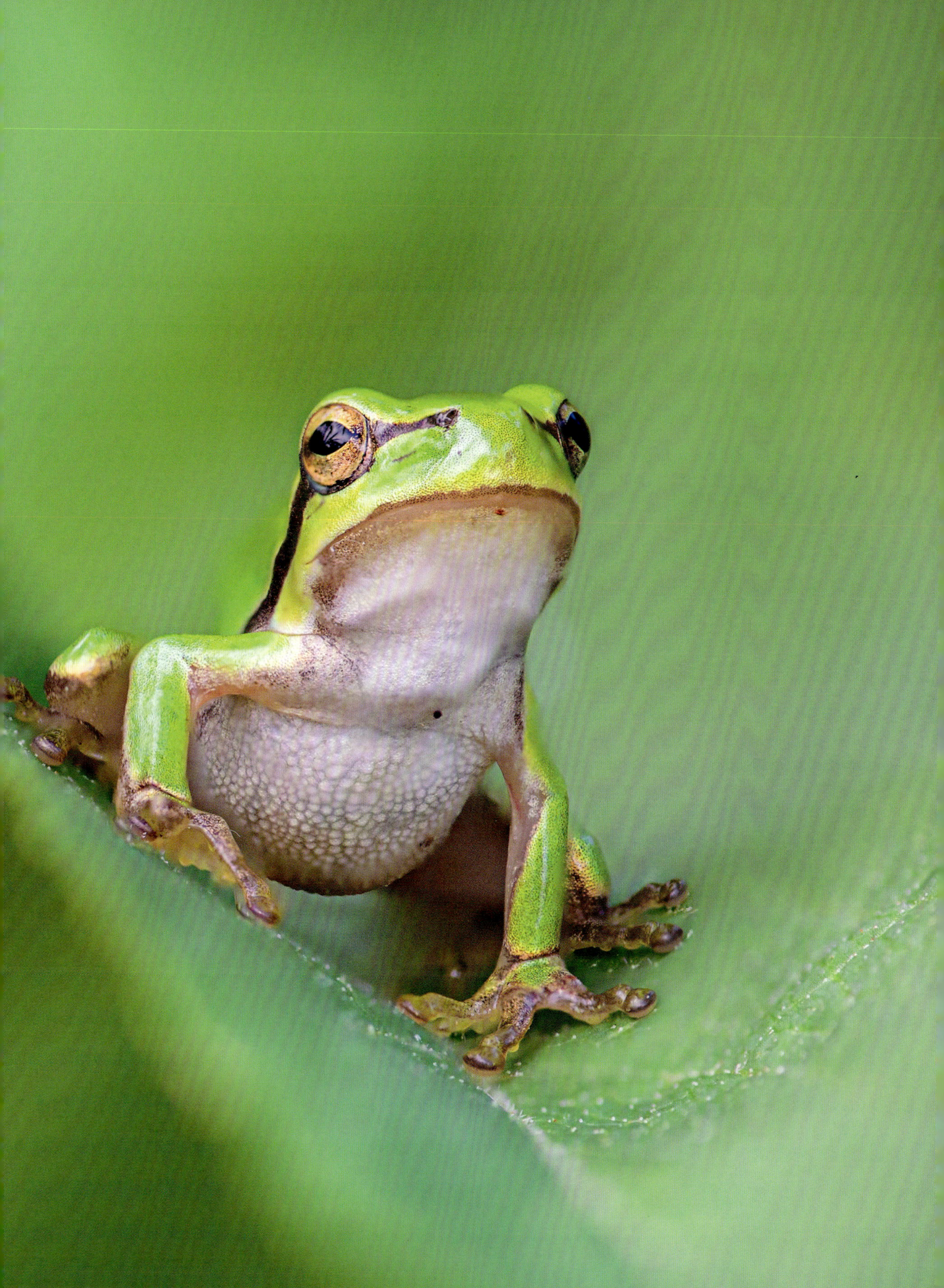

Exposure settings for macro photography

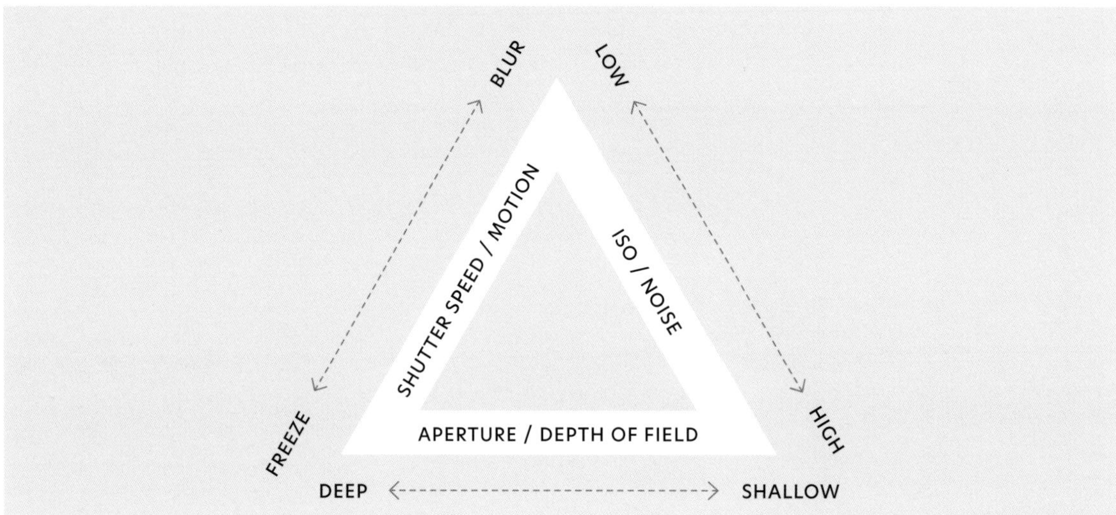

The word 'photography' comes from the Greek words *phos*, meaning 'light', and *graphe*, which means 'I draw' or 'I sketch', so it makes sense that light is the most important element in all photography. Light or lack of light can change how a photograph is formed, and for macro photographers, who often have to work with limited light, it is especially important to understand the factors that go into exposing a photograph properly.

Exposure refers to the amount of light that reaches your camera sensor, and it is determined by three factors: how large or small the aperture that admits light to the sensor is; how long the shutter is open, allowing light to reach the sensor; and how high or low the sensor's sensitivity to light is, known as ISO. Together, the aperture, shutter speed and ISO are referred to as the 'exposure triangle', and learning to balance that triangle is something all photographers need to master in order to take full creative control of their images.

Helpfully, modern cameras come equipped with an internal light meter that measures the amount of light in a scene, according to your settings, and lets you know if an image will be overexposed or underexposed. Allowing too much light in will overexpose an image, making it too bright overall, and losing detail in the highlights, while underexposing – which tends to be more of a problem for macro photographers – is the reverse. However, the exposure triangle is responsible for more than just how light or dark an image turns out. The aperture, shutter speed and ISO settings each play a certain role in how the image looks.

Above The exposure triangle is a handy way to visualize the interdependent nature of the three aspects of exposure.

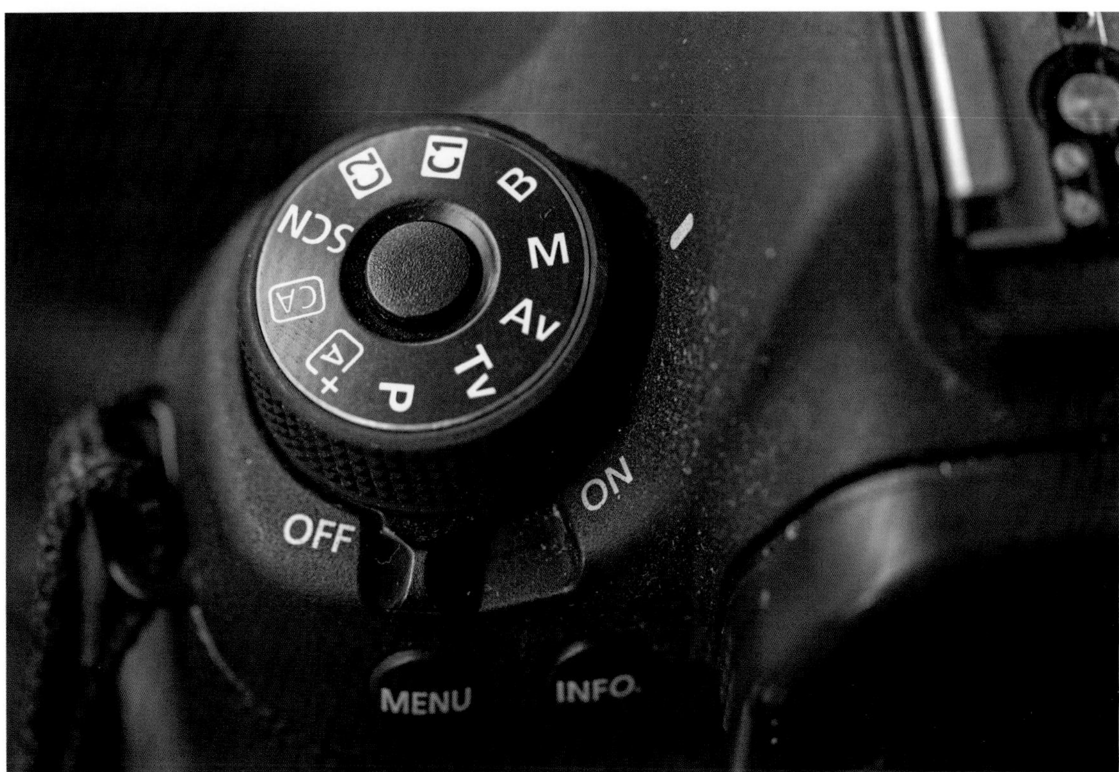

Above The mode dial on your camera lets you switch between shooting modes to explore the different aspects of exposure at your own pace.

Aperture

A bigger aperture allows more light into the camera, and results in a shallower depth of field – meaning less of your scene is in focus – and vice versa.

Shutter speed

The longer the shutter is open (the slower the shutter speed), the more light reaches your sensor; however, any movement in that time will cause blur in the image. A fast shutter speed can freeze movement, but you need to find another way to compensate for the short duration of the exposure.

ISO

You might think that increasing the ISO is the easiest way to compensate for the small apertures and fast shutter speeds sometimes required to capture a subject with enough in focus and no motion blur. However, when the sensitivity increases, it can also pick up unwanted signals and start making your images look grainy, an unattractive phenomenon known as 'noise'.

Thankfully, you don't have to dive into manually setting each aspect of your exposure straight away. DSLR and mirrorless cameras have a number of modes that allow you to experiment with different levels of control, which we will look at over the coming pages.

Automatic and program mode

In automatic mode, the camera chooses the settings for the aperture, shutter speed and sometimes ISO based on the scene and lighting to provide a proper exposure. This mode is designed to simplify the act of taking photographs, allowing you to master things such as composition and focus without worrying about the exposure too much. It is also a great way to learn how the exposure triangle works (see page 46). Automatic mode does have its limitations, and once your confidence develops you will find yourself wanting to explore other modes to expand your creativity and technique, and make the most of all the camera has to offer.

Program mode (usually labelled P) is an automatic mode with slightly more control – you can control the ISO and some other exposure features.

Aperture-priority mode

This mode is often found on the camera dial labelled A or Av. Aperture priority will allow you to set the aperture value, leaving the camera to choose the shutter speed needed to achieve the correct exposure. Using this mode allows you to control the desired depth of field (DoF), which is the area of the scene that will be in focus.

The term 'aperture' describes the opening in a camera lens that regulates how much light reaches the image sensor. It acts in a similar way to the pupil of the human eye, in that it changes size to let more or less light in. For example, an aperture of f/2.8 allows lots of light into the lens while an aperture of f/22 restricts the amount of light.

Depending on the lens, apertures can be as wide as f/1.4 and as small as f/32. There are numerous f-numbers, or f-stops, between these extremes, including f/2, f/2.8, f/4, f/5.6, f/8, f/11, f/16 and f/22. The difference between each of these f-stops represents one 'stop' of light. How wide or small the aperture is not only affects the amount of light reaching your sensor, it also impacts how much or little of the scene will be in focus.

The area of sharpness in front of and behind the point of focus is referred to as 'depth of field'. A shallow depth of field, where only a small portion of the image is in focus and the rest is blurred to some extent, is produced by a wide aperture (small f-stop) such as f/1.4 or f/2.8. This technique is frequently used in macro photography to separate the subject from the background. It can also create a pleasing effect known as bokeh, where any points of bright light in the background are rendered as blurred shapes, typically circles.

On the other hand, a small aperture (high f-stop) such as f/16 or f/22 results in a larger depth of field. This helps keep more of the image in focus, but can also mean capturing distracting elements in your scene.

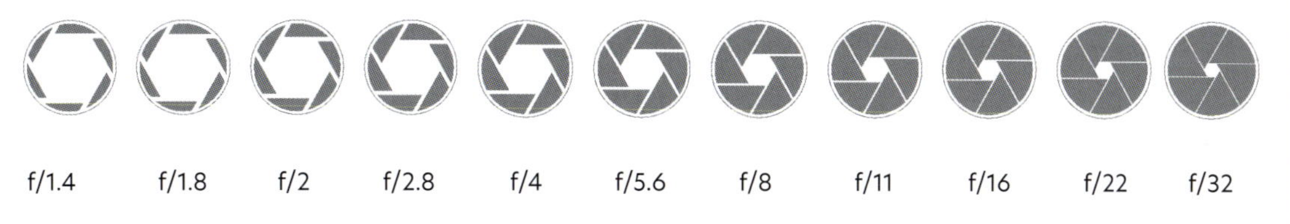

Above This graphic illustrates how each f-stop affects the aperture blades.

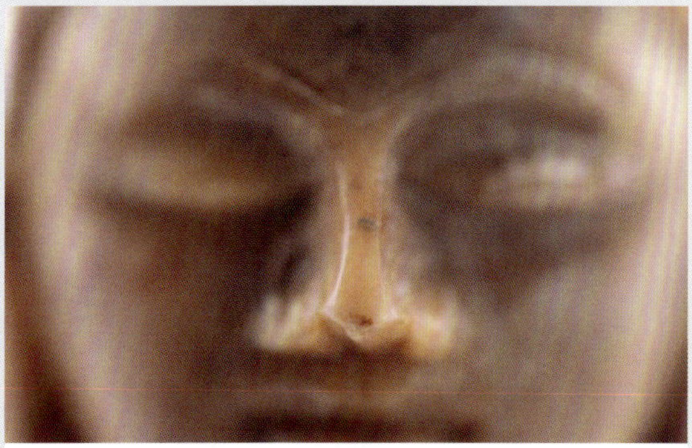

f/2.8

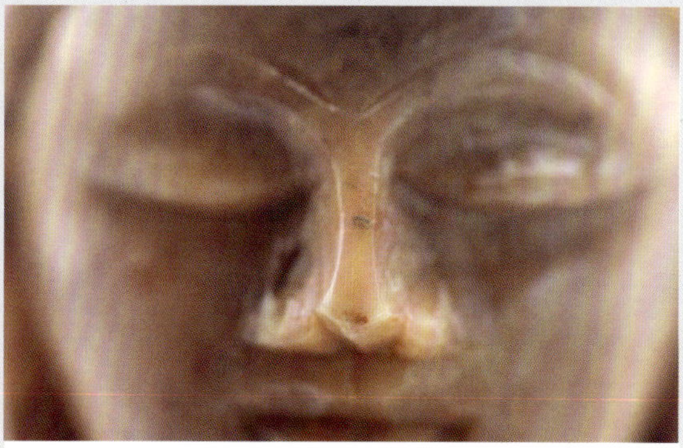

f/5

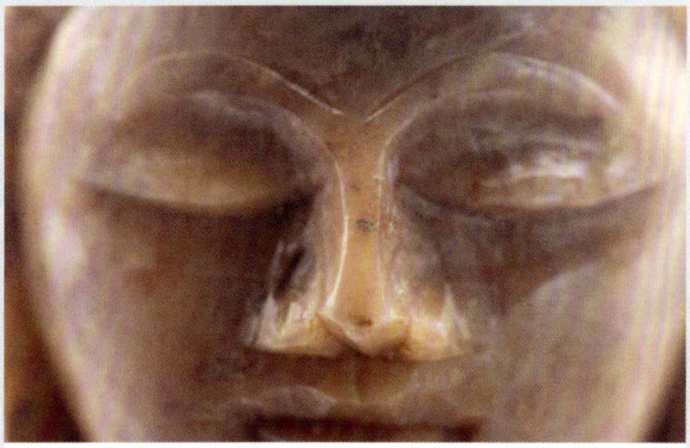

f/9

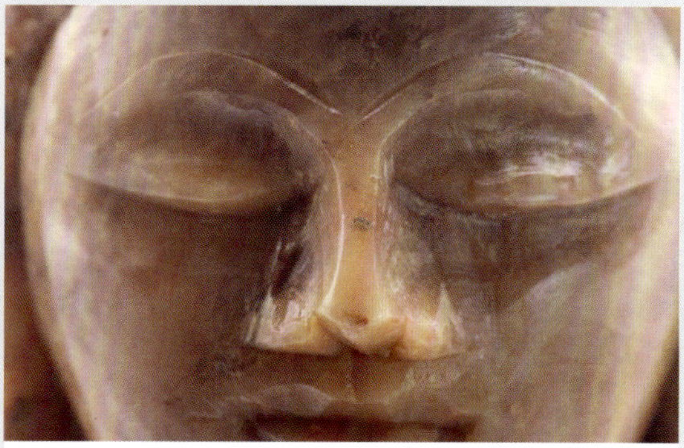

f/18

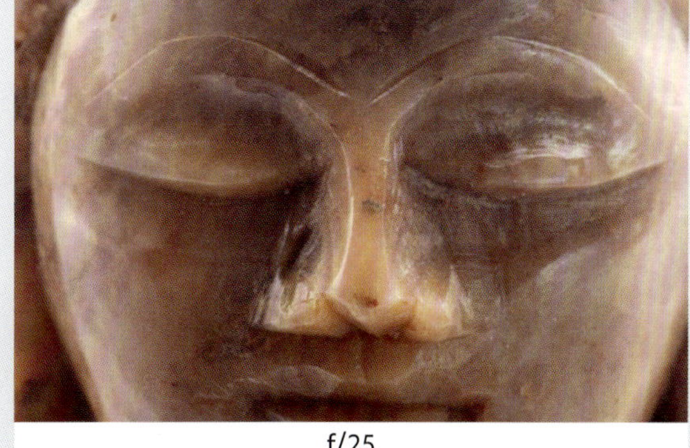

f/25

Above & left Your choice of aperture controls how much or how little of your scene or subject is in focus. Look at how each aperture setting changes the amount of the subject that is sharp.

Shutter-priority mode

This mode is usually labelled S or Tv on the mode dial. Utilizing this mode allows you to set the desired shutter speed while the camera chooses the aperture value needed to give a correct exposure. This setting is usually used when you want to capture or freeze fast-moving subjects, on windy days when flowers may be swaying back and forth, or for in-flight subjects such as dragonflies and butterflies. Shutter-priority mode can also be used when you want to reduce or add motion blur to an image.

When shooting handheld, using a shutter speed that is equal to or greater than the focal length of your lens can help avoid camera shake. For example, if you are using a 100mm macro lens, a shutter speed of 1/100sec or higher will help keep your focal point nice and sharp. Of course, this is also dependent on you as a photographer, how much your lens weighs and how steady you are.

When shooting macro at high magnification, any movement becomes more visible, something to keep in mind when opting to shoot handheld. Of course, you can also use a tripod to help minimize camera shake and allow you to use longer shutter speeds for that extra bit of light.

Shutter speed is expressed in fractions of a second, such as 1/1000sec, 1/250sec and 1/30sec, although it can also be expressed in whole seconds, such as 1sec, 2sec etc. The range of shutter speeds varies depending on camera make and model, but generally extends from the slowest setting of Bulb (a user-defined time period) all the way to a fastest setting of around 1/8000sec. How long the sensor is exposed to light depends on the shutter speed selected.

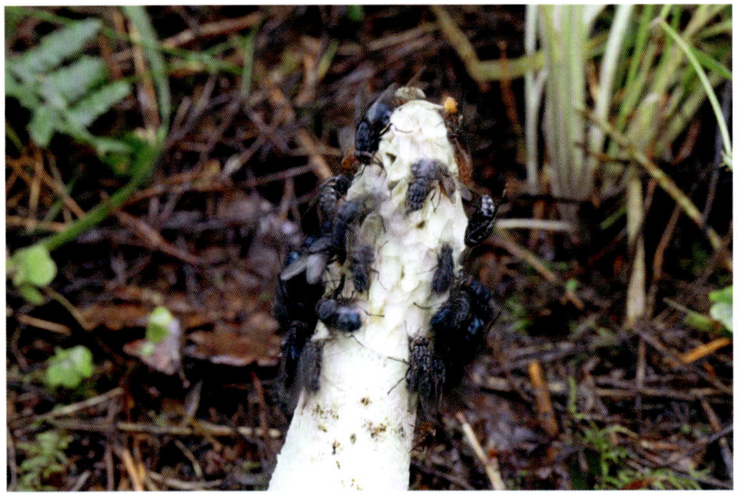

Left Without the use of a tripod, shutter speed not only affects the amount of light entering your lens, but also the amount of camera shake captured by your camera's sensor. In this photo, not only does a slow shutter speed add camera shake, but it is also not fast enough to capture the motion of the busy flies on this stinkhorn fungus.

Picture/style modes

Most modern cameras have various picture or style modes, given different name by different manufacturers. These modes are essentially presets accessible from your camera menu, with parameters that adjust the overall colour, sharpness, contrast and saturation.

They offer a quick and simple way to edit your image's appearance without using post-processing. Some cameras allow you to customize picture style settings or add extra parameters to suit your preferences. The most common picture style modes include:

- **Standard** – A basic preset that offers a balanced look with a slight boost to colours, contrast and sharpness.

- **Portrait** – Designed with skin tones in mind, this mode produces a softer and flatter look, reducing contrast and boosting warm tones.

- **Landscape** – Designed for capturing landscapes, this mode boosts sharpness and saturation.

- **Neutral** – Compared to the standard mode, neutral has less sharpening, contrast and saturation. It is meant for post-processing or finishing touches.

- **Monochrome** – This mode captures the image in black and white or sepia tones.

- **User-defined** – In this mode, you can customize parameters such as sharpness, saturation, contrast and colour tone and save them as a preset.

- **Macro** – This mode is specifically designed to help capture sharp and detailed images of small subjects.

It's important to keep in mind that the macro setting, which is typically represented by a small flower on the camera's mode dial, enables the camera to increase the aperture size so that more of the subject is in focus. Aperture, shutter speed and ISO are all controlled by this mode. Macro mode does not increase magnification as a dedicated macro lens would, and the mode's availability will depend on the camera model you are using.

Manual mode

Manual mode is labelled M on a camera's mode dial. This mode is for experienced photographers who are confident with the exposure triangle and want full control of aperture, shutter speed and ISO. When using manual mode, it's important to be aware of the changing light conditions in which you are photographing. For example, an overcast scene can quickly turn into an overexposed scene if the sun suddenly peeks out from behind the clouds. In automatic and semi-automatic modes such as aperture-priority, the camera will meter for this change, and adjust the settings to maintain a consistent exposure. In manual mode, it will not. The light meter will still display information on the LCD or viewfinder based on the scene's exposure, but it will have no effect on the settings, serving more as a guide.

With complete control over the exposure settings, you have the freedom to produce images exactly as you envision them. Using manual mode enables greater creativity and experimentation, and it will greatly enhance your understanding about how ISO, shutter speed and aperture interact with one another. It may take some trial and error, but this mode should be explored once you are comfortable with your camera.

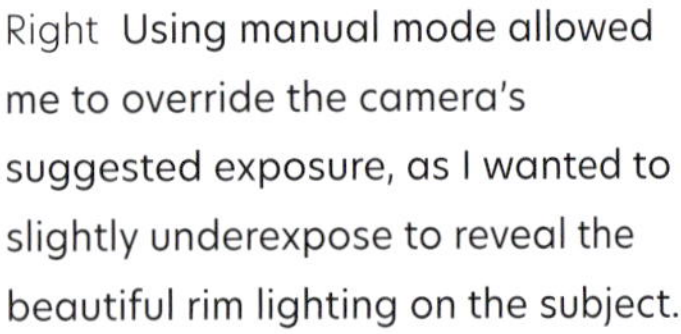

Right Using manual mode allowed me to override the camera's suggested exposure, as I wanted to slightly underexpose to reveal the beautiful rim lighting on the subject.

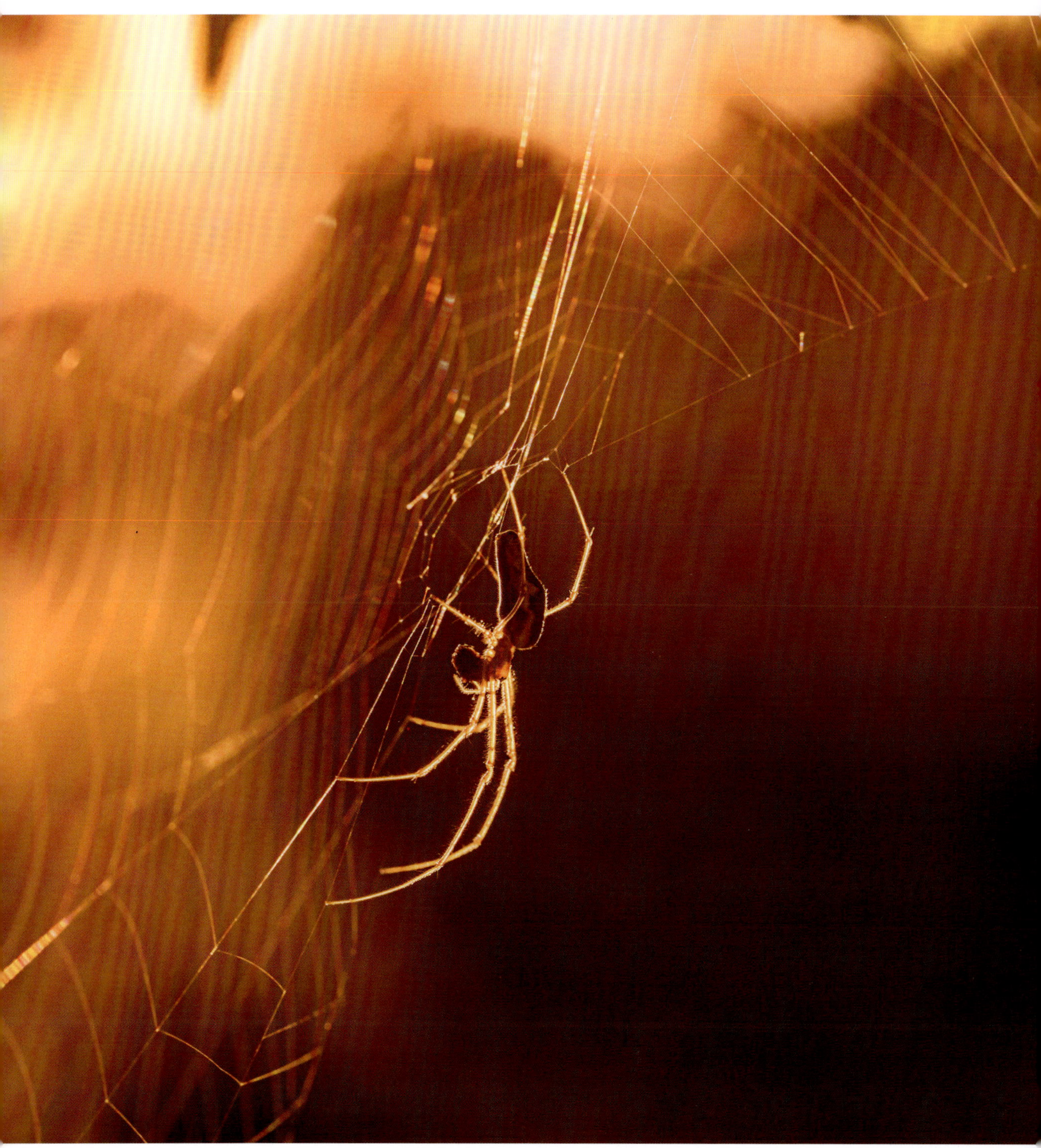

Exposure compensation

The light meters in our cameras generally do a great job at evaluating a scene, but can sometimes get it wrong and provide incorrect exposure settings. If you are shooting in manual mode, this will not affect you, however, it will impact the auto modes. Knowing when the light meter may struggle and how to override the exposure without switching to manual will allow you to capture detailed macro images with the desired level of brightness when you're still learning the exposure triangle.

In high-contrast lighting scenes, such as a sunny day, the deep contrast between shadows and highlights can really confuse light meters. They may try to expose for the shadows and increase the exposure, but by doing this the lighter parts of the scene are also increased in brightness and risk becoming overexposed and vice versa. Backlit subjects (see page 65) can also play havoc with light meters, as they will expose for the brighter light, resulting in an underexposed subject. Dimly lit environments and reflective and bright surfaces can also confuse light meters.

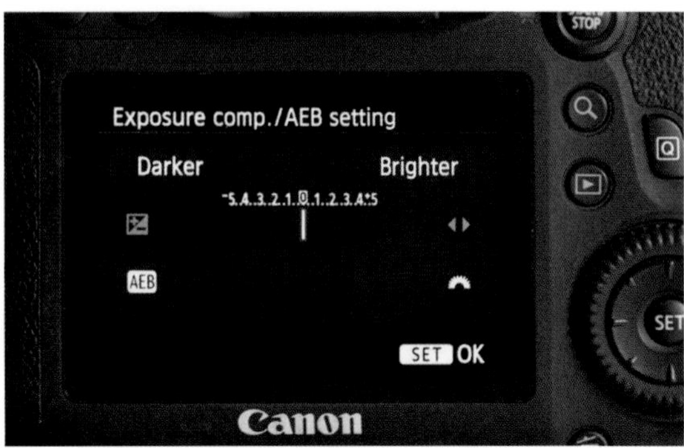

Above Exposure compensation can usually be dialled in via your camera's main menu, but sometimes it can also be found as a dedicated option deeper in the menu.

So, to avoid this ruining our shots, we can use exposure compensation to increase (+) or decrease (-) the exposure. To access this function, look for a button with a +/- symbol on your camera. Some camera systems have moved this to a menu feature. Once located, pressing it will activate the exposure compensation menu. From here, you can use the dials or buttons to adjust the exposure to suit your desired exposure. If the image appears too dark you would most likely want to increase (+) the exposure; if it's too bright you would want to reduce the exposure (-).

PRO TIP Exposure compensation only works in automatic and semi-automatic modes. It's a good habit to reset all adjustments once you have finished or you may use the new exposure settings on subsequent photographs. Consult your camera manual to locate the exposure compensation function first before trying it out in the field, and maybe even try it out at home on some household items.

Right I used exposure compensation to underexpose this scene to add some mood and allow the insect's wings to stand out.

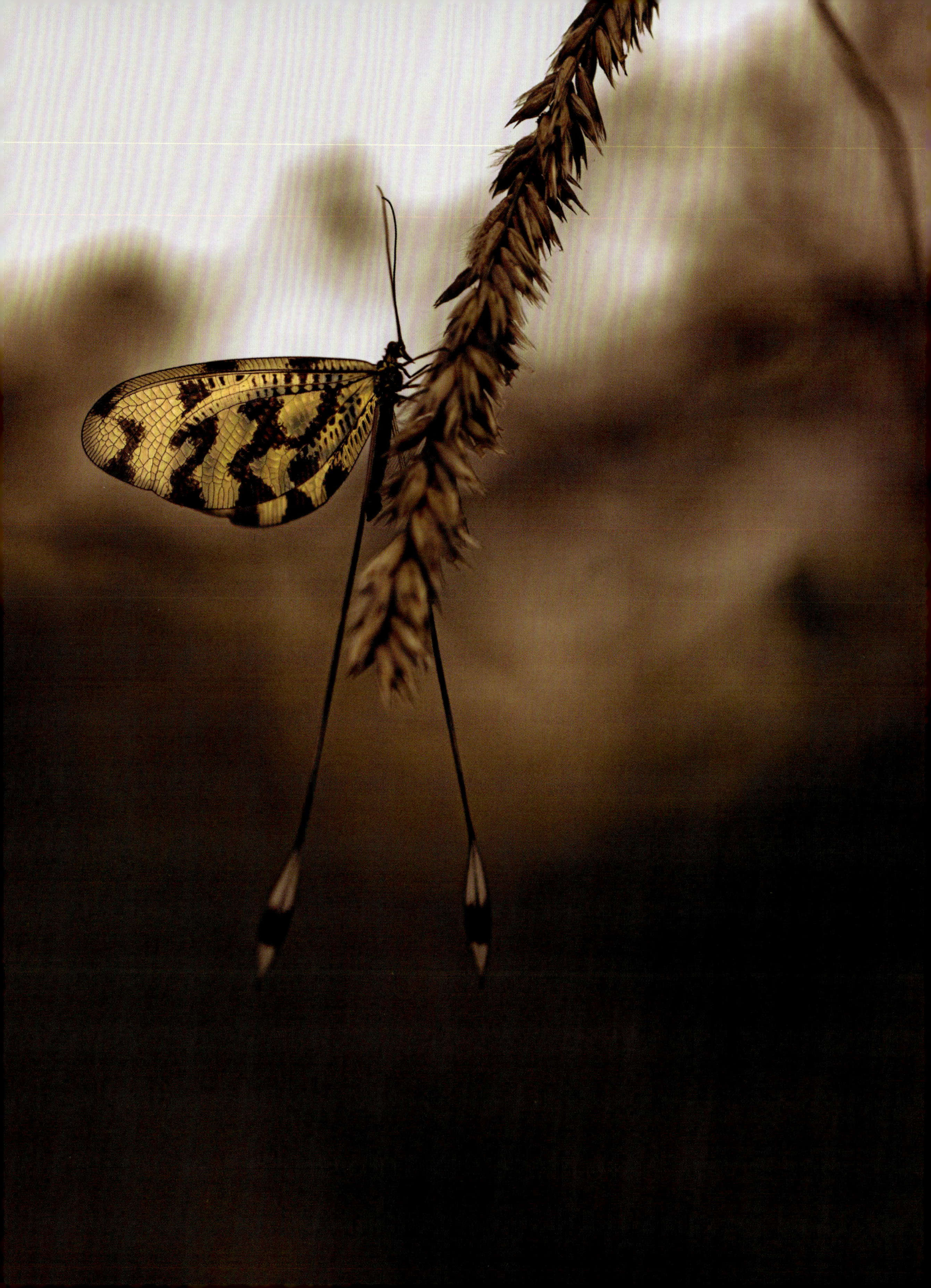

White balance

White balance is a vital aspect of digital photography that ensures accurate and natural colours in your pictures. Different light sources emit light with a different colour temperature, which if not accounted for can give your photographs a warm (orange/yellow) or cool (blue) tone. The white balance setting adjusts the colour temperature of your camera's sensor to match the colour temperature of the light source in the scene you are photographing. Most cameras feature white balance presets that have been designed to reflect basic lighting conditions such as daylight, flash and shade. You can choose your white balance profile by pressing the WB button or by accessing the white balance menu, then scrolling through the profiles and choosing the one that best matches your scene.

Most cameras have an auto white balance feature, often abbreviated to AWB. This works the same way as any automatic feature, in that once you select it you are relying on the camera's algorithms to evaluate the scene in front of it and, in this case, adjust the white balance settings accordingly. In situations where the light source is consistent, auto white balance works very well. However, in situations with a mixture of light sources, the camera may struggle to correctly adjust the white balance profiles for the scene. This also applies for scenes dominated by one colour. For example, if you are shooting in foliage heavily dominated by a flowering plant, such as gorse, the camera may assume the light source is a yellow light and incorrectly apply the wrong colour adjustments to the white balance. This can be avoided by using a white balance card, also known as a grey card.

A white balance card's primary purpose is to give the camera a neutral reference point so that it can determine the right colour temperature at the time of use. They are also very easy to use. You need to place the white balance card in the same lighting as your subject, and take a reference photo. The camera then uses this image as a starting point to calculate the precise colour temperature. You can get consistent and natural colour in subsequent photos taken in the same

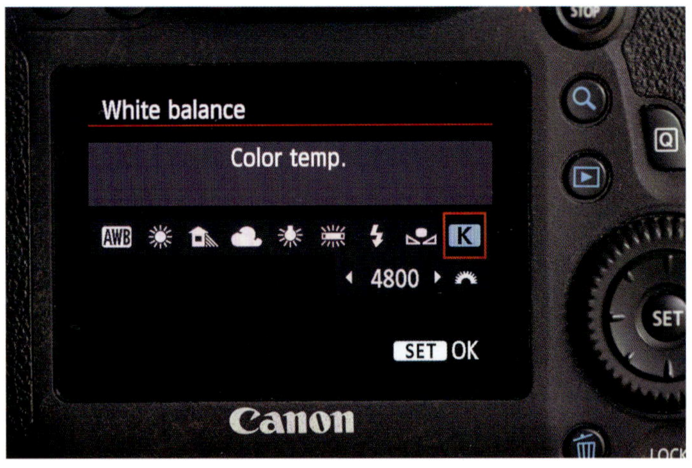

Right The benefit of modern cameras is the ability to change settings to suit your needs. In this instance, we are changing the white balance to suit the scene and lighting in front of us.

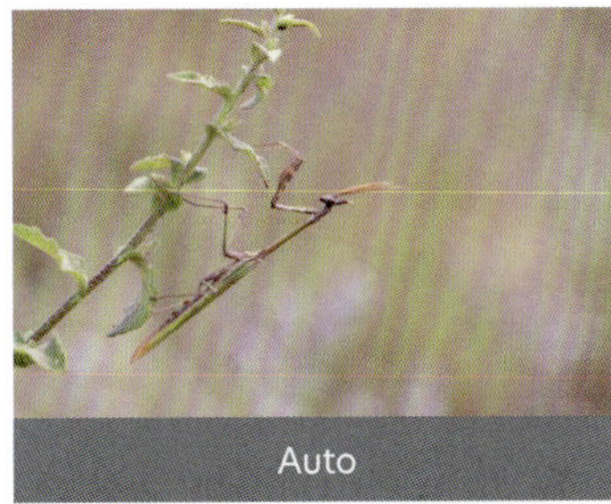

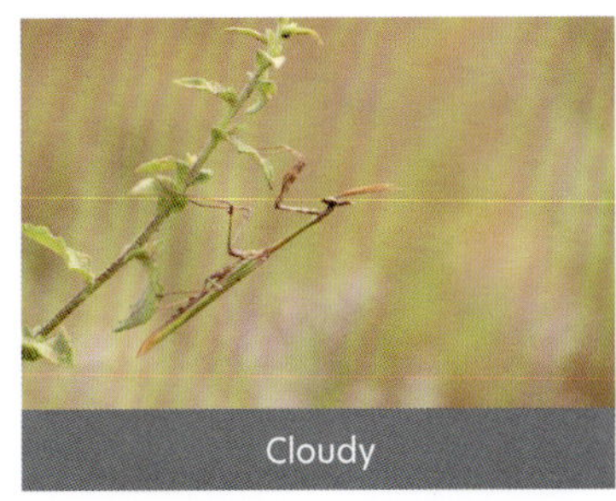

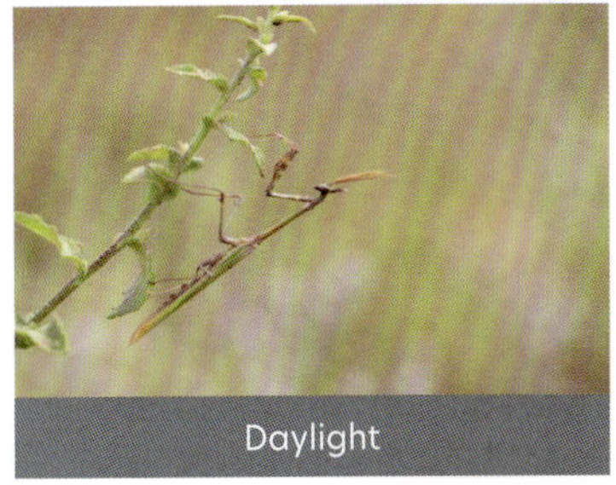

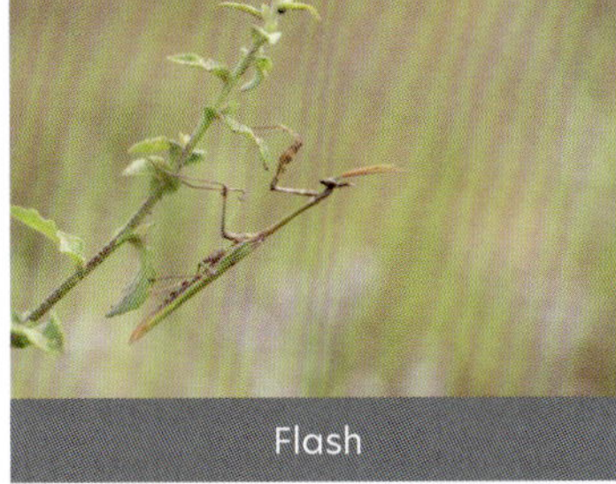

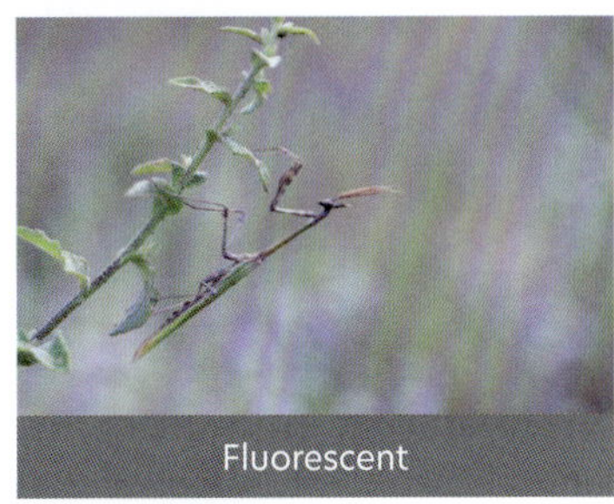

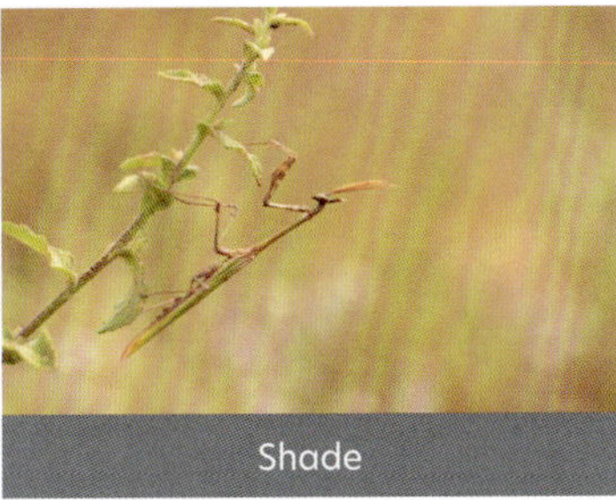

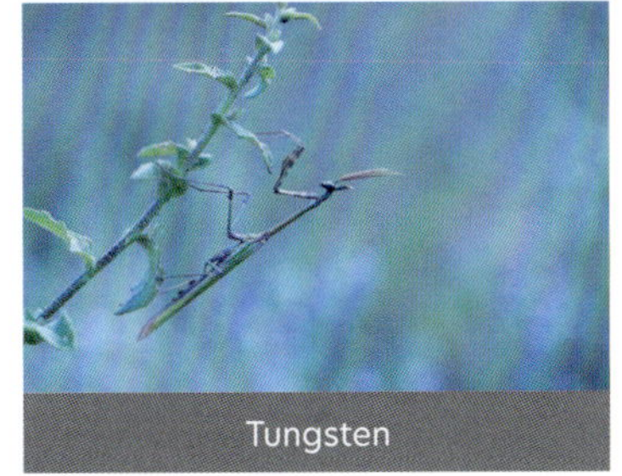

Above White balance can change the mood and feel of your images. It can be used intentionally to add warmth or a creative touch.

lighting conditions by adjusting the white balance settings based on the reference image you just took. Simply change the settings from auto to custom or manual to edit. In some camera systems you can even select the photograph taken with the white card and let the camera automatically make the adjustments for you. No matter the ambient lighting, the white balance card ensures that colours appear as they should.

The white balance setting may have an impact on how the image appears on your camera's LCD screen when shooting in Raw format, but in this instance it won't have a direct impact on the raw data itself. To avoid having this indirectly influence your exposure decisions, it is crucial to keep this in mind. If you are shooting in JPEG, however, the image displayed on the LCD screen will be very close in appearance.

Autofocus modes and manual focus

Capturing high-magnification photographs would be pointless if they weren't in focus, and having the ability to control that focus and knowing when to use automatic or manual is key to capturing pin-sharp images. Focus is split into two categories: autofocus (and its modes) and manual focus.

The technology inside modern cameras and lenses continues to advance at an impressive rate, as does the functionality of autofocus and its various modes. Each mode has its pros and cons, with some more suited to macro photography than others. When your camera is set up for autofocus, various modes can be accessed via the camera menu. The most common are:

- **Single-point autofocus** - Once you select a particular AF point, the camera will look for contrast in that area only, giving you pin-point accuracy.

- **Continuous autofocus** - Sometimes referred to as AF-C or AI Servo, this mode continually readjusts the focus as the subject moves through the frame.

- **Automatic autofocus** - This mode allows the camera to pick the focus point based on what it sees.

While it's true that there are many other automatic modes available, in my experience they don't do a great job when shooting high-magnification macro photographs.

Autofocus works in two ways: active and passive. With active autofocus, the camera fires a beam of infrared light onto your subject, which bounces back into the camera. The camera then calculates the distance and corrects the focus of the lens accordingly. Passive autofocus uses phase or contrast detection. Both methods can be problematic at high magnification.

Autofocus works wonders with larger subjects such as reptiles and amphibians, and even large beetles, dragonflies and butterflies, but when it comes to smaller insects, autofocus begins to fail and this is one of the major hurdles most amateur macro photographers face.

So, why does it fail? At higher magnifications, the working depth of field is very small and the autofocus systems struggle to find contrast or variations in camera-to-subject distance when you're so close to the actual subject with your lens. Also, insects blend in so well with their environment that the autofocus system can't tell the difference between the subject and its surroundings. This is why most macro photographers use manual focus.

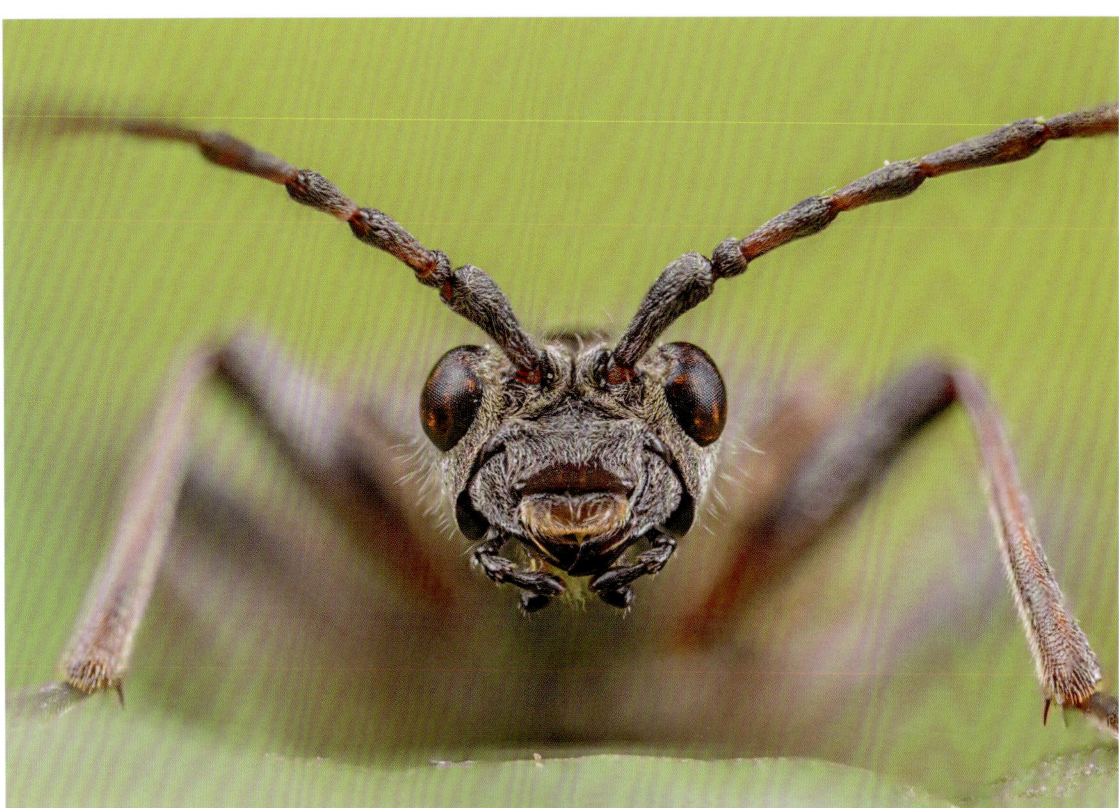

Switching to manual focus puts the control back in your hands – literally. By moving your camera's focus ring, you select where that focus lands. It can be the face of a butterfly or a section of its wings. It could be an abstract shot of an insect deep in a bush where autofocus may choose to focus on the bush itself rather than the insect. With manual focus, you get to adjust the focus to match your creative desires, and it is essential for some of the more advanced techniques we'll look at later.

Manual focus requires lots of practice and patience, but the time and effort spent mastering it will be rewarding.

Above A portrait of a two-banded longhorn beetle. Symmetry and a face-on approach can make a great composition. Try photographing your subjects at their level.

ISO

ISO is often one of the more confusing exposure controls for amateur macro photographers to understand, but it doesn't have to be. Put simply, ISO is a measurement of a camera sensor's sensitivity to light; the higher the ISO number, the more sensitive the sensor is to light, and the lower the ISO number, the less sensitive it is to light.

ISO is an essential part of the exposure triangle. You may find yourself in a situation where you have your desired aperture and shutter speed, but the image is still underexposed. This is where ISO comes into its own. By increasing the camera sensor's sensitivity, you can capture more light, increasing the exposure.

We have two options for setting ISO: auto and manual. As we've already discovered, setting anything to auto hands control to your camera and its algorithms and meters. When auto ISO is selected – either through a button located on the camera body or through the menu – the camera's light meter will evaluate the scene and increase or decrease the ISO to gain a balanced exposure. This works well with semi-automatic modes such as aperture-priority and shutter-priority. Auto ISO also works well in conditions where the lighting isn't constant, allowing you to work with your desired aperture or shutter speed values without having to worry too much about the exposure, as the camera will adjust ISO for you.

ISO does, however, have some drawbacks. Increasing it too much adds 'noise' to your image, as the images opposite demonstrate. For macro photography, this can affect how the image appears, making it look over-processed, less sharp and generally unappealing. Over the years, the noise-handling performance of modern cameras has advanced so much that even high ISO levels don't produce as much noise, so it's worth testing to find your own camera's acceptable limits.

ISO adjustments are the last thing I look at when taking photographs and I try to get my exposures balanced with the lowest possible ISO. At high magnification, any noise is really apparent, and I want my audience's attention to be on the subject and not the noise. This is why I manually select my aperture, shutter speed and ISO settings, as it gives me full control over the images I produce.

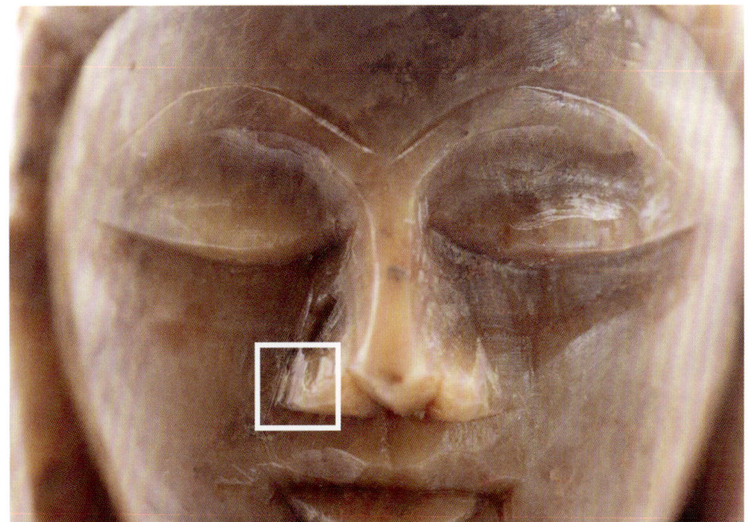

Below & left A high ISO value adds noise to an image. In bright situations, opt for a lower ISO value to reduce the noise.

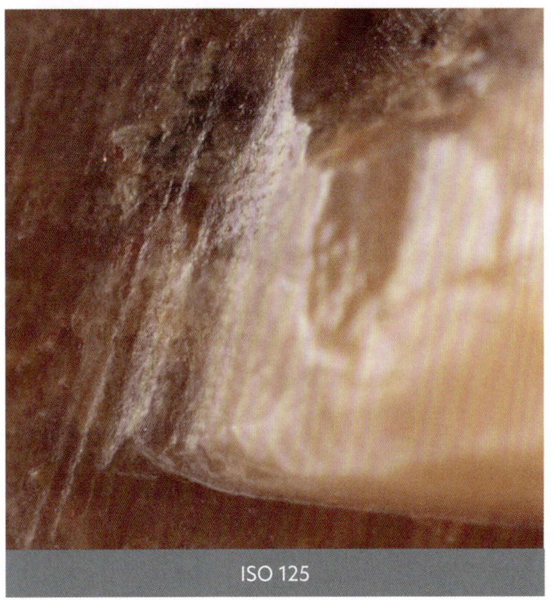

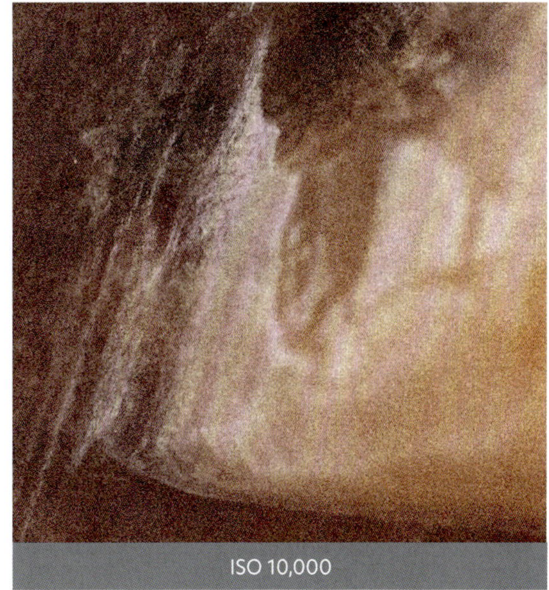

Quality of light

Choosing your light source and the quality of that light source are very important. So, what do we mean by the term 'quality of light'? We're referring to the features and impact of the light source, which can include:

Intensity

The brightness of your light source greatly impacts the overall photograph. A high-intensity light works well with macro subjects such as flowers and insects. These small subjects are full of complex details and having the correct light intensity can help to showcase them. On the other hand, intense light can blow out details and highlights. This can be avoided by altering the camera settings or light source to achieve the correct exposure needed.

Colour

The colour of the light also plays a big part in how your overall image will look and feel. Subjects photographed against a rising or setting sun give off warm light and tones, whereas cooler light, such as that produced in the blue hour or by overcast skies, can bring out the green and blue hues of a subject. If you are using flash or constant lighting such as LED lights, adding various coloured gels can help create a specific mood.

Direction

The light's direction can be used to produce a variety of aesthetic effects as well as change the overall atmosphere of your image. For example, a low rising sun can be used to add a beautiful rim light to your subject. Combining multiple light sources from different directions can add a dynamic look to a subject – a backlit subject with a side light to bring out the details is a great combination. We'll see more on this overleaf.

Hard light

Hard light creates deep shadows, usually cast from a small, focused light source such as an LED or external flash. This type of light gives a high-contrast look to your images with a sharp transition between the light and shadows. Think of how things look on a bright sunny day.

Soft light

Soft light is the opposite of hard light in that it casts a softer, more delicate light over your subjects with a smoother transition between light and shadows. Think of how the light appears on an overcast day, when the harsh sunlight is diffused through clouds. Soft, diffused light is often preferred by macro photographers who use flash and LED light sources.

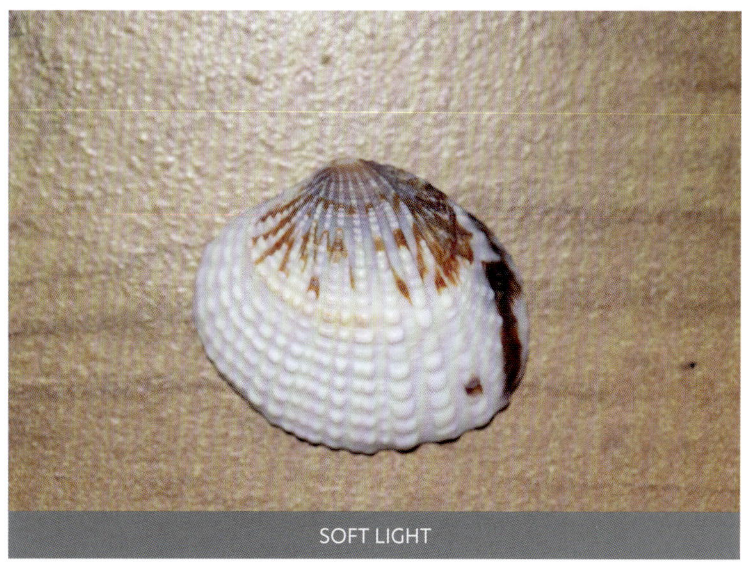

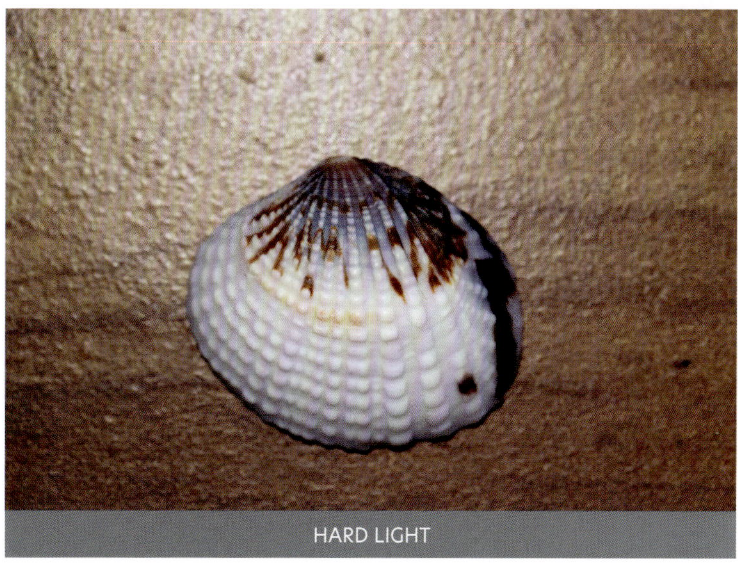

Above Whether the light is soft or hard will give a different look to your subject. With soft light, the light is more evenly spread; overall, there is less definition and contrast, and a softer feel to the image. Hard light can bring out more textural definition, as there is greater contrast between the highlights and shadows.

Directional lighting

Light and its direction can also be used to highlight details and contours of a subject. Below you can see how placing a light source in a north, east, south or west position of the sea shell completely changes how the subject appears.

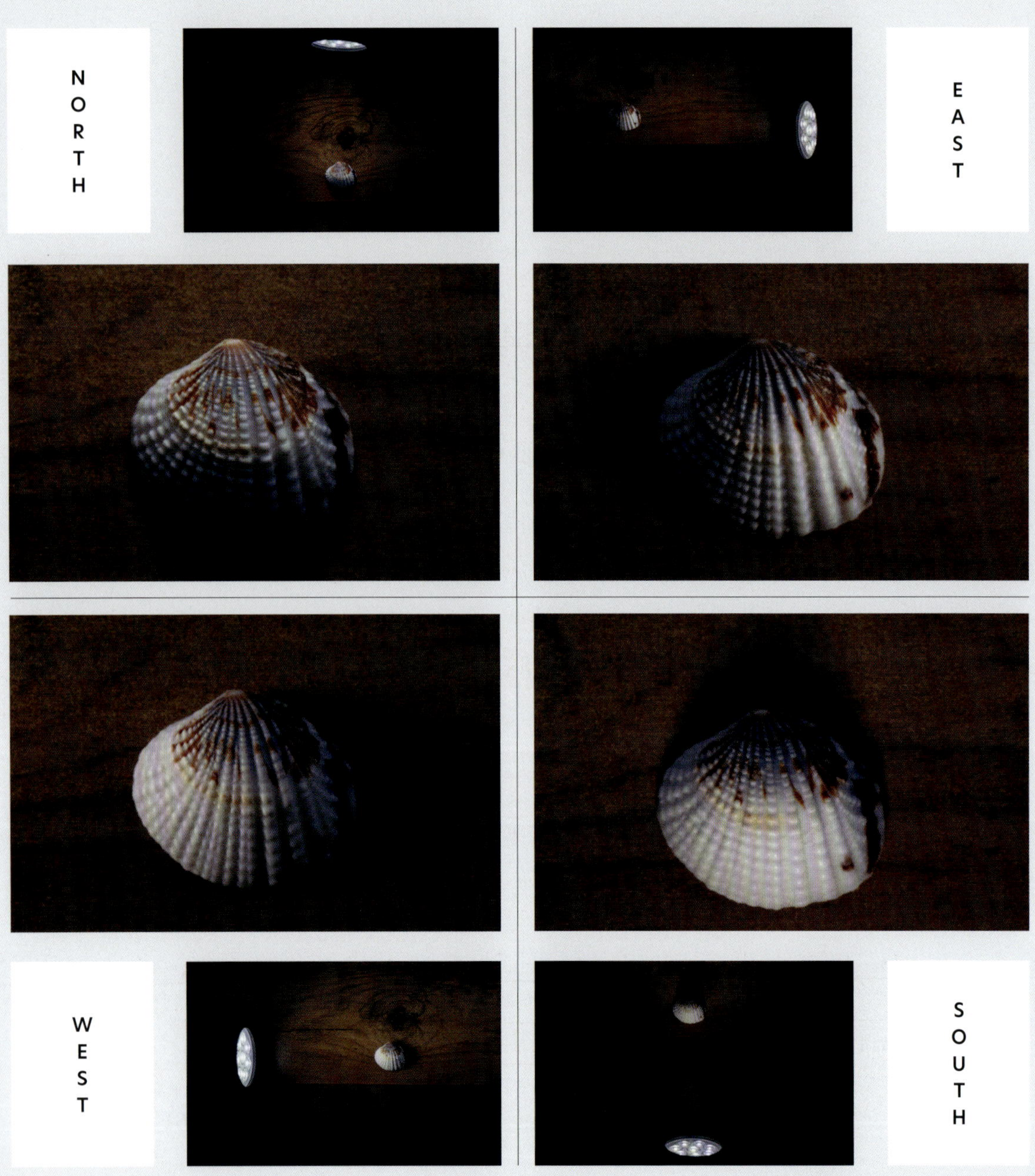

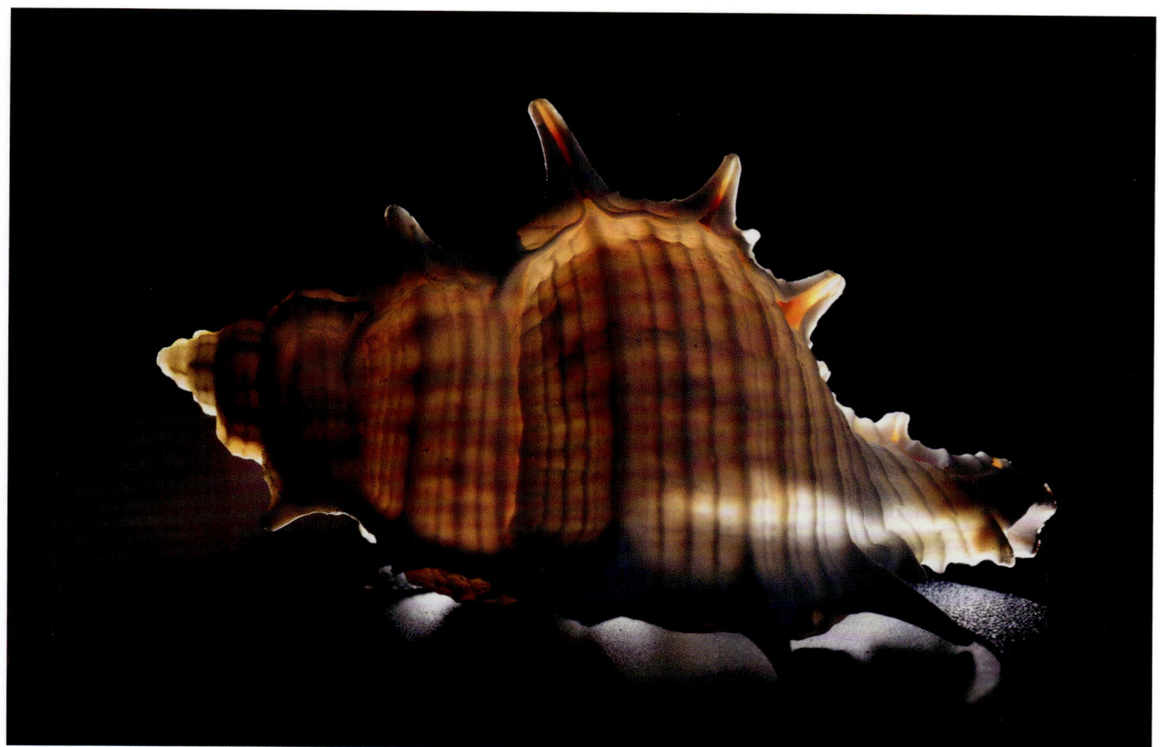

Let's take the light source that is placed to the west of the shell. By placing the light source to the west of our subject we have chosen to illuminate the left side while casting shadows on the right-hand side. The light and the elongated shadows help to define and reveal the structure of the shell. This technique can be used when working with subjects such as beetles to reveal intricate details of the elytra. I find that much of my more 'creative' work has come from when I've begun to experiment with light.

Experimenting with light can offer unique representations of the same subject. Rim lighting or backlighting your subject can turn the ordinary into the interesting. Backlighting involves placing the light source directly behind your subject and shooting towards it. When used successfully, backlighting can produce a glowing effect that brings your subject's textures and colours to vivid life. Experimenting with the angle of the light on your subject can also produce a beautiful rim of light around the edge of your subject, helping to separate it from the background and illuminating its contours.

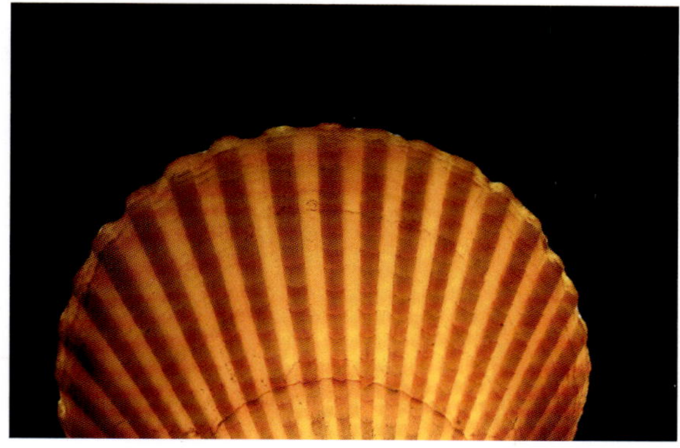

Using flash units

Your choice of flash unit can also determine how well lit your subject and scene is, and how that light affects the contours, shape and appearance of a subject. A single flash unit will give a completely different result to a diffused single flash unit, while a dual flash system changes everything again.

In the first example, a close up shot of an apple, using a diffused dual flash set-up. The broad illumination brings out all the details of the apple's surface, but you lose any sense of its form and volume. Notice the two white reflections, indicating the direction of the light, and the slight rim light at the top-right edge.

In the second example, only one flash head was used, placed to the left of the apple and slightly raised. This set-up causes shadows to the right of the apple, and we lose a little of the surface detail, but it gives a much more three-dimensional sense to the image.

In the previous chapter, we briefly looked at different kinds of diffusers (see page 38). To see the difference a good diffuser can make to your macro photography, consider the following examples. The first uses a single flash mounted on top of the camera, with a small white bounce card to help illuminate the scene. Notice how harsh and contrasting the light is; the highlights of the reflective white spot are also blown, which leaves an unpleasant flash hotspot on the apple.

In comparison, the final example, using a large diffuser (in this case the Cygnustech diffuser seen on page 39) with a single flash unit not only softens the light but it also spreads it evenly and over a wider surface, which is very beneficial for illuminating your subject and scene.

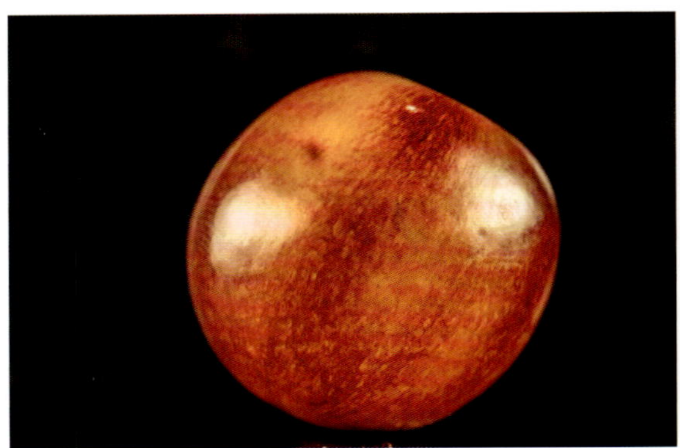

Above **Dual flash**

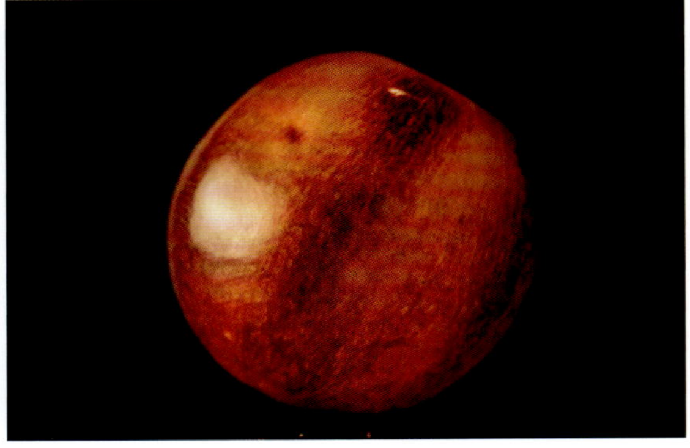

Above **Single flash**

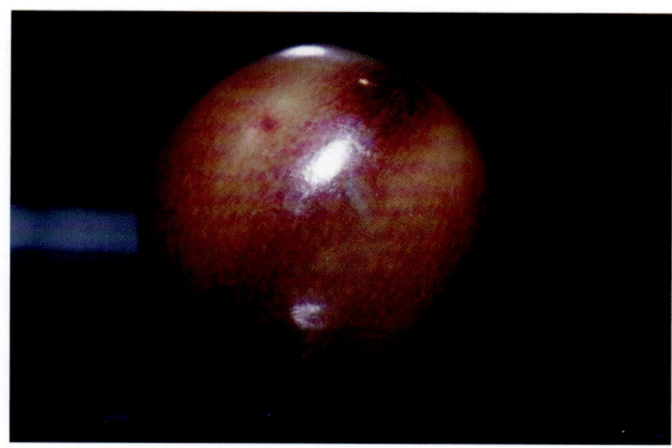

Above Single flash with bounce card

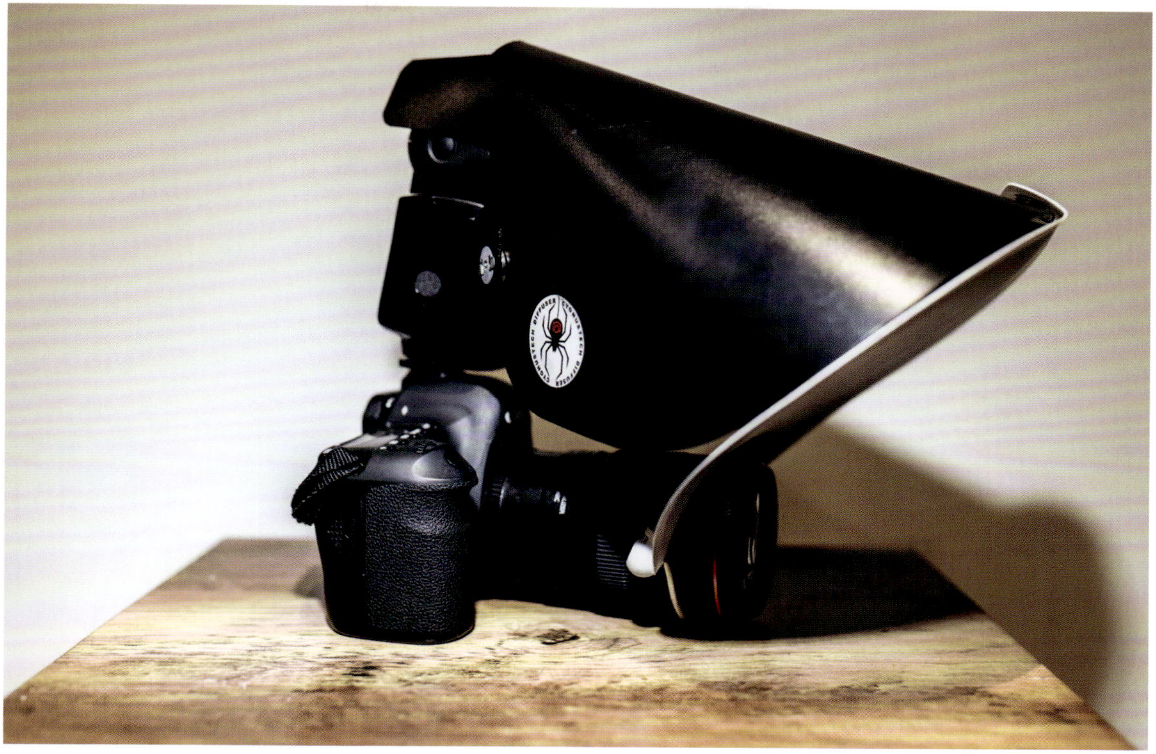

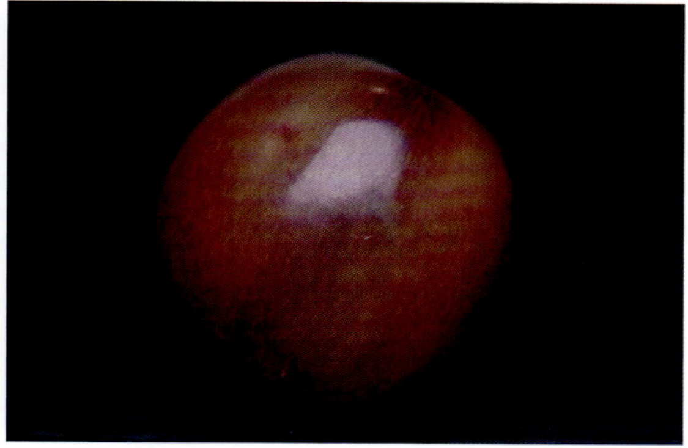

Above Single flash with diffuser

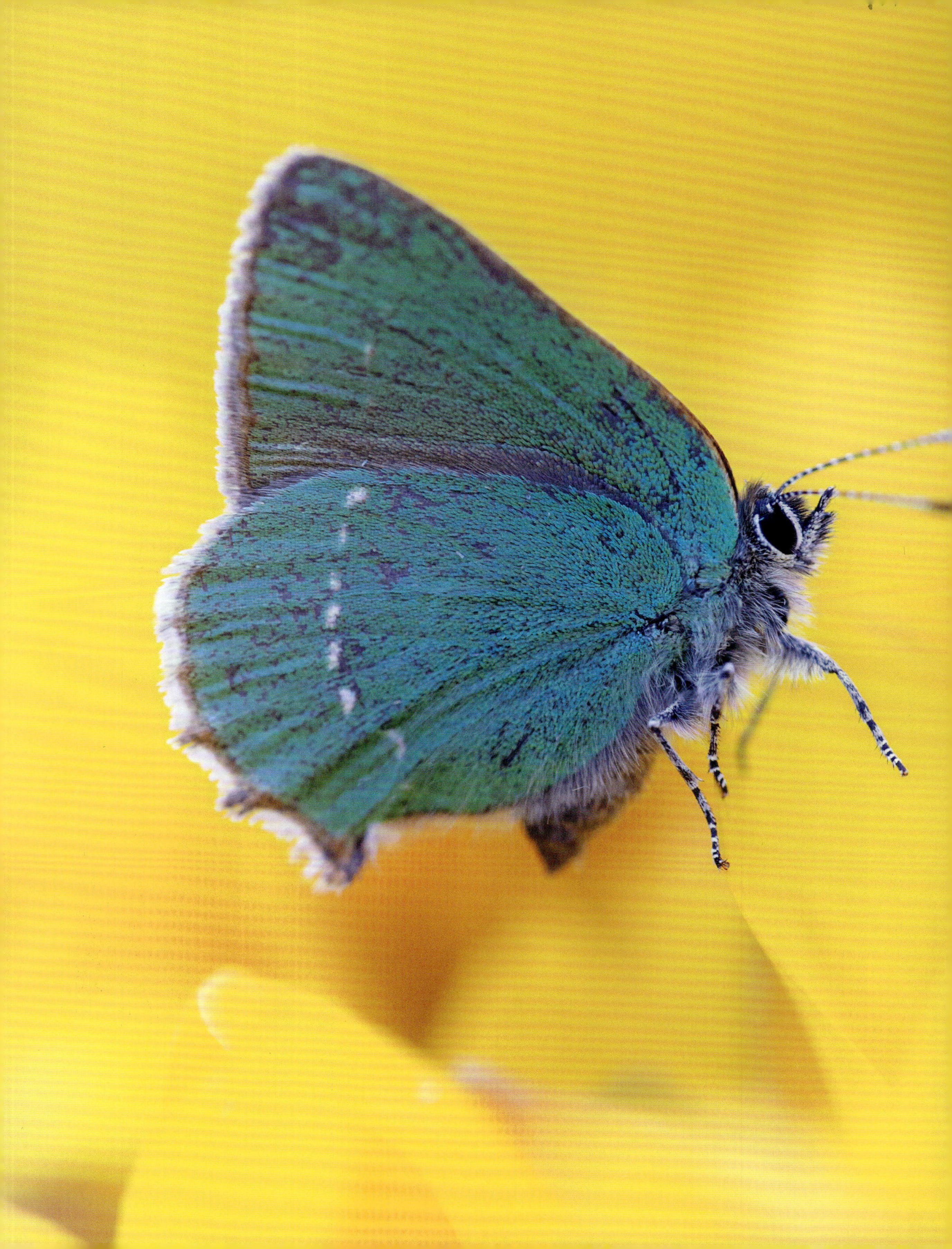

Three
WHAT
TO
SHOOT

A macro lens can be used to get extremely close to pretty much anything you want. In this chapter I will be showing you some of my favourite subjects to photograph at macro level. The most popular macro subjects are insects, flowers, amphibians and reptiles, but it doesn't need to stop there. There are plenty of ways to get creative with household objects, materials and even Lego figures.

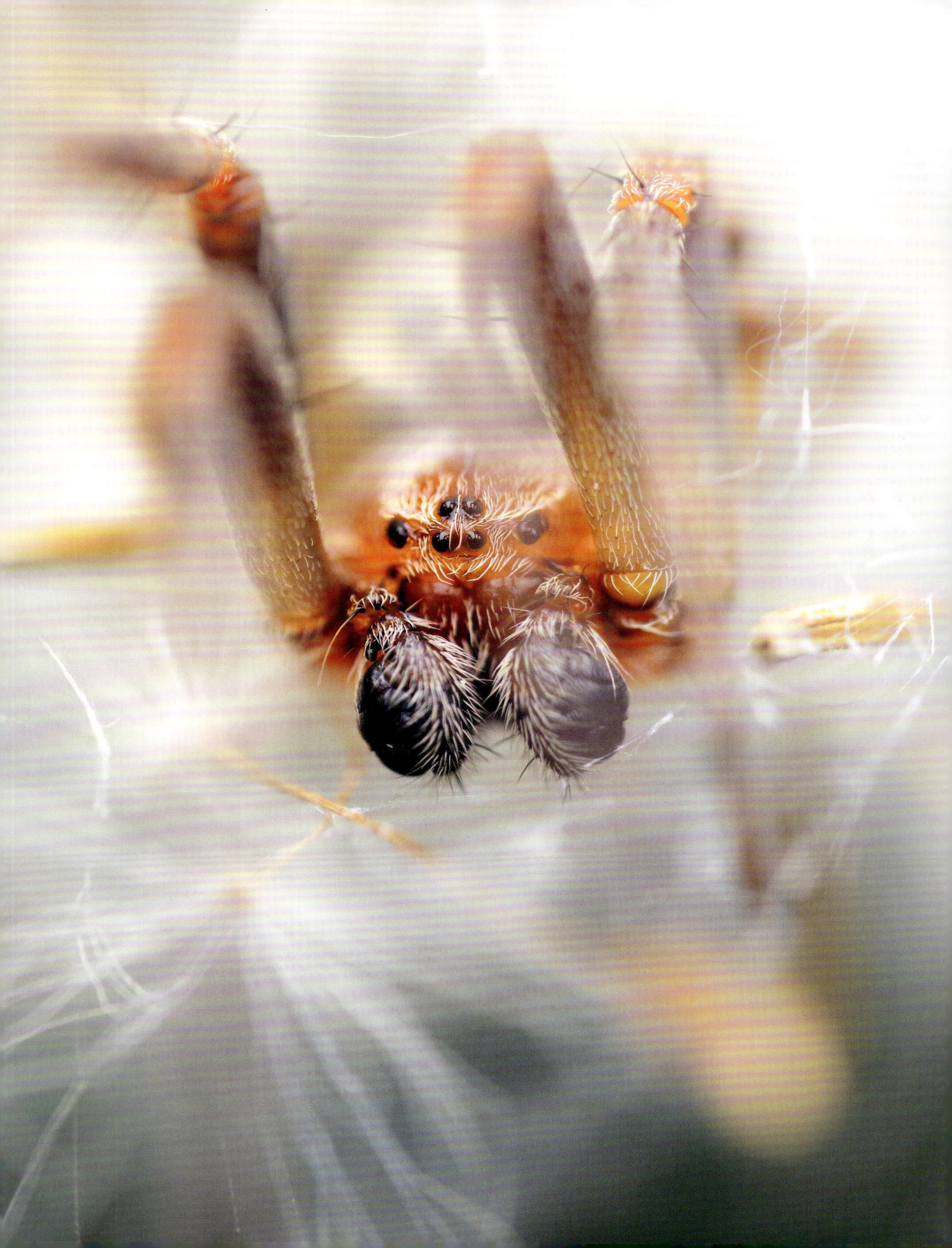

Spiders

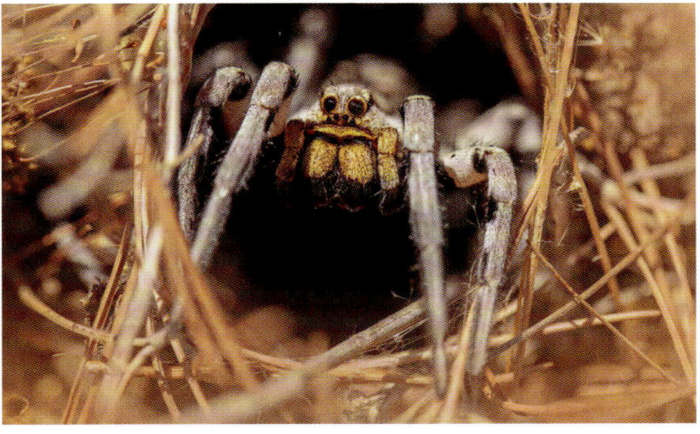

Above A wolf spider emerges from its burrow to see what all the fuss is about.

Love them or hate them, spiders are an essential part of our ecosystem and should be respected just as much as any other living creature. A lot of the fear around spiders is inherited fear from our childhoods. As children, we may see our parents, carers or friends scream and run from spiders. This makes us fearful too, but we don't have to be. Spiders are misunderstood, and they have been for centuries. Often the antagonist for sci-fi films and scary movies, these beneficial creatures are not usually harmful to humans – they're more interested in mating and feeding than they are in biting us. These fascinating creatures are also helpful in controlling insect numbers and even their own population, helping to maintain the ecological balance. Plus, they make fascinating subjects for macro photography.

With over 45,000 known species throughout the world, these arachnids come in all shapes and sizes, many with vibrant colours and patterns. Spiders can be very skittish, especially non-web-building spiders, so it's key to know how and when to approach them. As with most insects and arachnids, early mornings and late evenings are the perfect times. I don't recommend trying to photograph them in the heat of the day until you have studied and mastered your macro photography techniques.

Spiders are best approached from ground level and very slowly. Any shadows cast over them or fast movements will scare them away, so take your time, watch and study them, and understand their behaviours – you will soon be on your way to capturing amazing macro photographs of spiders!

Below Some spider species make fantastic webs, which make for interesting photographs. In this photo, the background is very busy, and the web would become entangled with the distracting elements behind it, but by using a shallow depth of field, you can blur out those elements, focusing attention on the spider and its web.

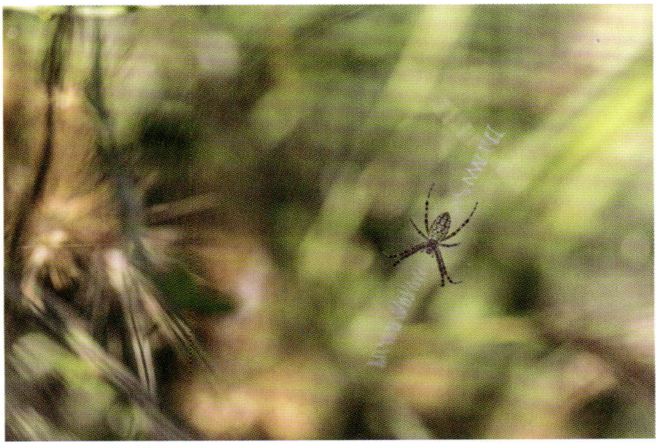

Left A spider waits unsuspectedly on a dandelion clock.

Butterflies

Is there a creature more graceful in flight than the butterfly? A true sign of spring and summer is when you walk in your local park or nature reserve and see butterflies on the wing. It is estimated that there are around 17,500 species of butterfly in the world, but due to habitat loss their numbers have started to plummet over the last few decades.

Like many of our macro subjects, the butterfly is a cold-blooded insect and generally will not fly on cold, overcast days. However, in full sun you can expect to see these beautifully coloured insects making the most of the warmth. In fact, butterflies can be found just about anywhere in the world except Antarctica, but knowing where and when to look is key to photographing this stunning creature.

Butterflies are more approachable in the early mornings when it's cold, as they need to spend some time warming up. If you're lucky you may even find them covered in dew. However, you'll need to set your alarm very early to photograph them like this, especially in summer!

Lots of butterfly species will roost in the evenings in grassy meadows, again providing an opportunity for you to get up close without too much disturbance. As with all wildlife, taking the time to study your chosen subject's behaviour will really improve your chances of locating and photographing them.

Right Getting out before the sun rises provides a perfect opportunity to photograph butterflies. This common blue butterfly had climbed out from the long grass, waiting for the morning sun to heat it up

Right A Cleopatra butterfly flutters from flower to flower in the heat of the day. A brief pause allowed me to get a photograph.

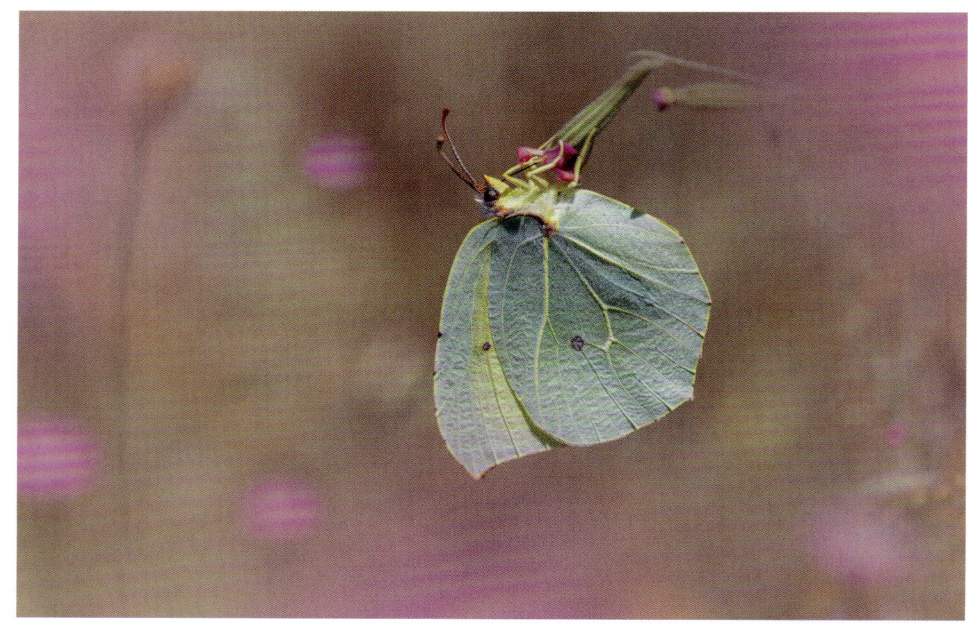

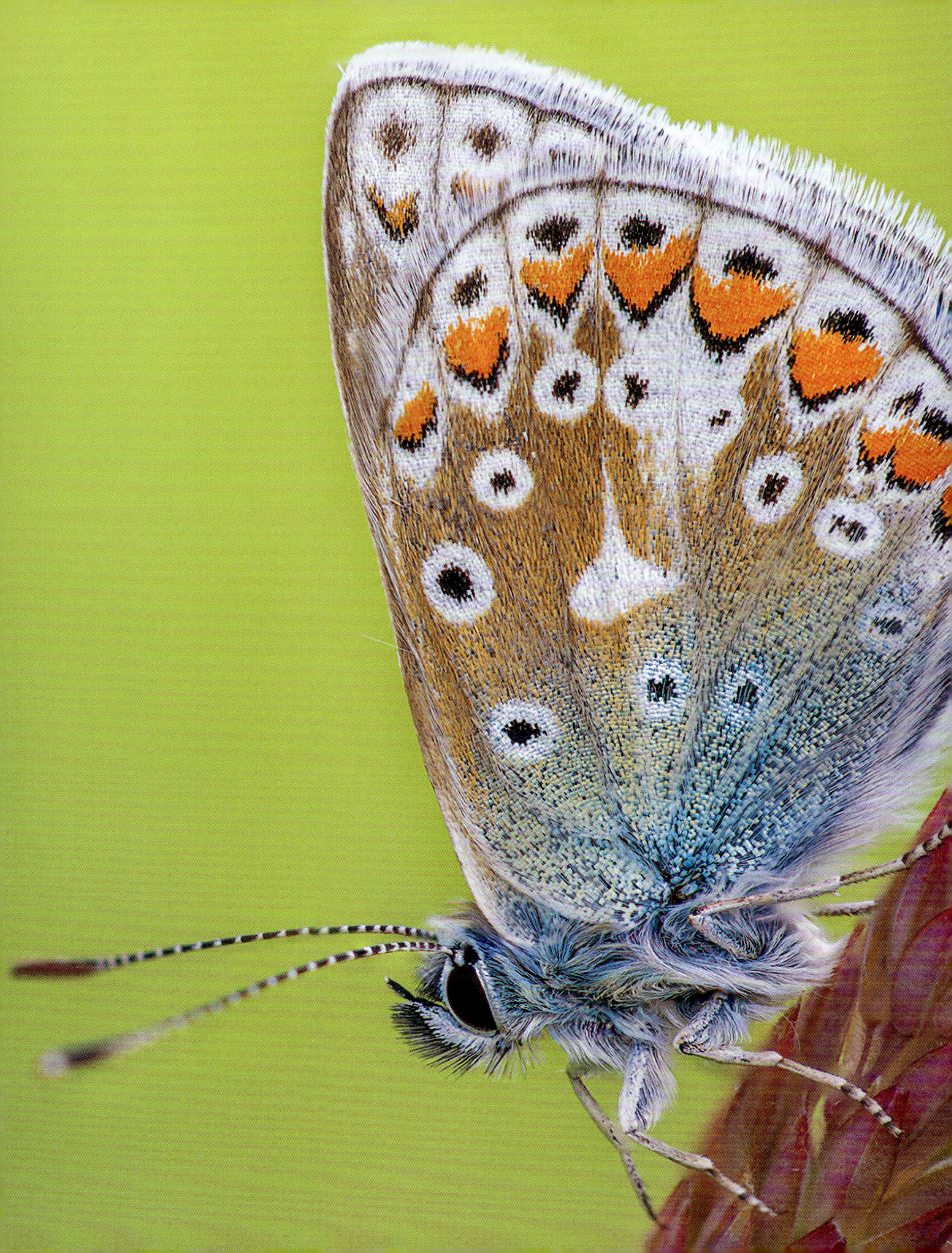

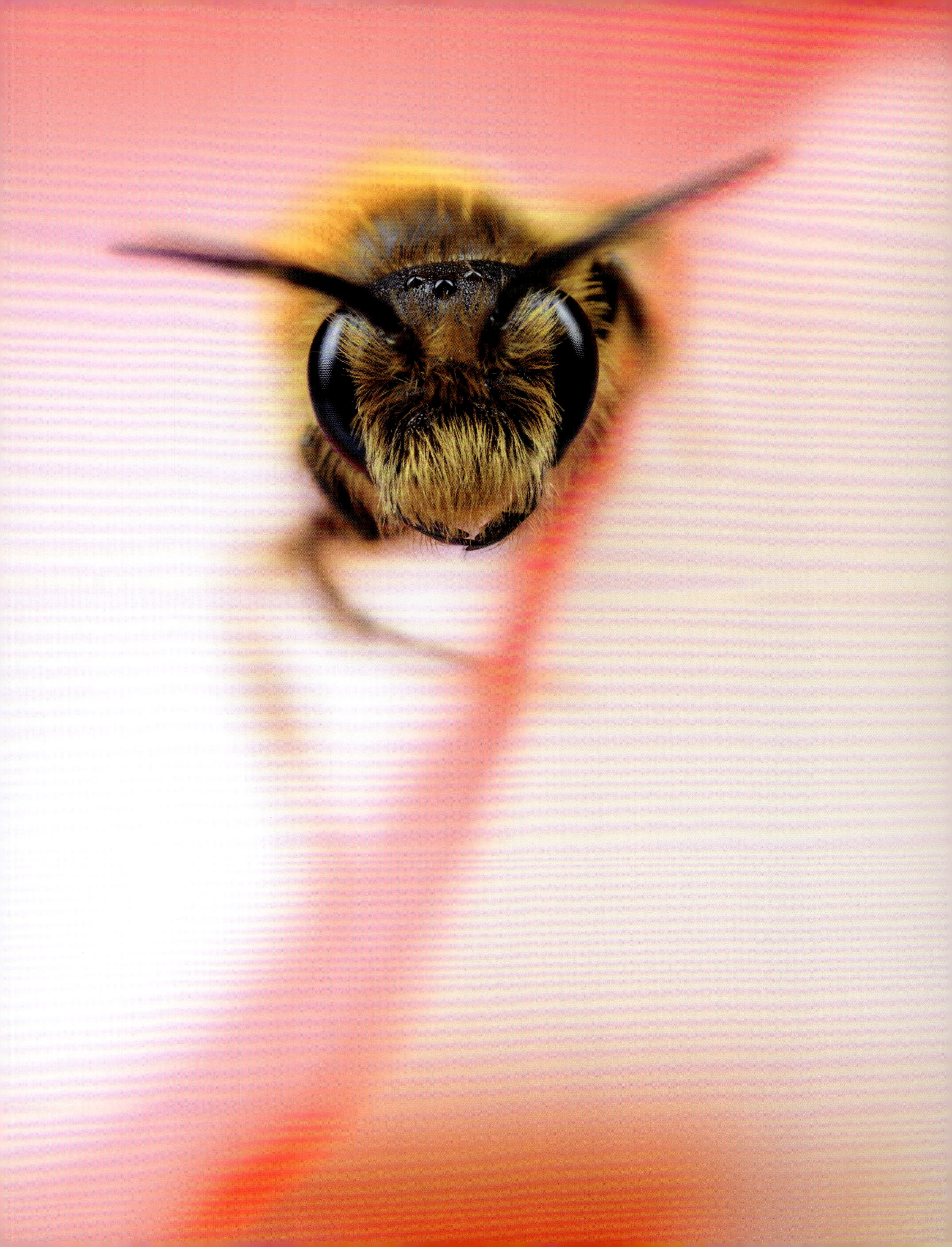

Bees

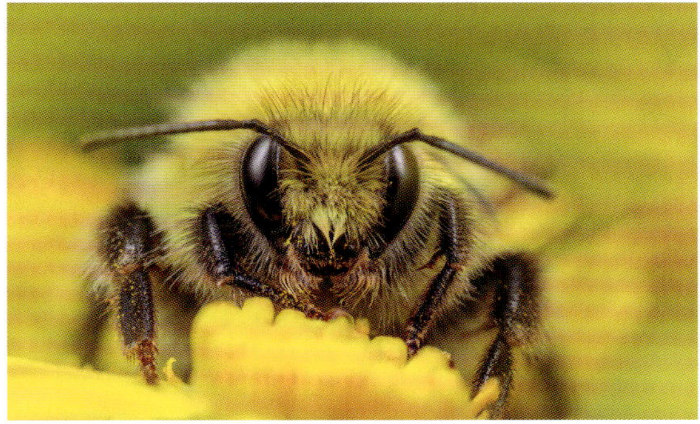

Above A bumblebee rests on ragwort.

Bees are the unsung heroes of the world. Without them, our planet would be a drastically different place to live. Bees and other pollinators are responsible for around 75 percent of the world's flowering plants, making them essential for agriculture and our ecosystems. There are approximately 20,000 species of bee, with the most well-known being the honeybee.

As a macro subject, bees can be tricky. They are usually on the move, flying from flower to flower and rarely staying still for long, so you must be prepared to move fast.

When it comes to bees, it's all about maximizing your chances. Find a meadow or area that has plenty of bees, decide what type of shot you want to capture, whether that's an in-flight shot or a close-up portrait, select the kit you will be using and be disciplined and stick with it. I often find that overcast days are best for bees, as they tend to move a little slower. Having your camera and lighting ready for action, and a fast shutter speed, will go a long way in helping you photograph these busy subjects.

Left A solitary bee peeks from behind a rose petal, investigating the waiting photographer.

Right A honey bee inspecting the hatching chambers of the honeycomb.

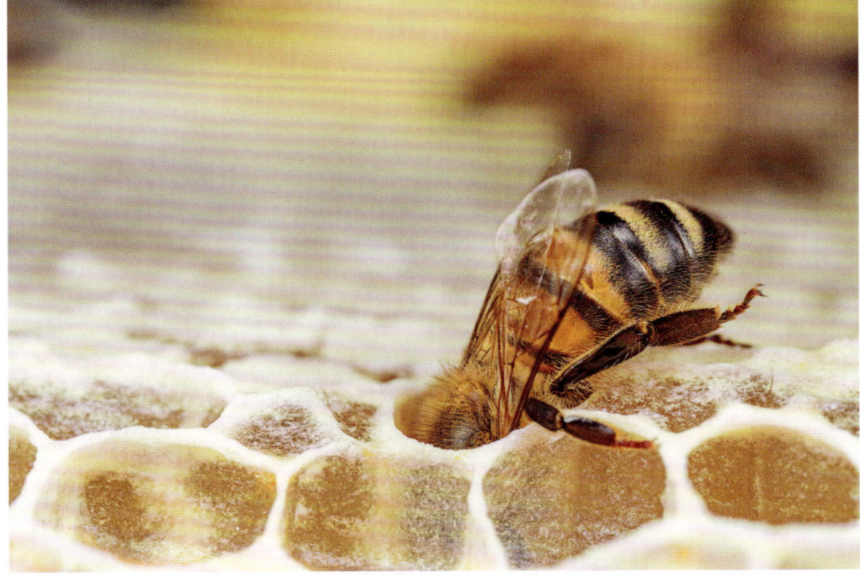

Praying mantises

Anyone who knows me will tell you that my favourite insect in the world is the praying mantis. These alien-like creatures belonging to the order Mantodea are one of the most intriguing creatures you will ever set eyes upon. Some of them display incredible mimicry; for example, the *Hymenopus coronatus* resembles a delicate white-and-pink flower, earning it the common name of the orchid mantis.

Most praying mantises are ambush predators, so they rely heavily on using mimicry to blend into their surroundings. This can make them tricky to find in the wild – but great to photograph, as they tend to stay very still.

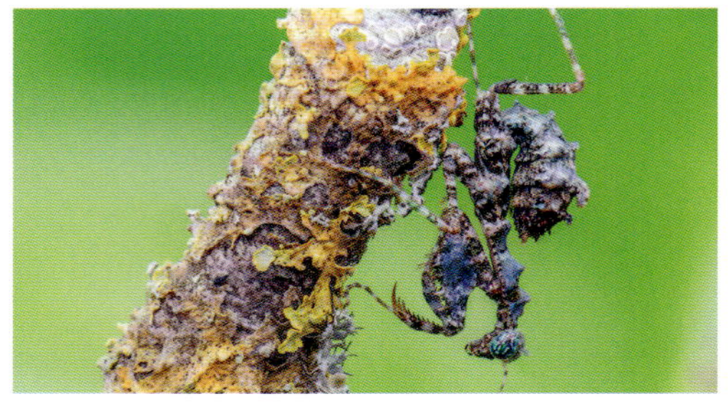

Above This lichen mantis hangs on a lichen-dressed branch, waiting for its prey.

The popularity of keeping praying mantises as pets has increased over the years, with many specialist breeders offering various species from around the world. However, anyone opting to buy one should consider the needs and the quality of life they are providing another living creature, rather than treating it as a disposable subject to photograph. Many mantises can be found in the wild, especially in Europe and Asia.

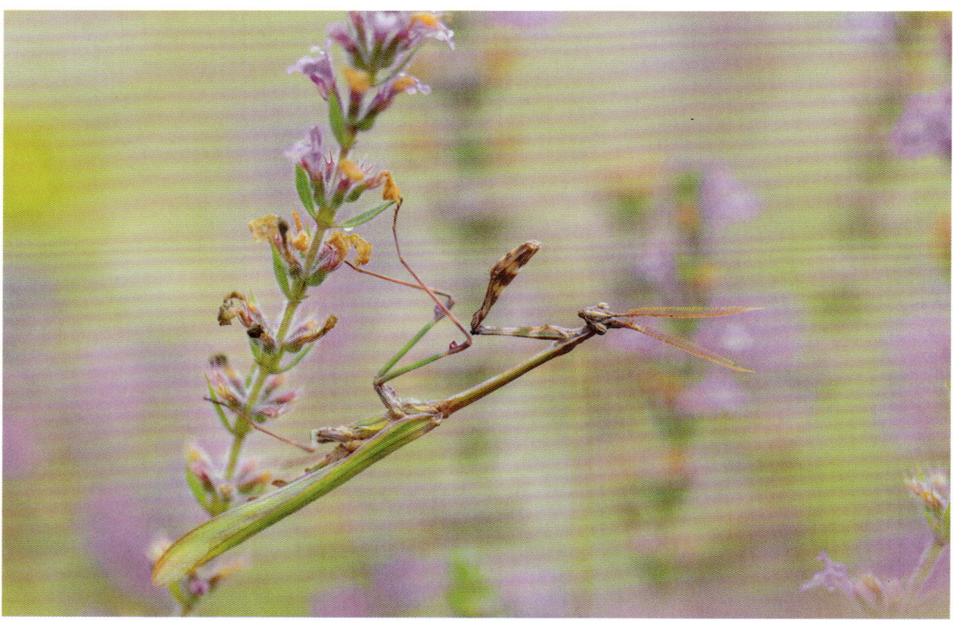

Left A master of stealth, this *Empusa spinosa* tries to blend into its surroundings.

Right The diverse range of colours and structures make mantises my favourite creatures to photograph.

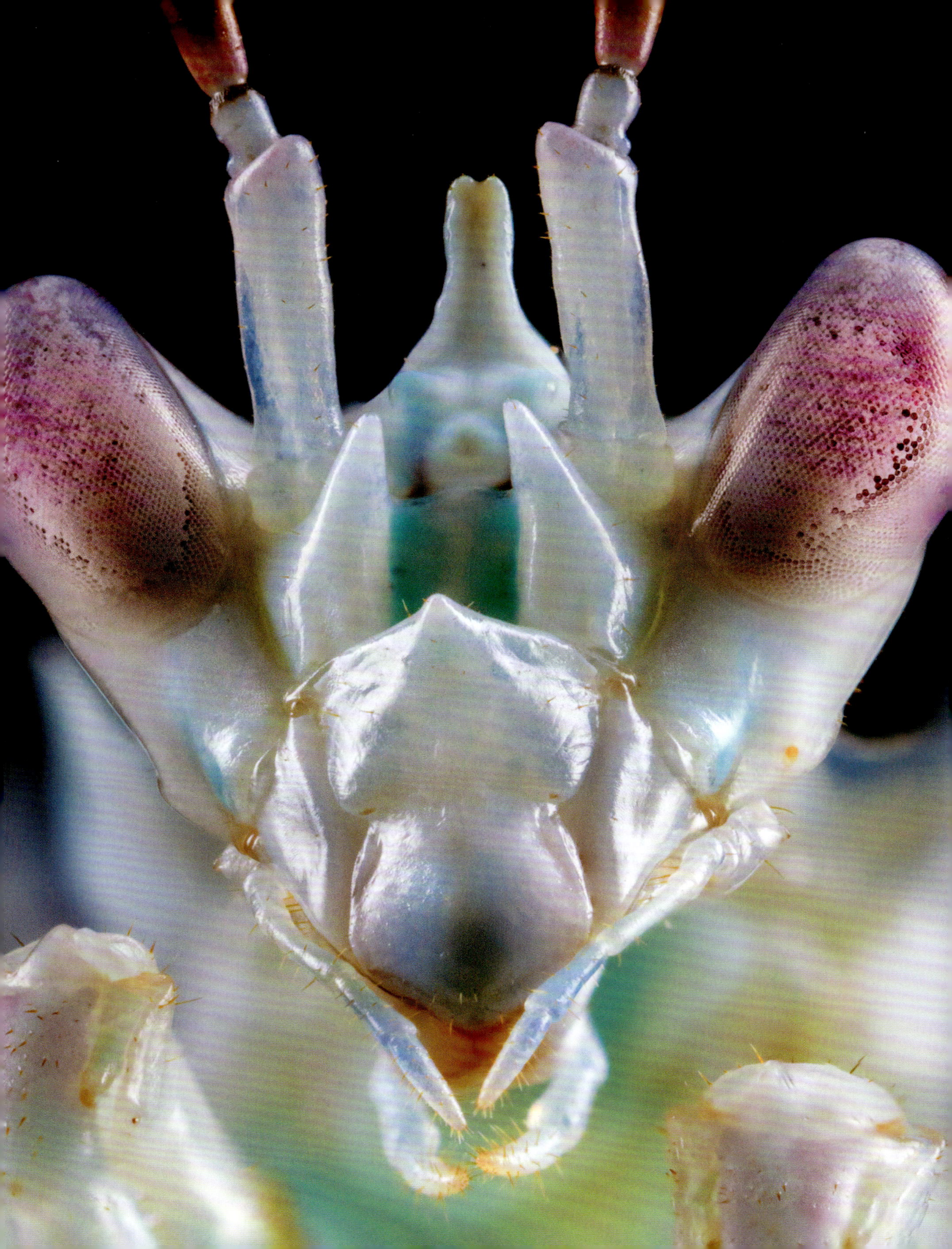

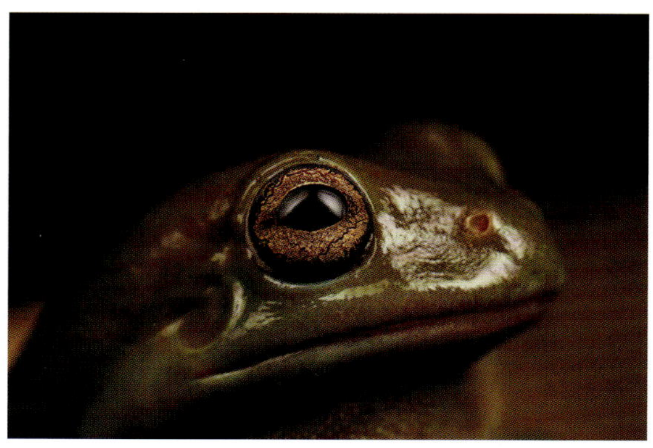

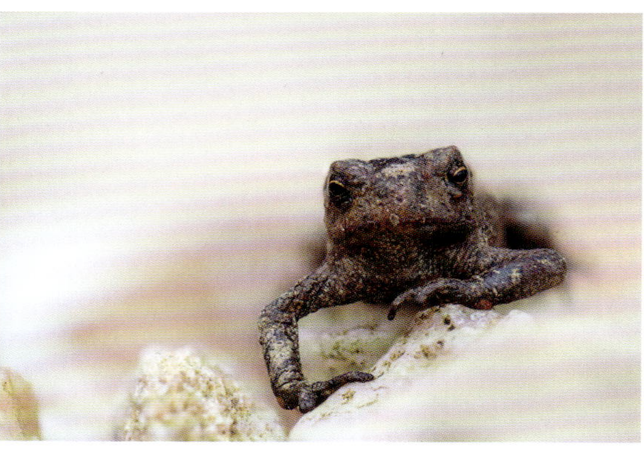

Above A toadlet pauses for a moment's rest before venturing into the pond.

Above A portrait of a tree frog displays its glossy skin and incredible golden eyes.

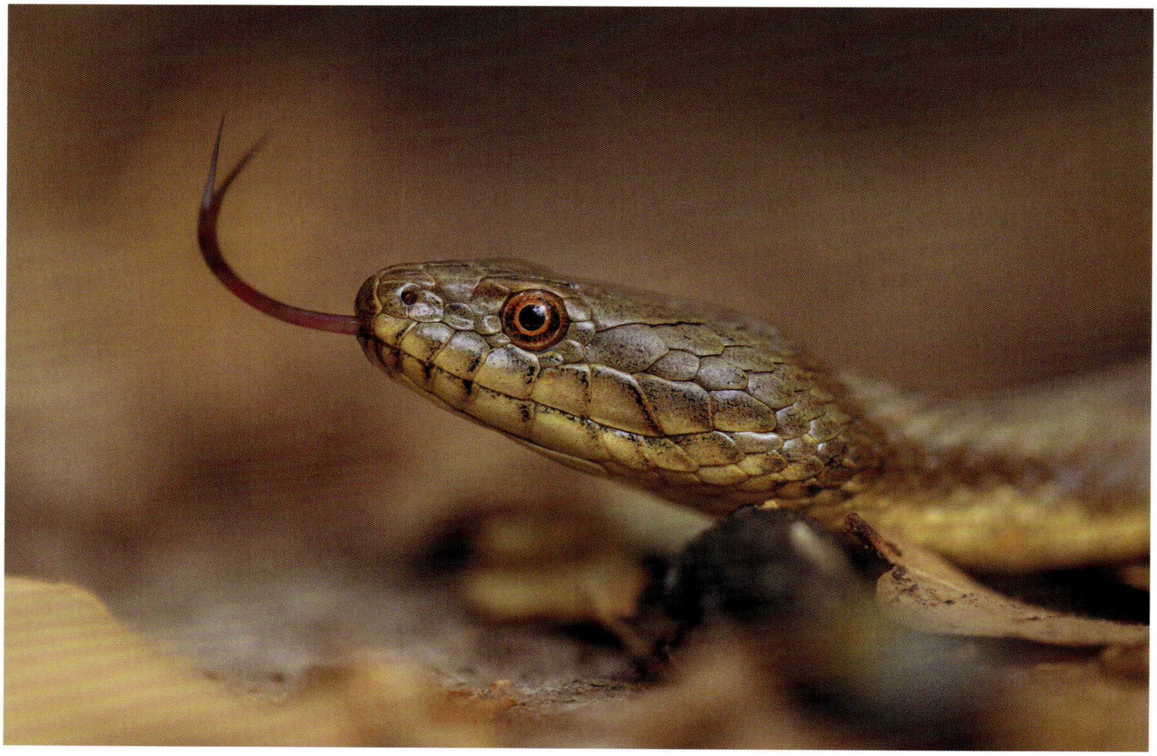

Above A dice snake navigates the undergrowth.

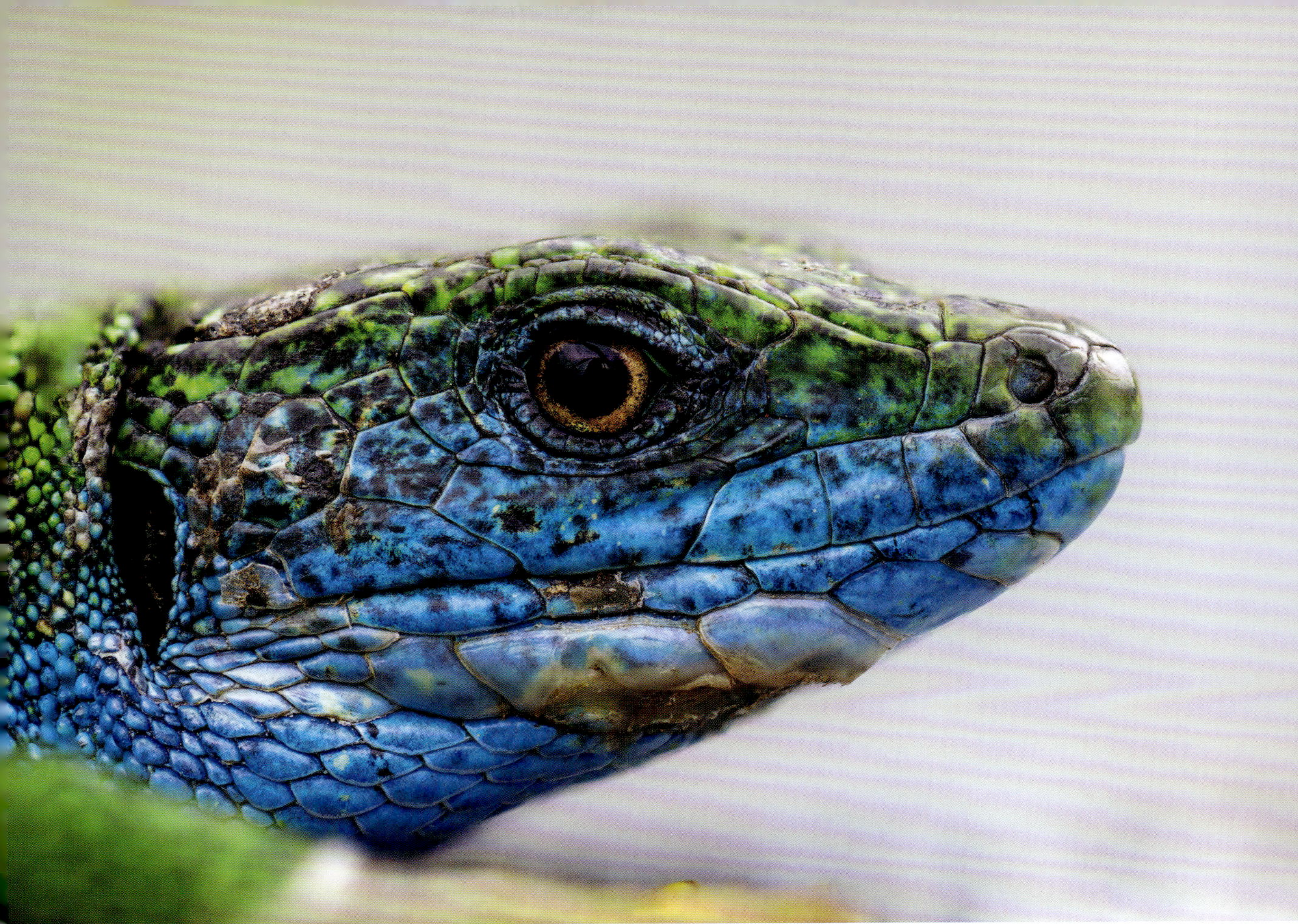

Reptiles and amphibians

Reptiles and amphibians are popular subjects for macro photographers as they are usually large and very detailed, with textured skins and fascinating eyes. Amphibians such as toads and frogs can be found in wetlands relatively easily. However, reptiles are a little more elusive, particularly in cooler climates. Snakes and lizards bask in the morning sun on large rocks and flat surfaces to raise their body temperature – if you can find them, this is an ideal opportunity to photograph them.

Plenty of research should be carried out before photographing snakes. A longer focal length macro lens works well for these subjects, as adding distance between you and your subject keeps everyone happy and safe. I prefer to use natural light for larger subjects like this. However, in dark forests, caves and even at night, a diffused flash will help you illuminate your subjects.

Above A male Balkan green lizard looking a little put out to be photographed so early.

Lichens

Lichens are neither plant nor animal, but rather a unique organism consisting of a combination of algae and fungus. Lichens can be found growing on trees, rocks, walls and even human-made objects. They make for great abstract photographs full of patterns and textures, and, as they are stationary, they make great subjects to practise advanced techniques such as focus stacking (see page 114).

I like to explore my local woodland to photograph lichens in the autumn months, which is when they are at their best. They come in various shapes, sizes and colours, from rustic browns and reds to leafy greens. Some have branching structures, some look like leaves and others can appear to be a rusty crust on the surface of tree bark and stones.

Lichens provide shelter for various insects, so the chances are you may stumble upon a few when photographing these intriguing organisms. They are also a food source for many animals and are the chosen material for the long-tailed tit to construct its nest from.

All The varied colours and textures of lichen make real works of art when you get in this close.

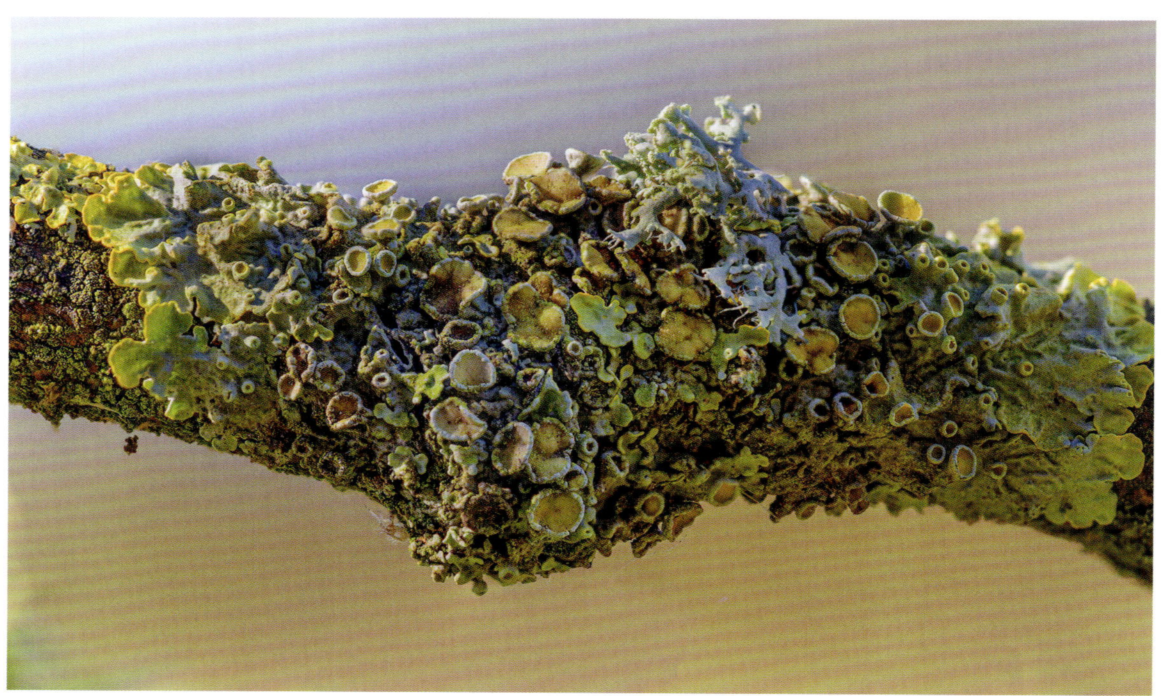

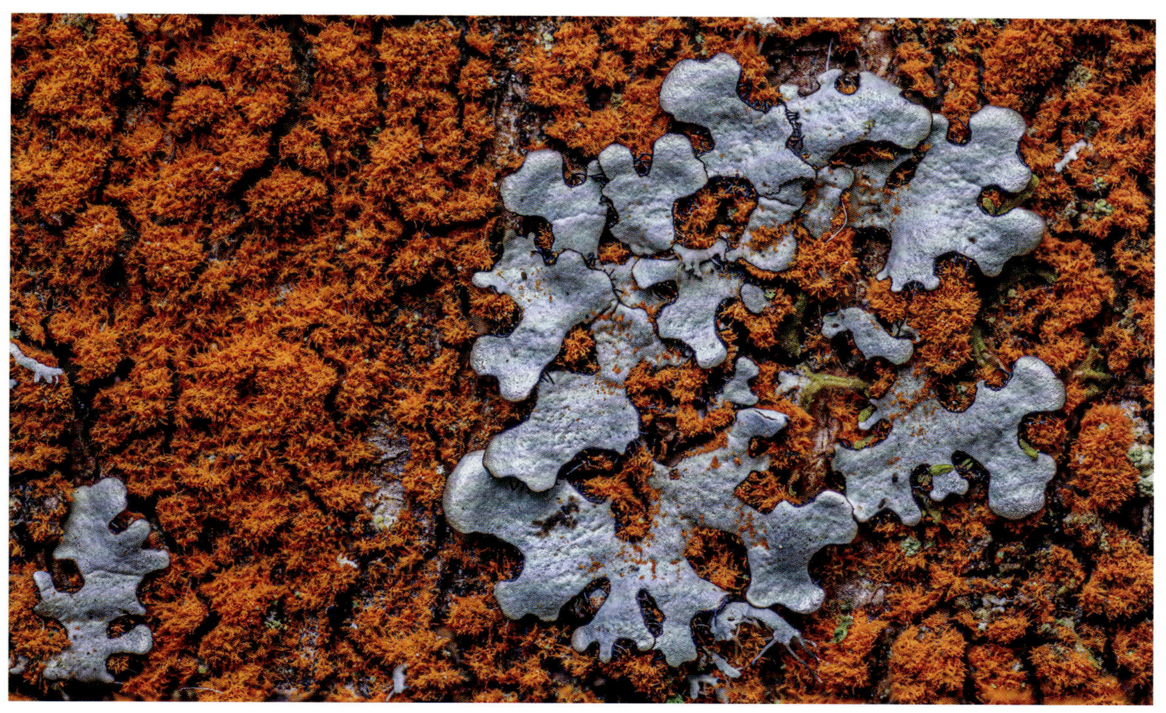

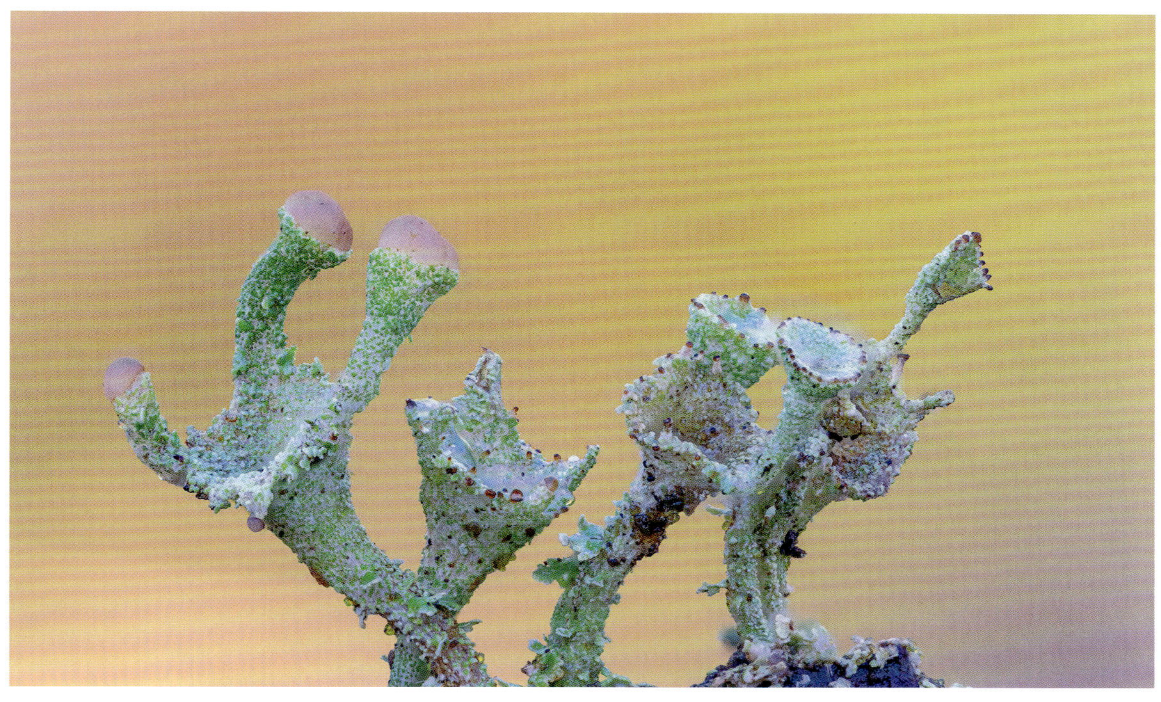

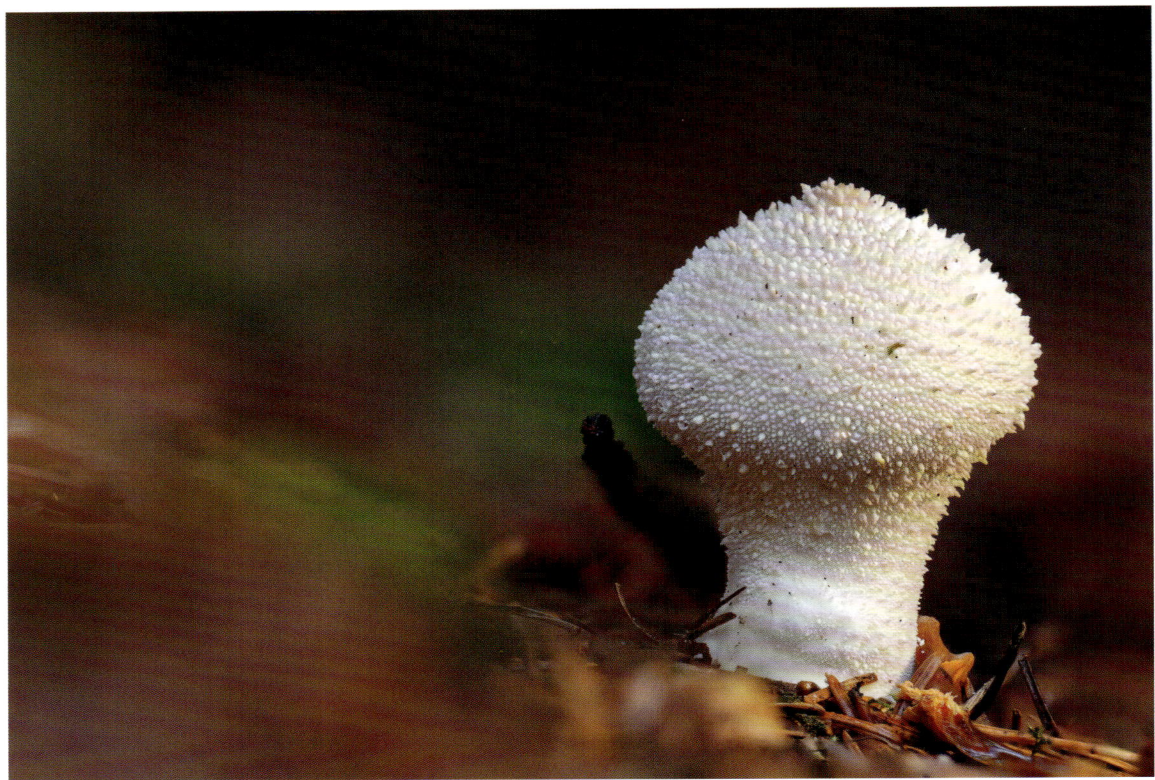

Fungi

With an estimated 3.8 million species existing worldwide (though no one can be certain the true figure), fungi are one of the most diverse and populous organisms on the planet. Some glow in the dark, some can be eaten and some can even turn insects such as ants into zombies!

The best time to spot fungi is autumn, as they thrive in warm, damp weather, and ancient deciduous woodlands and other moist environments are ideal habitats. Finding a subject that is undamaged and in a spot that offers a good composition can be tricky, so it may take some time and exploration to find the perfect subject.

Natural light, artificial light and even a mix of both works well for macro photographs of fungi.

During the autumn months, light is limited, even more so in woodlands, so don't be afraid to utilize flash or external LED lights to add fill or rim lighting. Be creative and look for patterns and abstracts – the underside (gills) of a mushroom can provide plenty of creative opportunities.

Above A puffball mushroom newly surfaced. Getting out early in autumn is key to finding freshly emerged fungi specimens.

Other subjects

There are many other subjects that can be photographed using a macro lens, including household items such as fruits, crayons, water droplets and flowers. A whole new world of texture and colour can be found in the simplest of items.

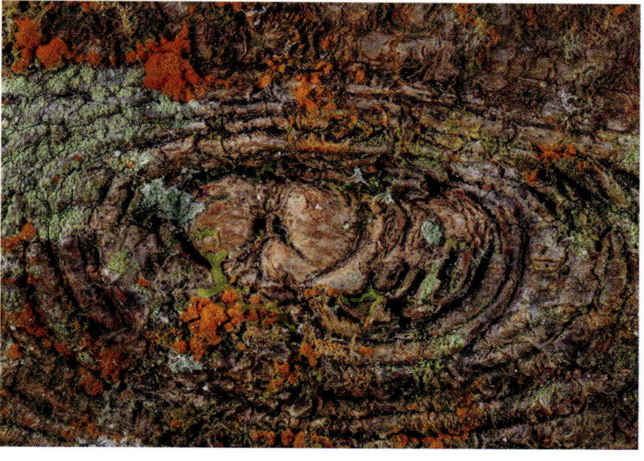

Tree bark and textures

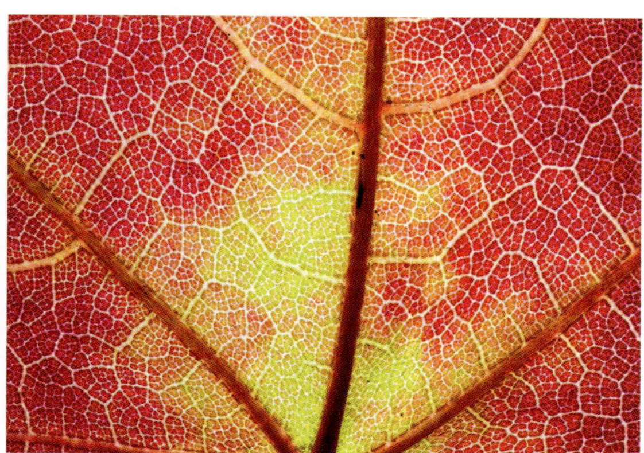

Backlit leaf

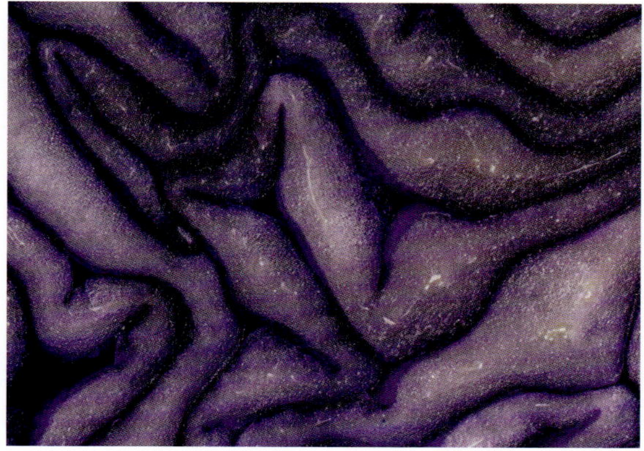

Purple cabbage

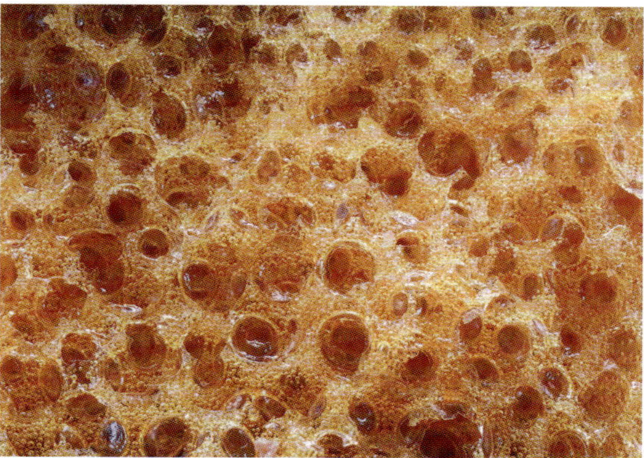

Honeycomb

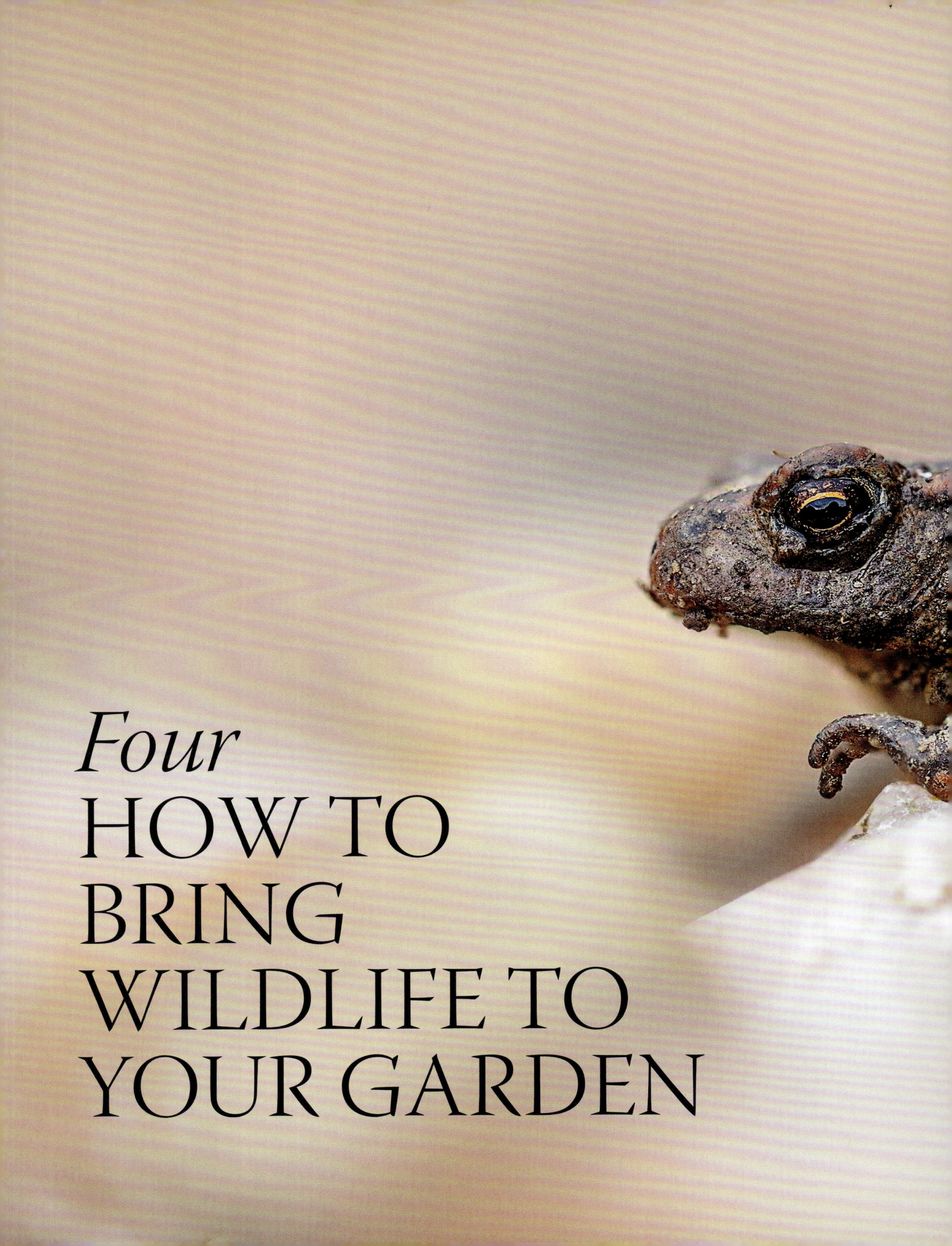

Four

HOW TO BRING WILDLIFE TO YOUR GARDEN

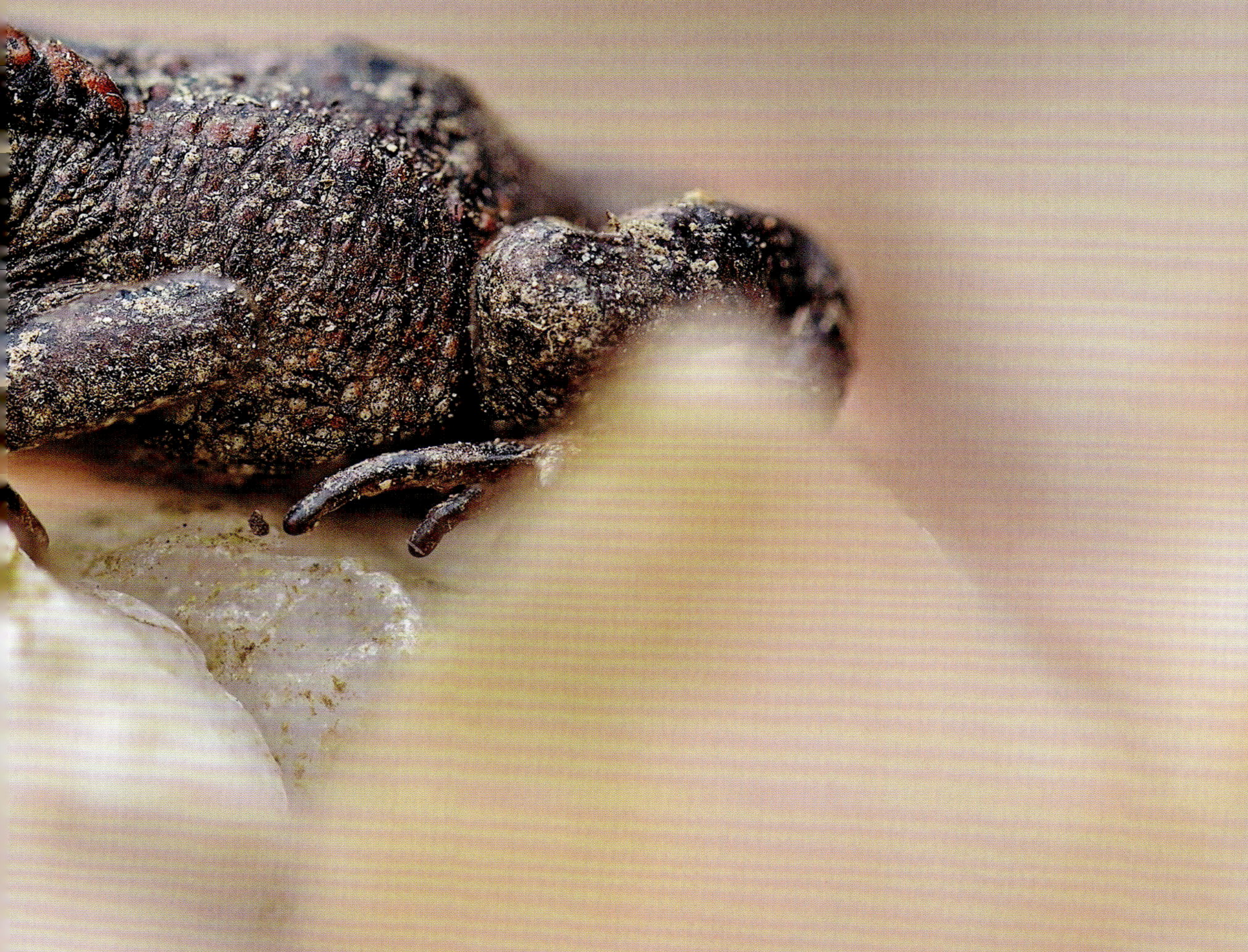

Our relationship with gardens dates back to ancient times; what began as agricultural communities and spaces transformed over the years to elaborate gardens to cultivate fruit, vegetables and plants. They have been part of our way of life for a very long time and you can track the history of gardens from all over the world; in ancient China, Egypt, Greece and across the Roman Empire, as well as the legendary Hanging Gardens of Babylon. For macro photographers, they play a vital role in bringing wildlife right to our cameras – but how can you attract more subjects into your garden?

Inviting nature in

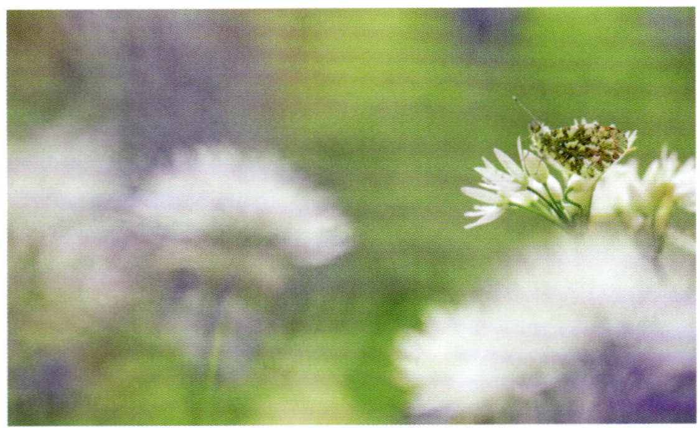

Above Encouraging native wildflowers to grow in your garden will attract all sorts of species.

Over the years I have lived in various parts of the UK, in different kinds of housing situations, and each has offered unique opportunities for macro photography. I spent the majority of my early career in the gardens attached to the place I was living at, honing my technique, researching my subjects and planting various flowers and shrubs to see what was or wasn't attracted. No matter what size, gardens are so valuable because they offer easy access to wildlife – you won't have to venture far to find some kind of insect, arachnid or plant subject. Being a father and working full-time often restricted my photography time, but having a garden allowed me to photograph after or before working hours.

Now you may be thinking, 'But I don't have a garden!' Don't worry – I've been in that situation as well. Lots of us live in town centres, flats or high-rise apartments, and not everyone is lucky enough to have a garden. There are still ways to attract wildlife, though, and I'll share some examples of how you can do that. You don't need much to start attracting wildlife to your garden; the smallest areas can still provide a home, shelter and food for an abundance of wildlife.

Grow wild

Allow a section of your garden to grow wild! That doesn't mean just ignore it forever, as it will still need some maintenance in the winter, but by allowing an area of your garden to just do its thing over the spring, summer and autumn months you may be surprised at what grows, and what is attracted.

Pick an area of your garden, ideally with grass, and mark it out, it can be any size, but ideally you want to go for something in the region of a 1 metre square or larger. Do not trim this area; allow the grasses to grow tall and natural.

Over spring and summer you will begin to see just how transformative this little section can become. I have been pleasantly surprised to see orchids, cuckoo flowers and even poppies erupt from the ground. I never planted anything in this area, I just let it grow. We never truly know what is waiting to burst through the ground if we keep trimming back that grass, so let it be. Each year also tends to offer something different, so be patient, sit back and watch your wild area bloom.

Long grasses also offer protection for wildlife such as small mice, which may take shelter there. Bees and other flying insects, such as butterflies, may choose to roost in this patch overnight, which offers you the unique chance to study them and photograph them in the evenings and early morning.

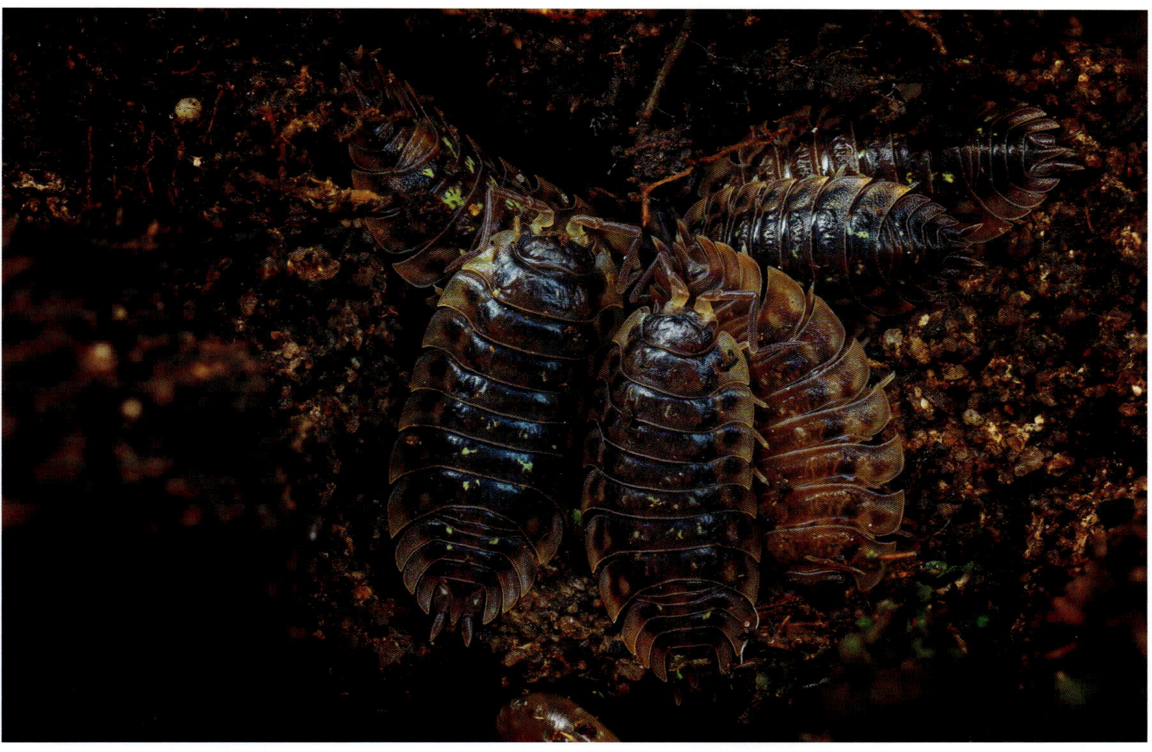

Leaf pile

If you have overhanging trees or vegetation that drop leaves, rotting wood and other debris, don't throw them away; instead, choose a section of your garden and pile them up. Piles of rotting vegetation are vital for your garden's ecosystem. They offer shelter to small mammals, and many larger animals such as hedgehogs love to make a leaf pile their home. They also make natural habitats for insects, arachnids, amphibians and reptiles, which will use them as hiding spots and breeding areas.

The decomposing pile is a valuable food source for microorganisms such as fungi and certain insects, which will, in turn, attract larger wildlife that may predate these subjects. Birds and other animals may forage from this area, using materials to build their nests. Some butterfly and moth species may choose this area to lay their eggs; the caterpillars hatch and pupate, completing a small section of its lifecycle in your garden. All of this provides you with great opportunities to get out with your macro gear and see what you can document and photograph.

You can upgrade your leaf pile by adding brick piles, small rockeries and larger chunks of wood. In the warmer months, these rocks and bricks become perfect hotspots for amphibians and reptiles to warm up. If you're lucky, you may even see courtship dances of wolf spiders as they scuttle about the rockery, or marvel as you watch small lizards bask in the early morning sun.

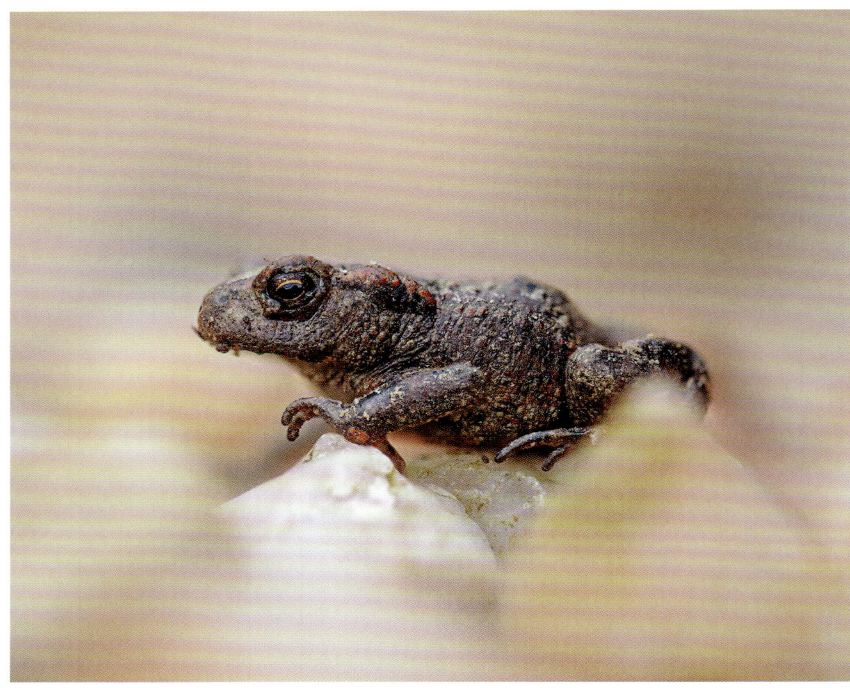

Left A toad makes its way across the land.

Below Even humble slugs and snails can make wonderful subjects, with their interesting shapes and textures. Their slow movements makes photographing them easy as well.

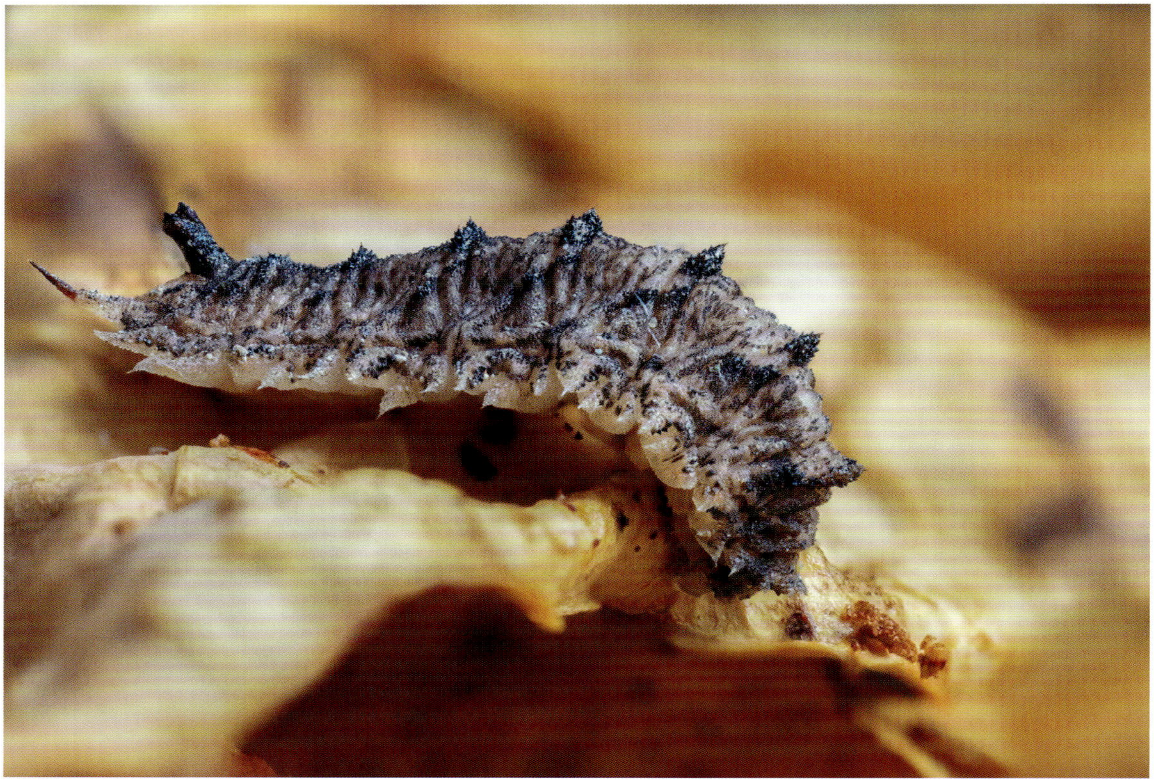

Plant native

You may be surprised to learn that a lot of the flowers available to buy from garden centres and supermarkets to plant in our gardens aren't actually native to our countries. It's important to bear this in mind, because native plants have co-evolved with the native wildlife, and much wildlife requires specific plants to provide their food and habitat. Many insects such as bees, butterflies, flies and moths have formed special relationships with the native plants in their area, and by honouring this relationship with the kinds of plants you add to your garden, you will help to promote vital pollinator populations.

While it's always worth considering how you can support the wildlife in your local area, it's also important to remember that planting native is not a rule. We've been planting and growing non-native plants in our gardens for years, and just because a particular choice of tree or flower isn't native, it doesn't mean it won't attract wildlife. Wildlife adapts quickly to its environment, and exotic plants may still have qualities that appeal to local populations. If in doubt, have a chat with the garden centre staff or do some research online. When there's a specific kind of creature you're trying to attract to your garden, this can be the best way to find out what kinds of plants and conditions will be ideal to lure them in.

Garden pond

Creating a garden pond, whether big or small, is a great way to attract and support wildlife in your garden. Ponds provide an essential water source and habitat for a large variety of flora and fauna. Making a pond doesn't have to be a daunting task. If space allows, you can create a large pond and make it a focal point of your garden, but a simple washing up bowl buried into the soil with some rocks and plants will be enough to draw in a variety of visitors.

When designing a pond, building it across different layers, with plants that grow at different depths, will help attract a variety of wildlife. Including a gently sloped or stepped entrance/escape point is essential to minimize the risk of drowning for any larger mammals that may use the water source for drinking or bathing. And it goes without saying that safety must be paramount when introducing a body of water into your garden, no matter how big or small it is.

When considering what plants to add, I recommend a mix of fully submerged, semi-submerged and floating plants. The fully and semi-submerged plants are beneficial for amphibians, whereas floating plants and reeds can provide a roosting spot for dragonflies and damselflies. From diving beetles, water snails, newts and a whole host of aquatic larvae, you will be surprised at just how much wildlife can reside in a garden pond – providing you with countless subjects to photograph.

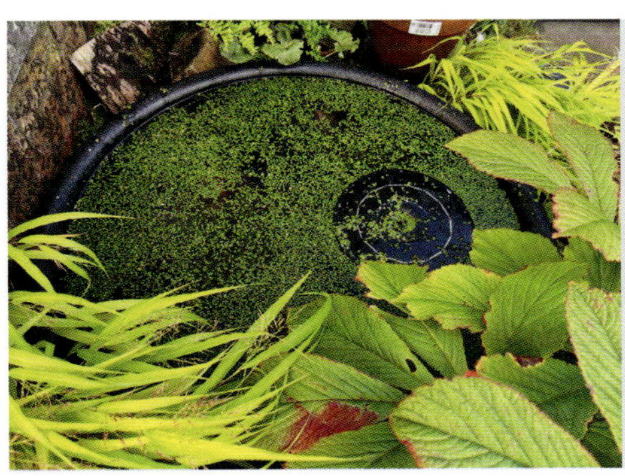

Create a pond habitat anywhere

We didn't have room for a large pond in my garden, so we utilized what space we had and filled a small tub with water and let the area grow wild. Each year, it is full of frogs and the odd damselfly too.

Right A bit of landscaping in the garden revealed this ant nest

Opposite This beautiful ruby-tailed wasp is a joy to see in the garden.

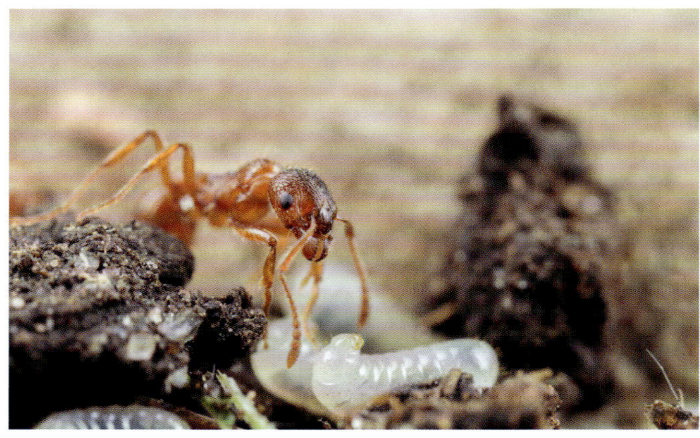

Balcony boxes and bug hotels

As I mentioned previously, not everyone is fortunate enough to have space for a garden, but that doesn't mean you have to miss out. Adding windowboxes, hanging baskets and other small containers planted with native flora can have bees, butterflies and birds visiting in no time. Vertical gardens, planted on walls, are also becoming more common in high-rise apartments and flats – you might be surprised at just how high a bee is willing to fly in search of food! Even just one small planted flower pot can be enough to sustain and help your local wildlife.

Man-made bug hotels also make a great addition to any garden, balcony or windowsill. These are boxes that are typically stacked with natural materials such as bamboo or pine cones, which attract insects to shelter among their nooks and crannies. Solitary bees, for example, lay their eggs inside the bamboo tubes, so by providing this space you will be actively contributing to the local population and helping conservation efforts. These bug hotels can be as small or large as you like. They're commonly available to buy these days, but you could also try making one yourself.

Whatever you decide to do, make sure everything is safe and secure. Always make sure you have permission before adding structures to rented properties, and if in any doubt, ask a professional for help with DIY projects.

Bird feeders and baths

Bird feeders provide supplementary food for birds, while smaller mammals and insects will make the most of the debris that falls to the ground. The bird feeder in my garden is one of my favourite spots to hang out and watch as ants come along and collect the discarded seeds and suet – not only is it great to watch, but it provides excellent photo opportunities.

Bird feeders are a great resource and an almost fail-safe way of attracting birds into your garden. If you can provide a selection of different food types you will notice that different species of birds each have their preferences; the more variety you can offer, the more species you're likely to attract.

Bird baths play host to bathing birds in the warmer months and offer a place to cool down. They also provide a valuable water source to passing insects that may need hydration. Getting low and close to water as a wasp stops for a quick taste can result in a superb photograph.

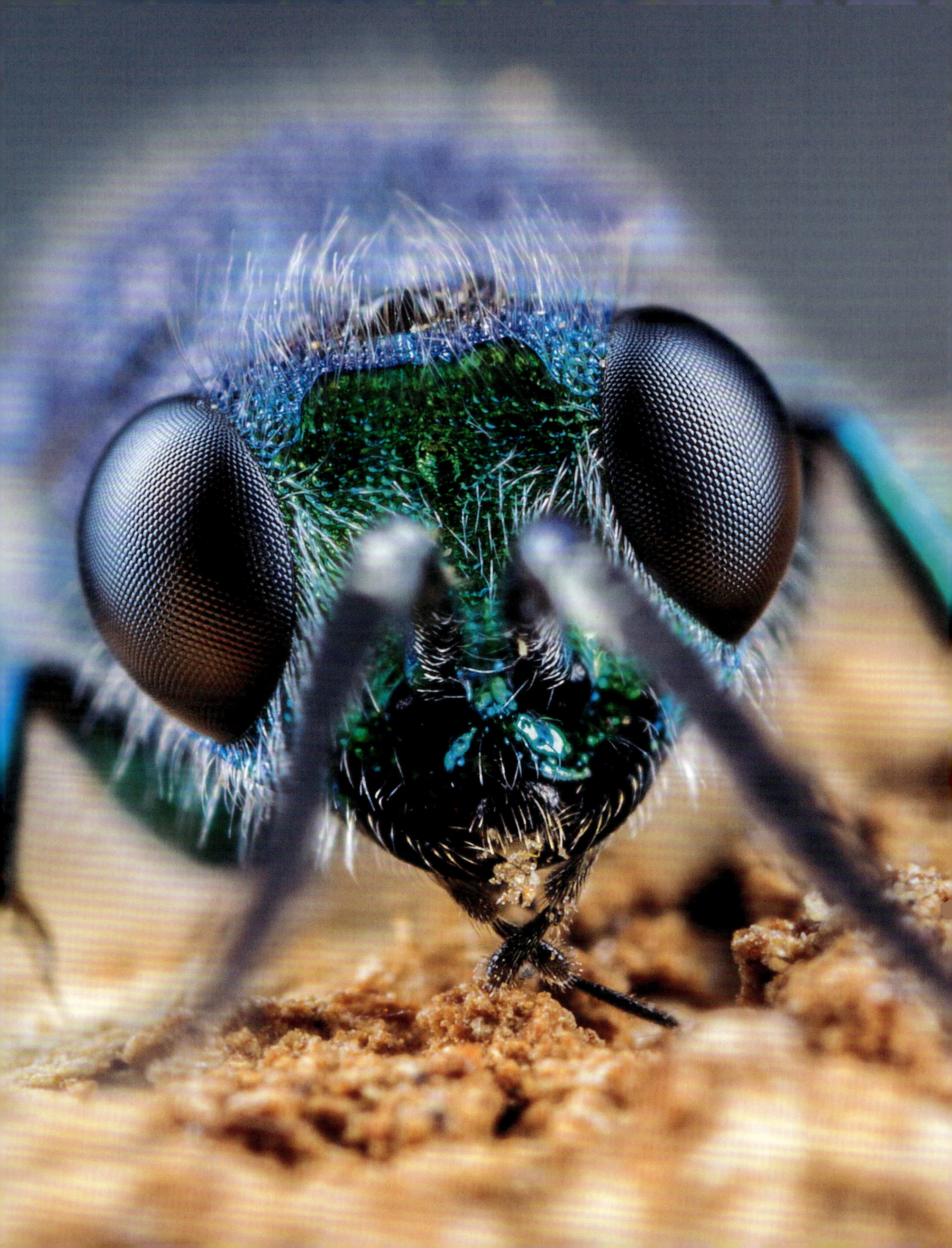

Many of our subjects are cold-blooded, so heat and time of day affect how they operate, which we can use to our advantage. But not only do we have to think about the time of day, we also need to consider the seasons and what they offer. Different seasons offer unique and interesting subjects, so knowing where and when your subjects will be active is crucial – there's no point looking for butterflies in the middle of winter, for example.

Five SEASONS OF MACRO PHOTOGRAPHY

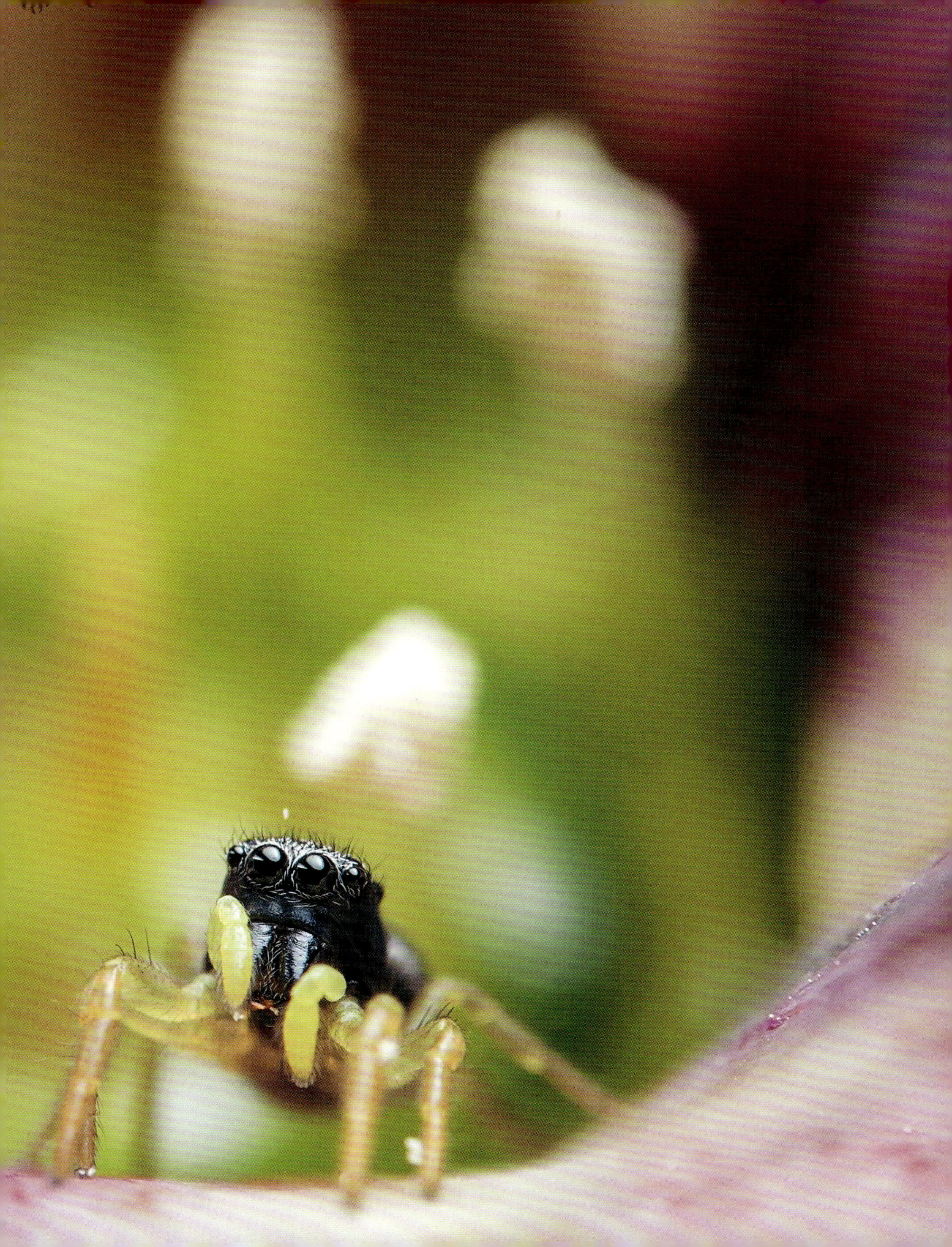

Spring

Spring means new life, new colours and new energy. It's the time of year that most wildlife photographers get most excited about. The natural world is waking up and rejuvenating our senses. What new subjects will we find? Have the flowers begun to bloom in the woods yet? Will I find some emerging dragonflies? These are just some of the questions bouncing around my head as spring erupts.

As the temperatures rise, so does the activity of the arthropods. Many species begin their lives here and some awaken from their winter slumbers ready to explore the natural world. Foraging, mating, finding the best habitat to raise the next generation; it's all going on and it's all there for us to witness and document.

Spring can vary in its arrival from country to country. In the UK, spring usually arrives in southern England first and slowly makes its way north to the top of Scotland, where I live, so I often have to wait a little bit longer for my subjects to awaken. And some springs are wetter than others, while some are much colder.

As we approach spring I start exploring my local green spaces, looking for the smallest signs, such as wood anemones growing in the woods or snowdrops decorating the woodland floor with a carpet of white. I look closely at rocks, old logs and emerging plants to see what wildlife has begun to stir. This is where fieldcraft really takes the lead (see page 110). It's all well and good knowing that spring will provide us with many subjects, but if we don't know where to look, we can waste a lot of time looking in the wrong place at the wrong time.

It's important to research your subjects. What time of the year will they be active? What type of habitat do they prefer? What is their food plant? Where will they lay their eggs? For example, the orange-tip butterfly flies from April to July, so I will look for them around early May, as this

is a great time to find newly emerged adults in pristine condition. I know that they prefer to lay their eggs on a food plant for the caterpillar such as lady smock, so I will look for this plant species in the hopes of finding a passing female laying her eggs. After July, I won't look for this species, as I know the chances of finding it will be slim. Dragonflies, damselflies and spiders all have their own preferred habitat, and by researching your subject's behaviour and life cycle you can drastically improve your chances of finding it.

Spring offers the chance to capture life as it starts, from metamorphism to mating; incredible behaviour waiting to be witnessed and documented. We get special access through our macro lens to the wonders of the natural world, but it doesn't have to be all insects. Some of the most beautiful flowers bloom in spring and they make fantastic macro subjects. The great thing about flowers is they tend to grow back in the same place each year, so long as the habitat isn't destroyed. They are one of the more reliable subject choices for spring, and if you're lucky you may even find some sleeping bees or roosting butterflies in the meadow too.

All in all, spring is an exciting season for macro photographers, offering us a plethora of subjects, with bees gathering pollen, butterflies gracing the skies, dragonflies skimming over ponds and ladybirds exploring the grass. The season evokes a real sense of wonder and hope as the winter months fade away and the world becomes full of life and colour once more.

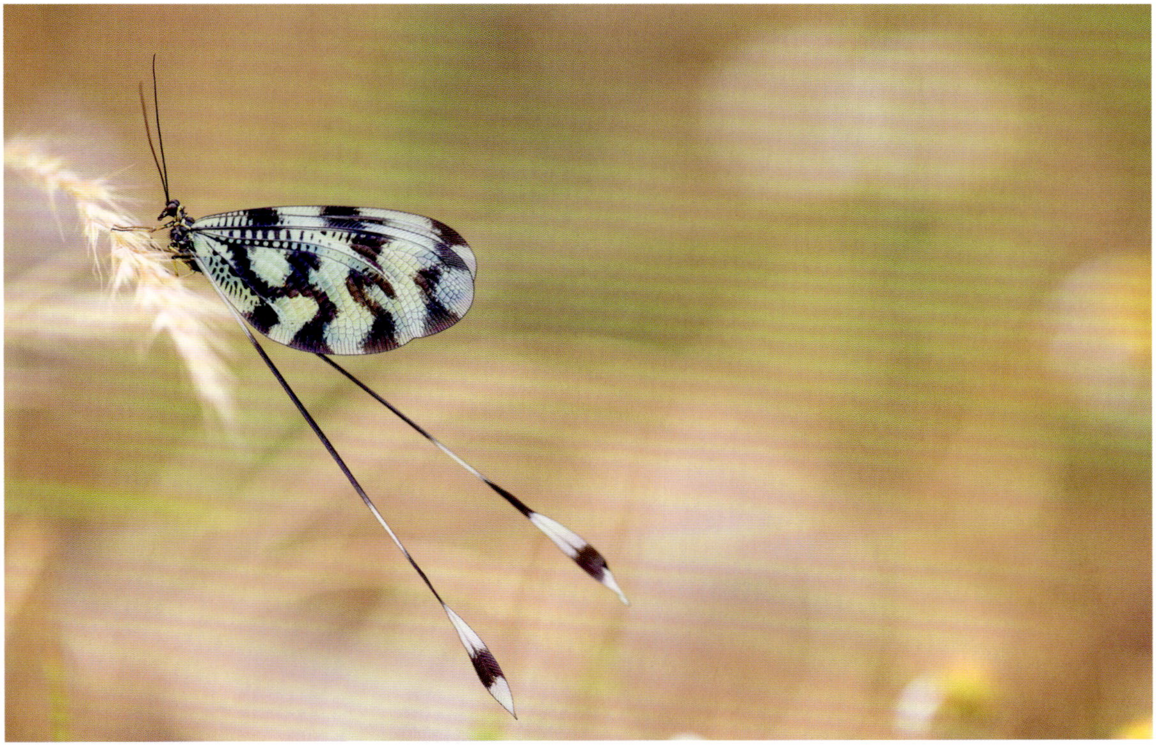

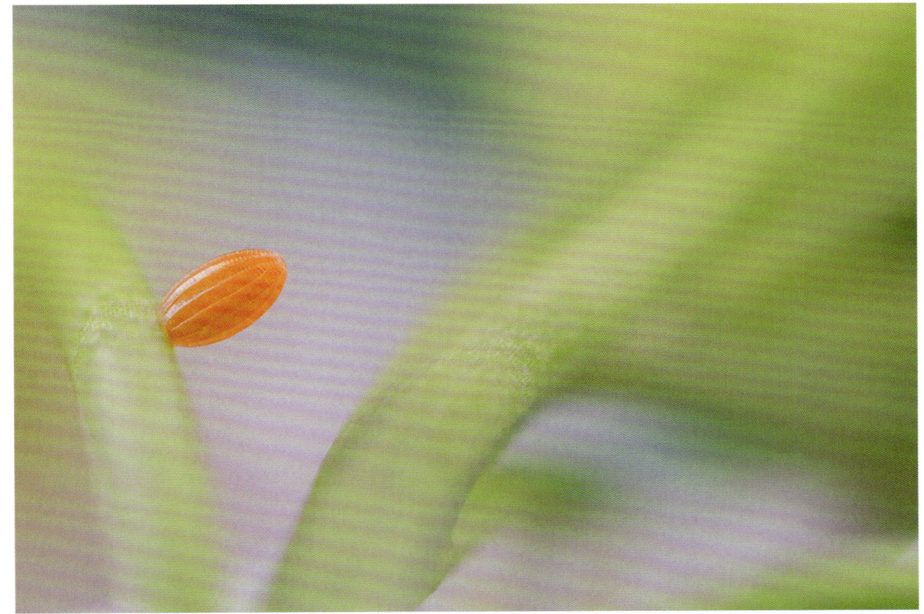

Above
A beautiful spoon-winged lacewing rests on a warm spring morning.

Right An orange-tip butterfly egg laid on the stem of a cuckoo flower.

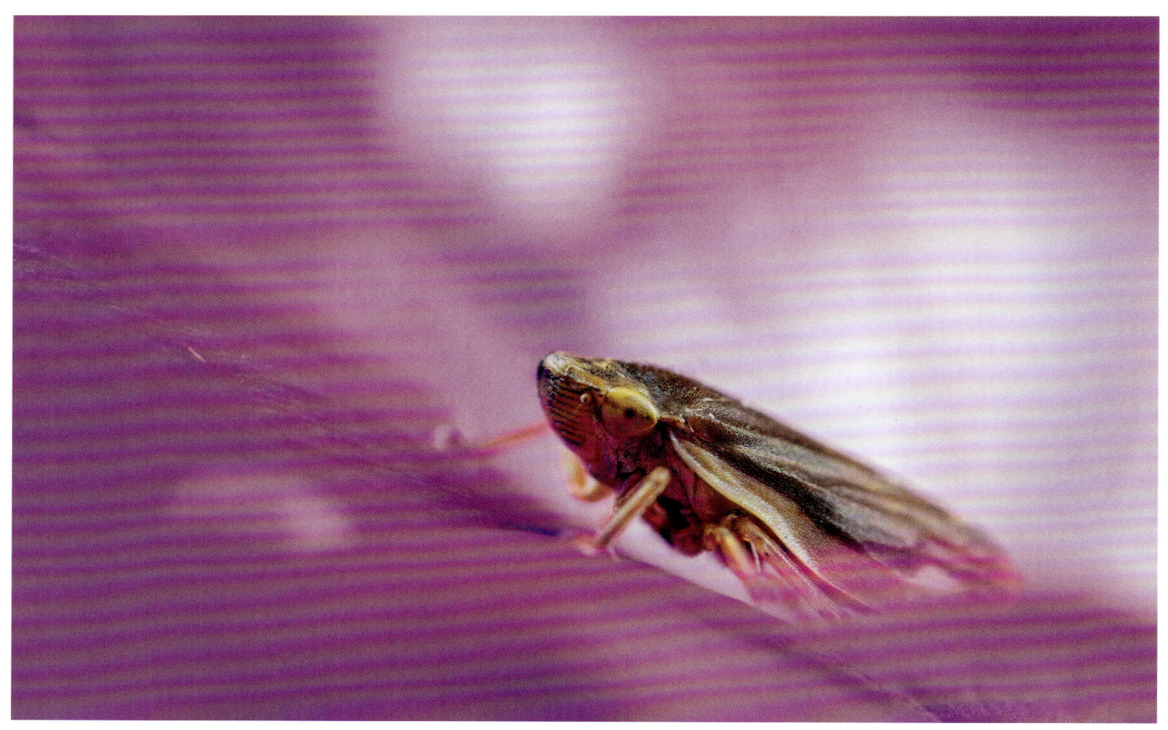

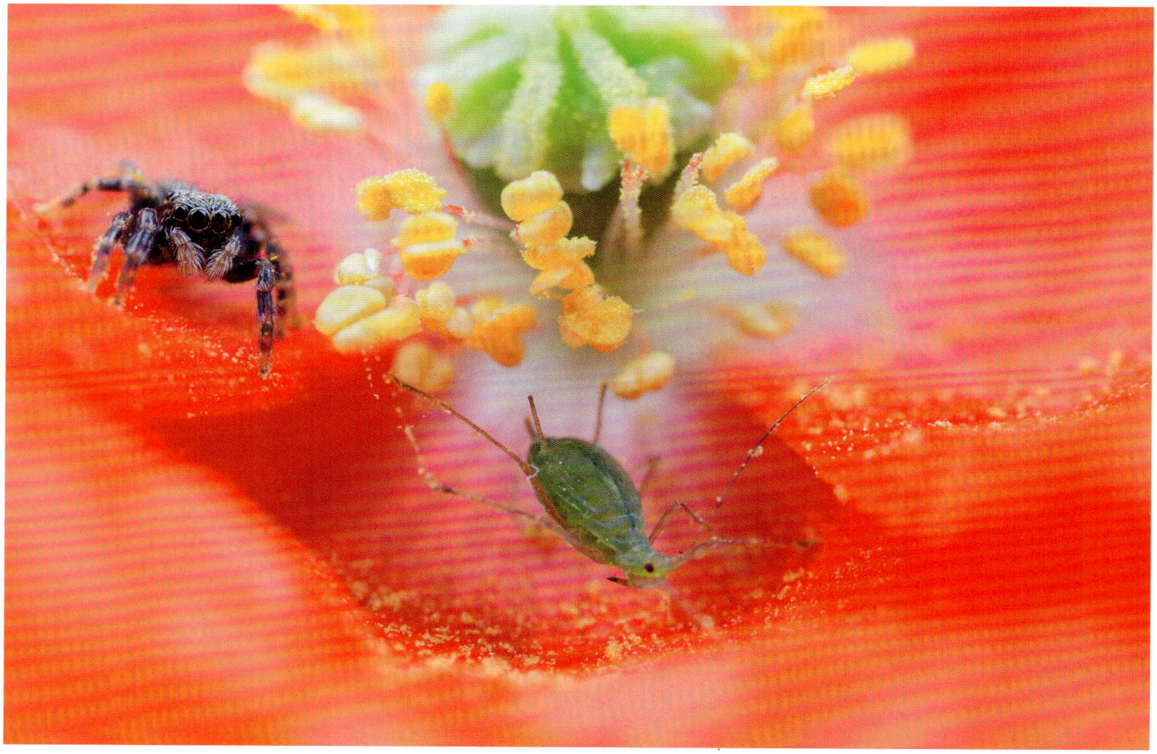

Summer

As spring fades, summer takes hold. Warmer temperatures and longer days provide the optimal conditions for plants, insects and arachnids. As the spring flowers slowly pass, new summer flowers emerge and wildflower meadows burst into life, attracting a host of pollinators and predators, while lush, green trees provide a home to insects and shelter from the hot sun. Summer is the peak season for many subjects, with grasshoppers leaping beneath our feet, ants busy building colonies and spiders constructing webs. But it's not just about arthropods – trees, leaves and bark can provide some interesting textures and abstracts too. We are spoilt for choice in summer!

Summer is the season in which I will look for more grounded species. It's also a great time to find a local pond alive with dragonflies and damselflies feeding and mating. A grass meadow will usually have my attention and I can spend most of the day there. I become more selective about what time of the day I shoot. Around midday, wildlife tends to be busy and active, which is great for seeing subjects, but not so great for photographing them, as they rarely stay still for long. So, I typically opt for early mornings and late evenings.

Most insects are cold-blooded, which means their body temperature is influenced directly by the environment around them. They are 'ectothermic' and rely on external heat sources to warm their bodies and regulate their metabolic processes, which is why you will find insects very still and lethargic in the early hours of the morning. A 4.30 a.m. alarm call will put most people off, but an early start will give you the chance to photograph your subjects while they are still and warming up for the day.

Dragonflies, damselflies and butterflies can all be found perched motionless as they wait for the sun to rise and warm up the land. This is the perfect opportunity to get up close and personal and I often practise various techniques in these moments, safe in the knowledge that my subject isn't going to fly away. I can get creative with lighting, composition and advanced techniques such as focus stacking. The rising sun can provide you with beautiful rim light and bokeh.

Early morning photography does have some drawbacks beyond the alarm clock. Light can be lacking, especially under tree canopies, and it's important to keep this in mind and choose your gear appropriately. Can you increase ISO without adding too much noise? Should you use a flash or tripod? It's important to answer these questions before you head out so that you are prepared.

If you're averse to early mornings, late evenings can work just as well. Species such as butterflies and bees begin to wind down for the day, carefully selecting a perch to rest overnight, and there's usually more light compared to the mornings, with the sun setting later in the day. I often revisit a spot the next morning to find the same subject still on the perch where I left it the night before. It doesn't always happen, as they may be disturbed or predated by larger animals in the night, but it is always worth checking.

Summer is a season overflowing with opportunities, and if you can utilize your fieldcraft and knowledge, you have the chance of capturing some beautiful images.

Left, top The froghopper is one of the more unusual subjects you will find in the summer months. Approach them too fast and they will 'pop' and disappear.

Left, bottom A jumping spider stalks an unsuspecting aphid.

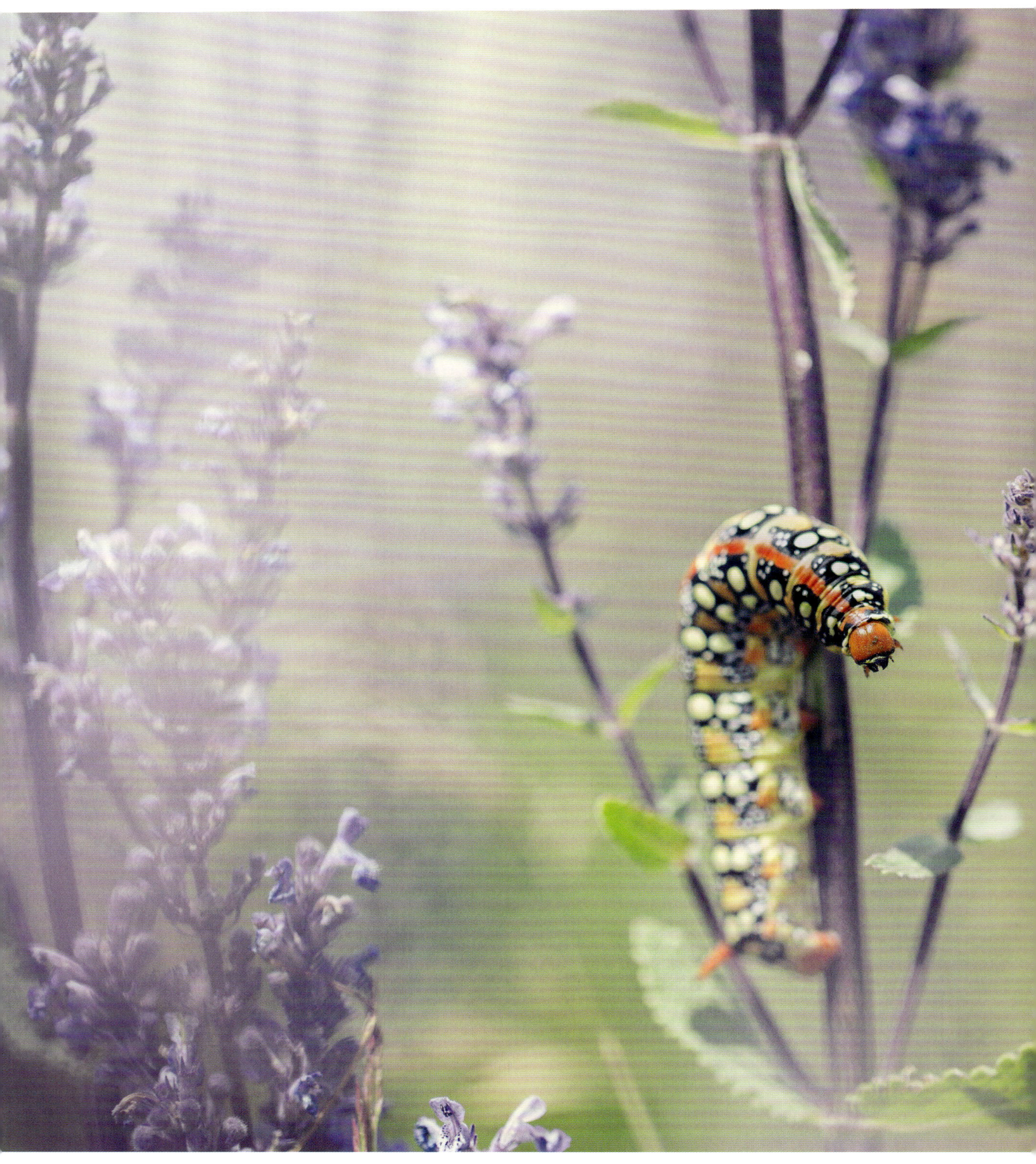

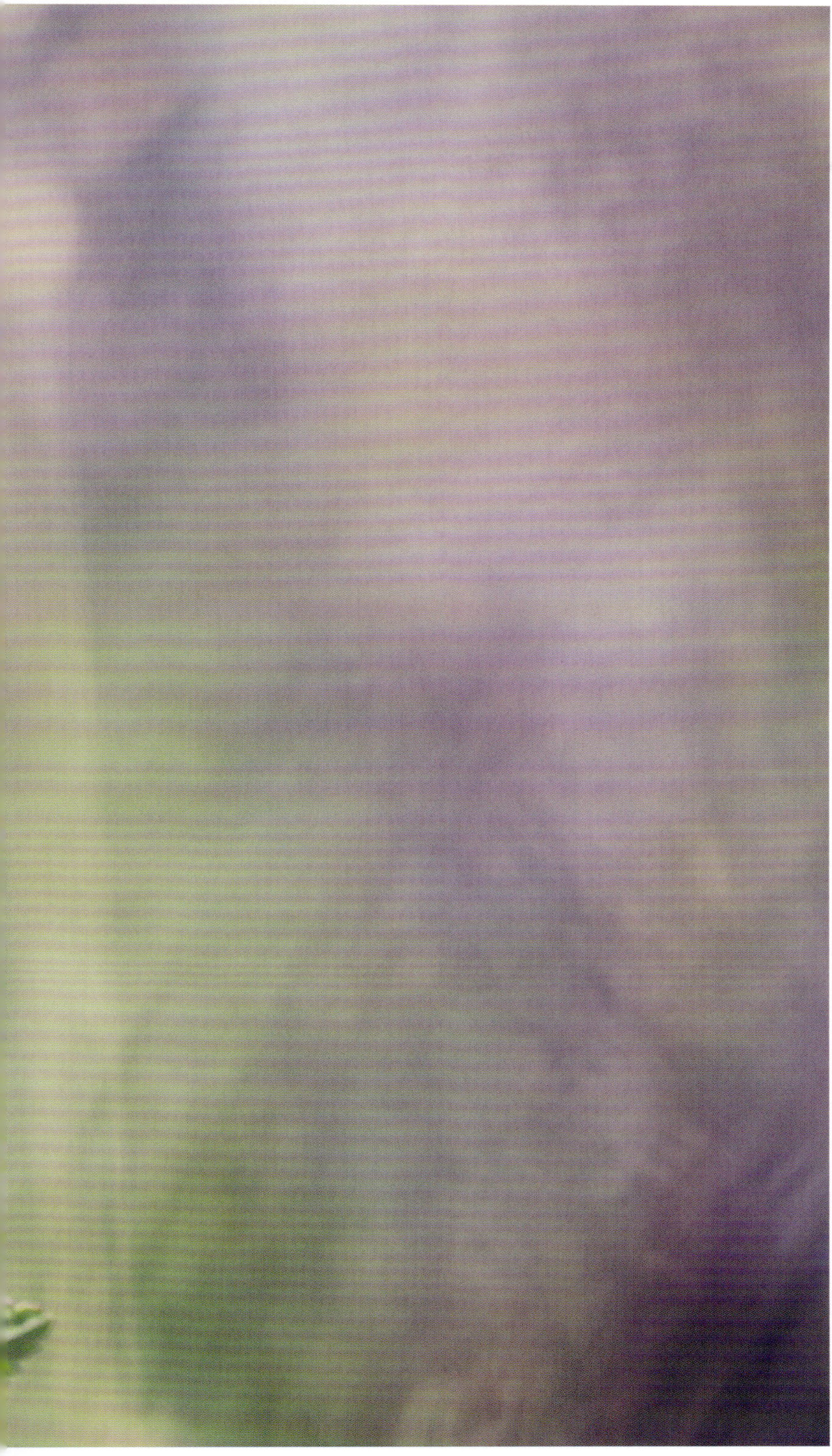

Left Fields of lavender are
awash with wildlife.

Autumn

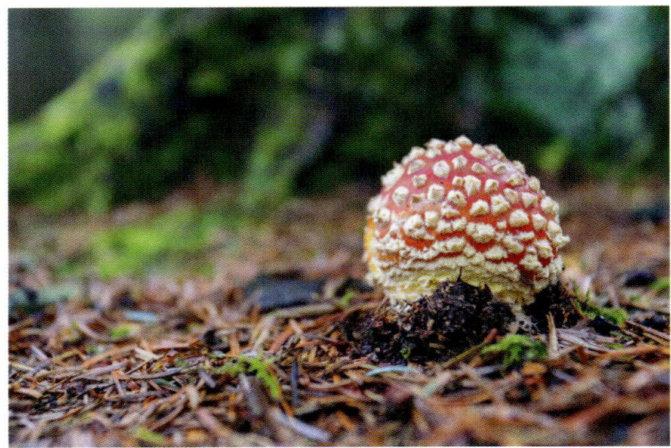

Autumn is the season of transition. The vibrant colours of summer are replaced by fiery reds and oranges in forests, while greens give way to golden yellows and earthy browns. The air smells crisp and fragrant; an aroma of ripened fruits and decaying foliage becomes a real feast for the senses. As the damper season begins, fungi, slime mould, lichen and moss begin to erupt from the ground, decorating fallen trees, branches, rocks and tree bark. The forests are transformed. Some insects go into hibernation; some cling on for that last bit of sun; some simply die off.

Autumn is one of my favourite months, as it forces me to be more creative and to look for new compositions or ways to photograph things such as the various fungi growing in the local woods. Despite the lack of insects, there is still lots to be found at a macro level.

Fallen leaves with their reds and oranges make perfect subjects and you can explore the textures, decay, shapes and sizes of the bounty we have on the floor. In some cases you may even find patches of green on these leaves, which means that inside lives a leaf miner. These insects live in and eat any part of a leaf that is still alive, despite falling from the tree. These areas are known as green islands and provide sustenance for the larval stage.

Autumn is a time when fungi, slime mould and lichen thrive, with delicate porcelain mushrooms growing on trees and fallen branches. They don't last long but are a real treat when you find them. You can experiment with natural light or get creative with a flash, adding some backlight to the mushroom and revealing the hidden intricacies of the gills underneath. Lichens make for great studies of texture and colour, as well as providing abstract opportunities.

Macro photography in autumn offers a chance to showcase the smaller, more intricate beauties of nature. You can take your time with your subjects and really push the boundaries of your creativity.

Above left Fly agaric is native to the UK – and very poisonous.

Right, top The leaf miner has a special relationship with the leaf, as it keeps part of it alive in order to feed.

Right, bottom A spider climbs a hill of fungi. Fallen trees are perfect spots to hunt for newly sprouting fungi.

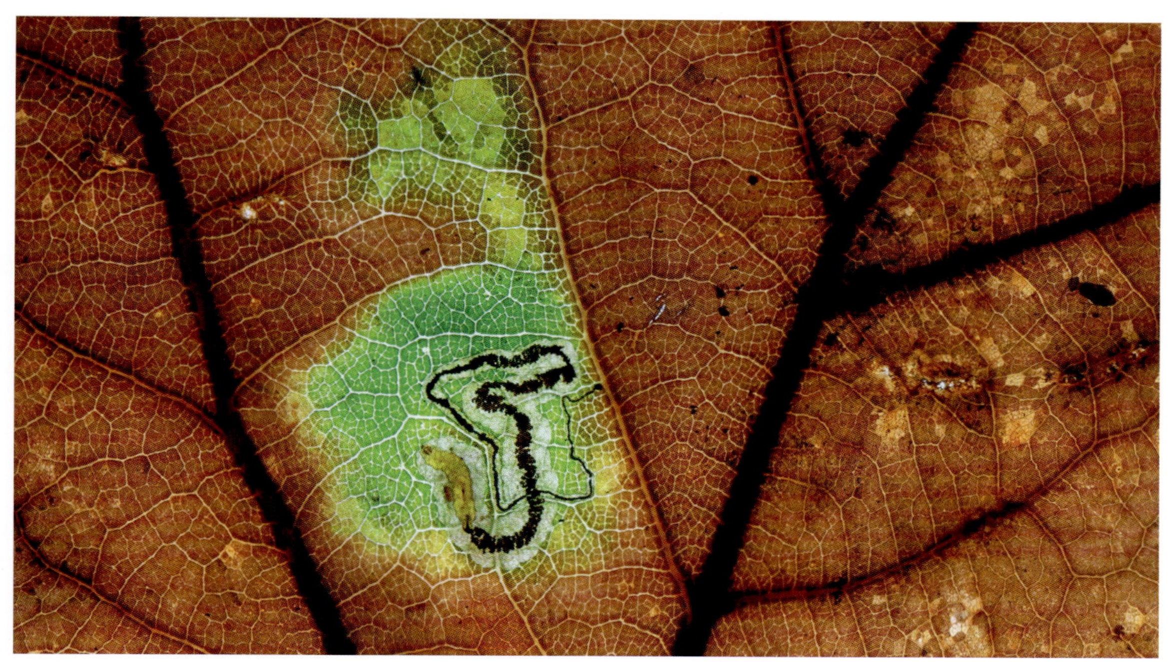

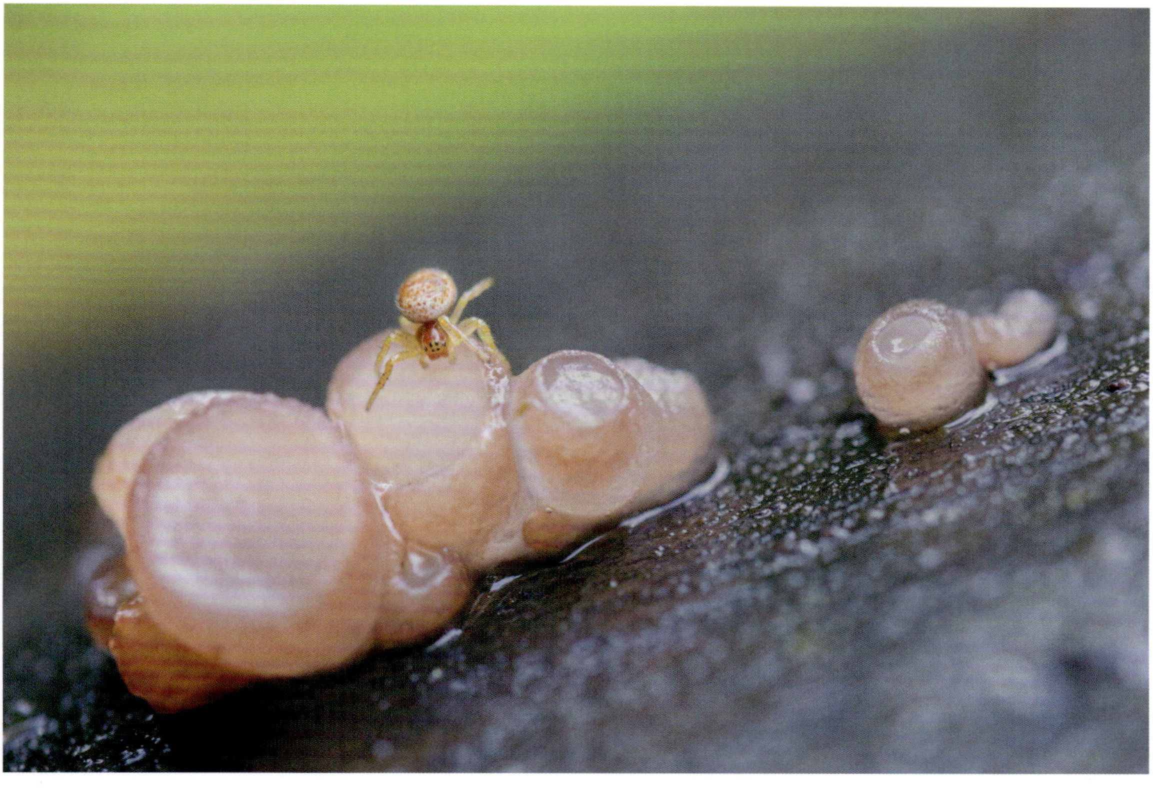

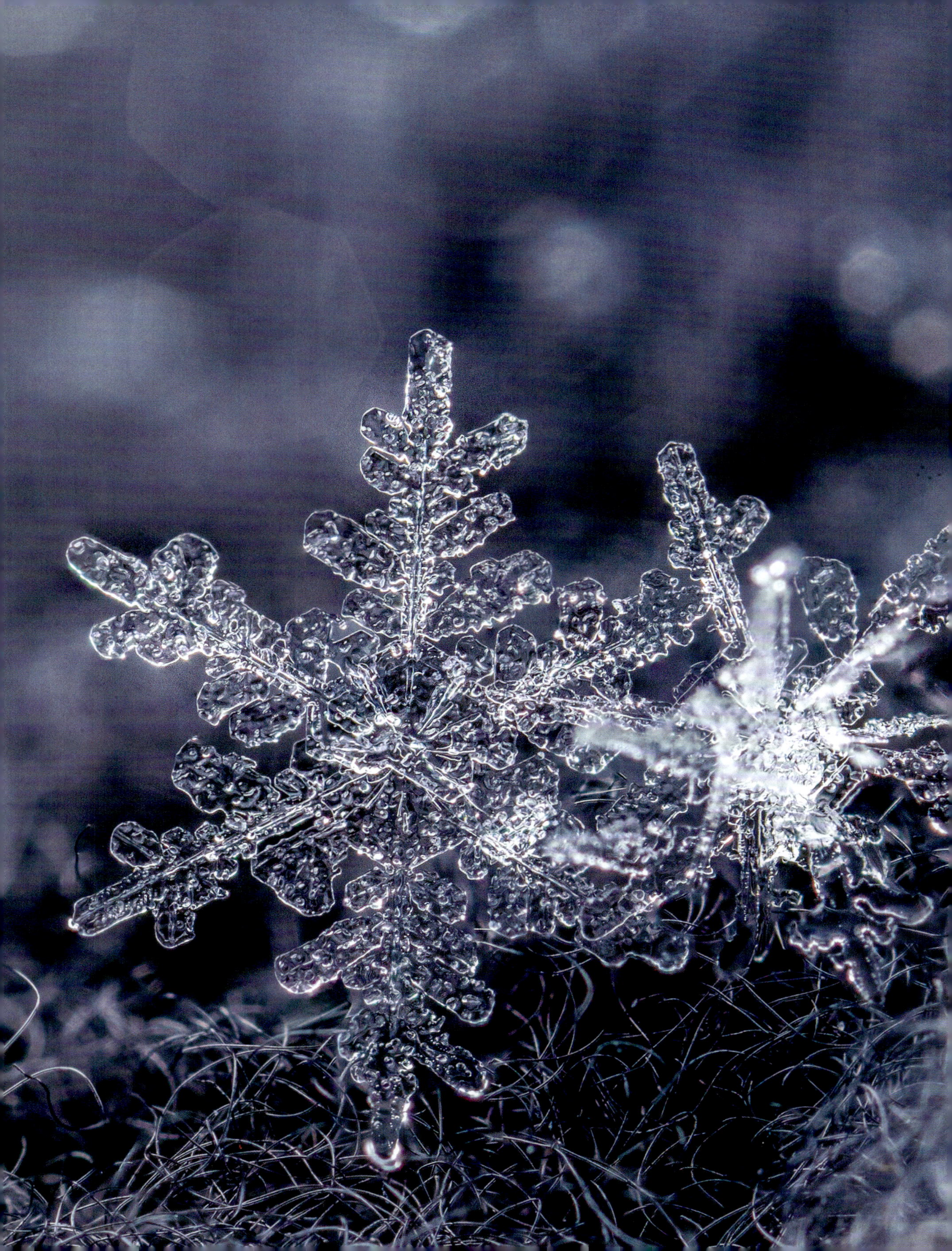

Winter

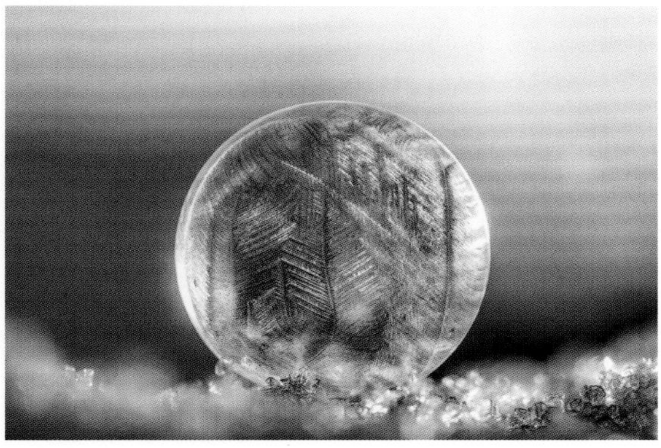

The air carries a chill, the trees are bare and even the fungi is no more. Light is limited and most of our subjects are gone, so what does winter offer the macro photographer?

As temperatures plummet, ice and frost begin to reveal the intricate details of the natural world around us. A fallen leaf now showcases a frosty edge that can be photographed at macro level. Frozen ponds and small puddles act as frosty mirrors and as the sunlight reflects and refracts through ice and frost crystals, a world of colour is revealed. Frost is one of the more accessible winter macro subjects to photograph; I tend to take a walk around my local forest or park areas and look for large shards of frost on the edges of park benches, leaves and even the grass. Check the weather forecast and look for a clear night – a blanket of cloud usually keeps the temperature above freezing and robs us of the frost, so clear nights are what we're after.

Ice formations create interesting sculptures that look incredible under a macro lens. For example, the last of the summer's spider webs, frozen in time and adorned with small crystals of ice, provide a great macro opportunity and serve as a reminder of the warmer months.

Snowflakes are my favourite winter subject, but they can be difficult to photograph. Typically, when they fall, they don't last long and any heat from your body or breath will melt them almost instantly. Up close, their delicate structures possess symmetrical patterns, each one unique in its formation. A top tip for capturing snowflakes (and cold-weather photography in general) is to have all your gear outside and fully acclimatized to the conditions, as this will reduce the chance of lens fog. Having material for the snowflakes to land on that is already frozen will give you some extra time once the snowflake lands.

A recent trend among macro photographers is photographing frozen soap bubbles. This requires very cold temperatures, some bubble mixture and a photographer willing to embrace sub-zero temperatures. It's fascinating to watch the crystals takeover the soap bubbles in real time.

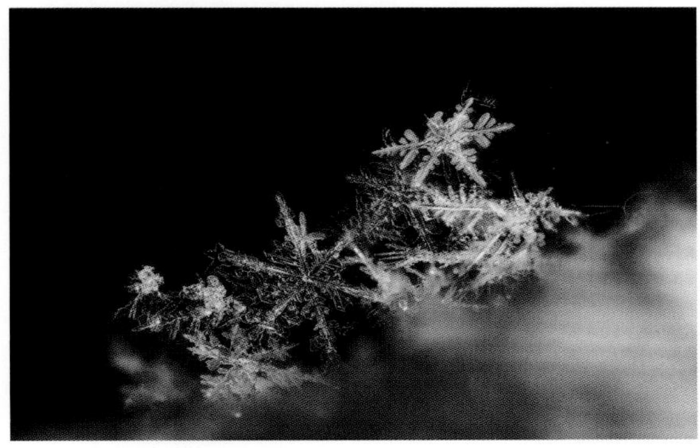

Top A frozen soap bubble, focus stacked and rendered in black and white.

Left Feel free to get creative. Here, I used a blue gel on my flash to add a cold feeling.

Above A black-and-white treatment can really transform a photograph.

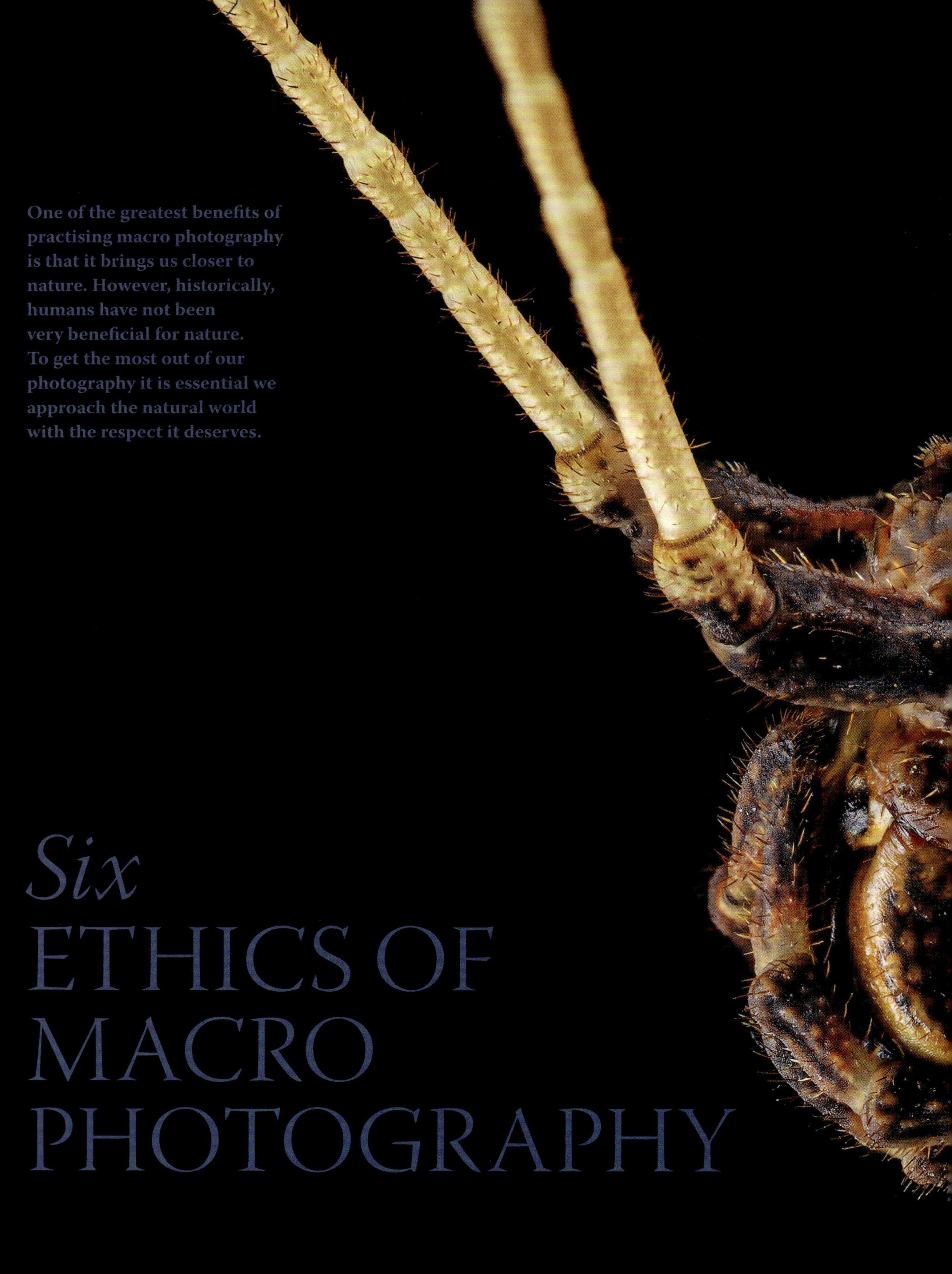

One of the greatest benefits of practising macro photography is that it brings us closer to nature. However, historically, humans have not been very beneficial for nature. To get the most out of our photography it is essential we approach the natural world with the respect it deserves.

Six

ETHICS OF MACRO PHOTOGRAPHY

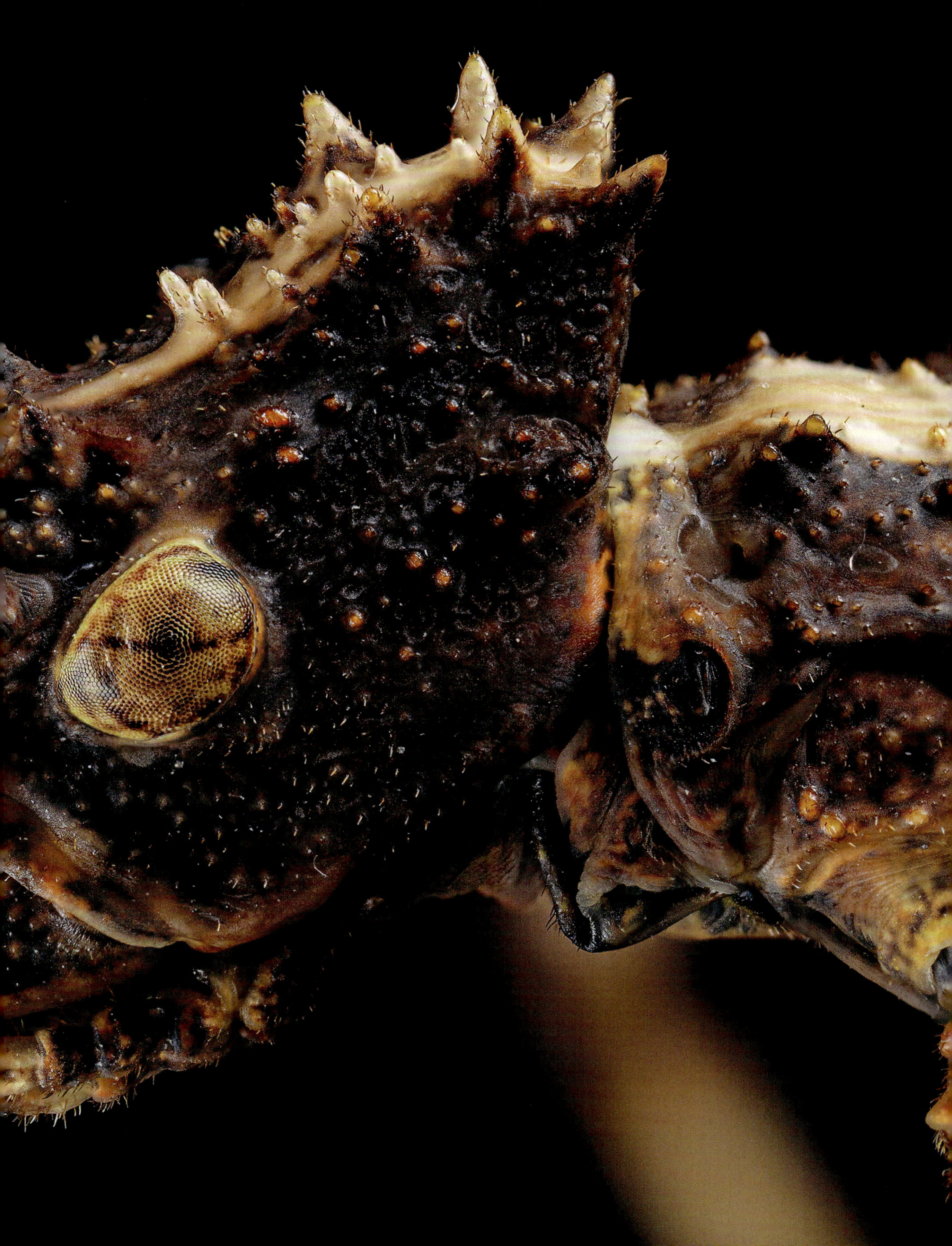

Ethical practice

Whether we are out in the field looking for our macro subjects, spending time photographing pets at home or even just out for a wander in a local park or wood, the welfare of the subjects we photograph and the environment they live in should always be a high priority. We are extremely fortunate to be able to enjoy the incredible flora and fauna this world has to offer, and we must respect, care for and understand it so that it can flourish.

'Take nothing but pictures,
leave nothing but footprints,
kill nothing but time.'

This is a quote that many landscape and wildlife photographers will be familiar with, and it sums up our aims. We share this world with countless amazing organisms, and we should act accordingly when we set out to photograph them.

Take nothing but pictures

Never remove an animal from its natural environment to photograph it at home in a controlled environment. Don't pluck or pull any flowers or foliage that are still growing to photograph it in a more aesthetic or convenient spot. Many can be found on the ground naturally and still make excellent subjects.

Leave nothing but footprints

When out in the field, we need to consider how our presence impacts the environment we are in. For example, where are we walking and what are we walking on? Be careful not to trample flowering orchids or kick sprouting fungi. Local hotspots for orchids can quickly turn into a mud bath in the autumn due to the volume of photographers visiting the area to get their shots. The same applies for bluebells in spring, and other seasonal beauties. We have a direct impact every time we set foot in these areas, and we should seek to minimize our impact as much as possible.

When we photograph the many organisms that live on this planet, we should pay special attention to not destroying their homes. A simple spider web represents hours of work for its creator. The same goes for any creature that has captured prey – try not to spook them into dropping it, as it could be the only meal they've had in days.

Right A single crocus flower, always a sign that spring is on the horizon.

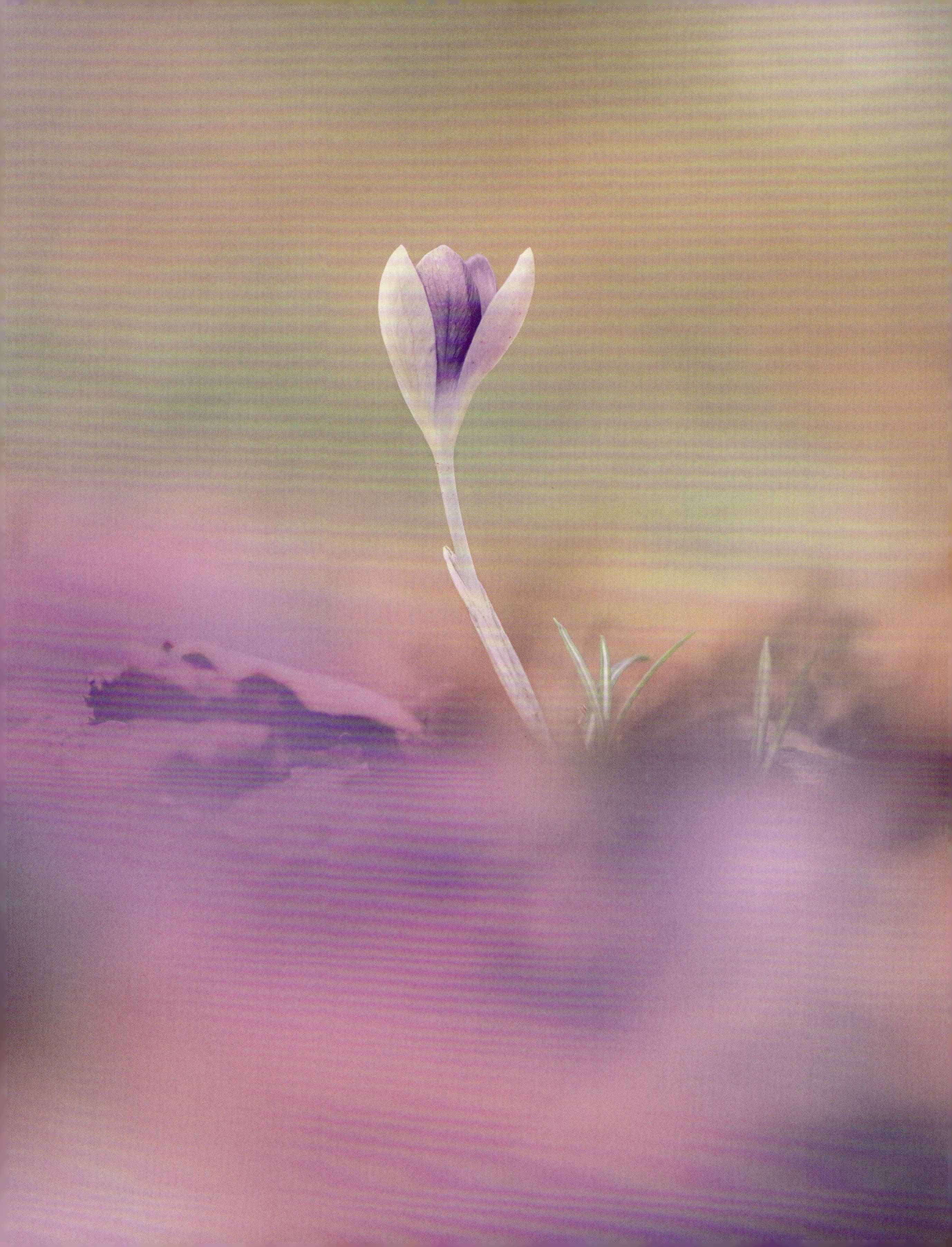

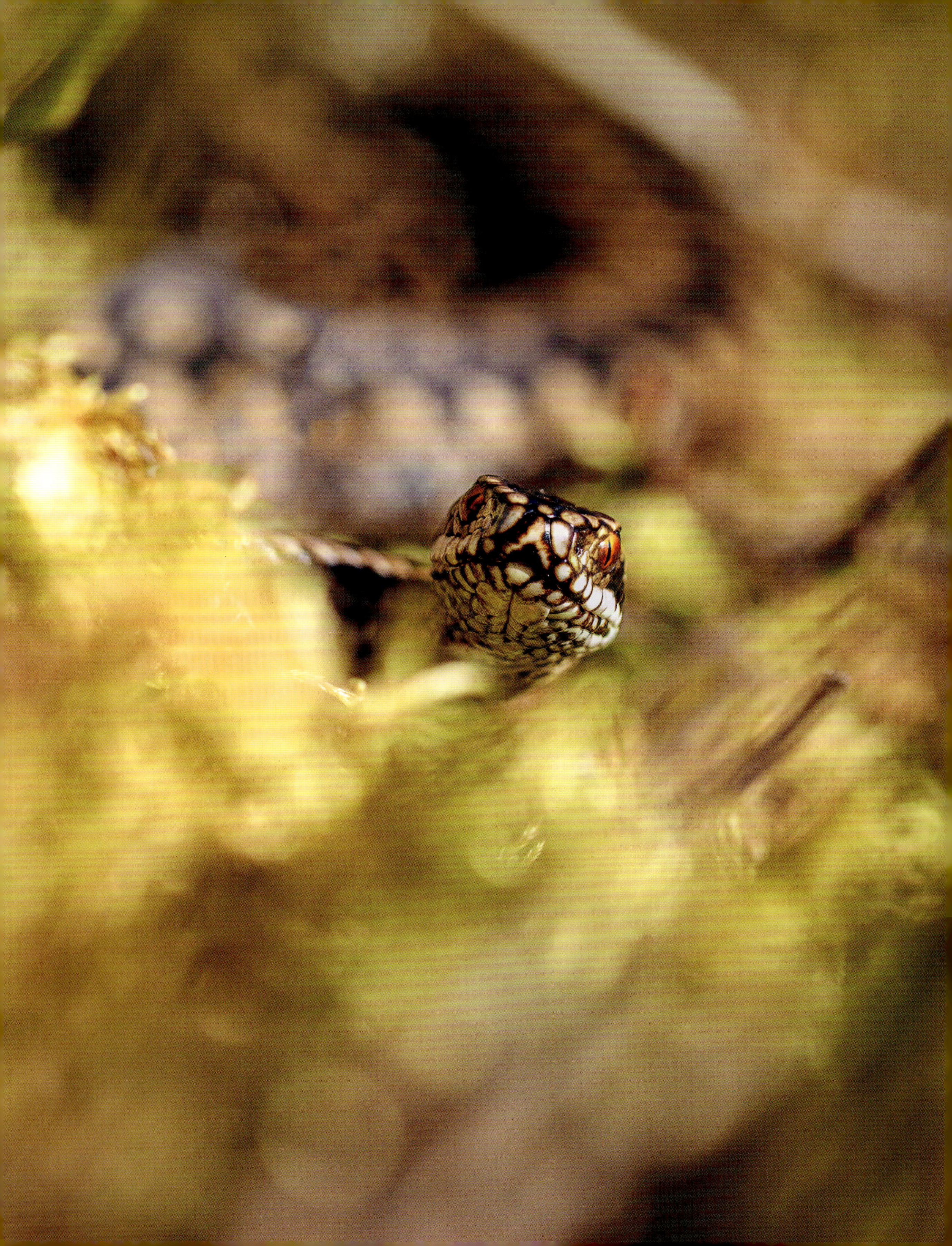

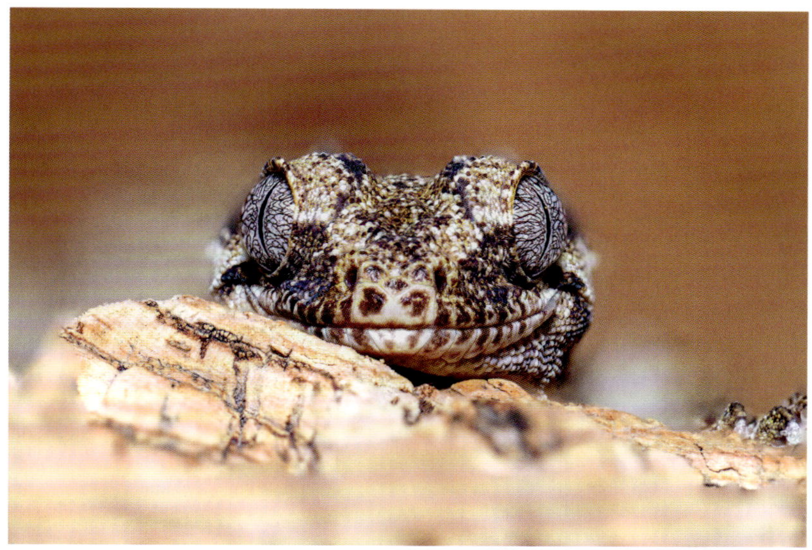

Left An adder emerges from the hibernaculum to bask in the early spring sun. It is important to not disturb these wonderful creatures; they should always be photographed at a distance

Right Gargoyle geckos make great pets and photography subjects, but remember that they are living creatures and deserve to be treated with care and respect.

Kill nothing but time

Insects, arachnids, amphibians and reptiles have been subject to some of the most unethical practices by photographers globally. Some of these approaches include freezing or cooling subjects. Many of our subjects are cold-blooded, so placing them in a cooler environment will naturally slow them down, but by freezing or cooling them to temperatures they would not normally face, you are most likely sentencing the creature to death. This is why many macro photographers choose to photograph early morning and late evening, when temperatures are naturally cooler and subjects stiller.

Other practices have included posing animals on other animals, gluing animals into position and even tying them with fishing wire, which is cloned out later in Photoshop. Not only is this highly unethical, but it also sets unreal expectations of what you may encounter out in the field. These are living creatures. They will run and they will fly, and chances are they won't cooperate with you for a photograph. Simply move on or be patient and wait for the creature to settle; if it becomes stressed, it's time to go.

As macro photography has gained popularity on social media platforms, so has the keeping of exotic pets such as praying mantises, jumping spiders and scorpions. Not only are they fascinating to observe, they also photograph well too. However, their popularity as pets hasn't always benefited their own health and well-being. As with any pet you might buy, do your research and learn how to care for it before committing to being responsible for its future welfare.

Most of our subjects are fragile and often demanding in the kind of habitat they need. Some species thrive in a hot and humid environment, while others prefer it to be hot and dry; getting this wrong can result in death. Before you intervene in any animal's life – whether it be moving an insect in the natural environment or buying a pet – consider the potential consequences for its welfare, rather than your own desires.

As macro photographers we can inspire our audiences to take a closer look and become enthralled at the beauty of this hidden world, and if we are to do so, we must first treat this world with the respect it deserves.

Fieldcraft

A part of committing yourself to photographing your subjects as ethically as possible is the study of fieldcraft. At its simplest, fieldcraft is the ability to approach and get close to your subject without causing it unnecessary stress. It is also the study and research of a subject and the environment it lives in. What is its food source? Where do they reside? At what time of the year can they be found?

Fieldcraft allows us to take a more nuanced approach to our photography – to seek our subjects more purposefully, leaving less impact on the environment. By knowing when and where a subject is likely to be found, and how it is likely to react, we can approach it on its own terms, select the appropriate kit and get the best out of our photography. Fieldcraft could be as simple as observing the habits of the spider in your bathroom, but there are several ways to learn:

Books
Books are a great tool for researching your subjects and there are plenty of options to choose from. You can get broad identification guides to national or regional flora and fauna, as well as more detailed publications on specific species, habitats and local environments. Remember when purchasing books to make sure that they are geographically correct for your location – wildlife varies widely from one region to another.

Recce
It is always useful to explore the area in which you want to photograph a species before you do it. First and foremost this will enable you to confirm that the subject is present and what your shooting options may be, but also – and just as important – to check out the area for any health and safety risks. As an example, dragonflies, damselflies and amphibians frequent wetland areas, which can have large bodies of open water and less obvious boggy or marshy grasslands. If you were to come out early in the morning or late in the evening, potentially when the sun is setting or later, would you be safe? It is essential that you assess the risks appropriately. Never put yourself or your subject in danger for a photograph.

Online
Online communities and forums are a great way to tap into local knowledge and share prime hotspots for certain species. YouTube can be a great source of information for researching your subjects and even their locations, and more generally there is a plethora of information available online for just about any subject. However, it is worth checking a source is reliable before putting too much faith in it.

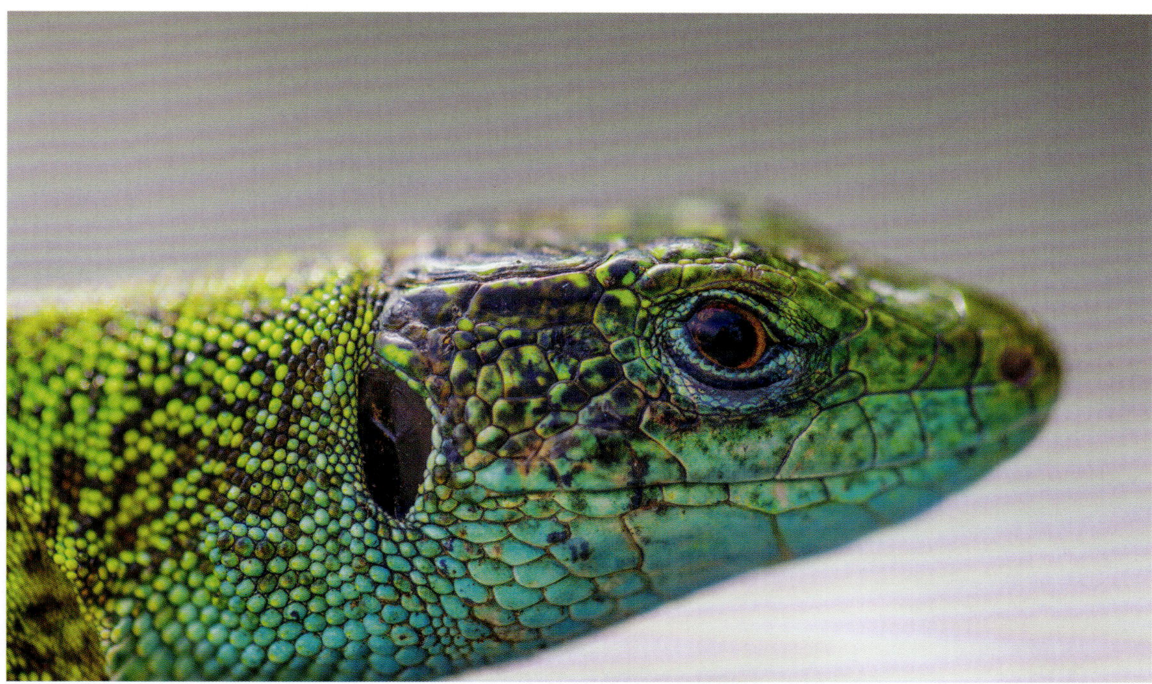

Fieldcraft: an example

How important is fieldcraft to your wildlife photography? It's extremely important! Here's an example.

Lizards are notoriously skittish, and macro photographers often favour longer focal lengths such as 180mm, as this allows them to get that macro magnification while maintaining a larger working distance, so the lizard doesn't become spooked and run away. However, with the correct fieldcraft techniques you can get extremely close with shorter focal lengths, such as 100mm. In the image above, I am so close – just a few inches between my lens and the subject – that you can see my reflection in this male Balkan green lizard's eyes (the shiny bald head is a giveaway).

When approaching lizards, the trick is to get onto your belly and crawl commando-style to close the distance. Do this very slowly, and with no sudden movements, or the lizard will run away. You can take photographs along the way – after all, you don't want to crawl halfway only for the lizard to run off – or you can commit and concentrate on getting as close as possible before taking your shots. The choice is yours.

By respecting the animal, learning it's habits and being patient enough to take the time, you will get shots impossible without this knowledge.

Above Never remove a wild lizard from its habitat, and always photograph pet lizards with the same respect as you would a wild animal.

Seven
ADVANCED TECHNIQUES

Once you have understood the basic principles and are comfortable shooting at 1:1 magnification there are some advanced techniques that will push your macro photography further. These techniques can really aid you in capturing more detail, help you create softer lighting and leave you with a beautiful photograph at the end of it. It's worth noting that these techniques are an addition to your macro photography, and you don't necessarily have to learn or use them all. Every photographer is different, and ultimately you will have to work out which techniques are suited to what you want to do.

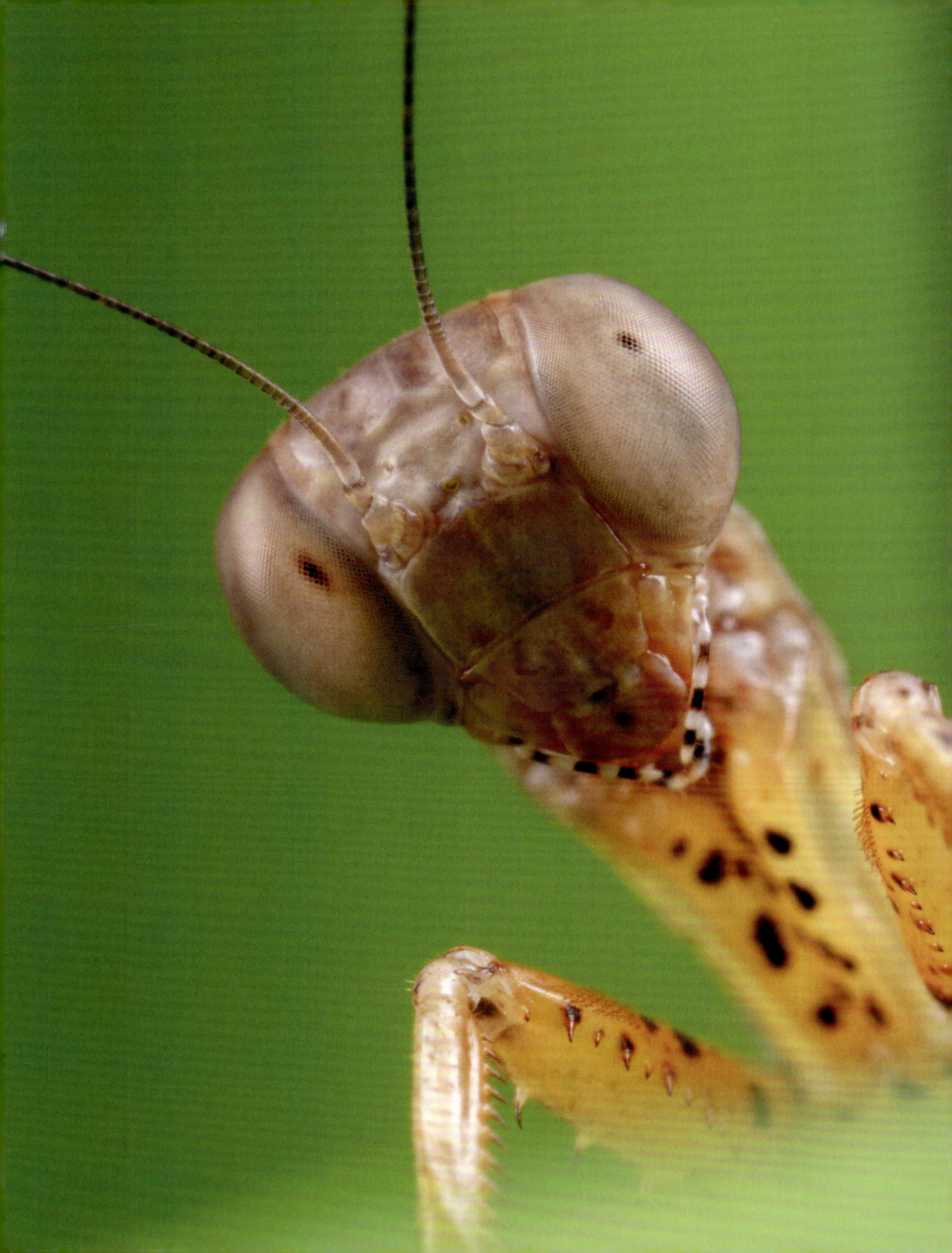

Focus stacking

One challenge of macro photography is getting enough of our subject in focus at high levels of magnification. Focus stacking is a technique that allows macro photographers to achieve greater depth of field and capture more detail than is possible in a single frame.

It involves taking numerous shots at varying focal points and then combining – or 'stacking' – them in post-processing software. There are many ways in which to focus stack, and I'll break the main ones down in detail over the coming pages.

Handheld manual focus stacking

Until recently, manual focus stacking was the only way to stack your shots. It requires a thorough understanding and mastery of your camera, lens and macro photography in general, but it's gives you a huge advantage in the field. So, how do we focus stack manually?

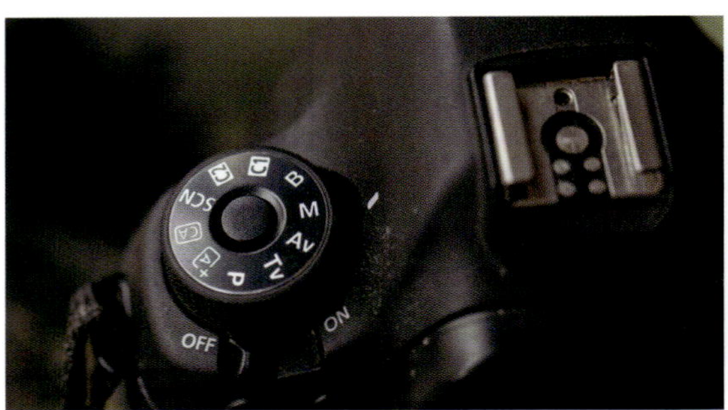

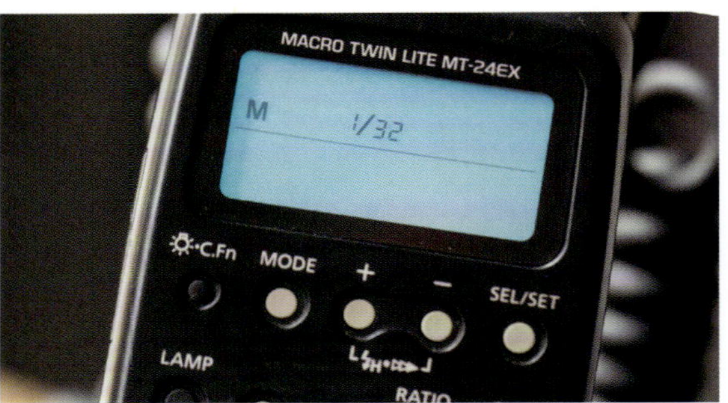

Step 1 Before we begin to stack our subject, we first need to make sure we have everything else set up and ready to go. Manual focus stacking can be done in aperture-priority mode, but if you are comfortable shooting in manual mode, I would always recommend this. More control over your camera means more precise results.

Step 2 Once you have selected your preferred camera mode, it is good practice to fire off some test shots around the area you are photographing to make sure you have the correct exposure. If you are using flash I would suggest switching the power mode to manual, as not only does this give you control of the exposure generated by the flash, but also the power level. A low to medium power level (1/16 or 1/32) will give you faster flash recycle times, meaning the flash will be ready to fire again sooner.

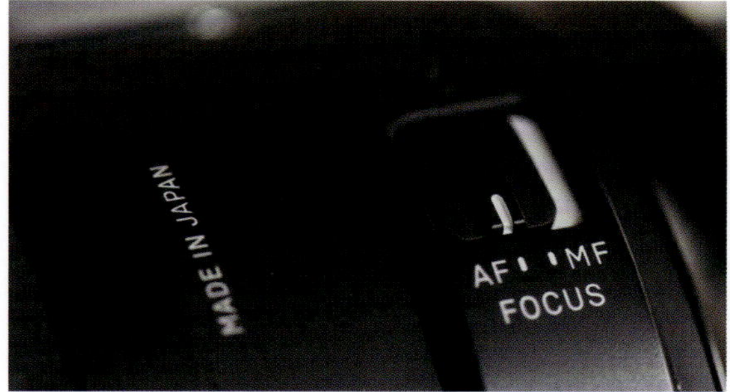

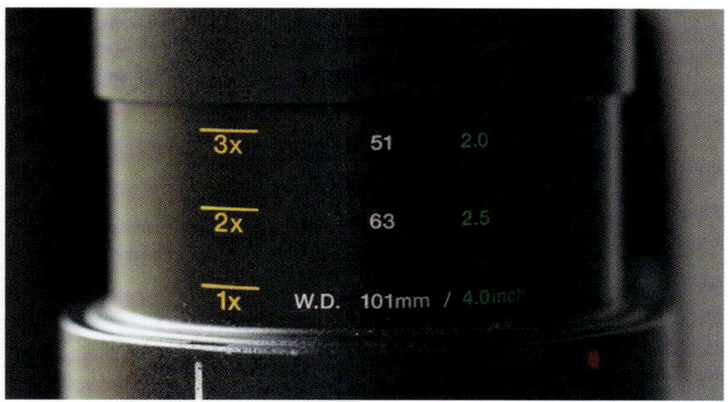

Step 3 Autofocus can struggle at high magnification and may choose different sections of the subject to focus on, which is why we need to be in full control with manual focus. Locate the autofocus/manual focus (AF/MF) switch on the side of your lens and flick the switch to manual.

Step 4 Set your magnification to the desired level and leave it there. Do not turn any part of the focus ring unless it is to change magnification for a new scene. It's worth noting that some newer camera systems now display focus and magnification on the rear LCD screen.

Step 5 We can begin to stack. Start by locating the subject in your viewfinder – this can feel strange if you are used to using autofocus but stick with it. Once you have located your subject, focus on the part of the subject that is nearest to you. By rocking back and forth in very slow and small movements, you will see the plane of focus shift over your subject. Once you are comfortable with this movement, find the nearest part of the subject and take a shot, then move forward ever so slightly and take another shot. Repeat this process until you have reached the end of your subject or desired point. Aim for 2–5 frames per stack and increase the number of frames as you become more comfortable. It is important that your subject remains still and your camera work is steady, as any movement will show once you process the frames in post-processing.

PRO TIP Focus stacking on household items such as fruit or confectionery is a great way to hone your technique. You don't have the pressures of a live subject and you can take your time, experimenting with lighting and composition.

Focus stacking using a tripod and focusing rail

This is the preferred method for a lot of macro photographers, especially those who enjoy early morning adventures out in the field. As we have discussed already, early mornings are a great way to get up close to various insects, as they are still and relatively motionless, sometimes even covered in dew. This is a great opportunity to take your time and fine-tune your focus stacking.

The principle and technique are the same as focus stacking handheld, but rather than rocking back and forth to bring the subject in and out of focus, you use a focusing rail instead.

The focusing rail is mounted on top of your tripod, and your camera or lens is then mounted onto the rail. When shooting with shorter macro lenses such as the 100mm, the camera will be mounted to the focusing rail. However, larger macro lenses such as the 180mm may come with a mounting plate already attached and it's best to mount the lens onto the plate, as this is the heaviest component. Note that it is important to turn off any image stabilization, as this now becomes counterproductive.

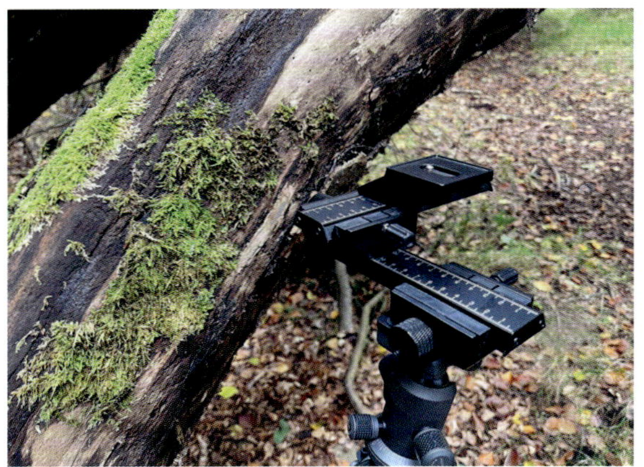

Focusing rails normally come with dials that can be used to fine-tune your movements in microns for all directions – front, back, left and right – although they do vary. Using a focusing rail in combination with live view and focus peaking (on a mirrorless camera) allows you to get pinpoint accuracy. This is how I like to work when shooting early morning macro photographs of roosting subjects.

Focus stacking using in-camera stacking modes

As camera systems have developed over the years, so too have the in-camera features they offer. Most recently, Olympus and Canon have developed in-camera focus stacking. This is a fully automated stacking feature and will require your lens to be set to autofocus. You can use this feature when shooting either handheld or with a tripod, and with or without flash, so the set-up is the same other than the activation and settings of the in-camera software.

Locate the feature in your camera's menu system – this is sometimes referred to as focus bracketing – and set how many frames you would like to take along with the focus increments (how much the focus shifts). Keep in mind that a larger aperture value will cover more focus increments than a smaller aperture would. I typically have this at the lowest setting.

Once you have this set up and have chosen your technique (handheld, natural light or flash etc.), you simply need to find your subject, focus on the nearest part to the camera and press the shutter button. Rather than rocking back and forth, you now must remain as still as possible and allow the camera to adjust the lens for the focus stack. Some camera systems will even process this stack as a composite in camera, leaving you with a fully stacked image and saving you the hassle of using post-processing software. They will also save individual frames should you want to edit them yourself.

Automated stacking is a great way to save time, but it is not without its faults. Sometimes, the composite may be wrong, especially if the subject moves halfway through the automated stack.

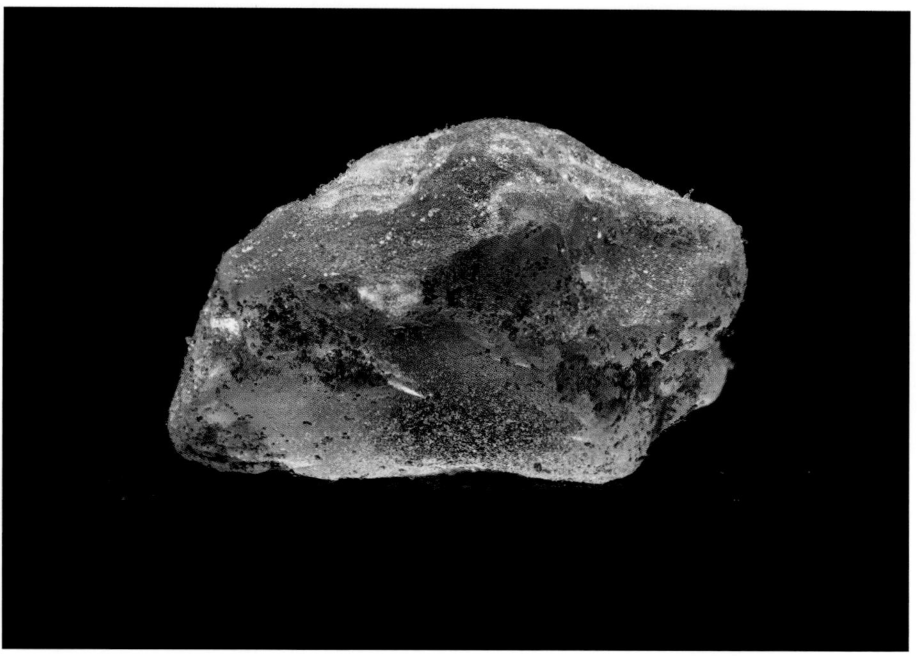

Left A tiny grain of salt is photographed at high magnification using the Canon EOS R7's internal stacking function. Over 150 frames were composited in camera, saving the need for additional hours of post-processing.

Backlighting using flash

How we use light can make or break an image. Too harsh and we have deep shadows, too bright and we overexpose the scene, too little and our subjects can look dull and uninspiring. Achieving the 'correct' exposure is usually the aim, but rules are meant to be broken. Purposefully overexposing your subject or subtly lighting it to reveal shadows and texture can also work.

One of my favourite techniques is backlighting subjects with a flash to add a rim light or change the scene. This technique requires you to use off-camera flash, and the easiest way to do this is with a set of remote triggers.

Once your flash is away from the camera, you will begin to see just how creative you can be with the light. You can place it below or behind your subject, use one or more flash units and add gels to add colour to your light source.

So, how do we use off-camera flash to get creative lighting such as backlighting?

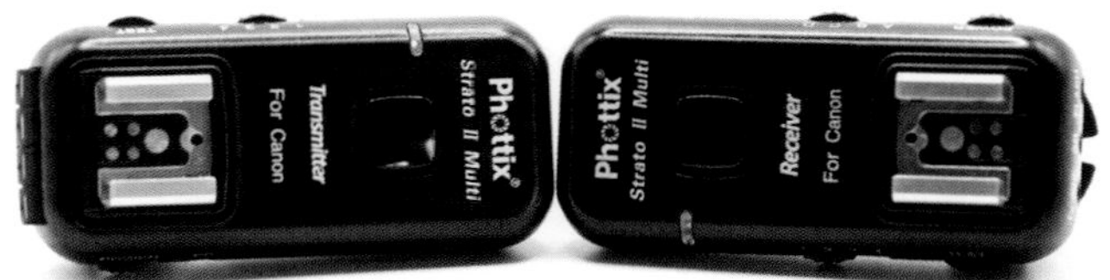

Right A remote flash trigger pairs with a receiver (or multiple receivers) to trigger the flash.

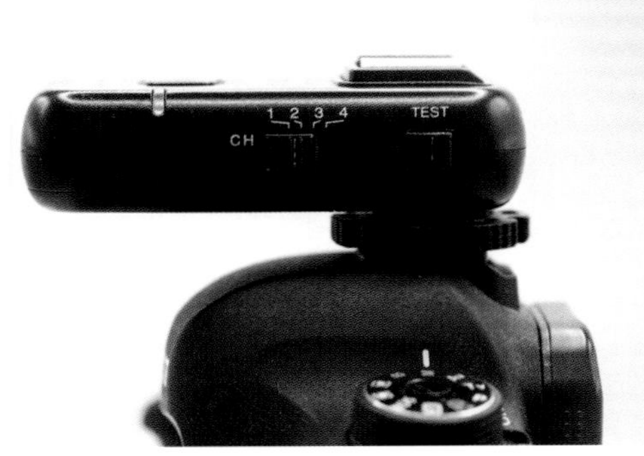

Step 1 Attach your remote flash trigger to your camera's hotshoe.

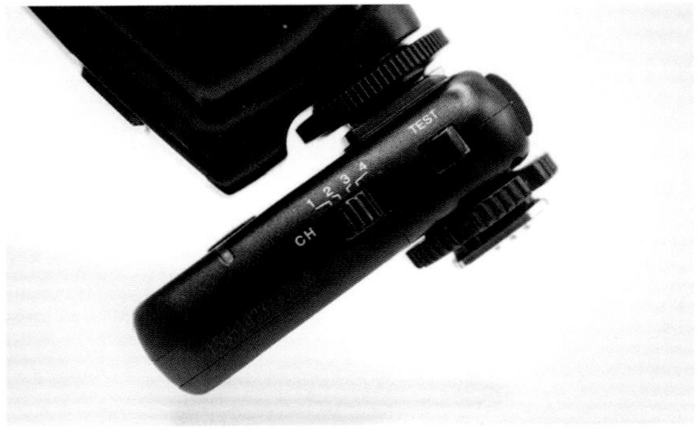

Step 2 Attach your remote receiver(s) to the flash unit(s) and make sure the trigger and receiver(s) are set to the same channel.

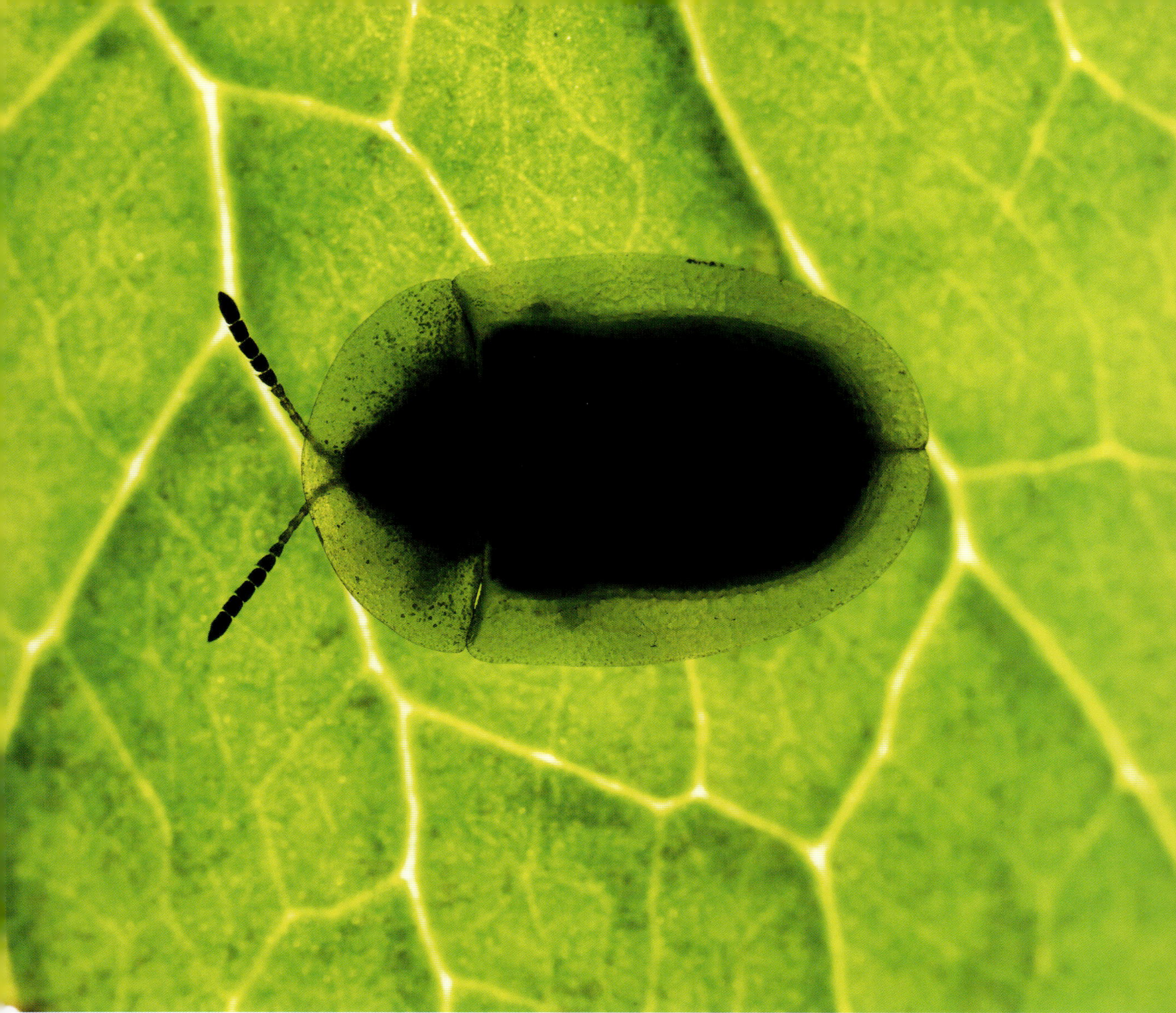

Step 3 Position your flash unit behind or slightly below your subject and take some test shots. If you find you are getting flare from the flash, adjust the camera/flash position until it disappears. For rim lighting I prefer the flash unit to be lower, but for backlighting I like the flash to be directly underneath or behind the subject.

Above A tortoise beetle lit from underneath creates a beautiful silhouette.

Composition

Composition is how your subjects or visual elements of a scene are laid out in front of you. Composition can be used to lead a viewer into your photograph; to direct a viewer to a certain section of your photograph; to highlight key points of your photograph; or can simply be an aesthetically pleasing arrangement of elements.

A good composition will pique your interest. Landscape photographers, for example, are masters of composition. They use the visual elements of the landscape in front of them to create images that immerse you, leading your eye through the scene or filling it with atmosphere. The best landscape photography is not just about capturing the rocks, trees, fields, mountains and various other elements that make a scene pleasing in the first place – it is about how these elements interact with each other in the frame. Now I'm no landscape photographer, but I can certainly be inspired by it and try to put the same principles to work in my own photography.

When it comes to macro photography it can often be very tricky to compose your photograph. Most of the time we are dealing with live subjects and, to put it simply, they aren't going to sit and pose for you – 'Just tilt your head to the left Mr Jumping Spider', or 'That's fantastic, Mrs Bee, just keep your wings like that.' I'll be honest, I have actually said these things to various insects in my time! Joking aside, we don't have a lot of time to frame our subjects in a great composition, but that's not to say it can't be done. It just takes a little practice and forward thinking.

Framing your subject beautifully is just one aspect of successful composition. Lighting, symmetry, patterns, colour and negative space are all things to think about when approaching a scene. Sometimes the subjects themselves provide all that's needed – think of a millipede curled up, for instance, or how a centipede curls and twists as it roams on the ground; just by themselves, these natural shapes and formations make for a pleasing photograph. Often, it's the limits of our equipment or the available lighting that help us find the composition – a shallow depth of field will blur distracting details into a smooth colour or pattern, naturally drawing the eye to the sharp subject.

Over the next couple of pages I will give a few examples of the way I might use the principles of composition in my photography. However, there are many different approaches, and no true hard-and-fast rules. The important thing for me in composition letting my creativity flow, so don't be afraid to try new compositions and experiment.

PRO TIP I have mentioned this a few times already, but practising at home on inanimate objects is an excellent way to build the experience that will help you in the field. Learning how the elements of an image interact, or how framing a subject in different ways can completely change the look and feel of a photograph, is a great way of getting into the habit of thinking about composition. You can then apply these principles to live subjects.

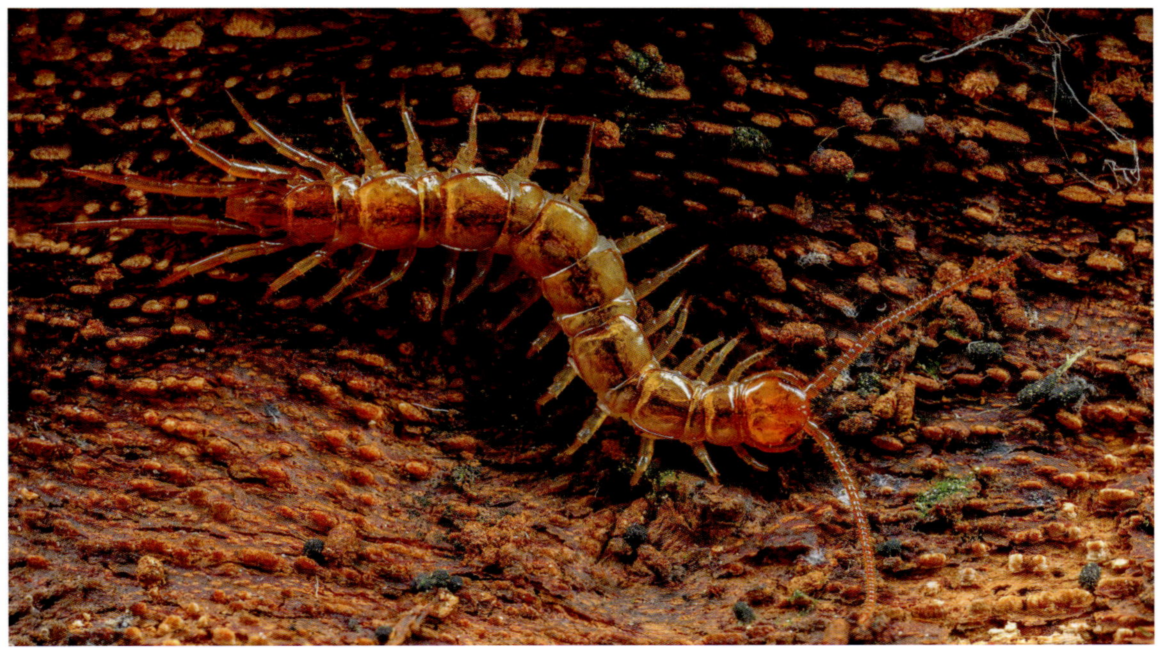

Above The natural curl of this centipede allows for a simple, central, but nevertheless interesting composition.

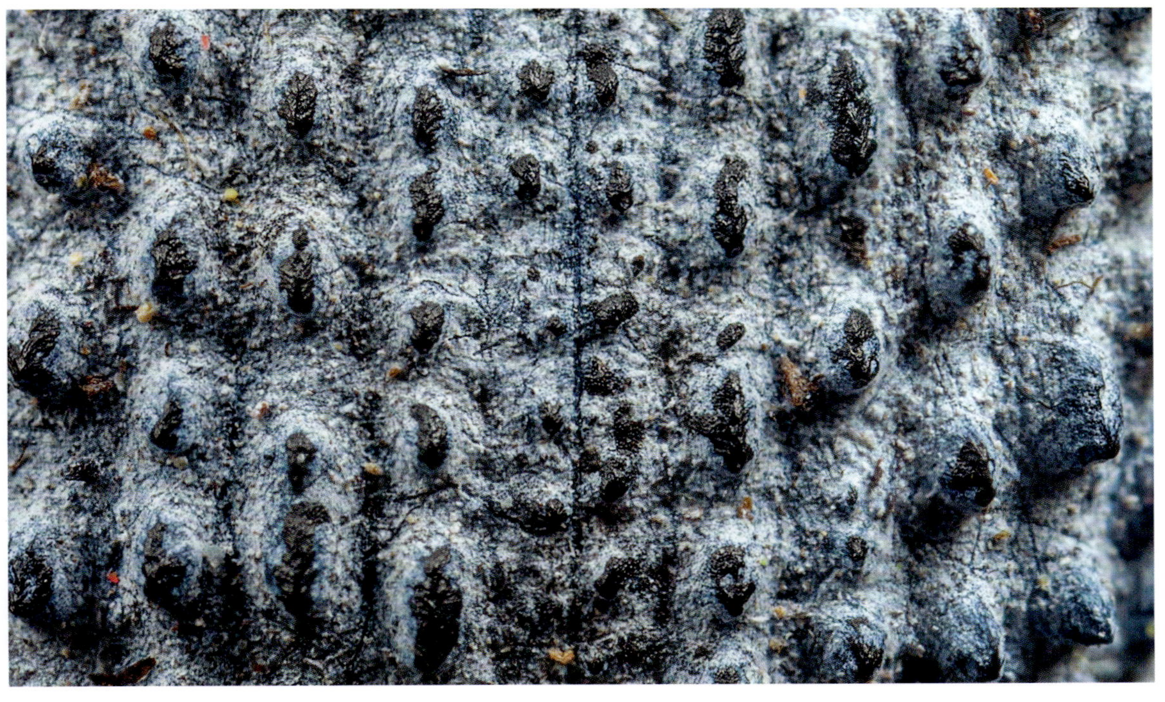

Above A close-up of the death-feigning beetle showcases its interesting textures and patterns for visual interest.

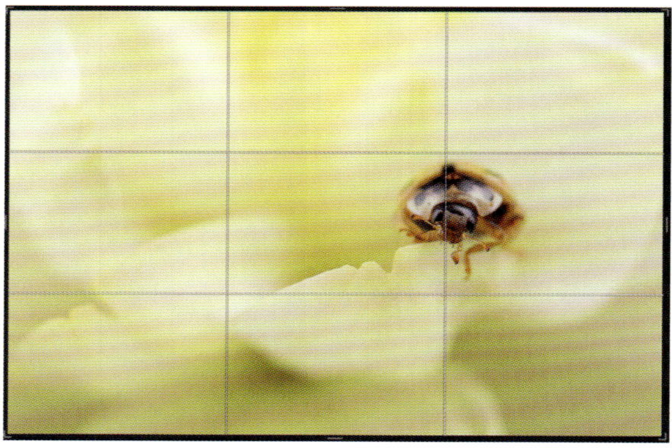 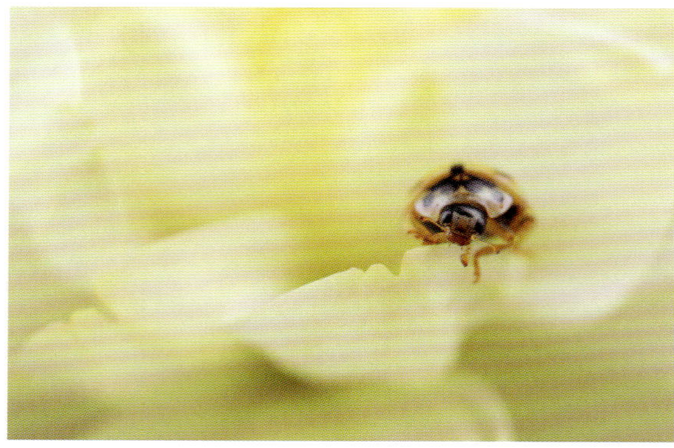

Rule of thirds

One of the most commonly used approaches to framing is the 'rule of thirds', where you place an imaginary 3 x 3 grid over the scene and aim to place your subject or key elements on one of the grid lines or their intersections. The idea behind this 'rule' is that placing your subject in the middle of the frame doesn't tend to make the most interesting image. By placing it to one side, you can use other elements in the scene to give context, contrast or lead the eye more slowly through the image.

In the example shown here I placed the subject – a ladybird – on the grid line to the right of the frame, between the two intersections. I also allowed just enough depth of field to capture the soft, delicate petals that curl up towards the ladybird, which leads the viewer's eye to the subject. Another thing to consider is the angle of your camera to the subject: here it gives an elevated feel to the subject, so you can get the feeling that the ladybird is perched on the edge of the petal.

Now take a look at the image below:

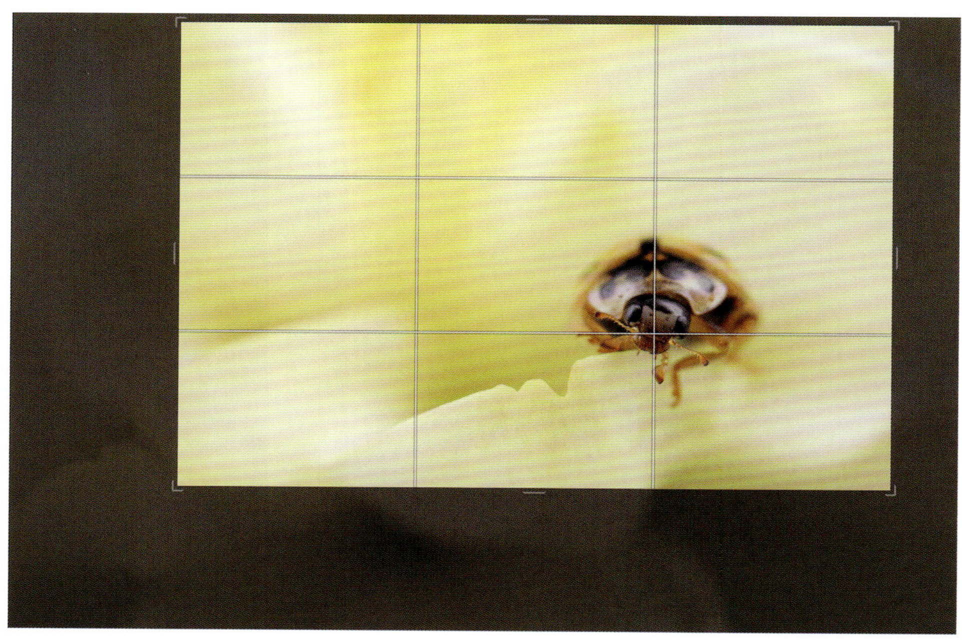

In this version I have cropped the original image in post-production to place the ladybird on the bottom right intersection of the 'thirds lines'. Cropping is a great way to experiment with composition after you have taken your photograph, and there are times when it can save the day. As these are live subjects who don't always play ball and pose perfectly for you, cropping can help improve the composition.

However, this does come with a warning: if you crop too much it can lead to a loss of quality in your image. Relying on cropping can also make you start to become dependent on it, and you risk missing out on learning a vital skill out in the field. As much as possible, aim to get the composition right when you take your shot.

Here, cropping makes the subject appear closer and it has greater impact as it fills the frame more:

Below Don't be afraid to experiment with cropping your images in post-production to see if the composition can be improved.

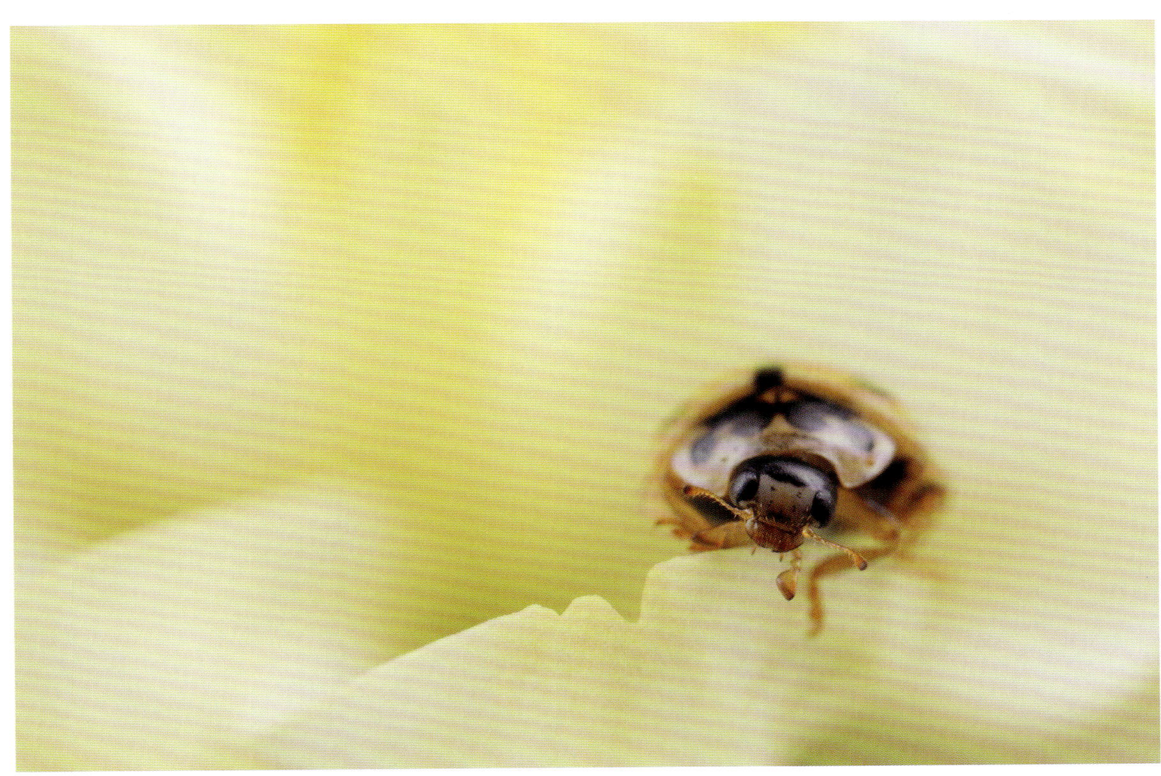

Light and space

Other elements, such as light and negative
space, can also help you in your composition.
When the scene is largely empty, with few visual
distractions, the viewer will naturally look for
something of interest – and find your subject.
Negative space also allows for the use of selective
lighting to enhance the composition even further
by concentrating the light on the subject alone,
leaving the rest of the scene less illuminated.

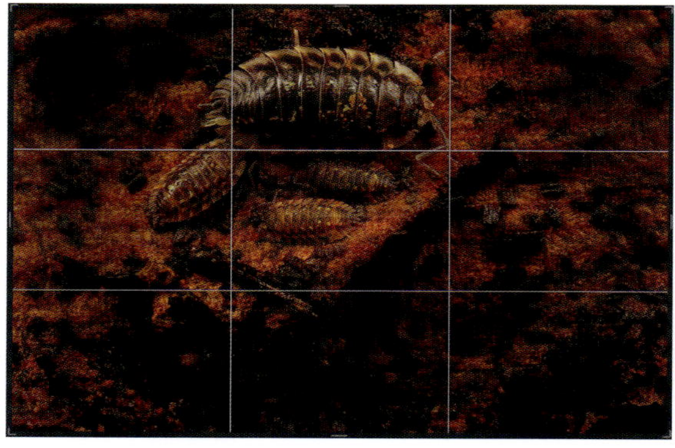

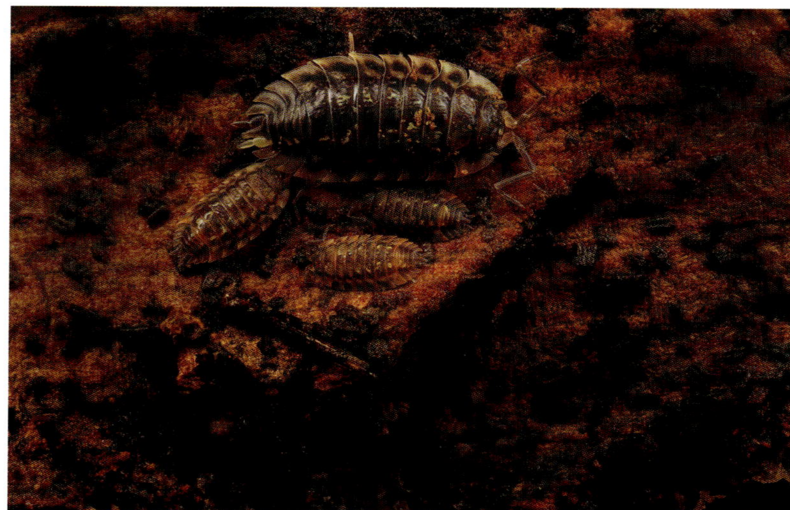

Left The viewer's eye will
naturally be drawn towards
the brighter, more detailed
areas of the image.

Right Muted colour palettes
can be just as effective as
vibrant ones.

Take this image of a huddle of woodlice. Using
the 3 x 3 grid overlay (shown top right), you can
see I haven't adhered strictly to a rule-of-thirds
placement – my subjects spill over the gridlines.
However, as a whole they have been placed
within the four 'blocks' at the top left, leaving
the other five empty and creating the negative
space I am after. You will also see the woodlice
are illuminated slightly more than the rest of
the scene, which is another way to naturally lead
the viewer's eye, highlighting the subjects and
emphasizing the details I want the viewer to see.

Light and colour

The colours, light and background of your
scene can also influence the look and feel of a
photograph. Although many of the colours of
nature are eye-catchingly bright and powerful as
seen in many of the images in this book, a muted
or monochrome palette can be just as effective.
Take a look at this shot of a small pearl-bordered
fritillary. The butterfly was roosting in the early
morning, and there wasn't much light available.
However, framing the subject in front of the rising
sun shining through the trees created a beautiful
bokeh, highlighting the butterfly and suffusing
the scene in a warm orange glow.

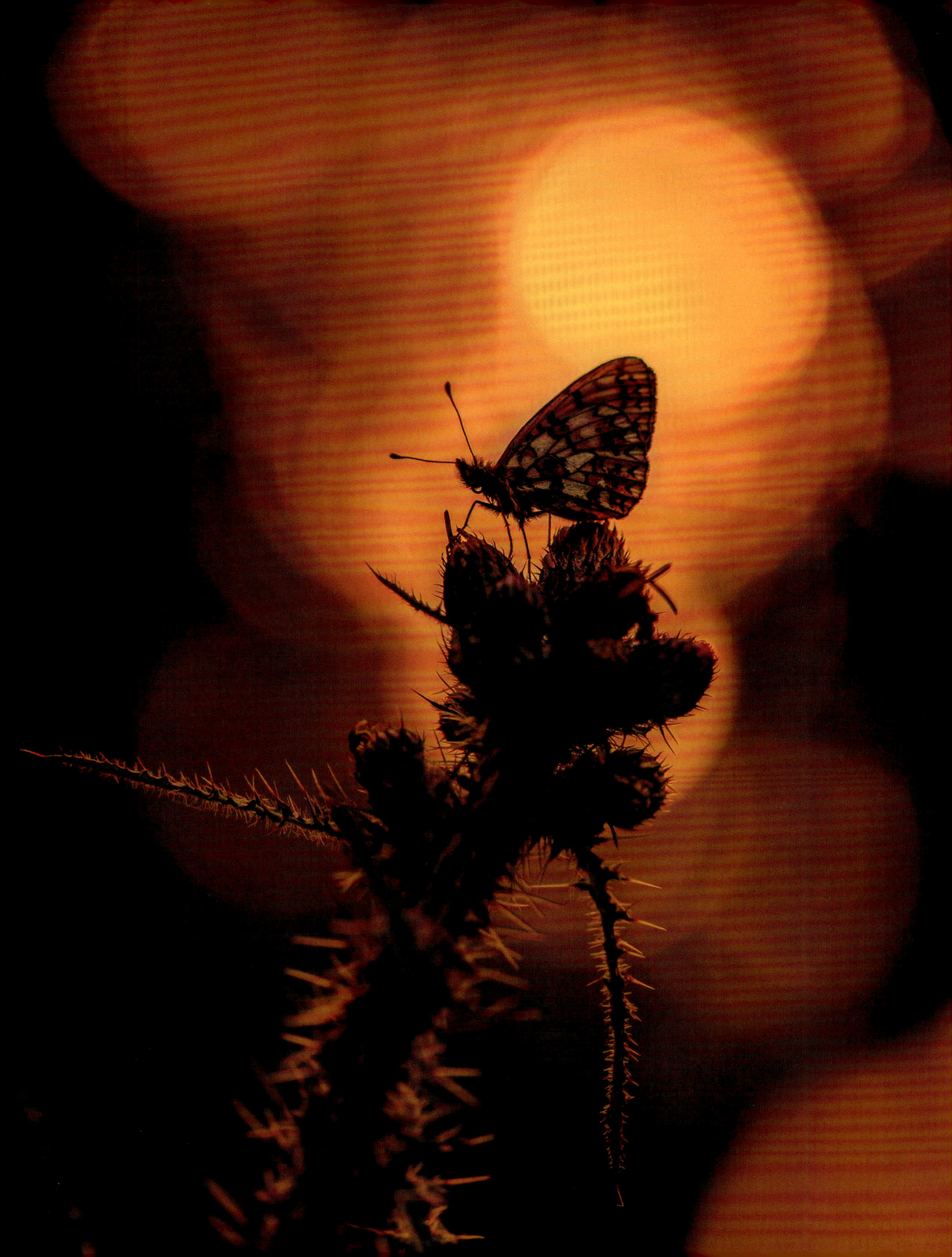

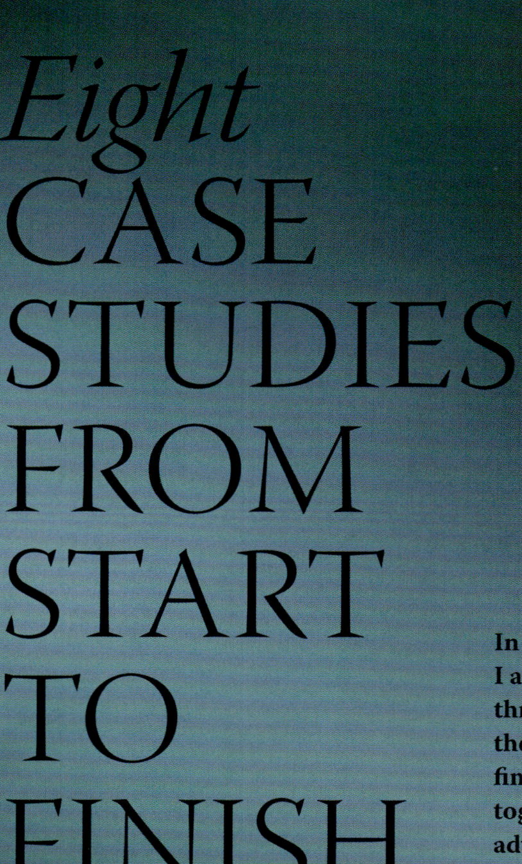

Eight CASE STUDIES: FROM START TO FINISH

In this section of the book I am going to take you through a full shoot from the start all the way to the final photograph, bringing together some of the basic and advanced techniques we have already discussed.

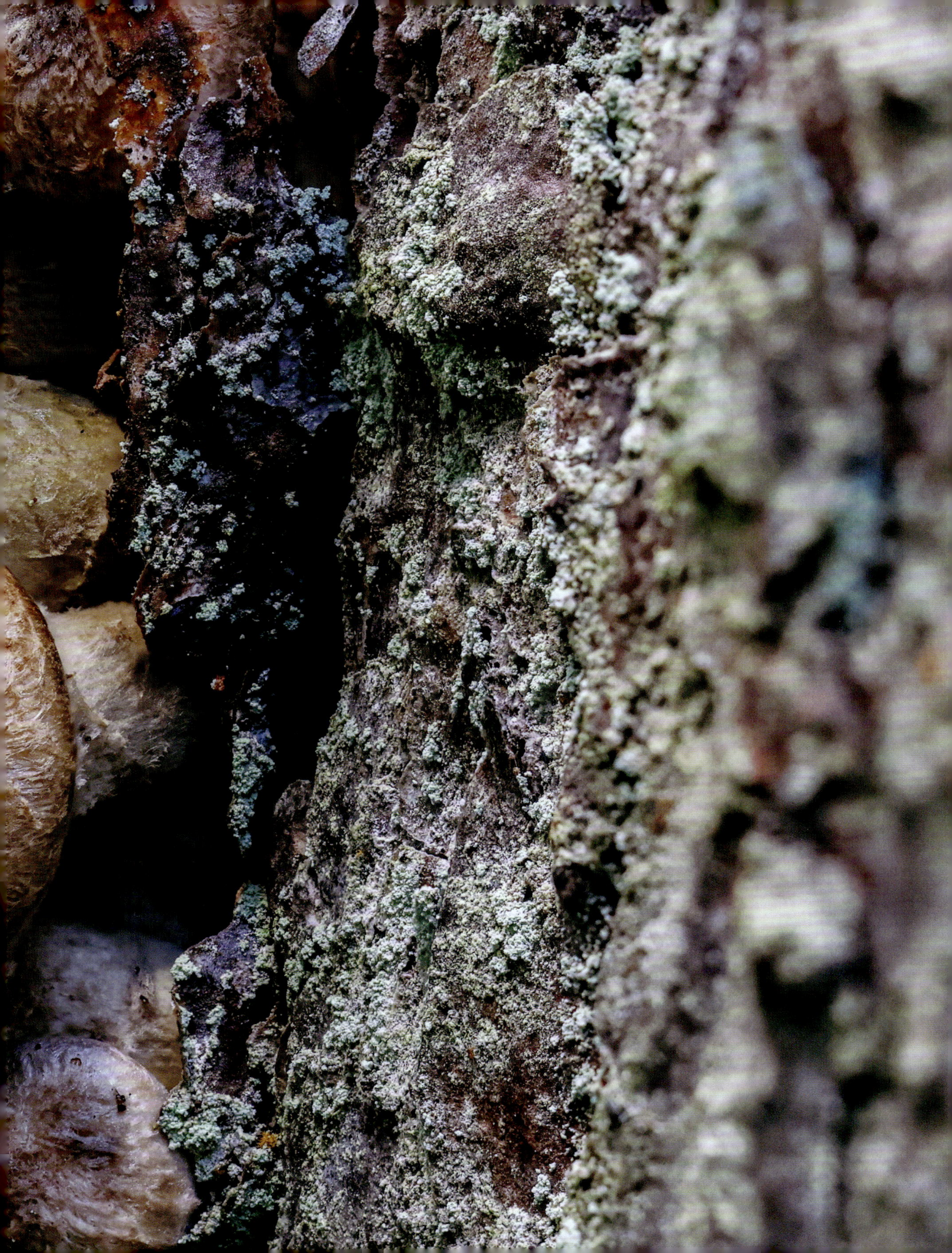

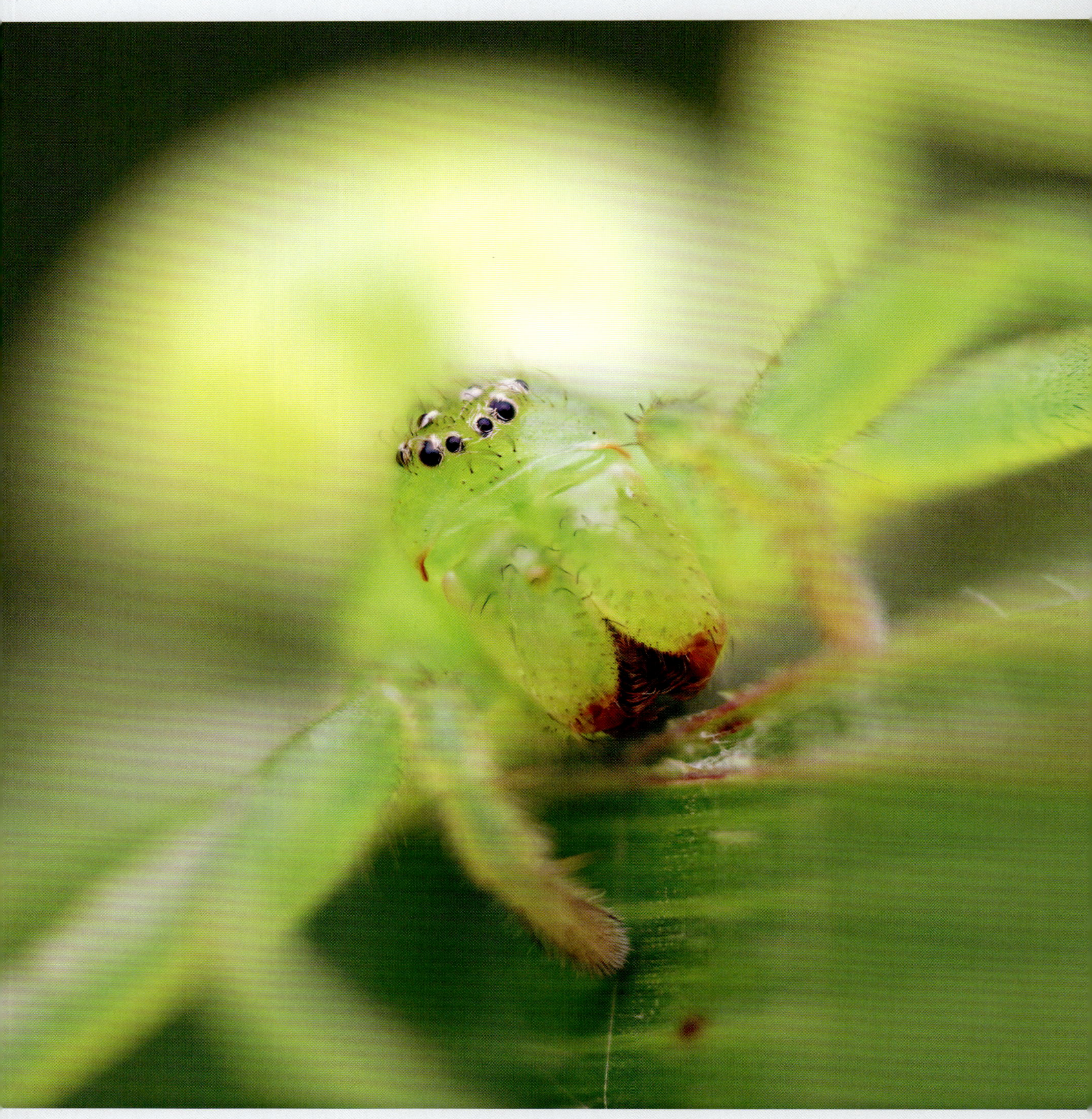

Case study 1

Focus-stacked huntsman spider

Focus stacking can seem like a daunting technique when you're starting out with macro photography. However, at high levels of magnification, our plane of focus is very shallow indeed, so mastering focus stacking will add so much to what you're able to do in this genre. This case study breaks down every part of the process.

Selecting your gear

When I first started with macro photography, I would take all my gear with me on a shooting day. I'd want to photograph dragonflies, as well as tiny jumping spiders, meaning I would always be changing my lens and set-up and this led to lots of missed opportunities. If the subjects you want to photograph live in completely different habitats, lots of time can be wasted venturing from place to place.

I quickly learned that if I concentrated on one species for the day, I could tailor my fieldcraft and equipment, shedding excess gear so my bag was lighter, and not waste time chasing different subjects. This led to my capture rate improving.

It is important that you have all the gear needed to photograph your chosen subjects so packing the night before a shoot, and having all your memory cards cleared and batteries charged is a great habit to get into.

Locating the subject

With subjects like this green huntsman spider I am using as a case study, fieldcraft can be the difference between getting the shot or not. The green huntsman spider is a rarity in the UK, found mainly in the south of England, but is common throughout mainland Europe.

Spiders, like many macro subjects, are cold-blooded, which means they need sunlight to warm their body temperature and become active. So, by venturing out early morning, I'd already increased my chances of finding a specimen. Plus, the spider should be lethargic at that time of day, making it easier to photograph.

Research suggests that this species of spider prefers the edge of woodlands, longer grass and branches of trees. Every huntsman I have ever found has been on low-hanging tree branches or tall reeds at the edge of a lake, proving the research is correct. So, I make this habitat my first choice when hunting for the huntsman. It can be a slow and painstaking task turning over leaf after leaf, and macro photography in general requires a lot of patience. However, once you locate your subject, you will feel a great sense of accomplishment even before you start taking photographs.

PRO TIP Often, the subjects we choose to photograph can be gone in the blink of an eye, so preparation is everything. Always have your camera out and be ready to shoot at a moment's notice.

Right The kit I take out with me these days is relatively simple and tailored to the subjects I am planning to photograph.

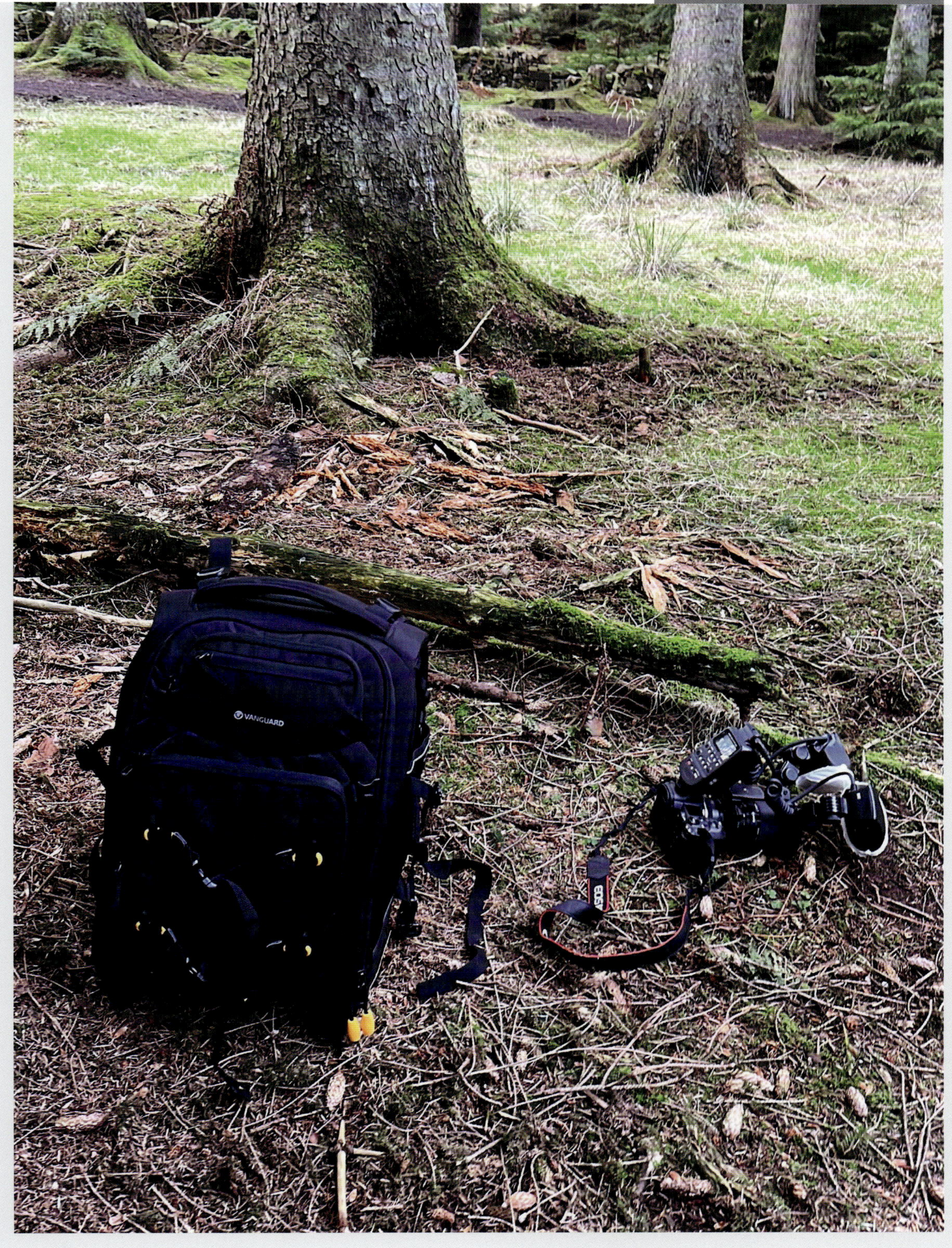

FOCUS-STACKED HUNTSMAN SPIDER 131

Photographing the subject

Once you have located your subject, it's good practice to spend some time assessing the area. First and foremost, make sure you are in a safe spot to take some photographs, then have a look at the environment the subject is in. Can you incorporate this into your shot? Will it add or detract from your image? These are some of the many questions I will ask myself. Sometimes, the subject isn't in an ideal photographic spot and that's fine — not every shot has to be perfect. Sometimes, it's just about capturing a record shot of your subject, especially if you've spent all morning looking for it.

On this occasion I had decided that I would attempt to shoot a small stack of 10–15 frames if possible. The reason I chose to shoot such a small stack is that this species of spider is notoriously skittish, even when warming up. In fact, your breath can provide enough heat to get things going.

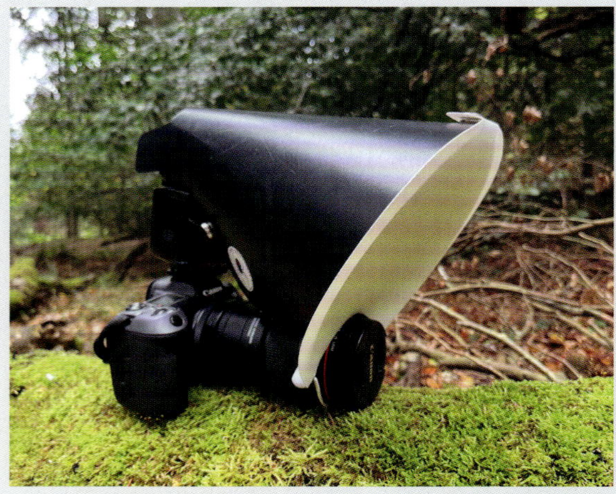

Left The Cygnustech diffuser, mounted to my flash, helps soften and spread the light.

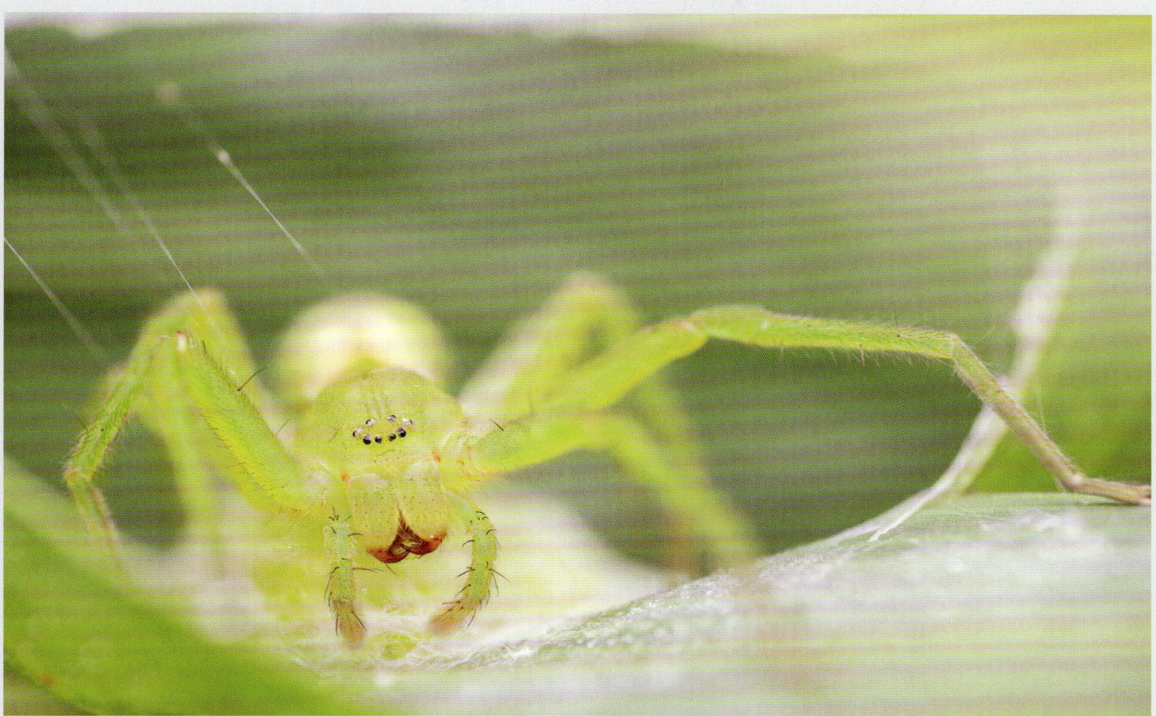

Above A green huntsman spider guards her nest.

As the green huntsman is a larger species of spider, I could be confident that a 100mm macro lens at 1:1 magnification would be enough to capture the portrait I was after, again proving how essential fieldcraft is to your work (see page 110). I opted to use a Cygnustech diffuser to soften and spread the light coming from the camera-mounted flash. This set-up is also lighter than the higher-magnification set-up, which allows me to be more agile. Again, knowing the species and set-up required to perform my stack, I was confident that a handheld manual stack was all I'd need, with no tripod to worry about.

With my camera set up, I approached the spider slowly, making sure not make any sudden movements that would cause the vegetation to move too much. I started by locating the spider in my viewfinder and then began to perform my handheld manual stack (see page 114). I continued to take photos until I was happy I had enough.

Once I'd finished, I took a quick look at the images on my rear LCD. It is important to note that some camera's LCD screens will enhance brightness, saturation and even sharpness, and if you are shooting Raw files this will not be how they appear when viewed initially on a computer.

Processing the stack with Photoshop

The first thing I do when I get home from a shoot is backup my files, transferring them from my memory card onto two external hard drives. This isn't a must, but I find it's a good idea to always backup your photographs – I once lost 1TB of images so I learned the hard way.

So, how do we combine and edit our sequence of stacked images? There are several software options: Adobe Photoshop, Zerene Stacker and Helicon Focus. For this case study I will be using Adobe Photoshop. It's vitally important that your individual frames are edited in the same way: the easiest way to do this is to use Adobe Camera Raw, so this is where we will start.

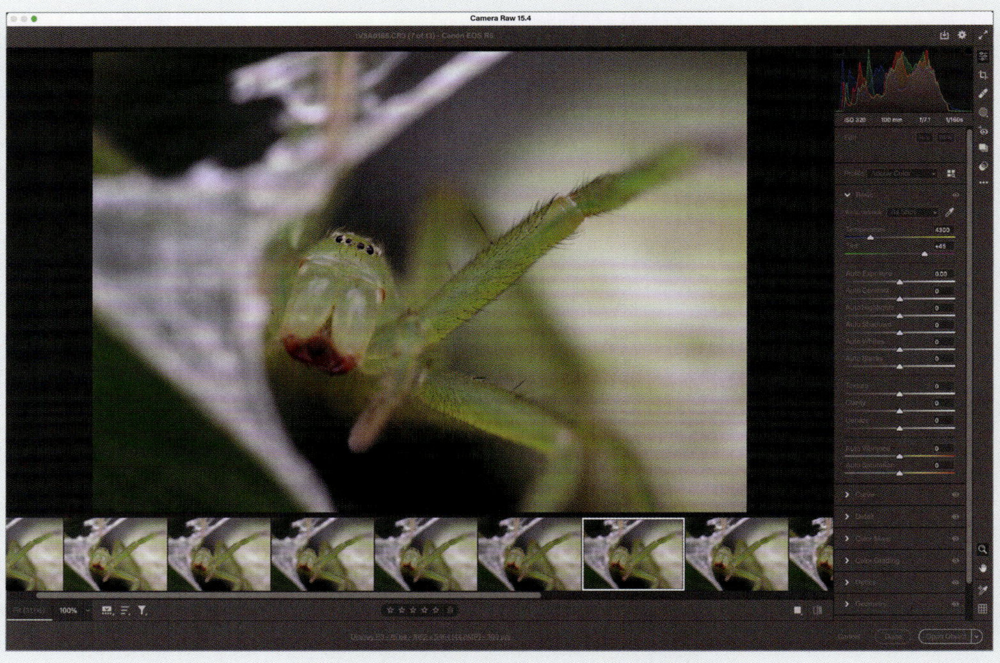

Step 1 Open Photoshop and load your stack sequence into Camera Raw.
It will look something like this.

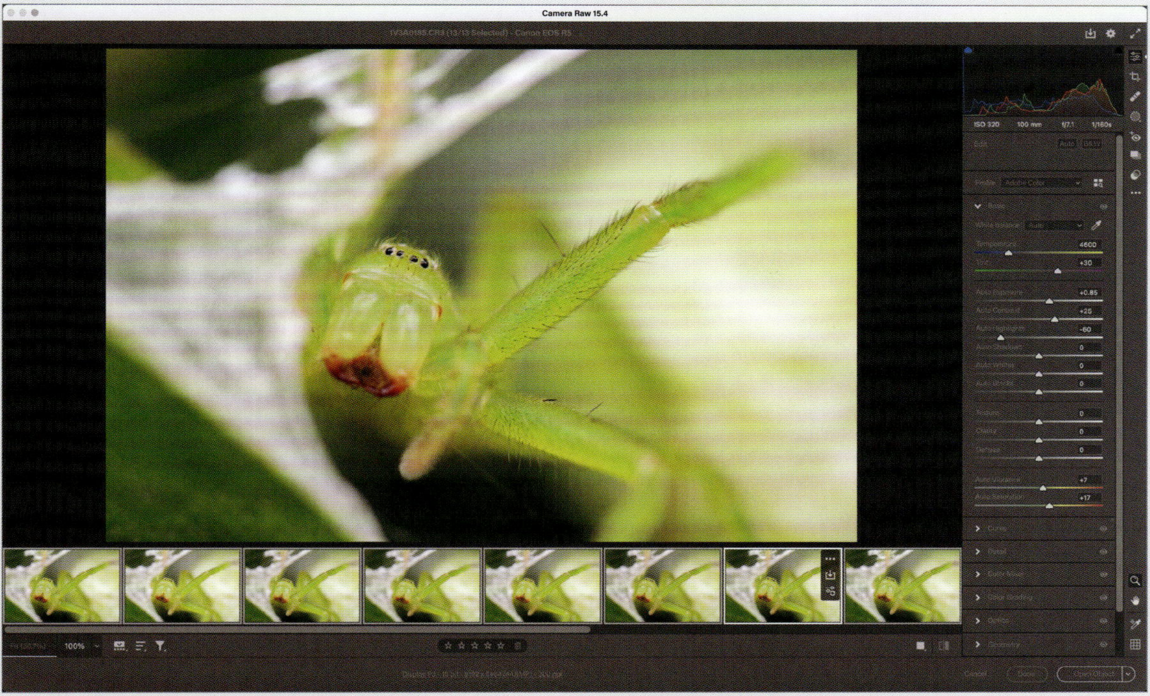

Step 2 You can now make your adjustments. Remember that Raw files will lack contrast, saturation, white balance profiles or any real sharpness, so enhance these using the sliders and panel you see on the right. JPEGs will already have these adjustments made, but feel free to tweak them to your style. How much you edit is a question of personal preference, but I'd recommend you don't add too much sharpening or saturation; too much sharpening will add noise, while too much saturation will make colours look unnatural.

Once you have edited the first image in the sequence, you can use it to sync the adjustments for the rest of the sequence.

To do this, select all of your images (Ctrl + A for PC, Command + A for Mac). Once the images are selected, hover your mouse over the edited image, which should be highlighted by a white box. A small menu will appear – click the Synchronize button.

Step 3 The Synchronize menu
will now open. Check the boxes
for the adjustments you would
like to apply across all of your
images and press OK. Allow a few
minutes for the adjustments to be
made to all your images.

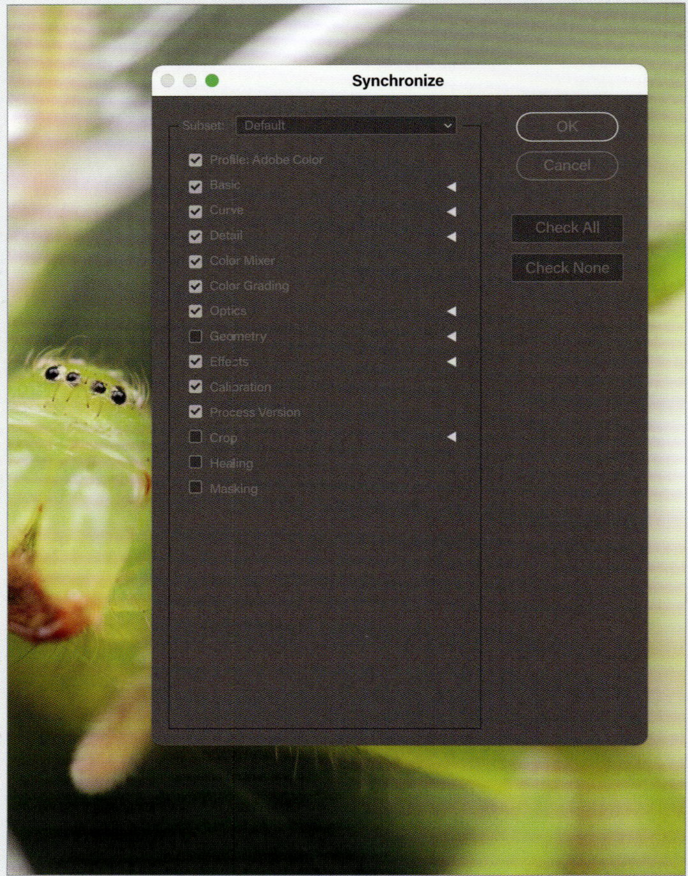

Step 4 Once all your images are synced, double-
check that the edits are consistent across the
sequence. If you are happy, select all of the images
again (Ctrl + A for PC, Command + A for Mac) and
hover your mouse over one of the images to bring
up the same menu you used to sync the image edits.
However, instead of selecting the Synchronize button,
click the Save button.

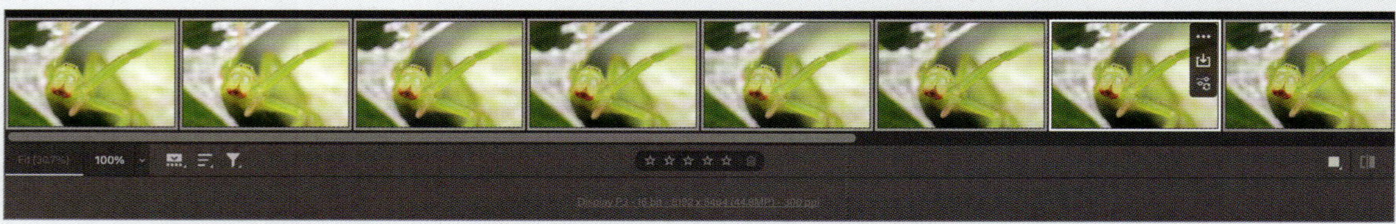

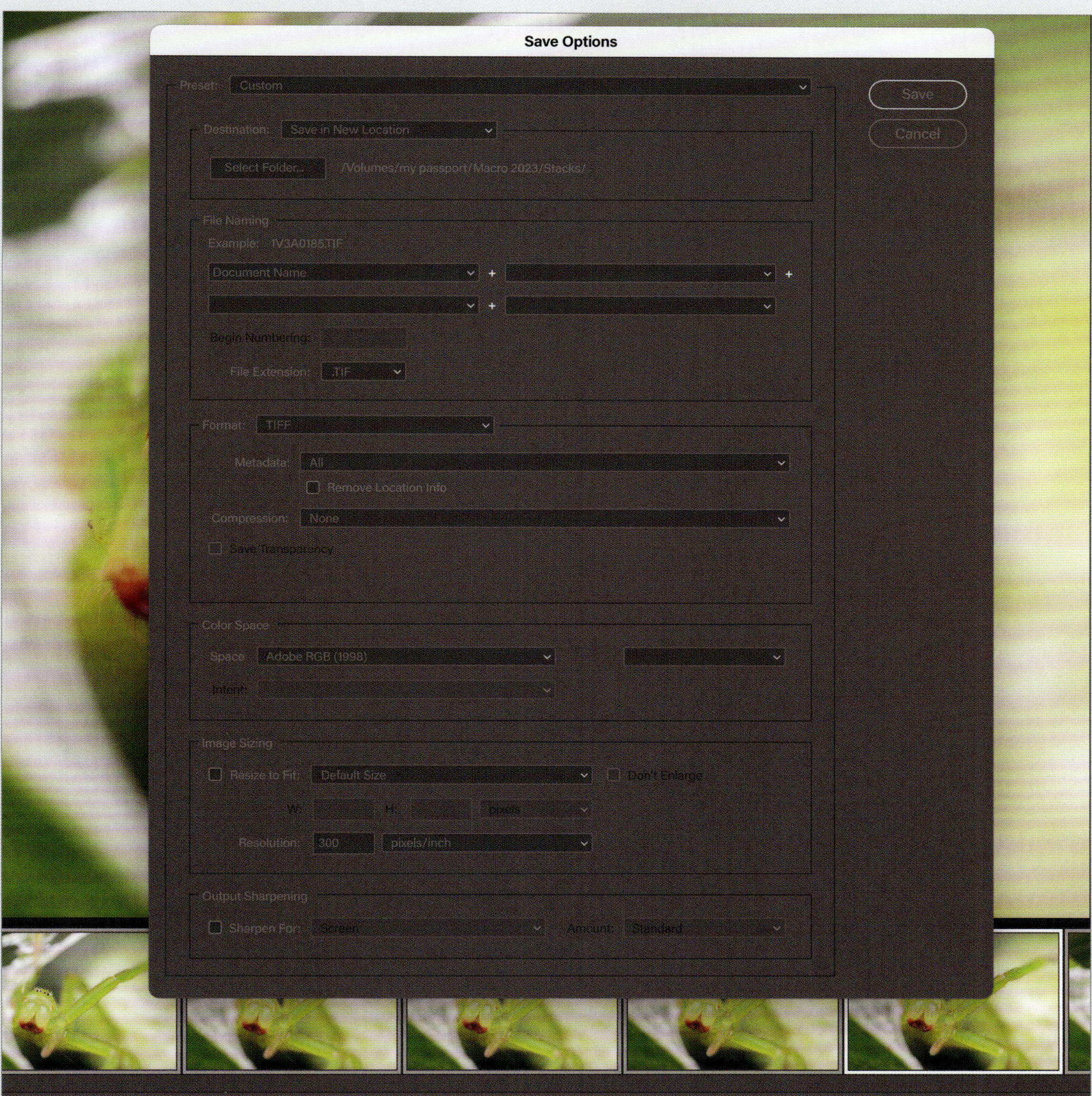

Step 5 The Save menu will now open. Here, you can set certain conditions, such as the file destination, name and file type for your saved images. I tend to keep my stacks in a separate folder and leave the file names unchanged for transparency. I always save Raw files as TIFFs or JPEGs and add no resizing conditions. Again, this is your choice.

Step 6 Once you have saved your images, you can move onto the alignment and stacking part of the process. Open Photoshop and go to File > Scripts > Load Files into Stack.

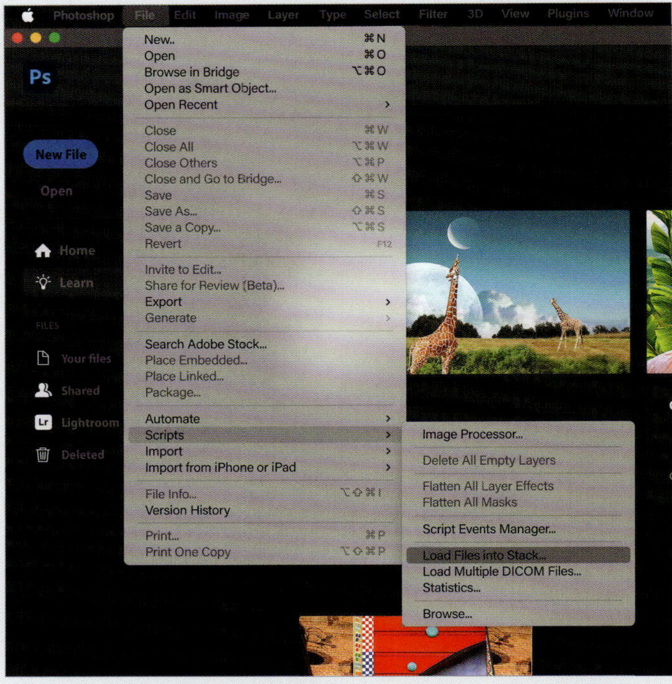

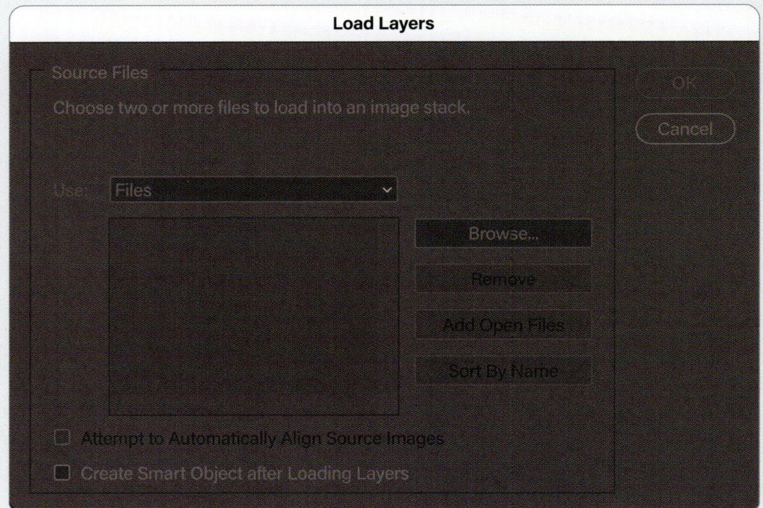

Step 7 A Load Layers menu will open. Click Browse and locate and select the images you want to be included in the stack.

Step 8 Once the images are listed, check the Attempt to Automatically Align Source Images box and press OK.

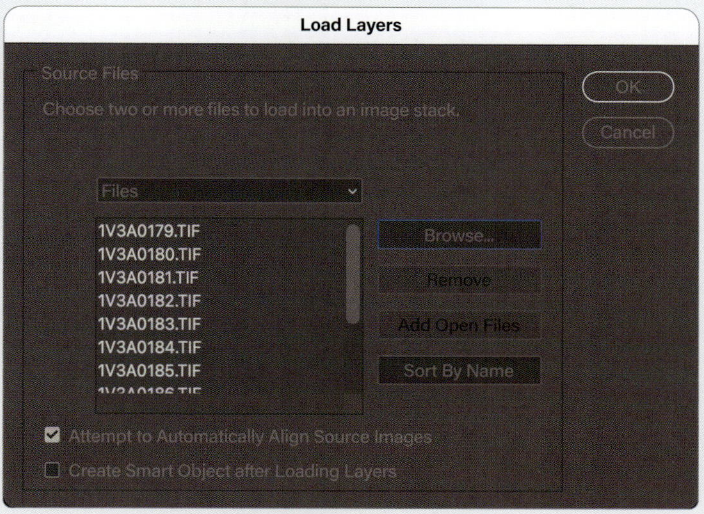

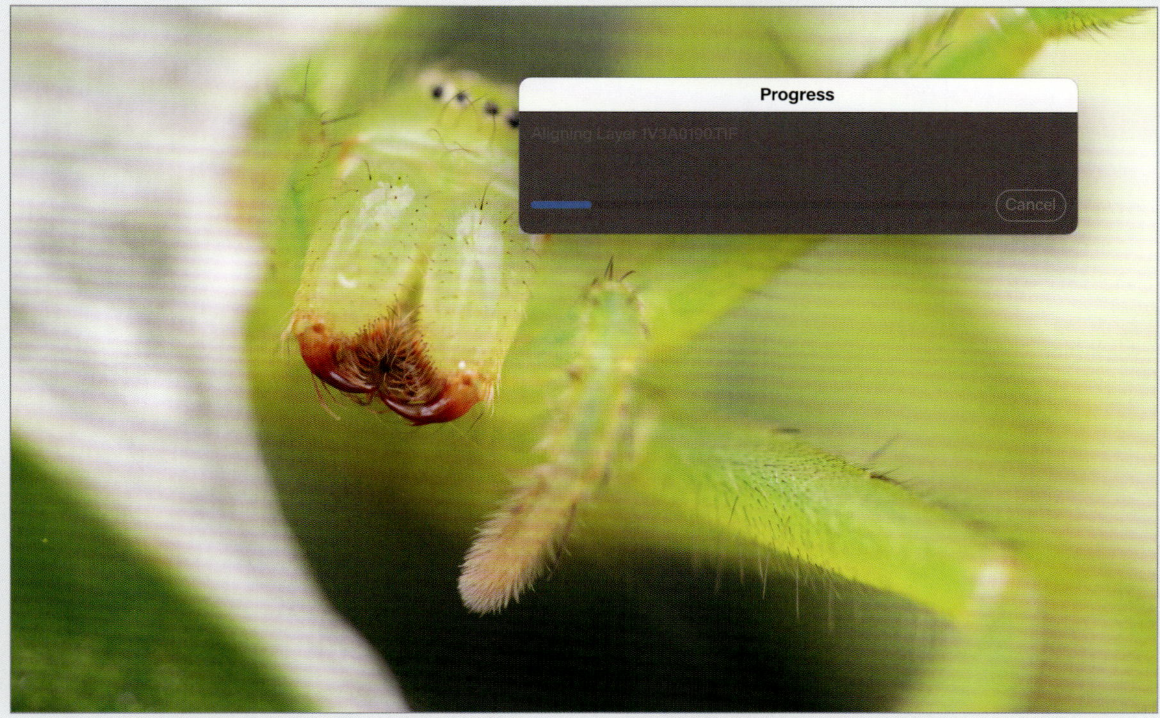

Step 9 Photoshop will start to load and align your images.

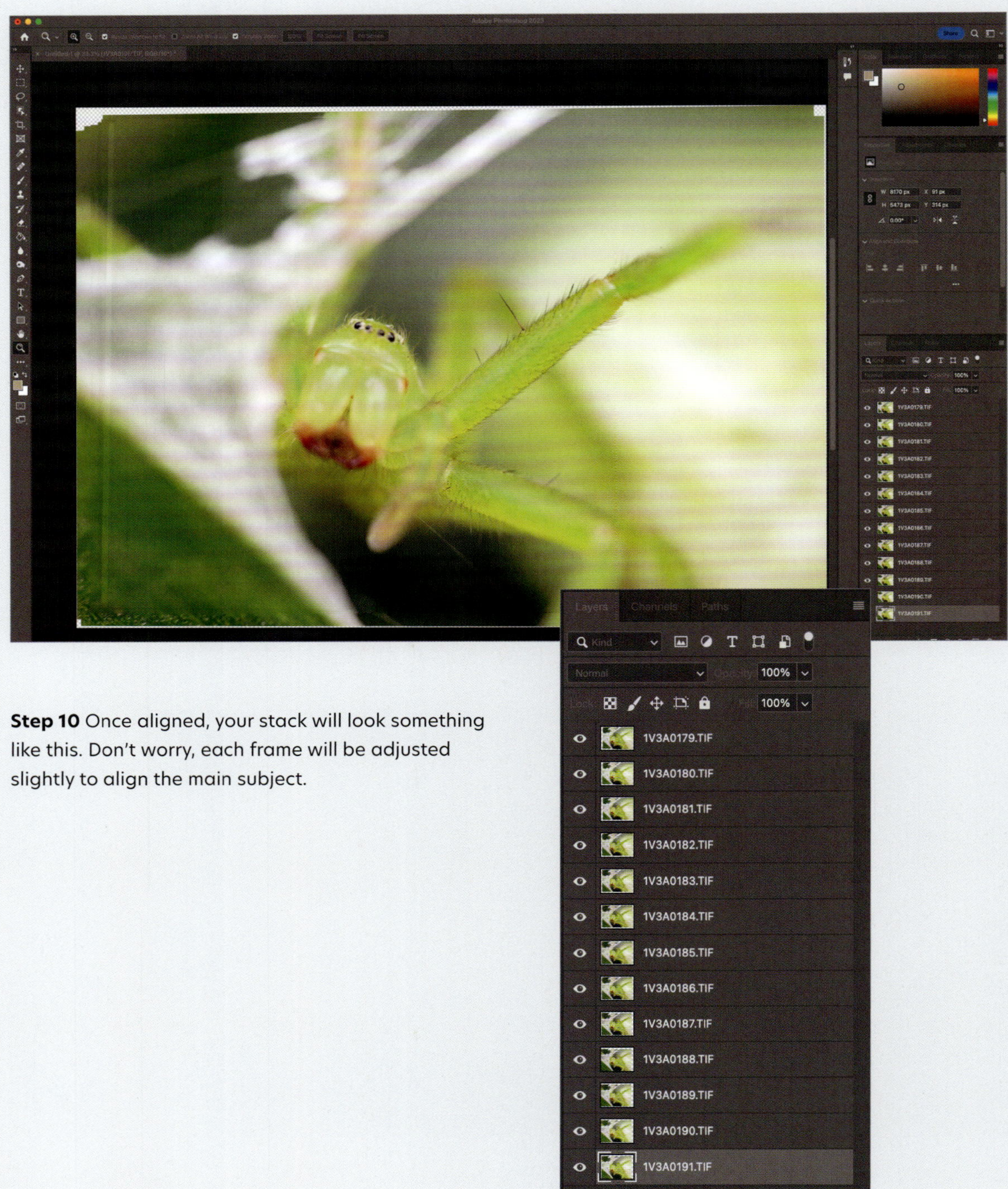

Step 10 Once aligned, your stack will look something like this. Don't worry, each frame will be adjusted slightly to align the main subject.

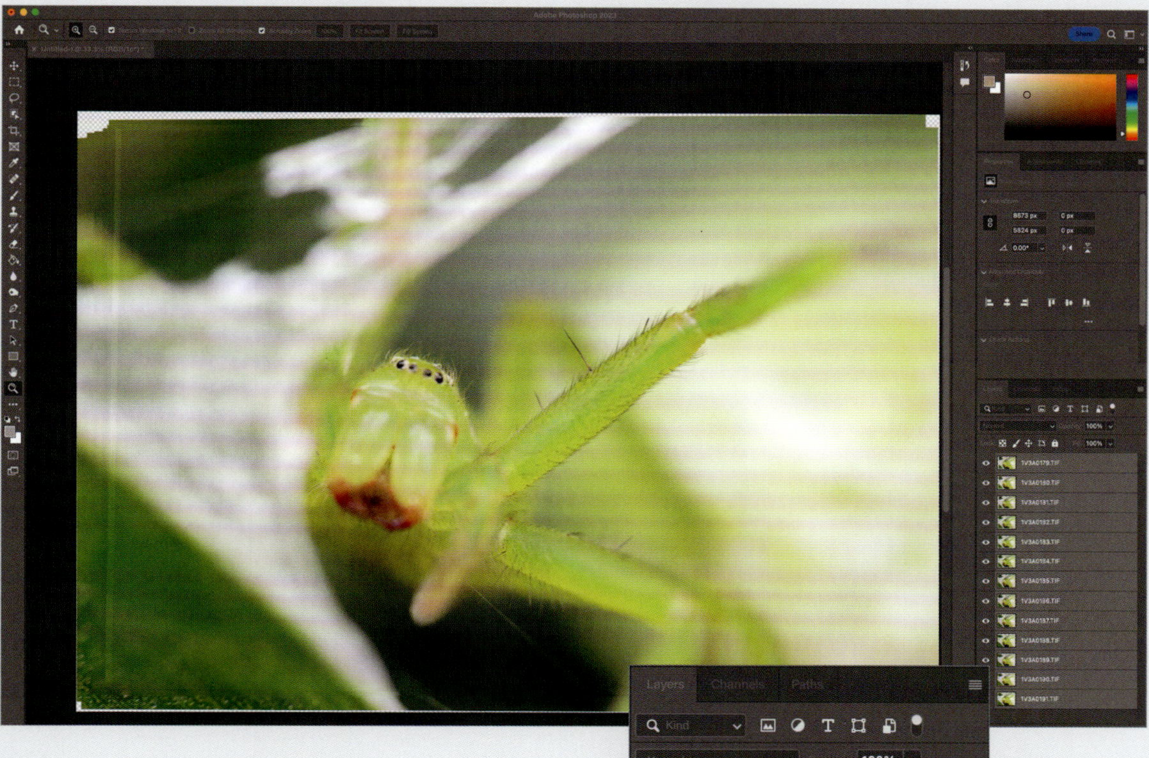

Step 11 All the images should now be aligned and listed as layers in the same editing window. Select all of the image layers by clicking on the top one in the list, holding down the Shift key and selecting the bottom image layer. This should highlight all of the image layers in the list, turning them grey.

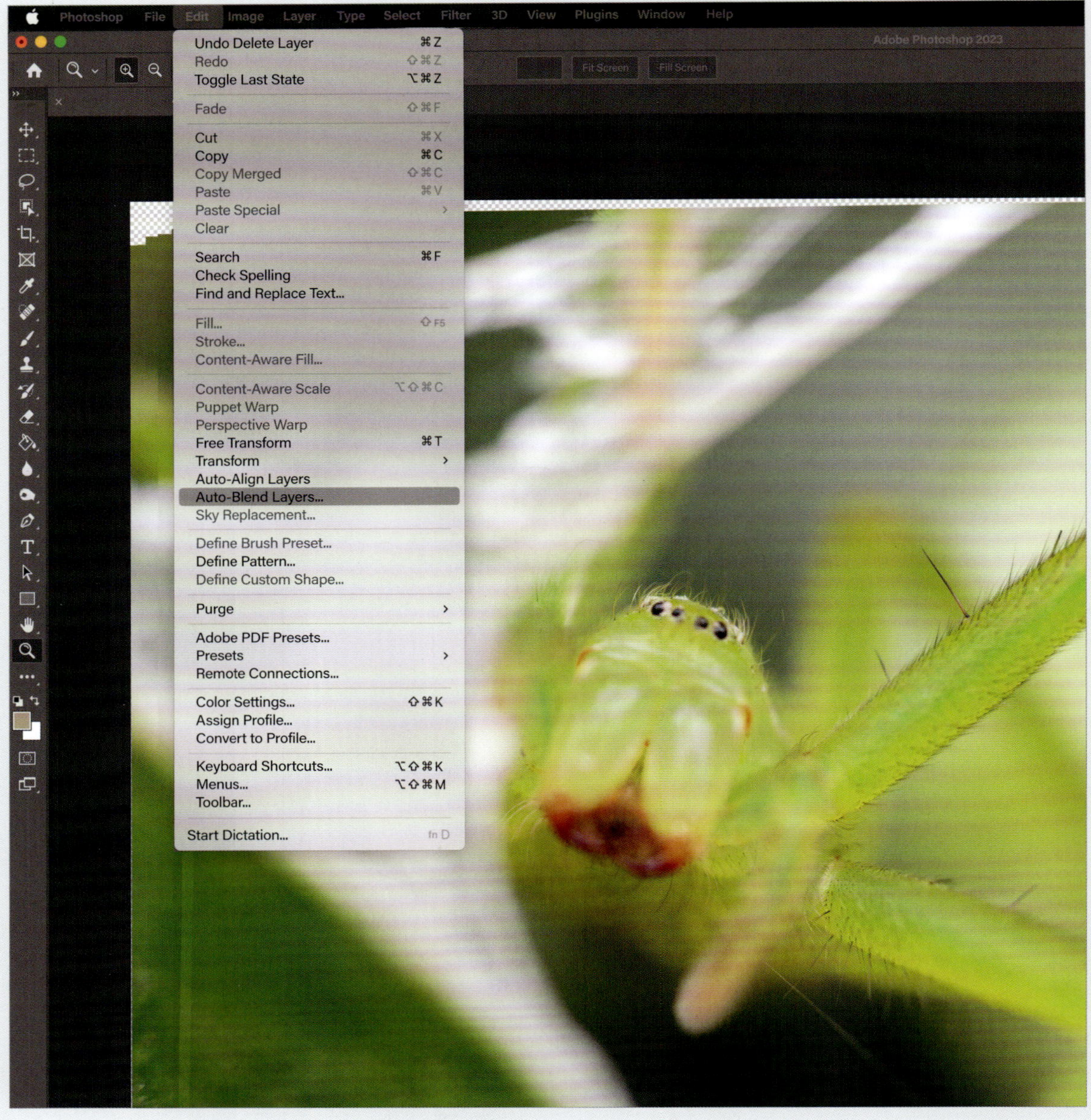

Step 12 Once all the image layers are selected, you can begin the stacking process. Go to Edit > Auto-Blend Layers.

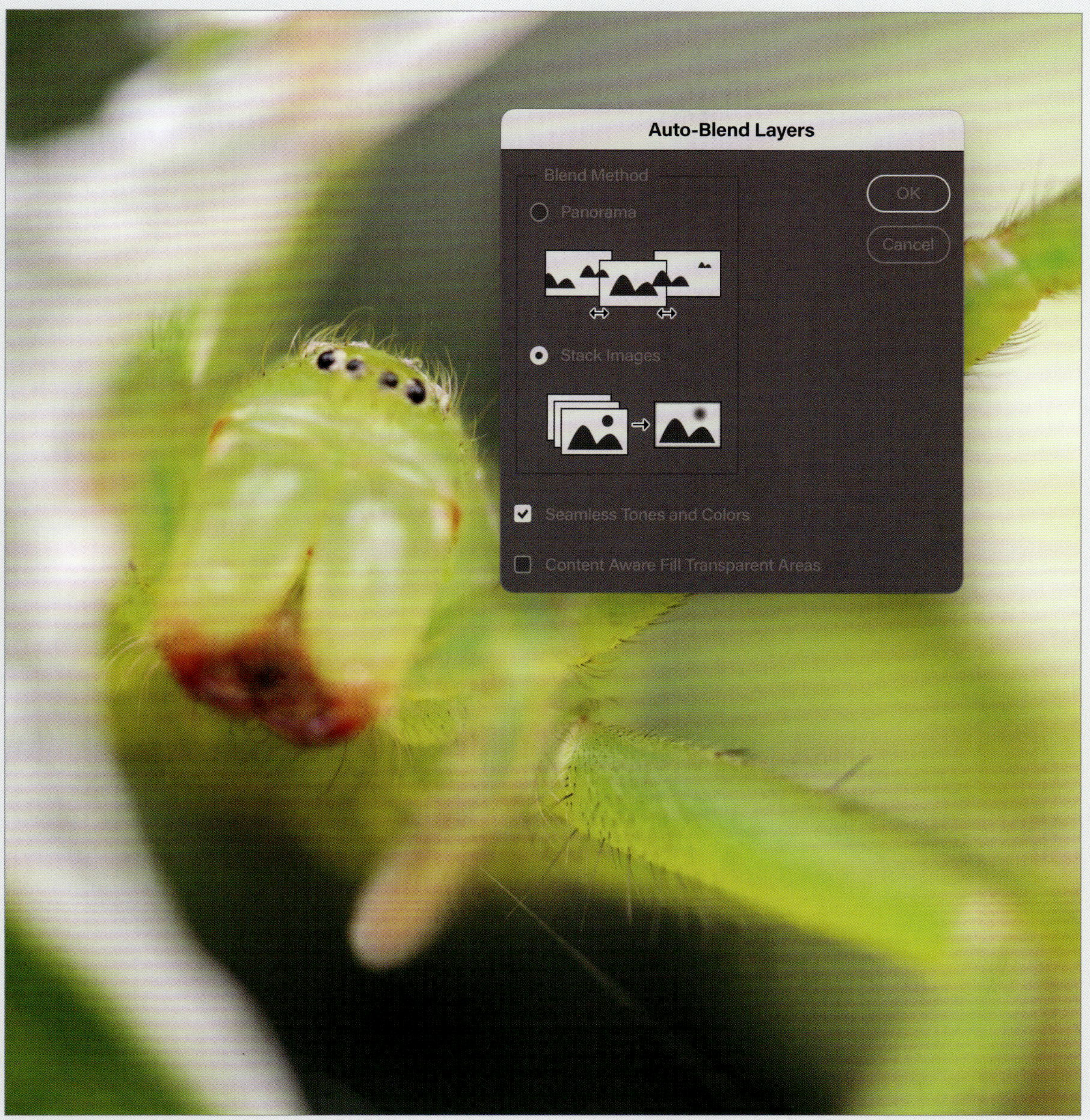

Step 13 In the Auto-Blend Layers dialogue, select Stack Images and check the Seamless Tones and Colors box.

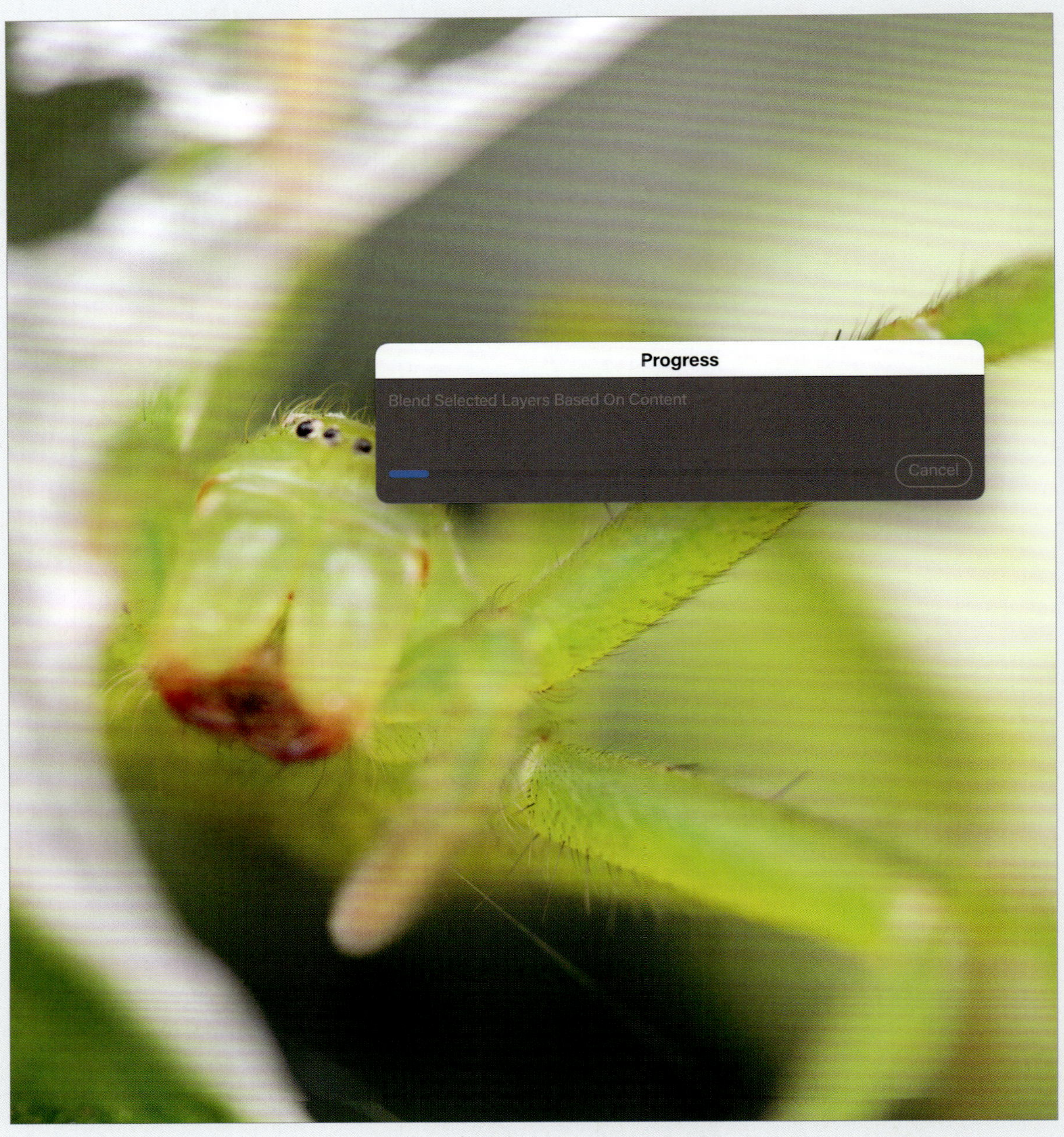

Step 14 Photoshop will now begin to stack your images.

Step 15 Stacking the images may take some time, depending on how complex the image is, how many image layers it contains, file type and size, and how powerful your computer is. If you find it takes too long, or scratch disks become full, try and complete the stack in smaller batches. For example, rather than trying to stack 30 images at once, try three smaller batches of ten, resulting in three composite images. You can then stack those three together to get your result.

Your final stack will look something like the image below. If there's any misalignment of the subject, this could be because the subject moved too much during the picture-taking process, or you adjusted your position. Handheld stacking is considered to be one of the most advanced and difficult techniques, but stick with it. Try smaller stacks to begin with and work your way up to larger ones.

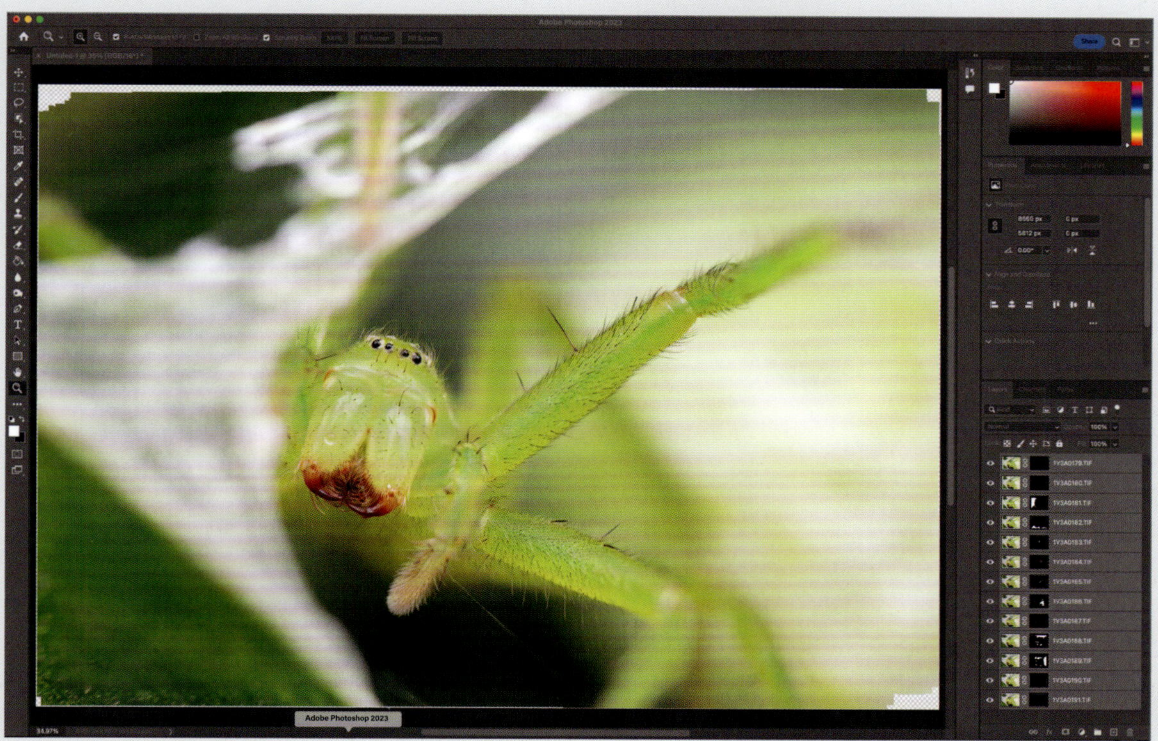

If you are happy with the result, it's time to flatten the layers into one image. Simply select all the image layers, right-click and select Merge Layers.

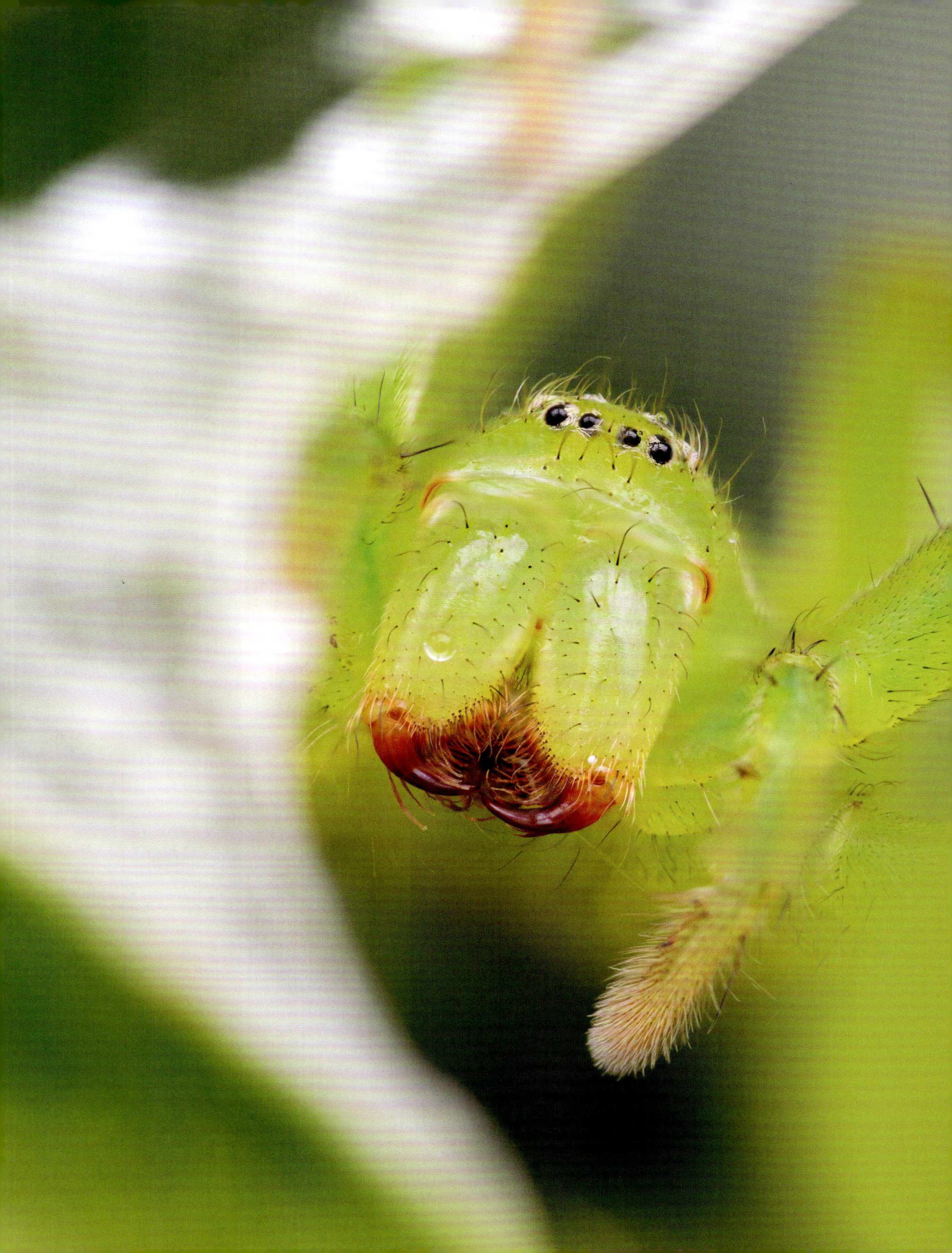

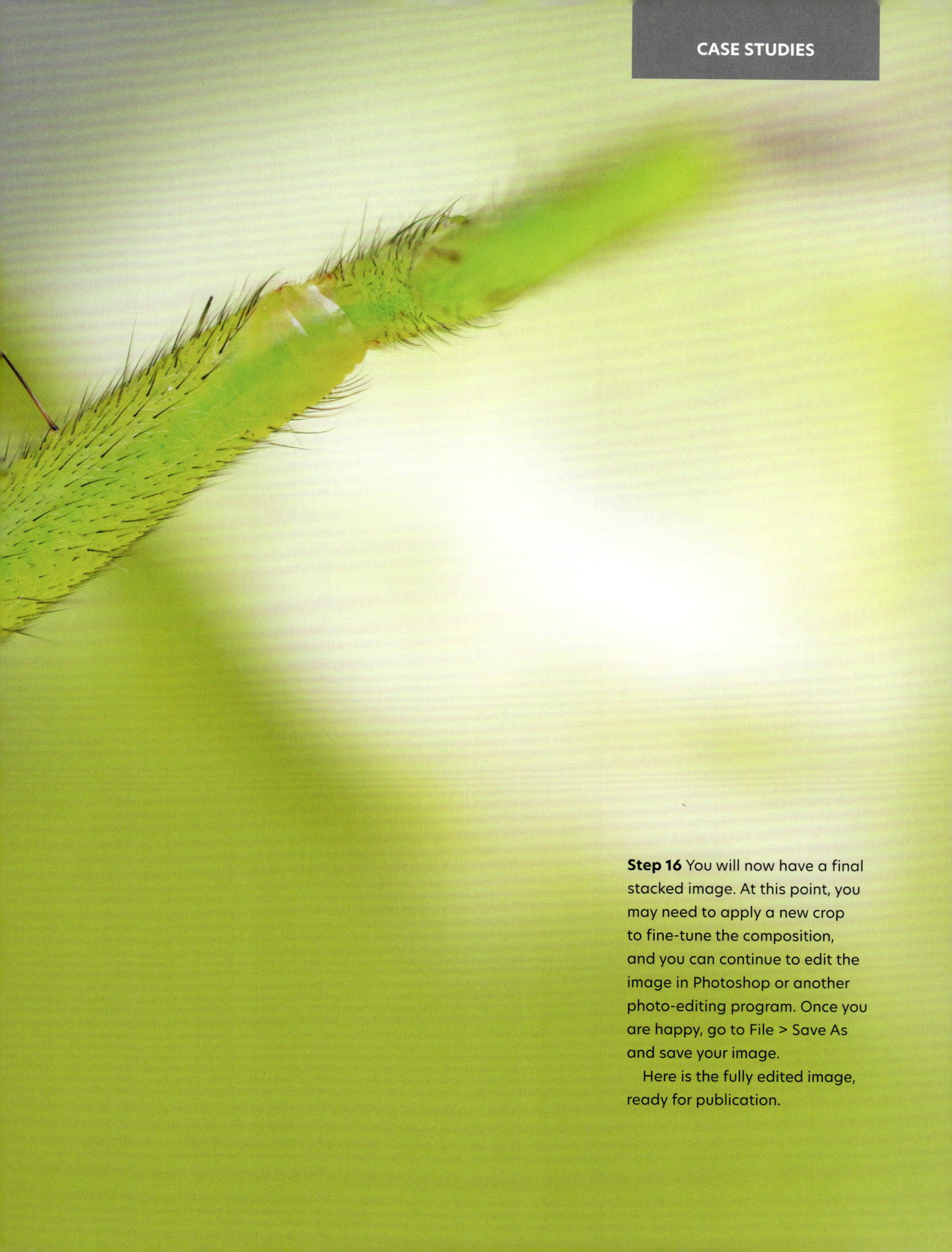

Step 16 You will now have a final stacked image. At this point, you may need to apply a new crop to fine-tune the composition, and you can continue to edit the image in Photoshop or another photo-editing program. Once you are happy, go to File > Save As and save your image.

Here is the fully edited image, ready for publication.

Processing a stack with Zerene Stacker

Photoshop isn't the only stacking software available, and some programs stack images better than others. For subjects that are very still or dead (for instance, entomology collections), I find Zerene Stacker is more efficient. It also works well with larger stack sequences, which Photoshop can sometimes struggle with.

Here, I will show you how to stack with Zerene Stacker using a specimen of a Menelaus blue morpho (*Morpho menelaus*) butterfly from the National Museum of Scotland's incredible Entomology collection.

Step 1 Start by opening Zerene Stacker on your computer – it should look something like this.

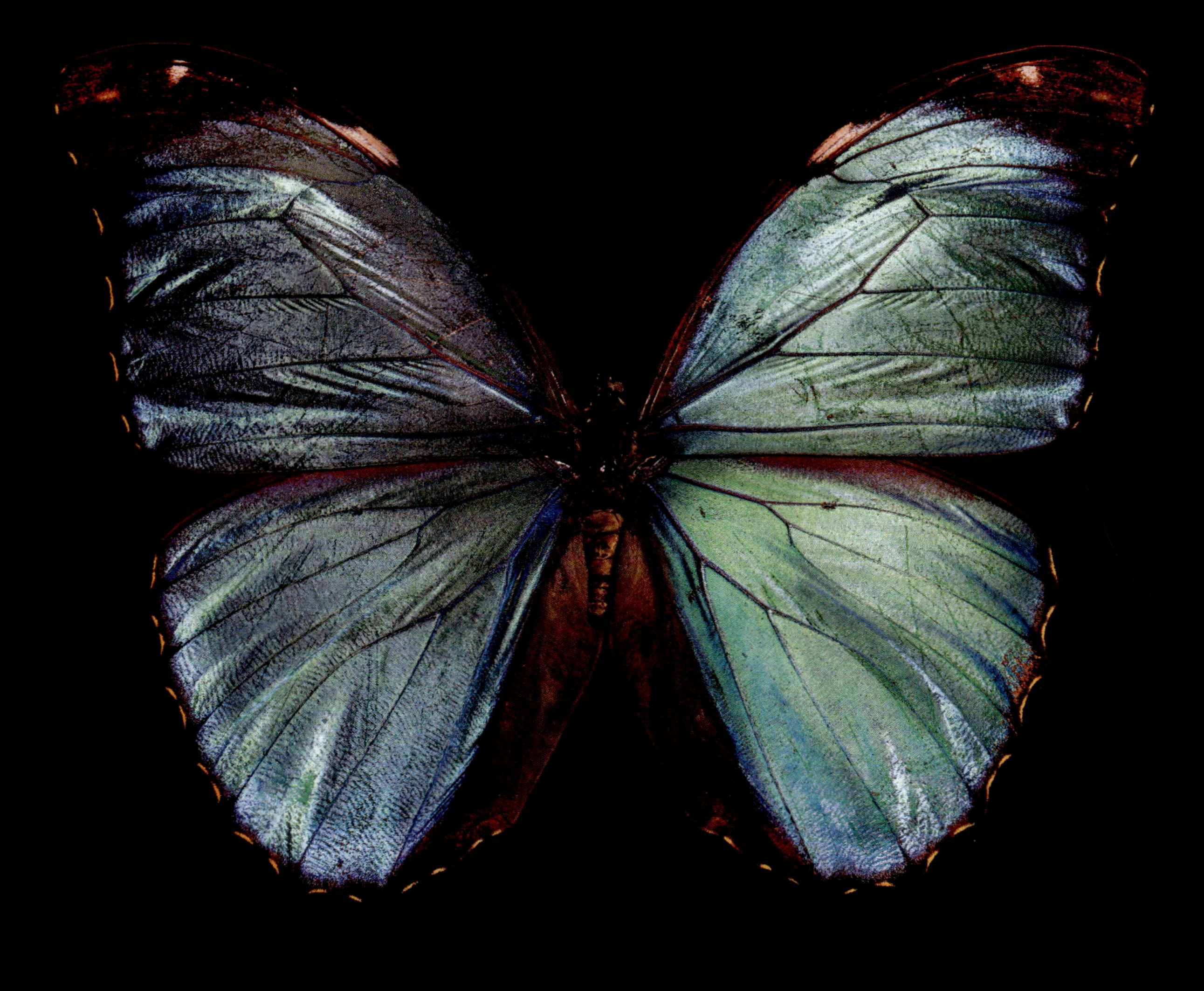

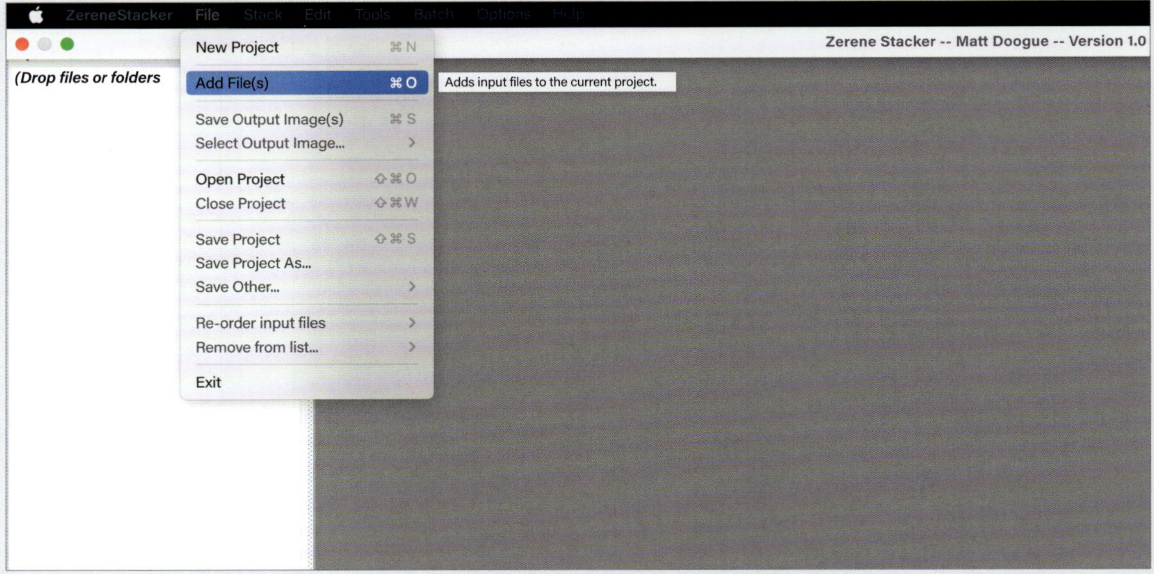

Step 2 Go to File > Add File(s).

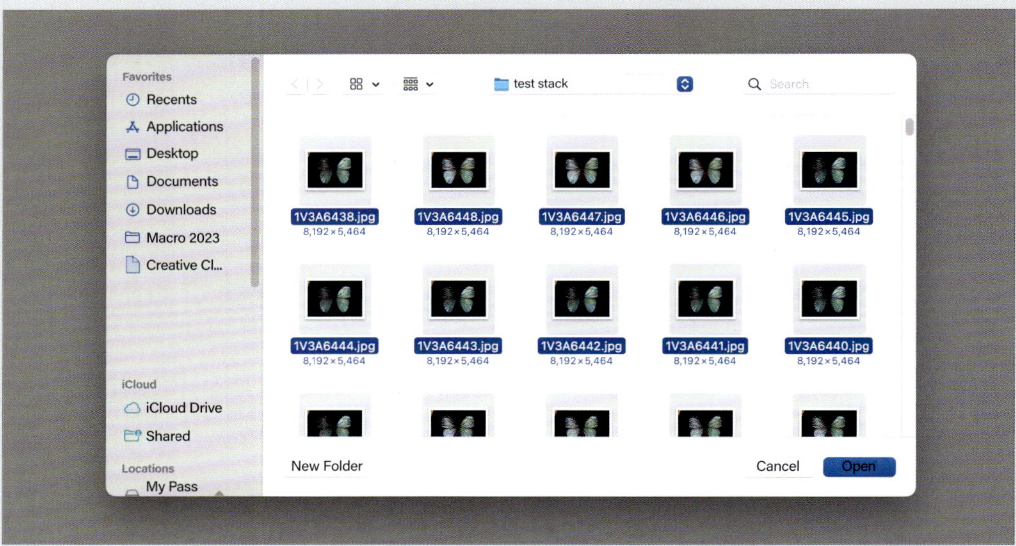

Step 3 Locate the image files for your stack sequence, select them all and click Open.

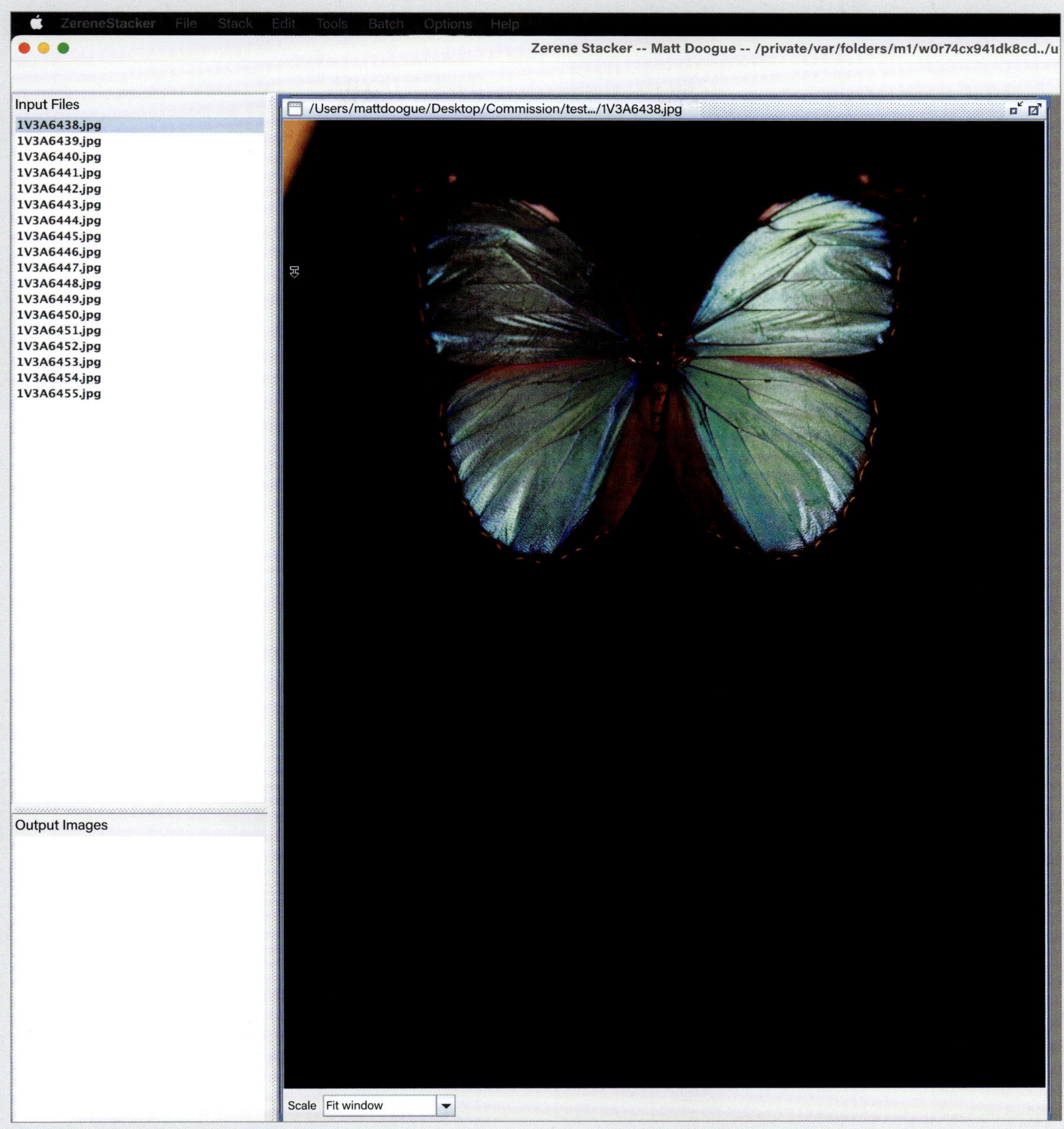

Step 4 With your images loaded, it should look like this.

Step 5 Select all the files listed in the left-hand column –they should all be highlighted with a blue box.

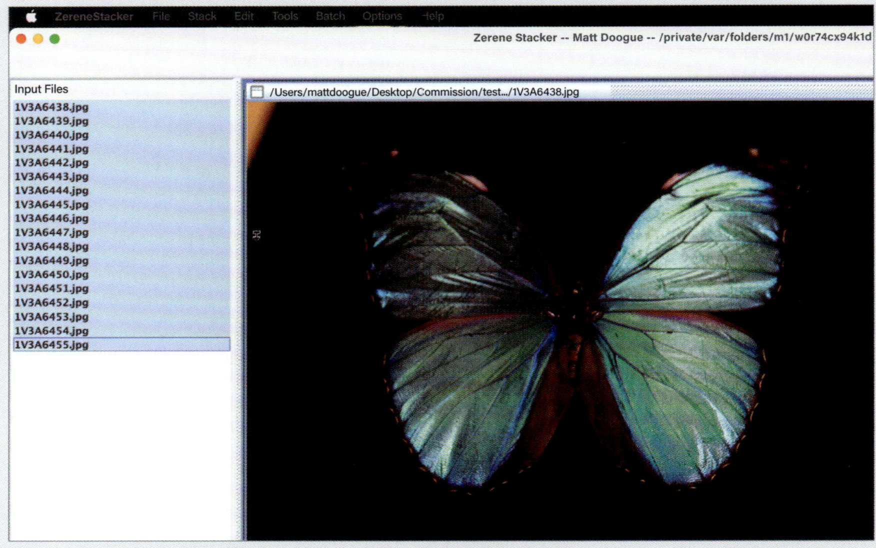

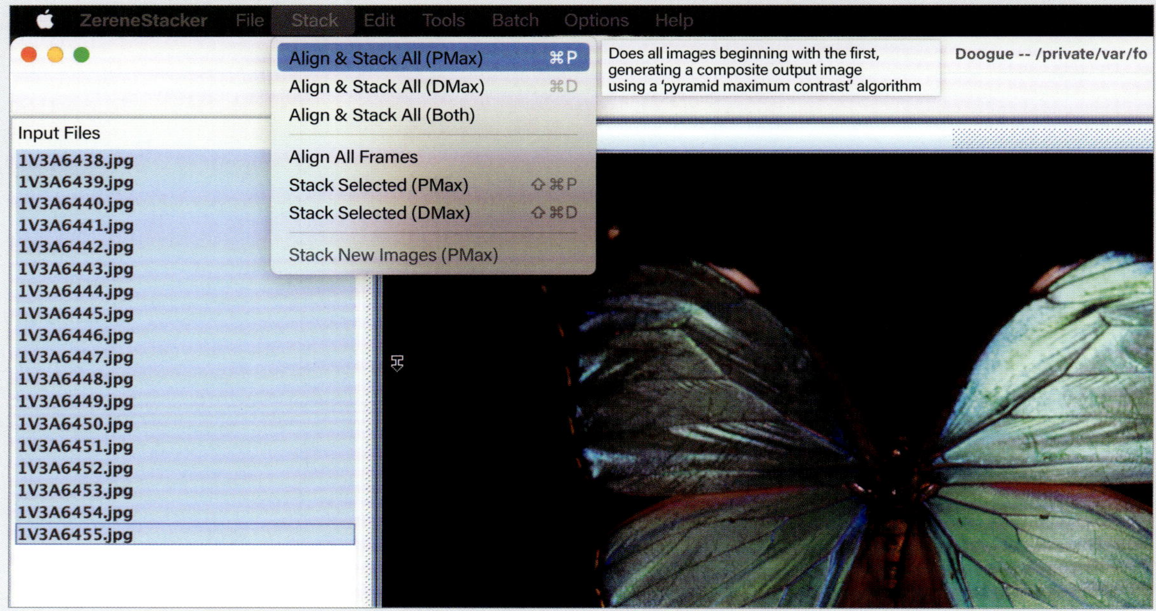

Step 6 You have various stacking options to choose from – I prefer Stack > Align & Stack All (PMax).

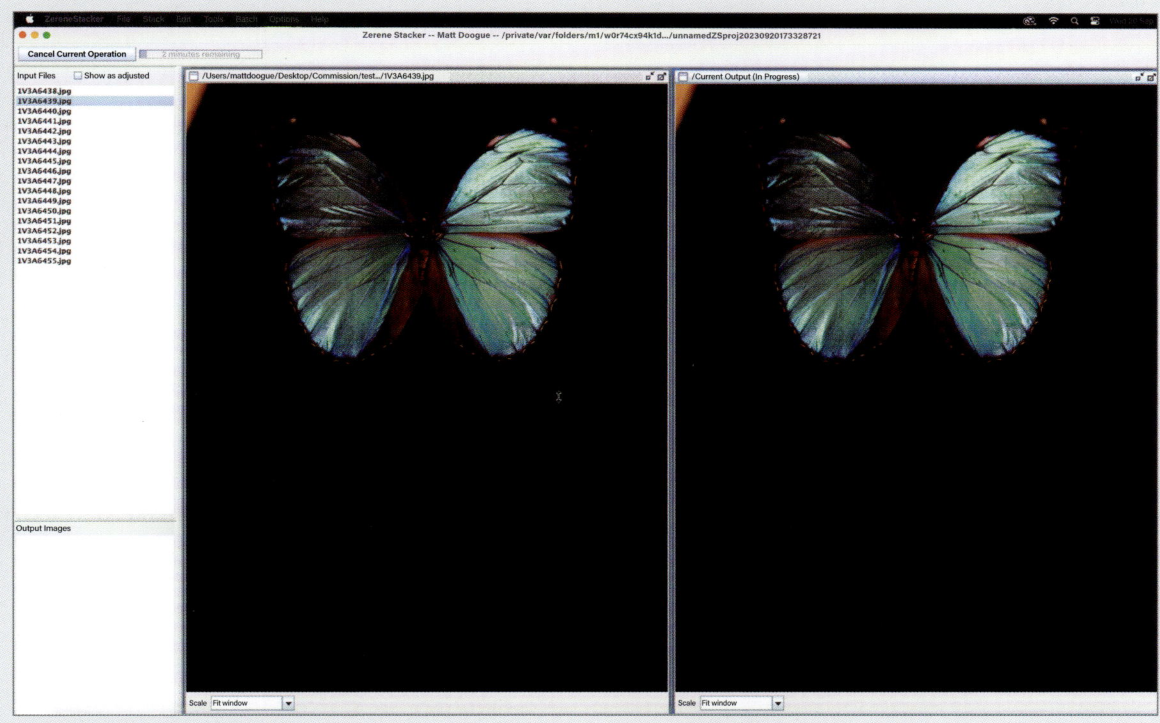

Step 7 The software will now begin to align and stack your images. The stacked image being generated is shown to the right of your original image on the screen.

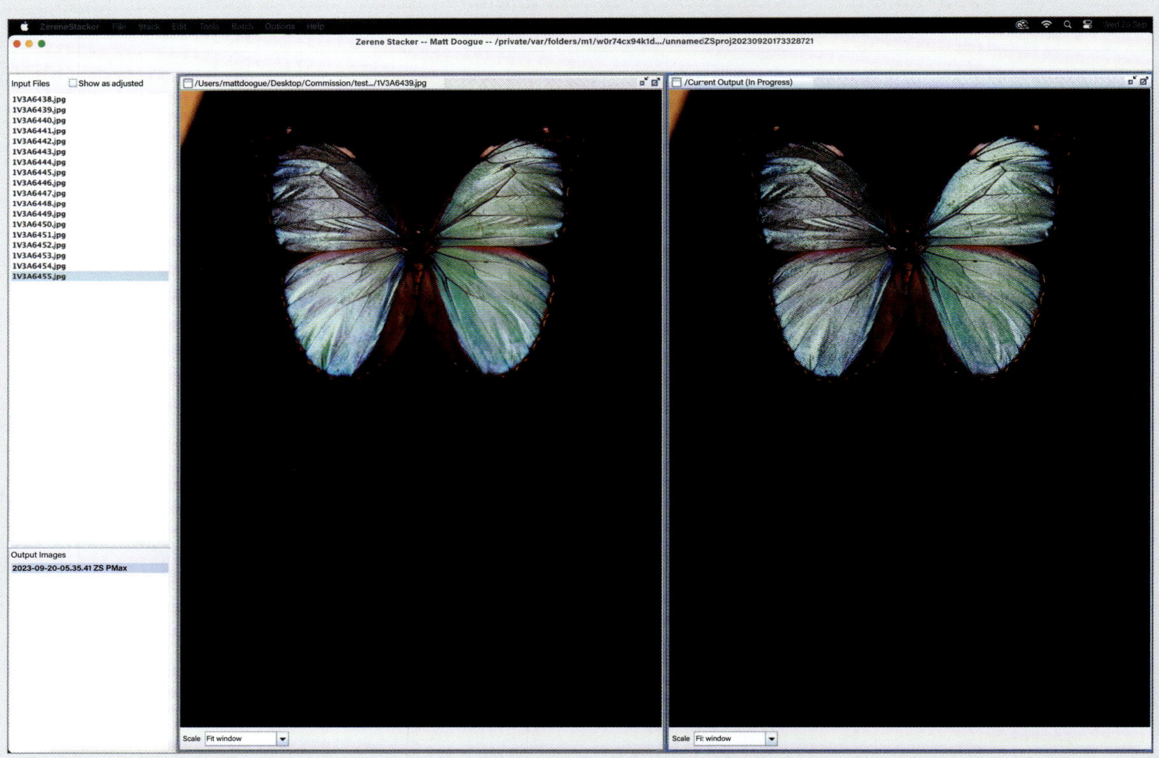

Step 8 Once completed, you will see the fully stocked image on the right. An output image has been generated beneath the Output Images window, at the bottom left of the screen.

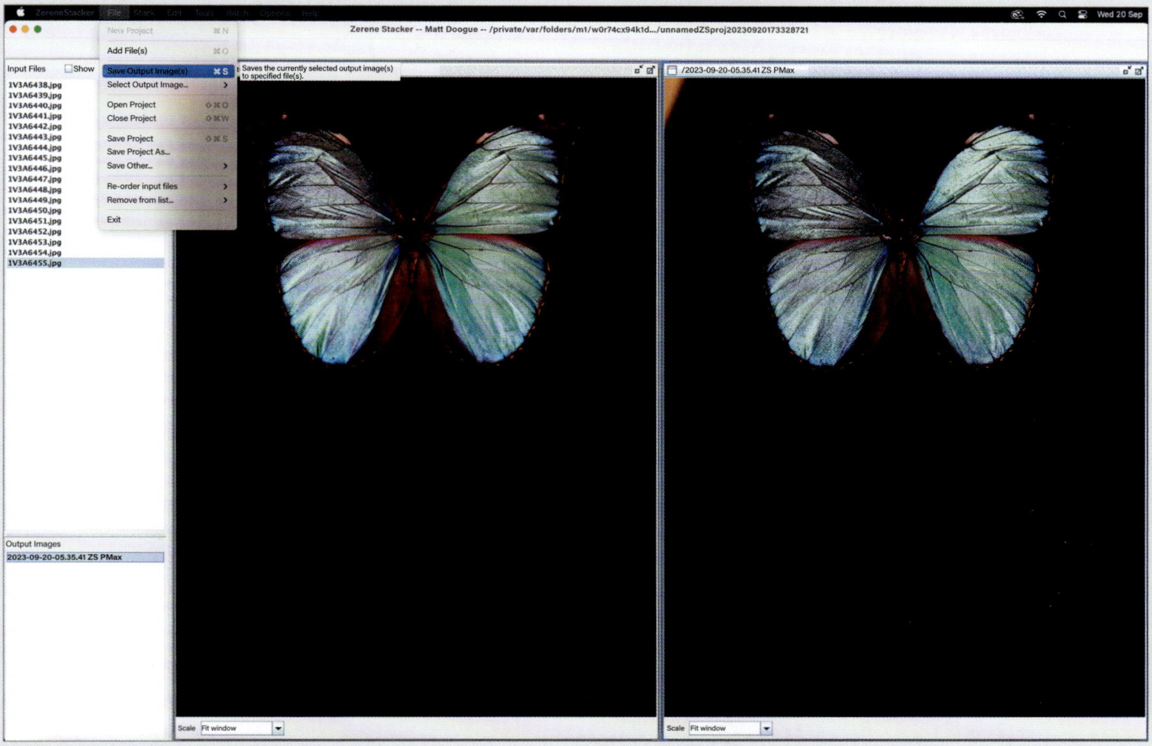

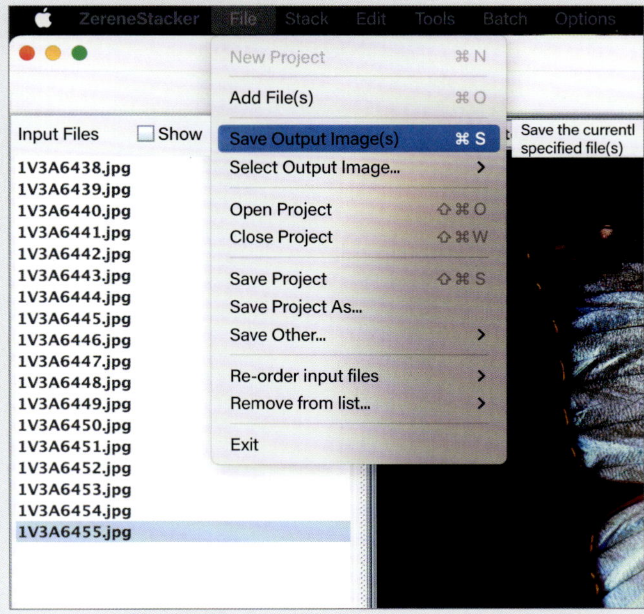

Step 9 If you are happy with the result, save your output image by going to File > Save Output Image(s).

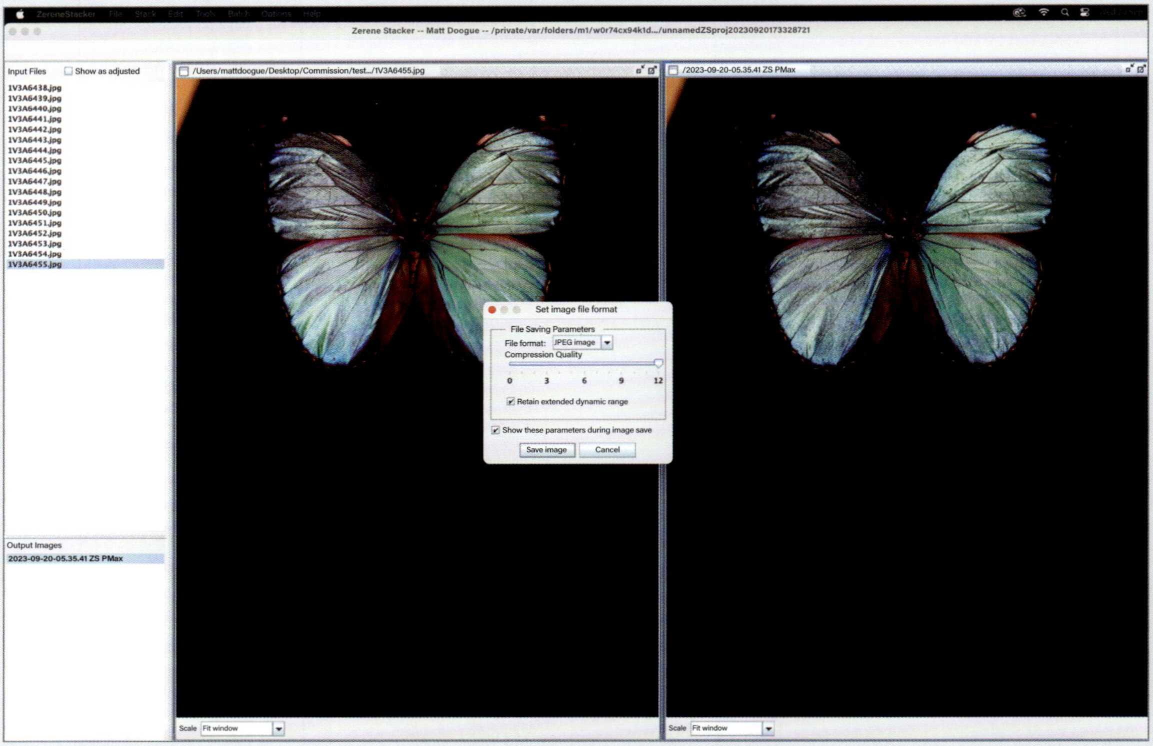

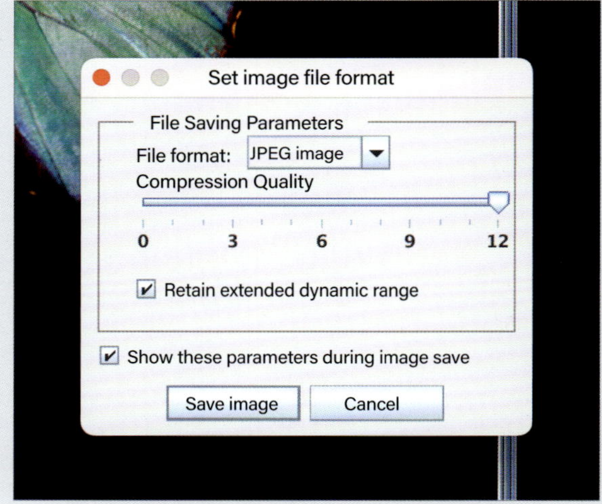

Step 10 A Preferences menu will display your output options. If you are saving your stacked image as a JPEG, select the highest Compression Quality and click Save image.

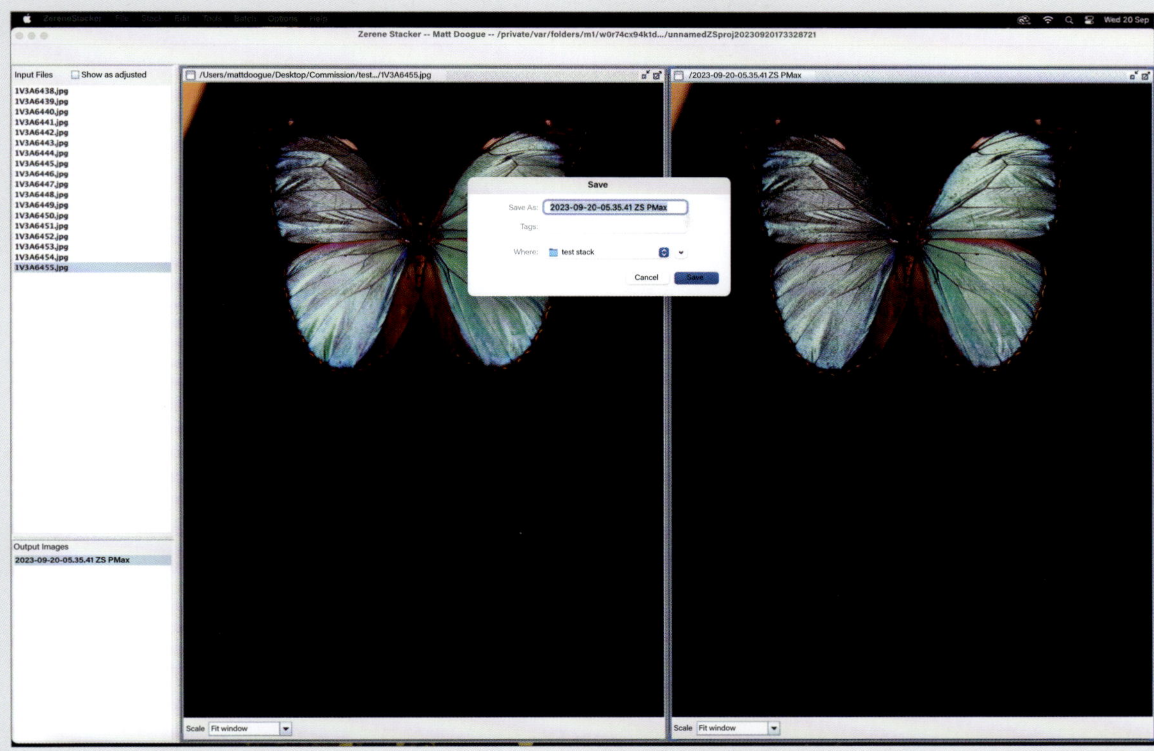

Step 11 A submenu will appear where you can rename the image and select the save destination.

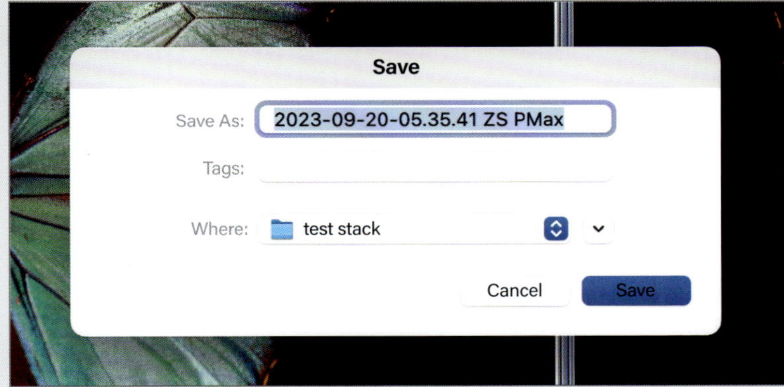

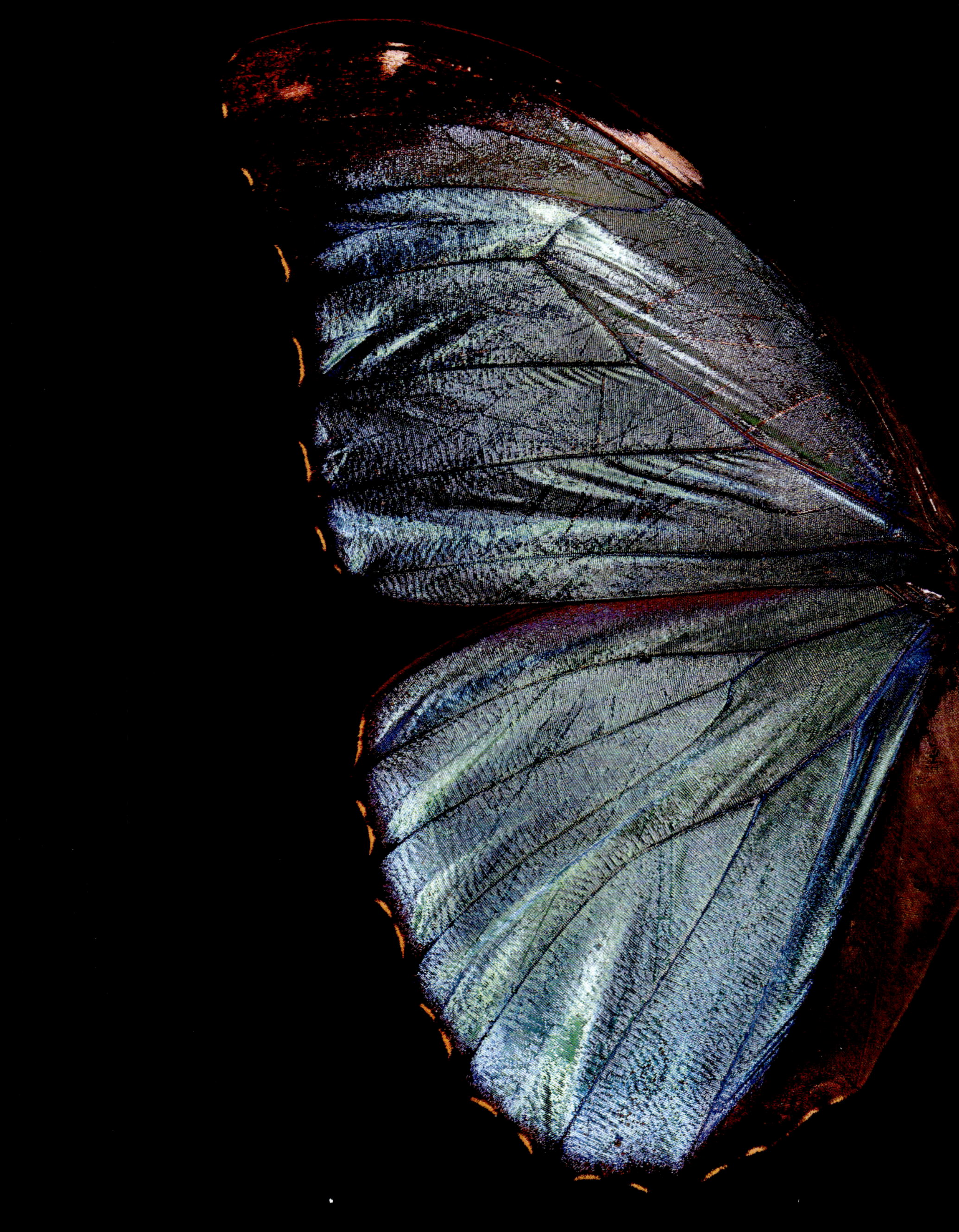

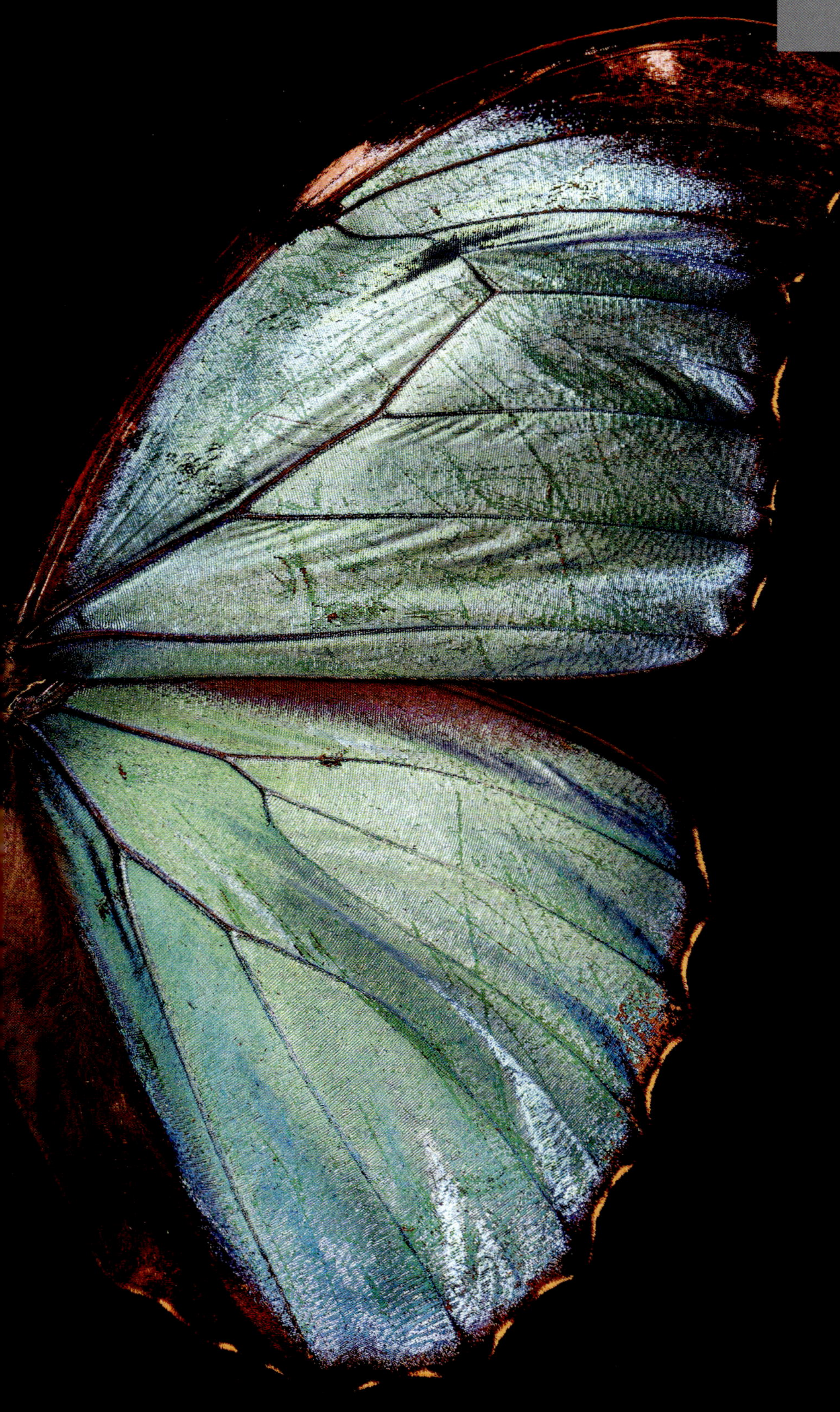

Step 12 The fully edited image, ready for publication.

Using focus peaking on the stinkhorn

Autumn is one of the quieter seasons for insects and arachnids, but what it lacks in beautiful critters, it makes up for with fungi and lichen!

I tend to wait until we have had some damp weather before I go on my fungi forage, as I've found that just after a downpour, the forest floor blooms all over with fungi. I have a list of favourites to look for – including fly agaric, puffballs and porcelain fungus – but there's one that tops them all for me, and that's the stinkhorn.

These stinky, sticky fungi erupt from the forest floor, particularly favouring coniferous woodland during the autumn months and they truly are fascinating. The Latin name, *Phallus impudicus*, roughly translates as 'shamelessly phallic', and when you look at the shape and size, well, you can understand why.

These mushrooms give off a foul, rotting smell and you will often smell them before you find them. They start off egg-shaped, slightly soft and gelatinous, sticking out from the forest floor, before they erupt into the phallus-shaped mushroom. The cap of this mushroom produces a sticky and smelly substance called a 'gleba' and this is what attracts the flies. This gleba contains the spores of the mushroom and the flies become coated in it, thus spreading the spores to new places to grow.

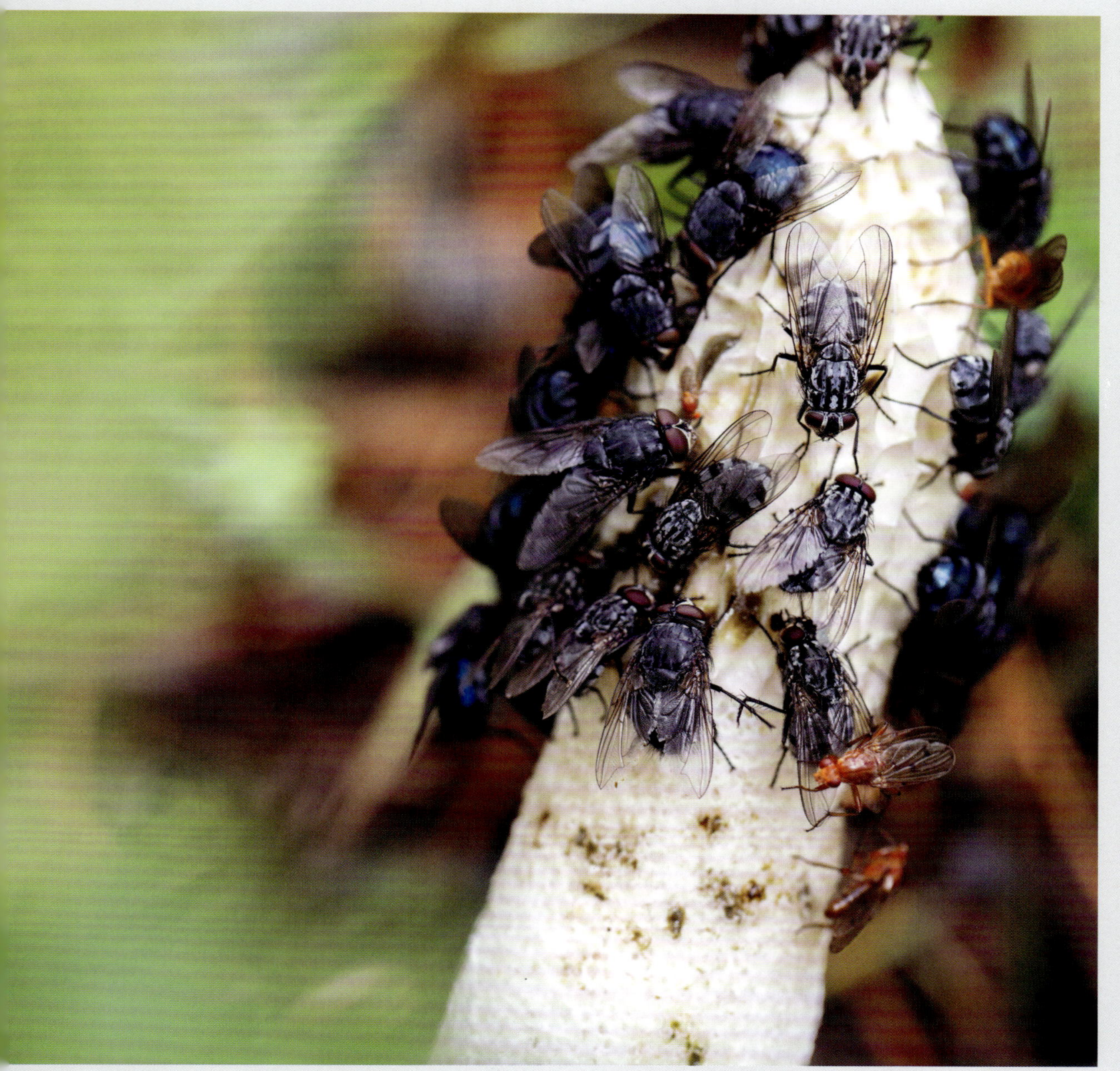

Photographing the subject

Photographing fungi can sometimes prove tricky. First and foremost, the majority of our subjects are on the forest floor, meaning we have to get down low in order to compose our shots. However, due to its large size and odd shape, it is sometimes possible to photograph this particular mushroom from a slightly elevated angle. The joy of photographing fungi is that the subject is going nowhere – it isn't going to fly away or scuttle behind a leaf. This allows you more time to compose your shot and look for varying angles that suit your artistic creativity, experiment with depth of field, add and remove any extra lights as needed.

For this particular shot I decided to use a tripod. The forest can be very dark, especially on a dull, overcast day. Utilizing a tripod meant that I could use a slower shutter speed to achieve the correct exposure, allowing me to set the aperture to achieve the depth of field I wanted, and keeping my ISO relatively low.

When you are using a tripod it's important to turn off any image stabilization, either in camera or on the lens. This function works to stabilize any movement, reducing camera shake and blur, but when the camera is stable on a tripod, it begins to work against itself. The system is still 'searching' for any movement, and as a consequence it can add unnecessary vibrations, which in turn may cause blur.

Because this subject was full of flies, I knew a focus stack wouldn't work. The flies were very active while feeding, with lots of new arrivals and lots of departures – it was pure chaos, and trying to focus stack would be a nightmare. I made the decision to focus a little closer instead, and concentrate on a group of flies feeding on the cap of the mushroom.

Because of the slight angle and lower shutter speed I was using I didn't want to compromise the composition or add any unnecessary movement to the camera, so I utilized the rear LCD screen and a timer to take my shots. Manual focus was used since autofocus would struggle to deal with the number of flies moving around and in order to help me further, I used a great feature of modern mirrorless cameras: focus peaking.

Right Using the tripod and adjustable head allowed me to get above the subject and at a slight angle in order to maximize my depth of field and reduce my shutter speed.

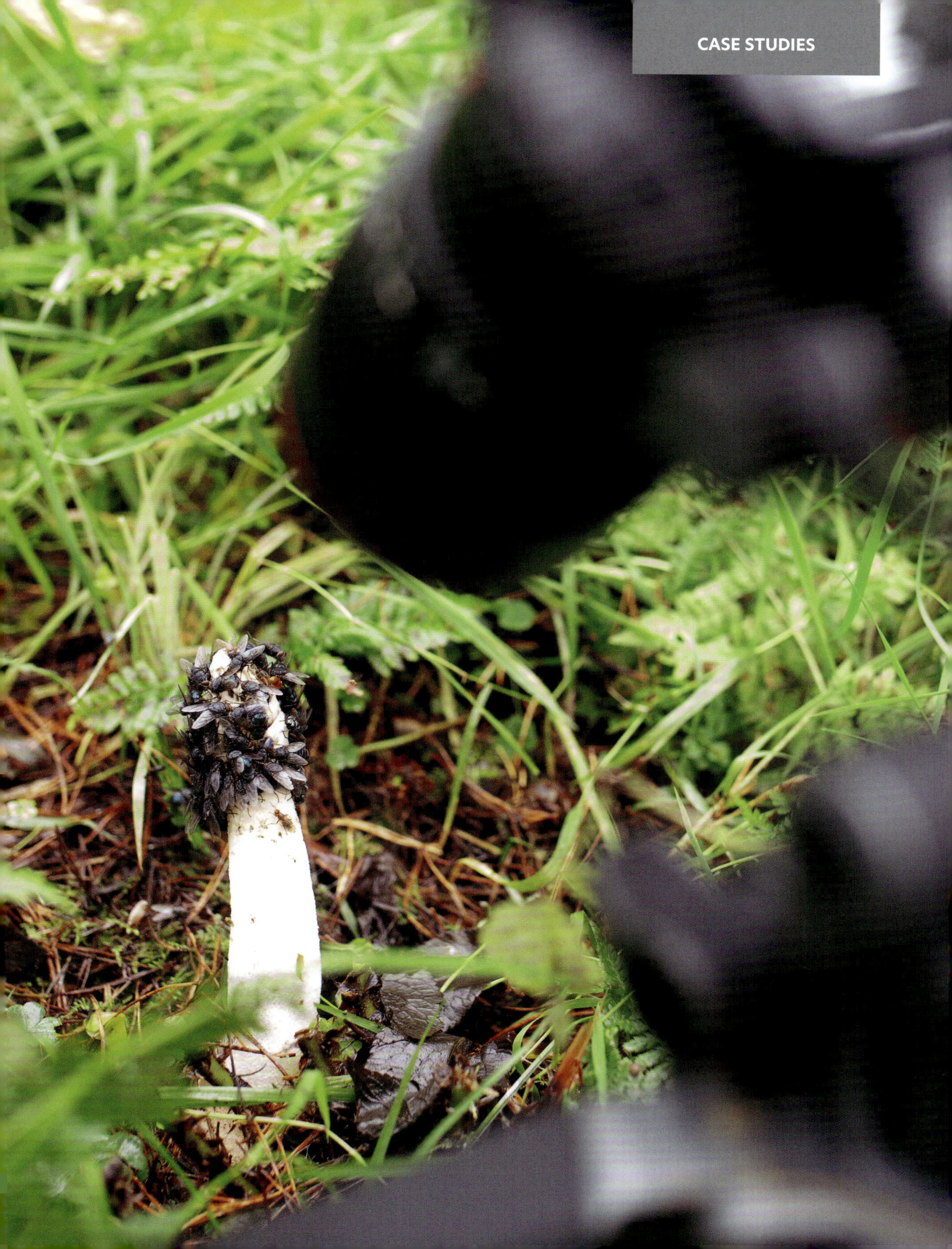

Using focus peaking

Focus peaking can be activated when you are using manual focus, and will allow you to focus incredibly accurately. It works by identifying areas of high contrast (which typically indicates that these areas are in focus) and adding a coloured overlay so you can easily see which part of your subject is in focus. You can usually set the overlay colour, and I typically set it to red as I feel it stands out more.

A large rear LCD screen is a huge benefit for using this function, but most digital viewfinders will display the same thing, only smaller.

As you start to adjust your focus you will see the highlighted area shift over your subject, allowing you to select the exact area you want to be in focus. The focus peaking feature may vary slightly from camera to camera, but here's an example of using it with the Canon EOS R5:

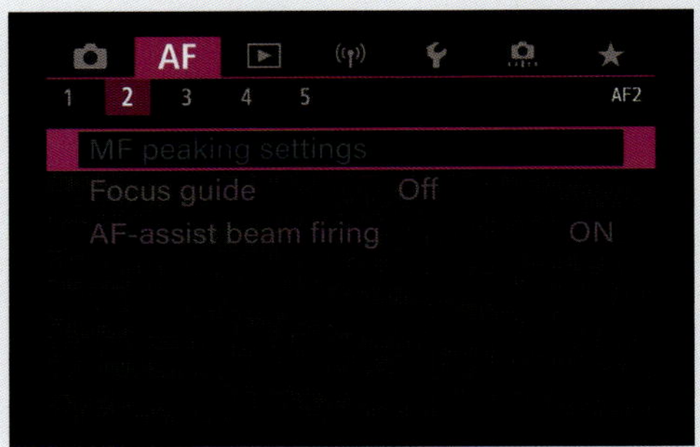

Step 1 Scroll and find the MF peaking settings.

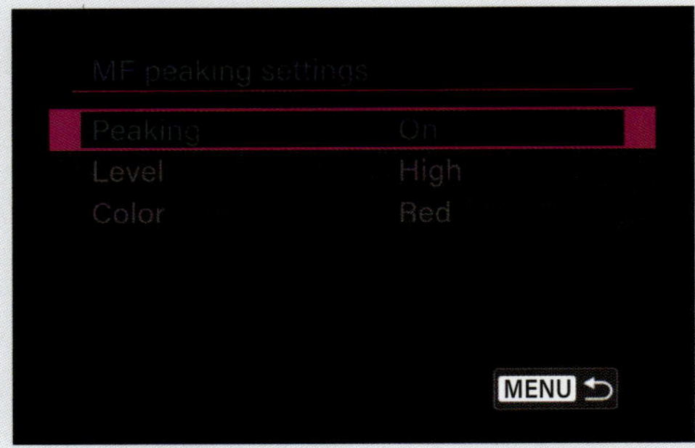

Step 2 Switch Peaking to On.

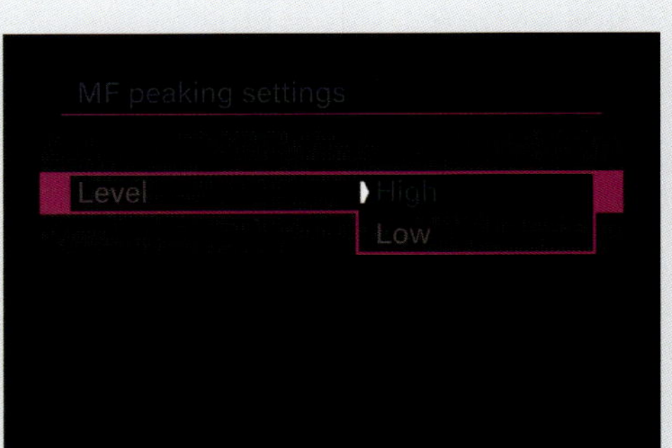

Step 3 Select the Level of focus peaking. For macro photography I always choose High.

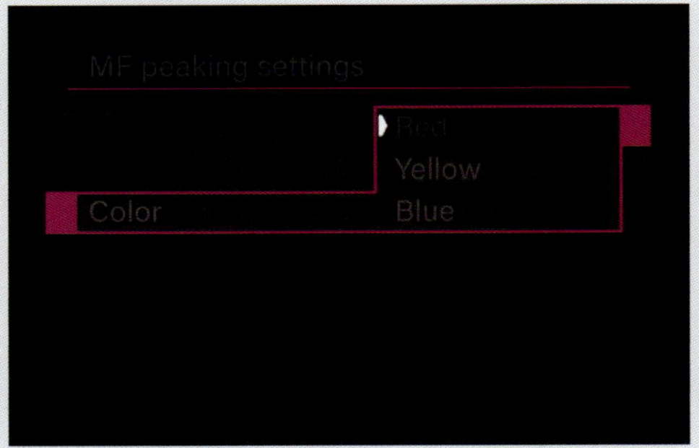

Step 4 Finally, select your overlay Color choice. Once selected you can exit the menu.

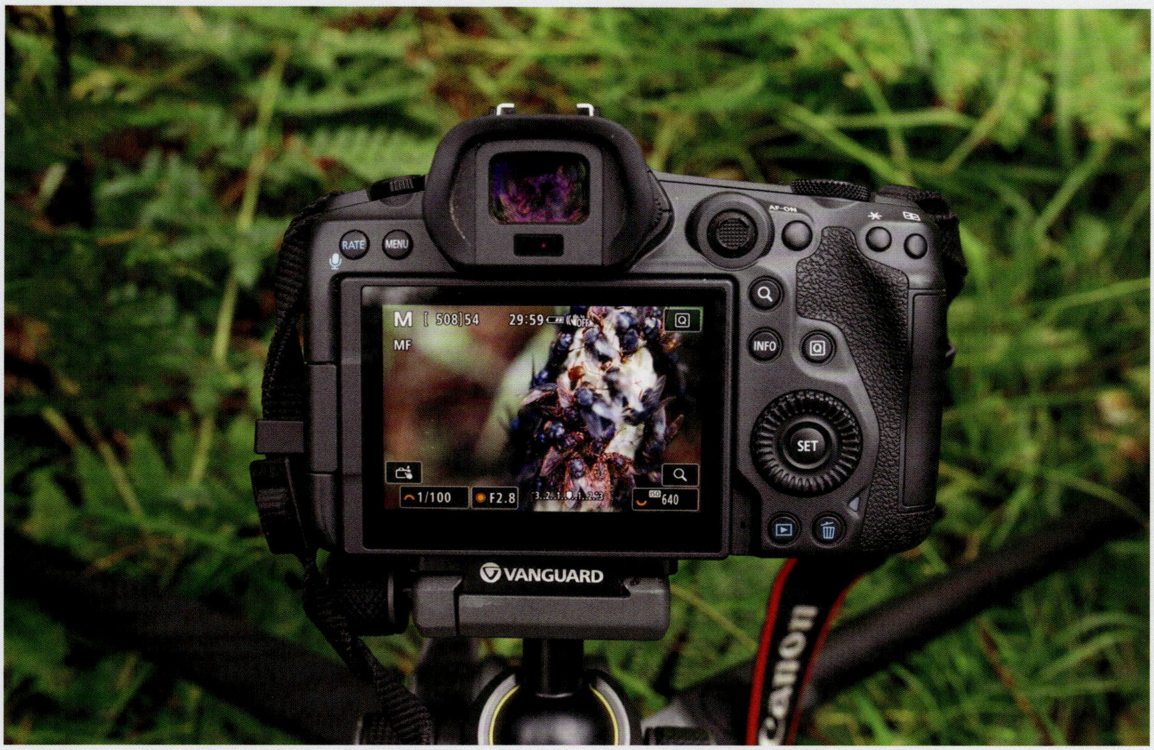

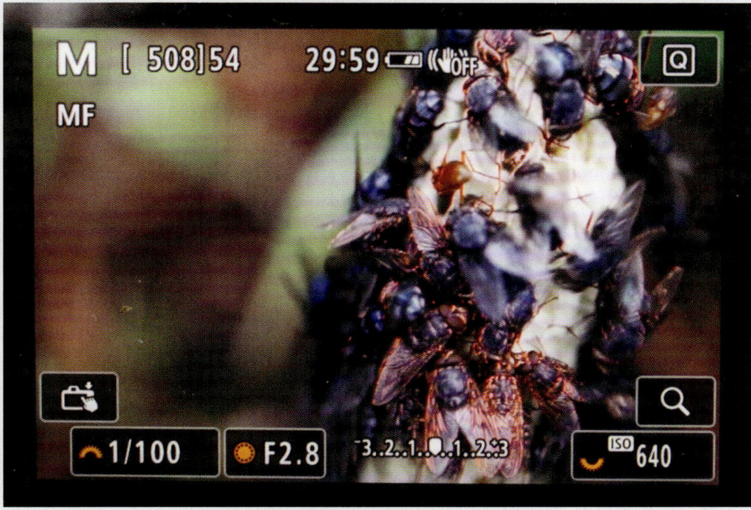

Step 5 As you look at the rear LCD screen (or through your viewfinder) you will now see the coloured outline, which indicates the areas that are in focus.

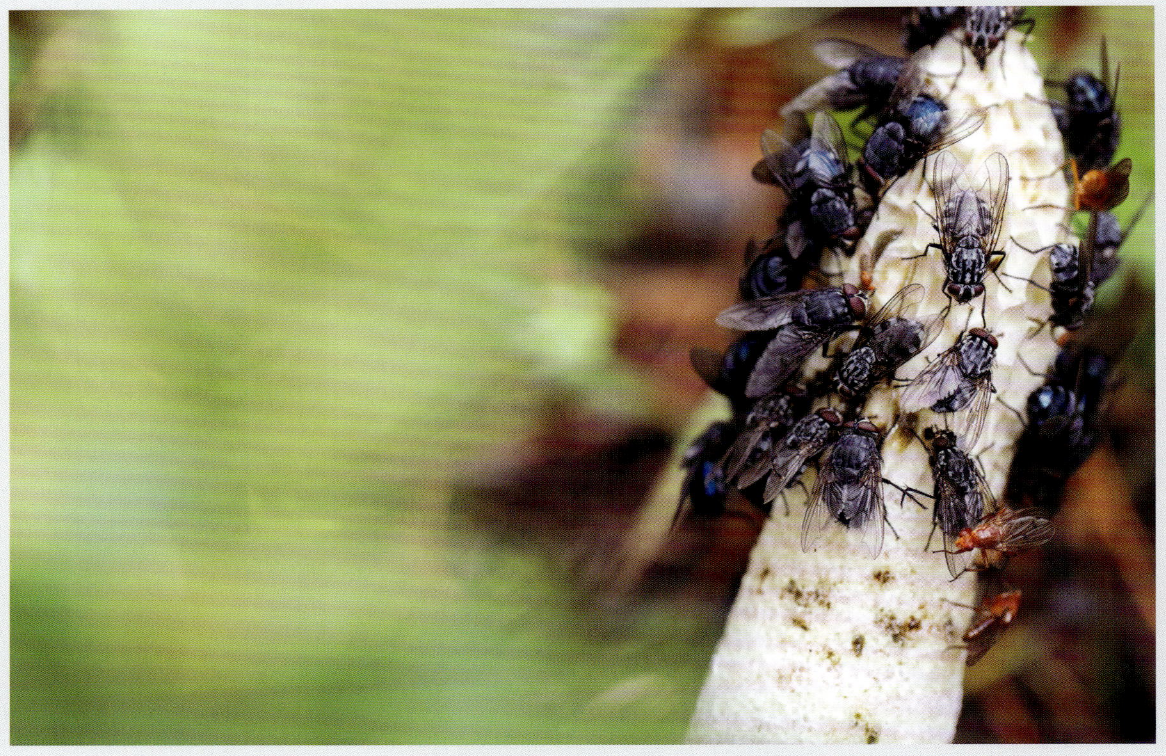

Step 6 Once I was happy with the area I wanted in focus, I set a timer for the shutter, as manually triggering it at slow shutter speeds can cause a shake.

PRO TIP Focus peaking is a great feature that works very well in low-light scenarios and with tricky compositions when you need to be confident you have the area you want in focus. As with other techniques, I recommend practising focus peaking at home on inanimate objects and subjects such as flowers or toy figurines. Get used to adjusting your focus and see how each turn of the barrel shifts the plane of focus over your subject.

Right Focus peaking helps you achieve a sharp image, even when your subjects are in constant motion.

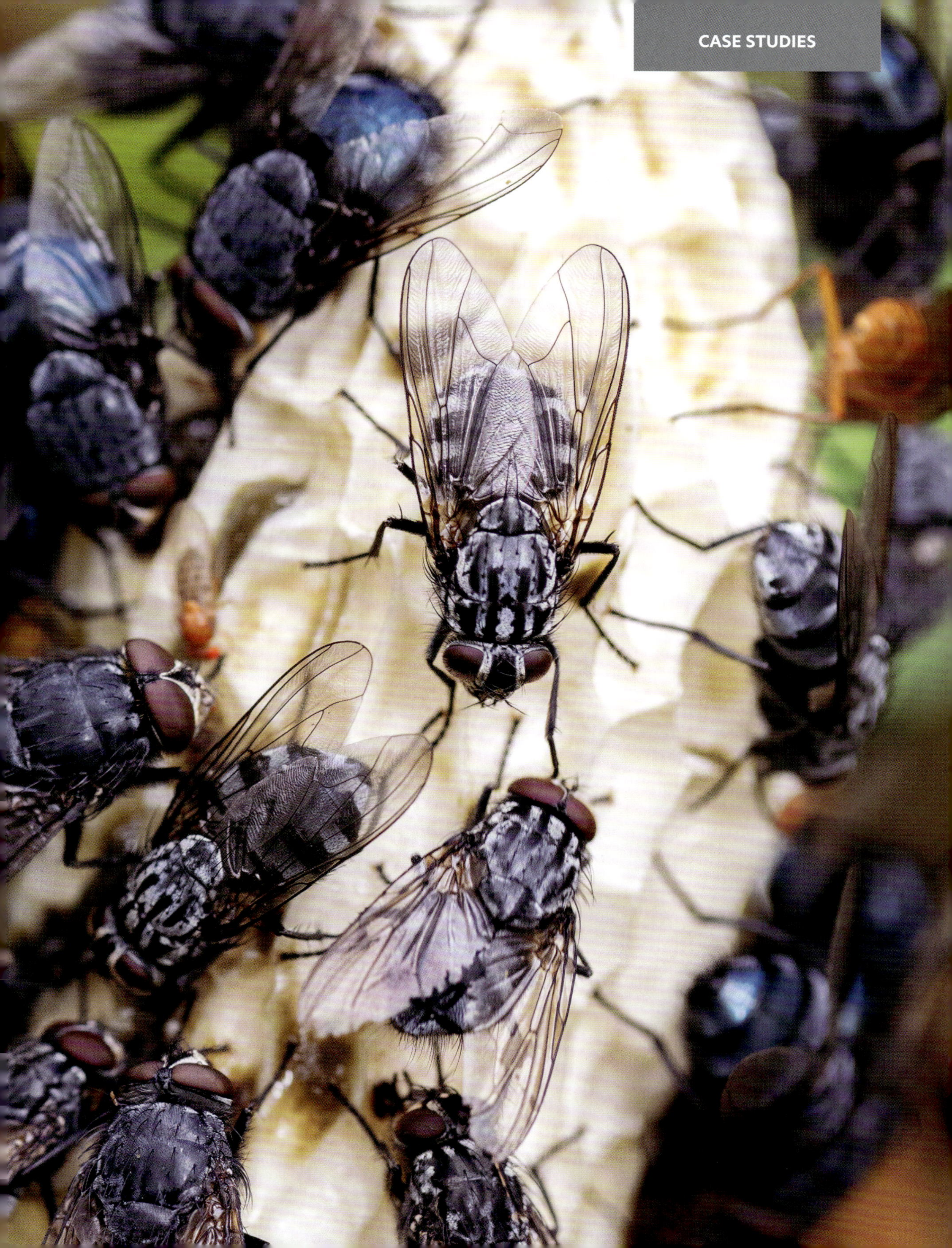

Forest fungi using in-camera focus stacking/bracketing

When it comes to focus stacking your images, doing it manually is not necessarily the only option available. In recent years, camera systems have become so advanced that they not only perform the stack sequence for you, but will align and merge the sequence into a final composite, all within a few seconds. It's fast, it's efficient and it can save you hours of post-processing time.

In-camera focus stacking doesn't always get it 100-percent perfect, but that is to be expected with any automatic feature on a camera. Auto focus stacking can be used for live subjects if they are very still, but if they move, then the stack will show this. However, for inanimate objects, flowers, fungi, lichen and similarly motionless subjects, it can work very, very well.

The focus stacking feature is sometimes referred to as 'focus bracketing' so if you don't find 'focus stacking' look for bracketing instead, the principle is very much the same. The camera I'm using for this case study uses 'focus bracketing', so that's how I'll be referring to it.

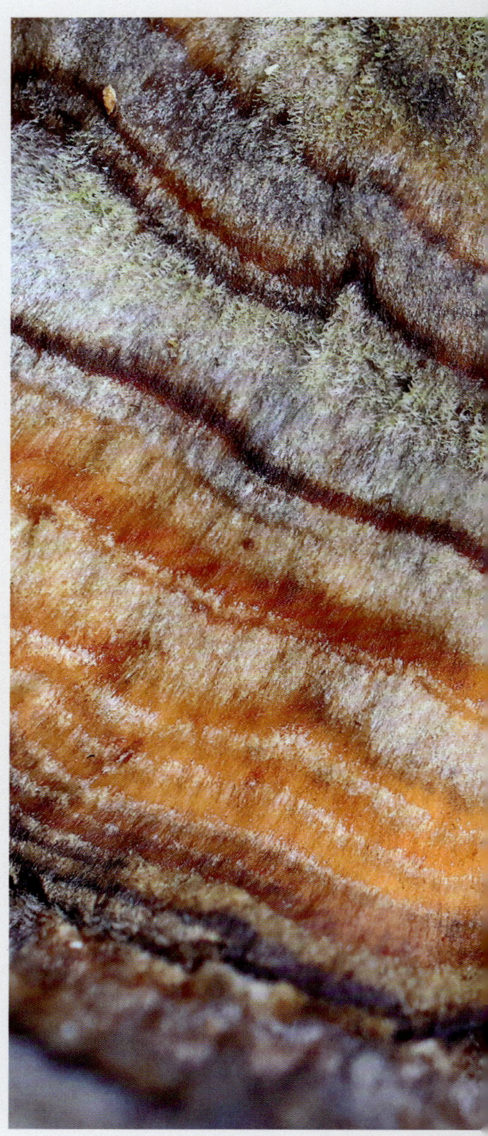

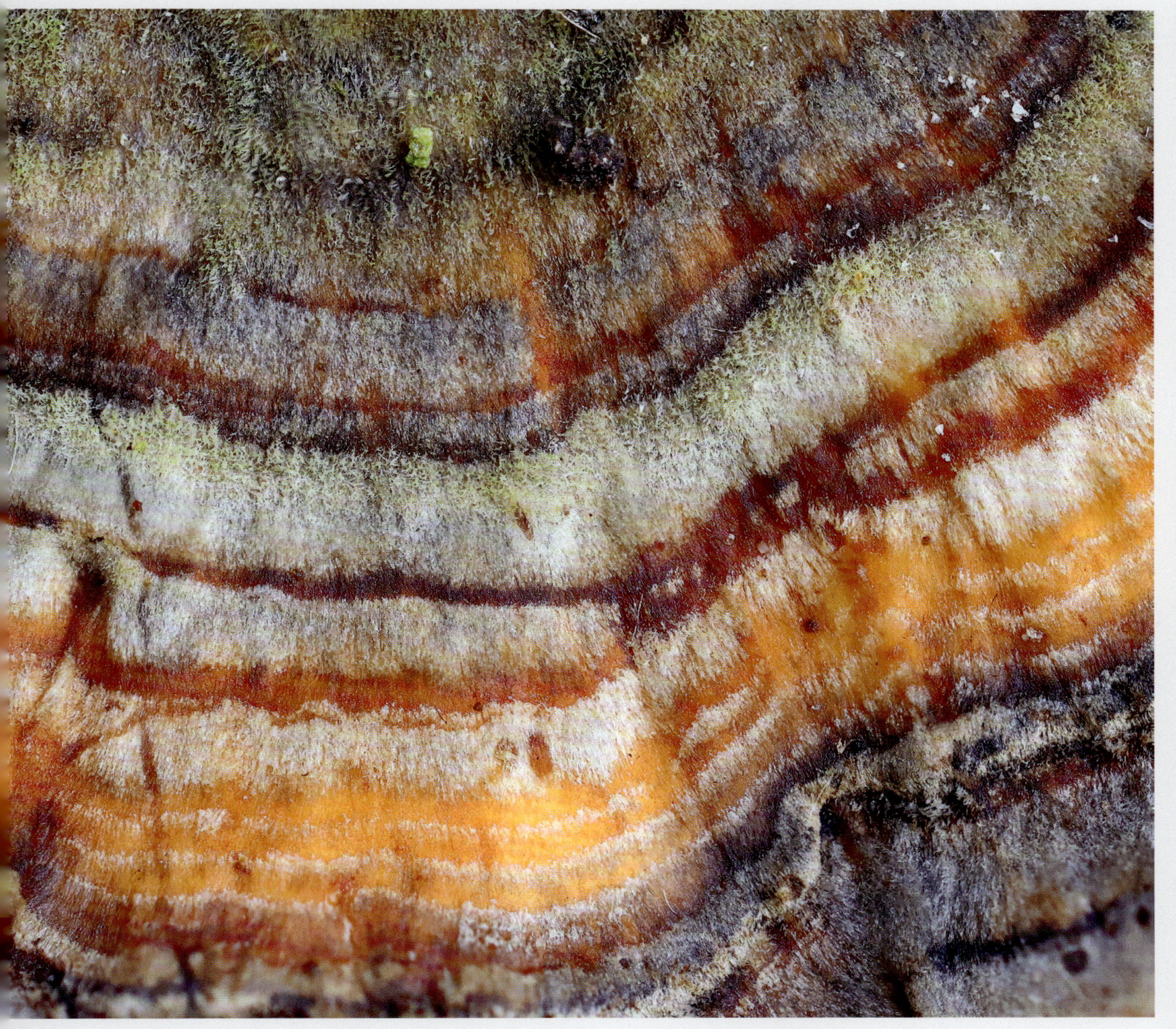

Photographing the subject

Gear

- Canon EOS R10 mirrorless camera
- Canon 100mm f/2.8 IS lens
- Vanguard tripod
- Lume Cube

As always, I head for the woods when I'm looking for lichens and fungi. After a short forage, I managed to find some good subjects – some low down on fallen rotten trees, as expected, and some growing out from the side of a tree.

For the mushrooms I found lower down, my intention was to capture as much detail, texture, pattern and colour as possible. These polypores were the perfect subject for this. The top side has all the colours and textures you need for an interesting composition, whereas the flip side isn't as interesting.

As my subject was still and easily accessible, and the light wasn't great, a tripod was a great addition to my kit, keeping the camera completely motionless as it did its work.

Right Using the rear LCD allows you to compose your shots with ease and offers a larger preview of the composition than a typical viewfinder.

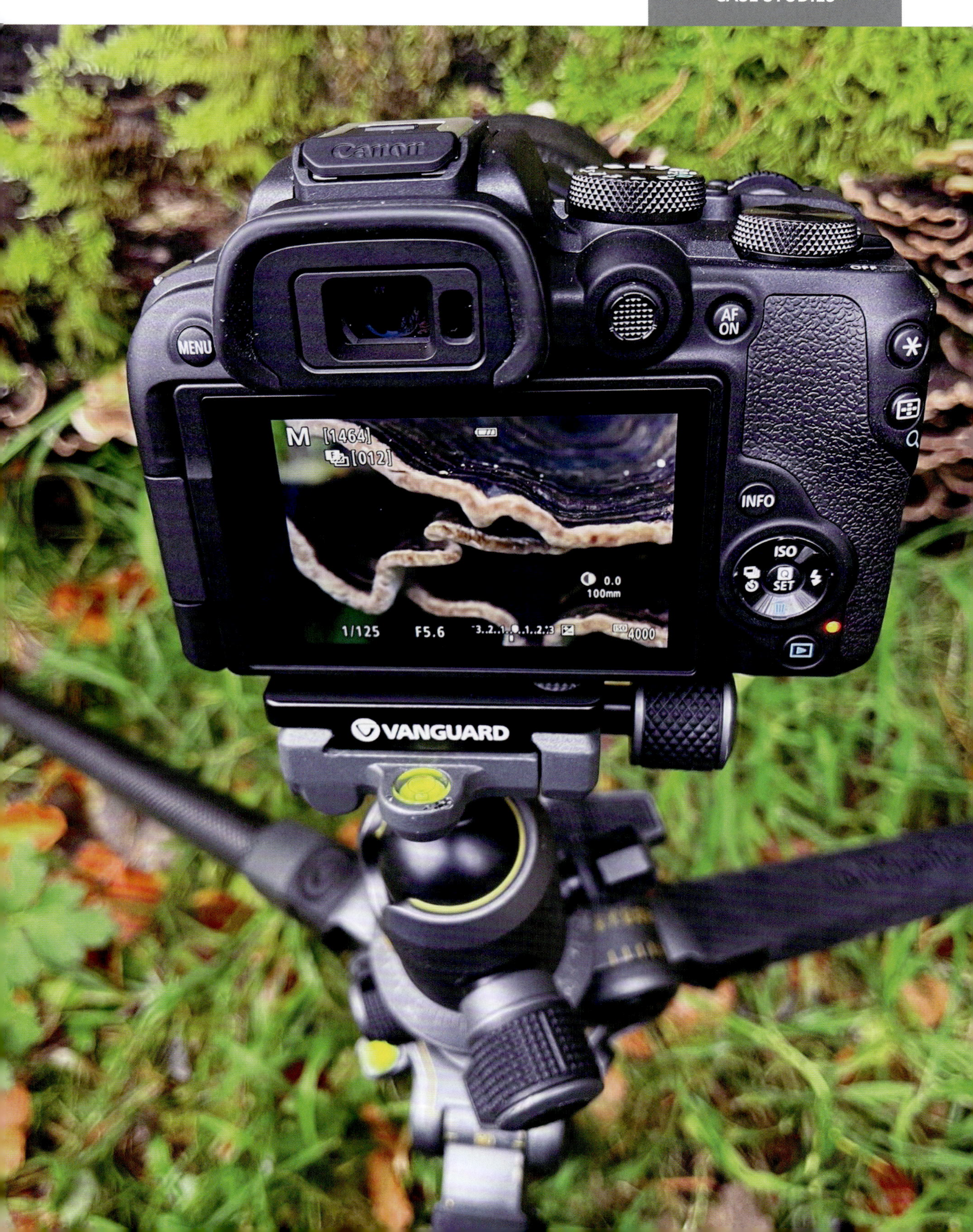

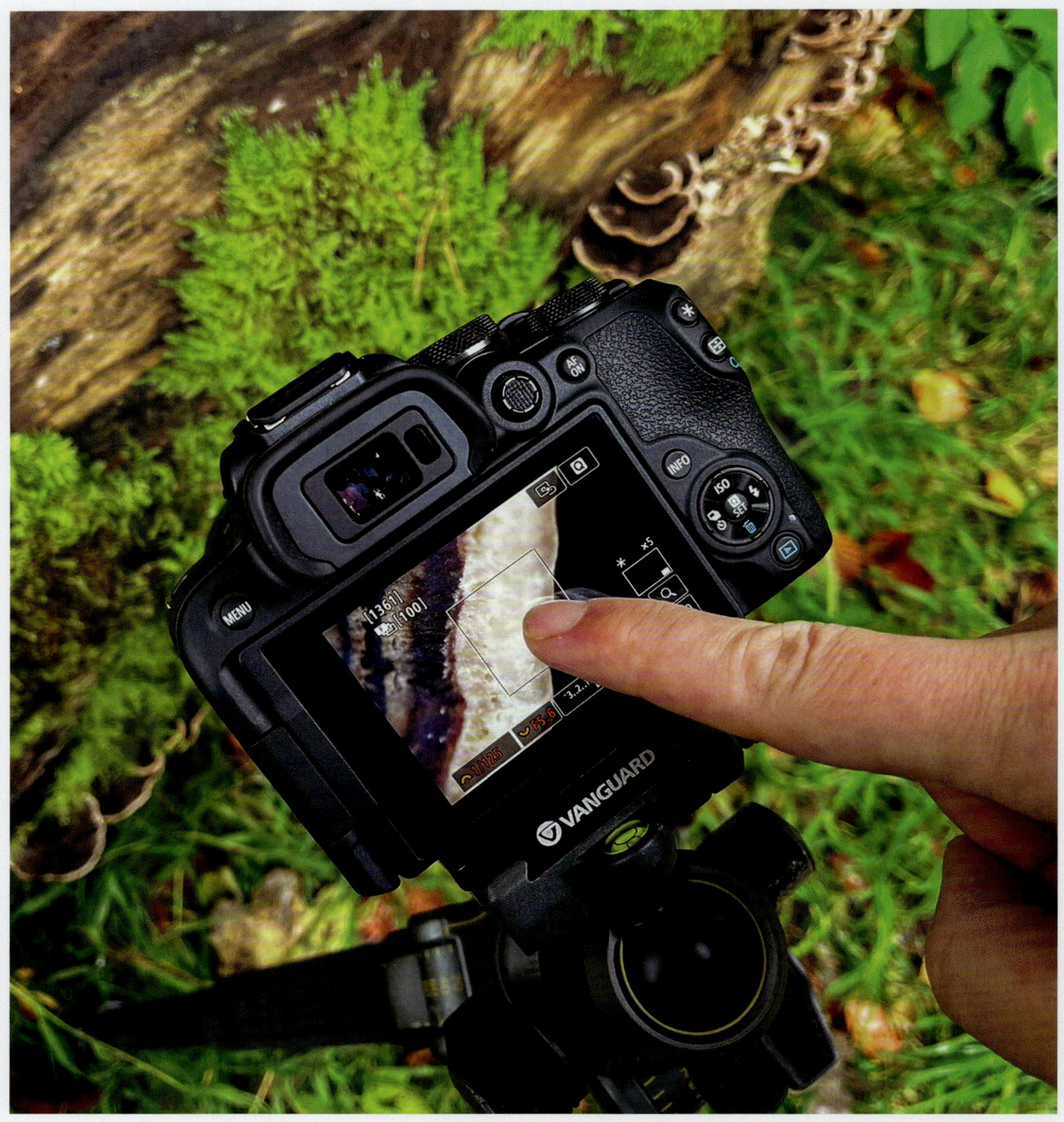

Above The LCD screen can also be a great tool to use when fine-tuning magnification and selecting a start point for your stack sequence. Using the screen's zoom function, you can pinpoint your starting place, which is usually the closest part of the subject to your lens.

Using focus stacking

As with all systems, the menu options vary – I'm using a Canon EOS R10 for this shot, which refers to focus stacking as 'Focus bracketing'.

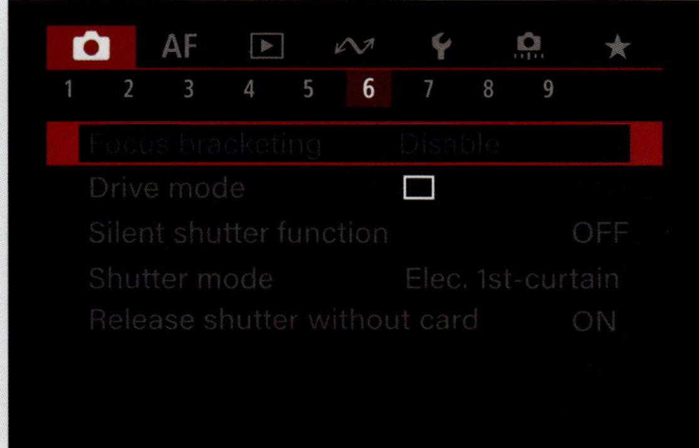

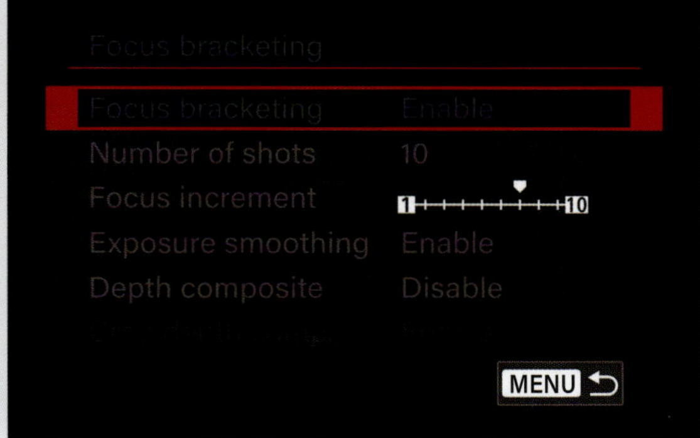

Step 1 Enter the menu system and scroll to the screen that contains Focus bracketing. Change it from Disable to Enable.

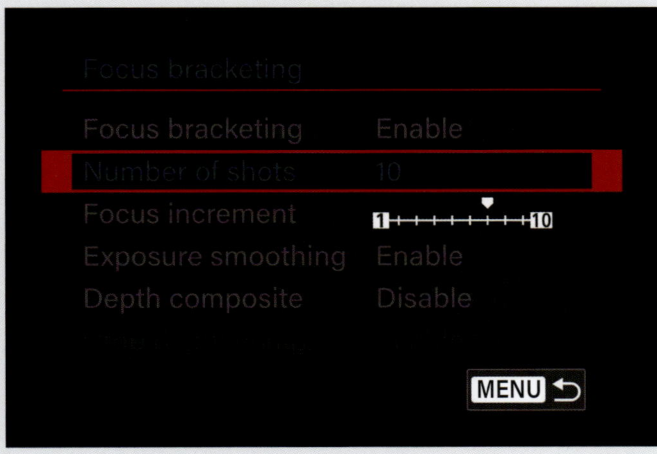

Step 2 Select the Number of shots you would like in the sequence. This number will vary depending on subject size, the depth of field chosen and the focus increments you select, so play around and experiment with it until you find a number that suits your shot.

Step 3 You can now select the Focus increment, which is how much the focus shifts over the subject. Larger aperture values will automatically shift the increments to cover a wider range so it's worth considering this when you select your aperture.

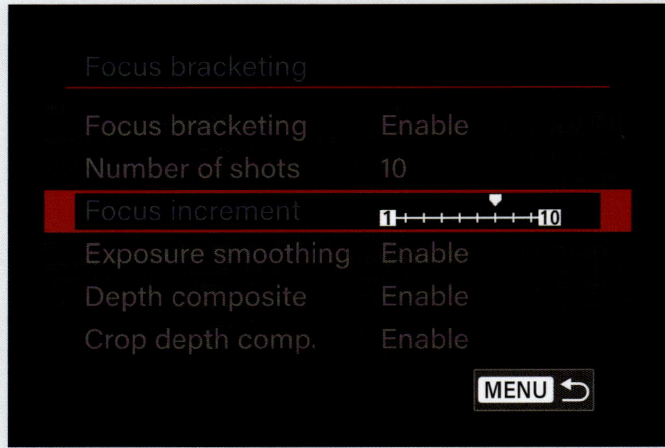

Canon's Focus bracketing feature allows you to activate additional functions, such as:

Exposure smoothing, which helps to compensate for any changes in brightness.

Depth composite, which saves both the composited stack and individual stack frames.

Crop depth comp., which crops the images as the stack is aligned.

I turn all of these options on. It's important to note that Focus bracketing only works if you use autofocus, as it requires full control over the lens as it shifts the focus over the subject.

Step 4 Once you have selected your start point for the stack, it's simply a case of pressing the shutter button and allowing the camera to do its work: the camera will shoot the focus stack, process the composite and then display the final image. If you're not using a tripod, it is important to remain as still as possible when using Focus bracketing.

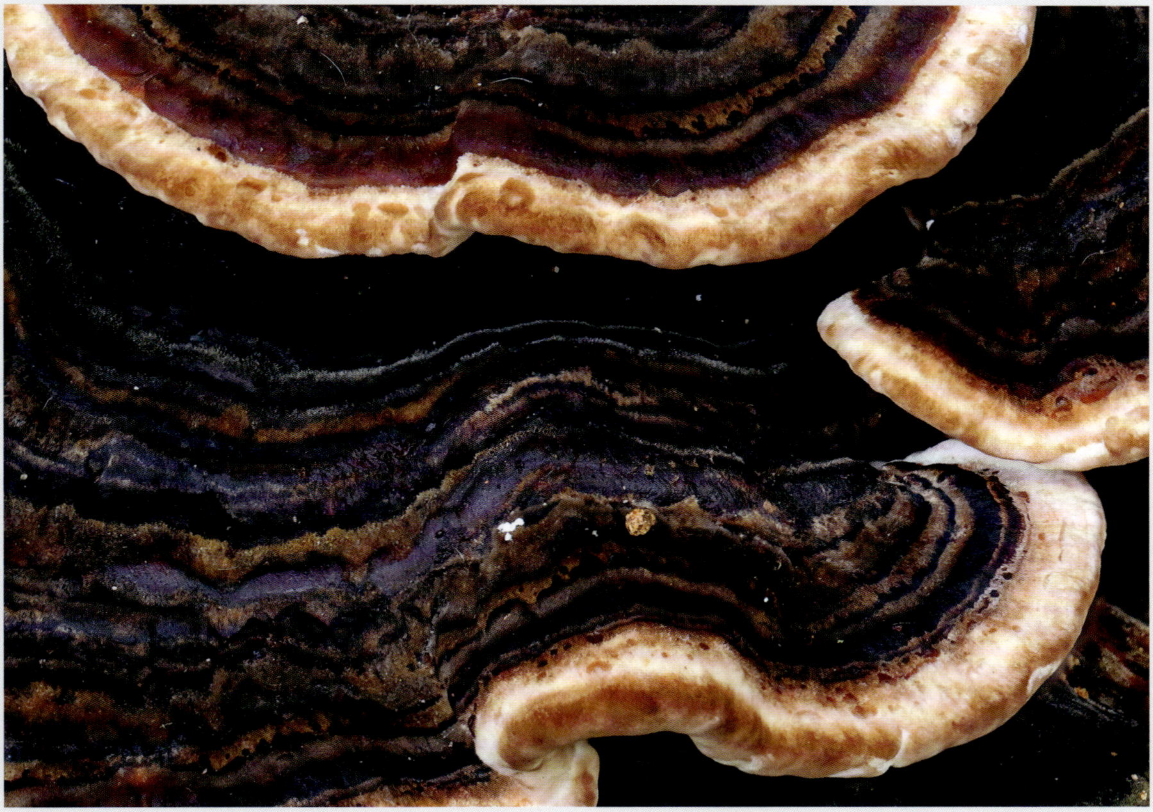

This page Just like flowers, fungi is the perfect subject to practise your technique and lighting on.

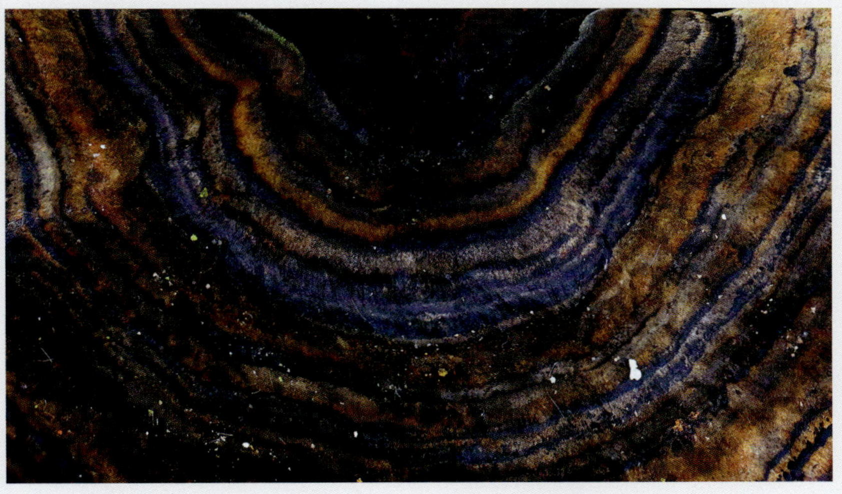

Right & below Bracket fungi come in a variety of shapes and colours, and this turkey tail was perfect for some abstract close-up stacks. Look for overlapping layers and interesting colours and textures when photographing these fungi.

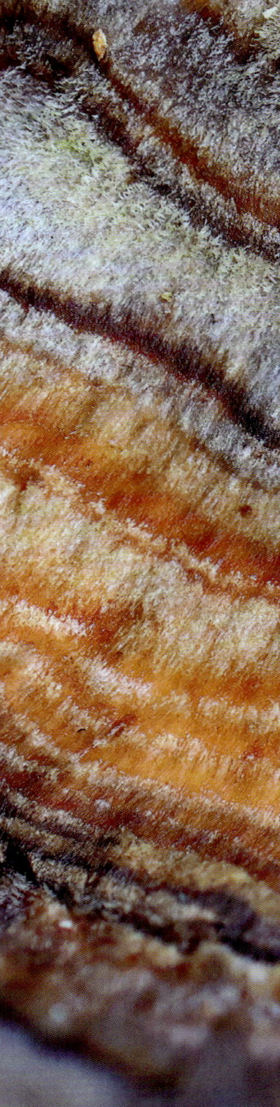

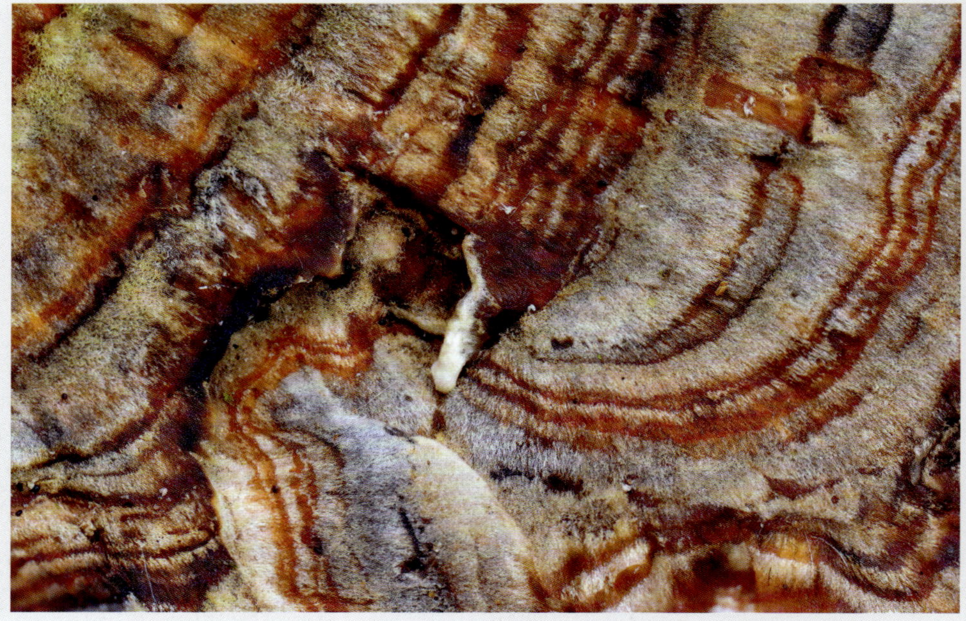

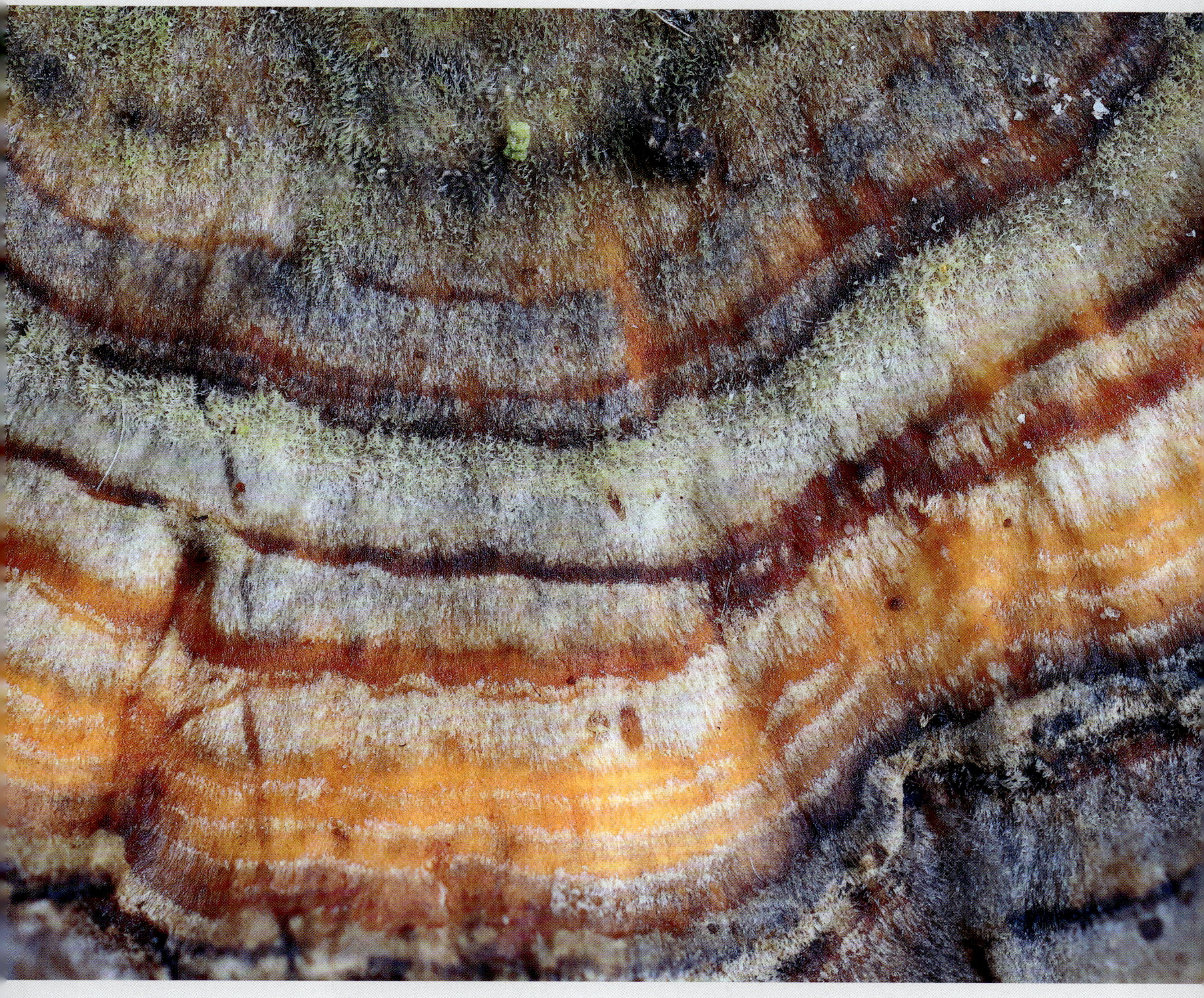

Lighting with in-camera focus bracketing

One of the many benefits of using in-camera focus bracketing with a tripod is that it allows you to free up your hands while the camera performs the stack. Knowing this, I packed a Lume Cube into my bag for some extra lighting on a trickier, more hidden set of mushrooms growing out from the side of a tree. Once again, I used the in-camera Focus bracketing feature, and while the camera worked away I held the Lume Cube above to add some lighting to the scene.

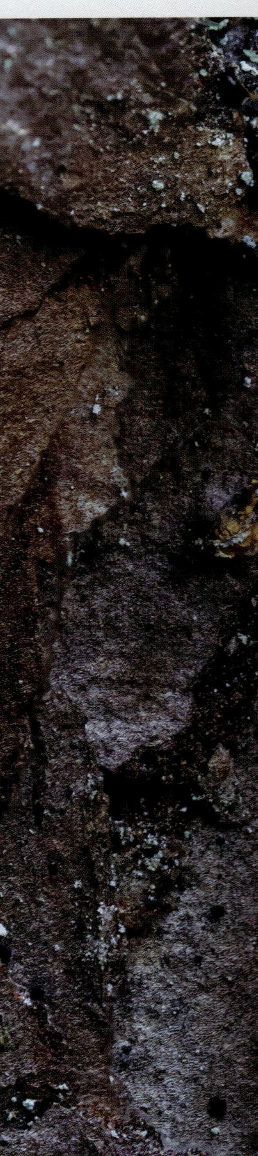

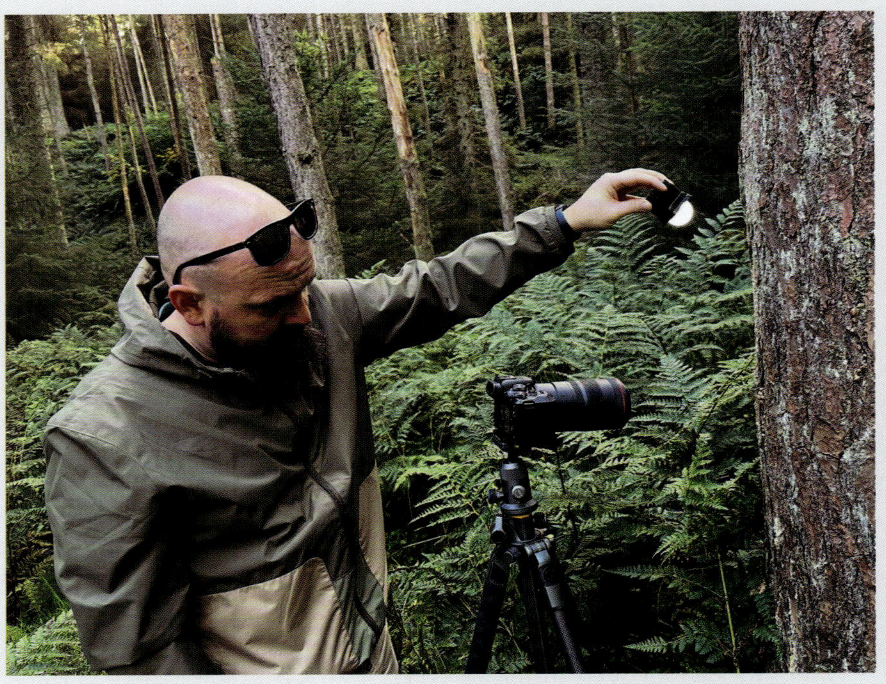

Above A benefit of using a tripod is that it frees up your hands to light your subject.

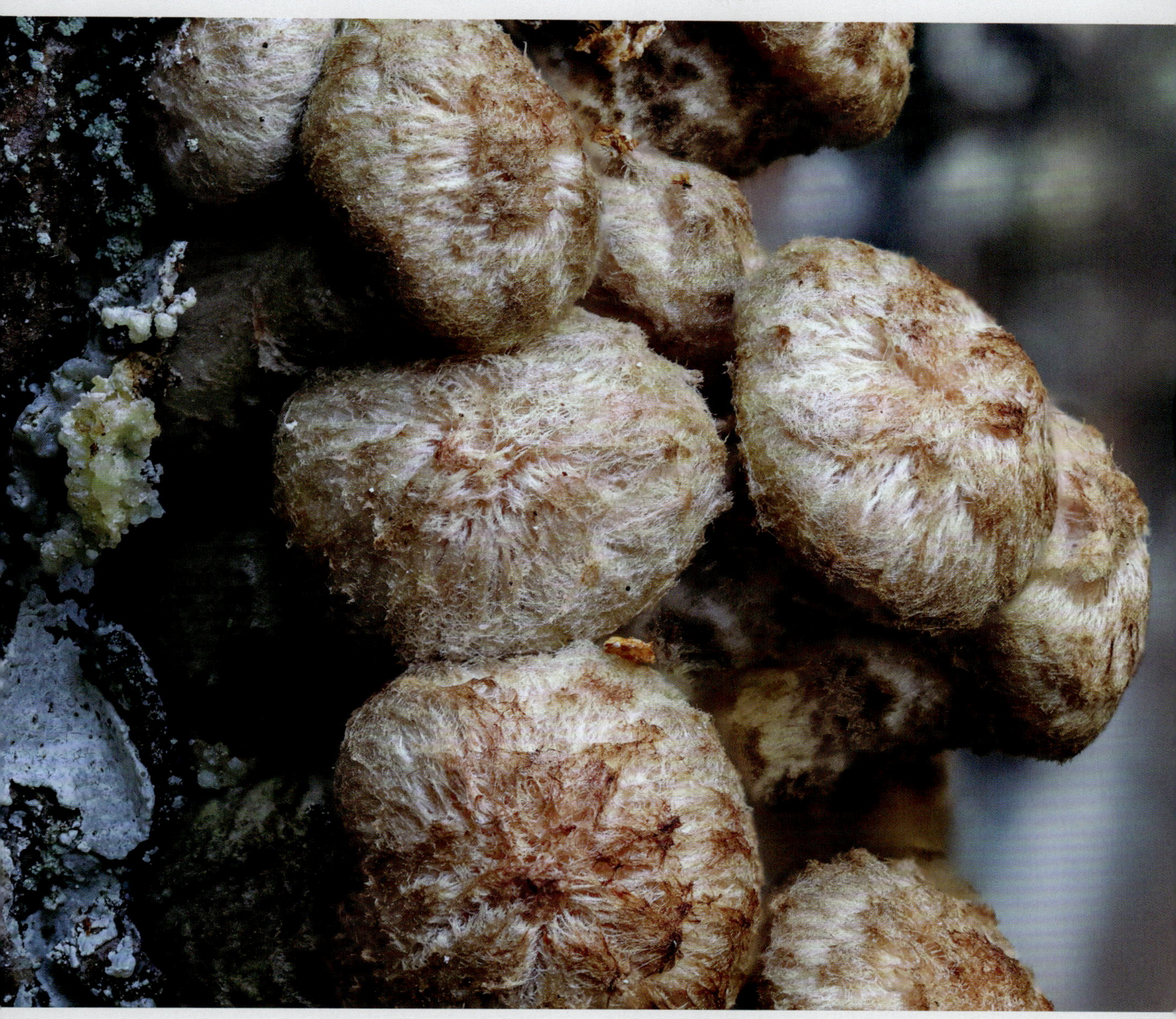

Above Subject shot under natural light.
Overleaf Subject shot with Lume Cube.

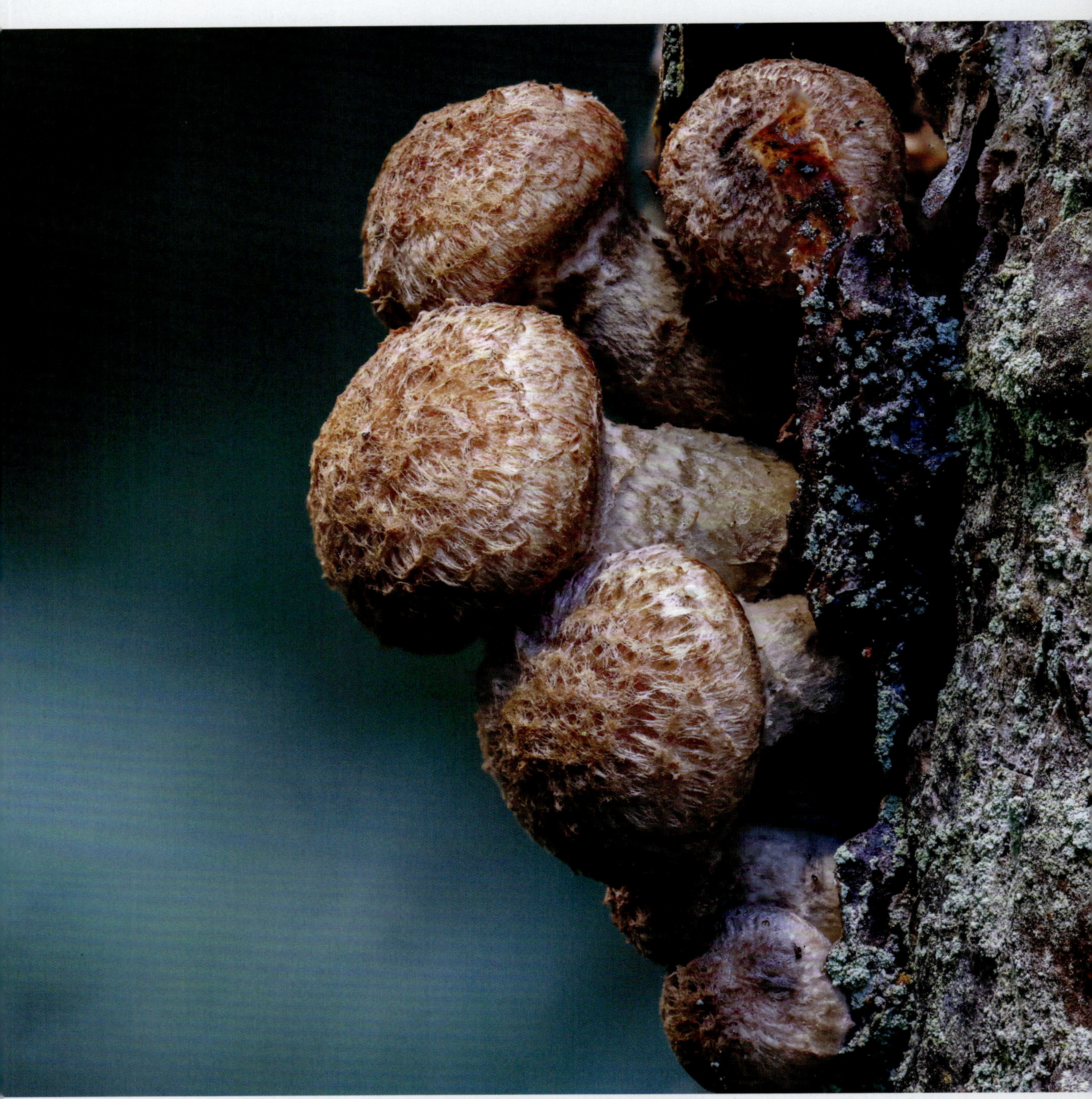

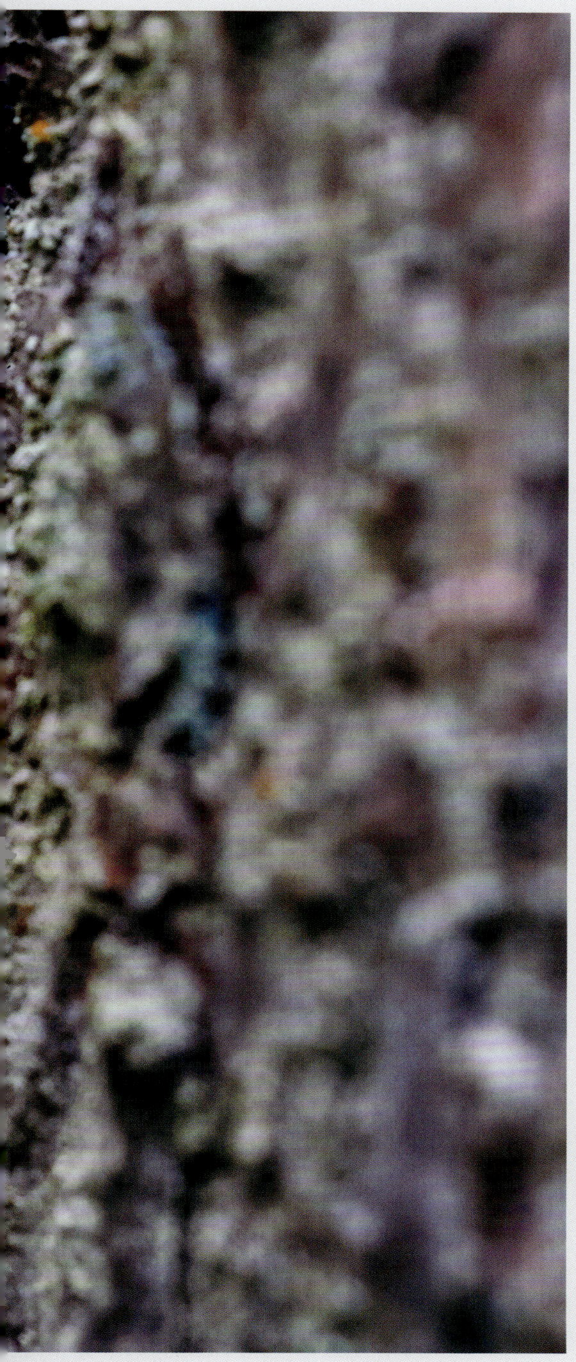

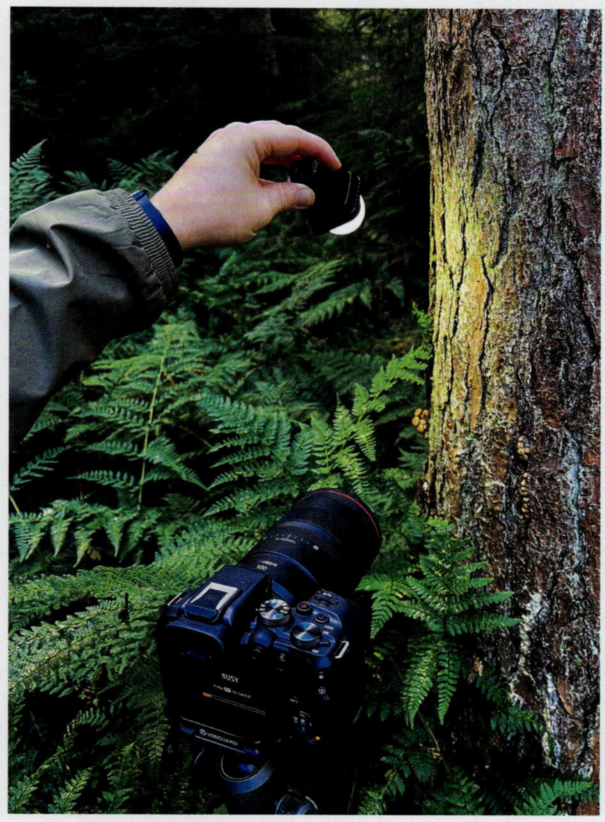

Left & above I used a Lume Cube to light my subject from above, bringing out all the lovely texture.

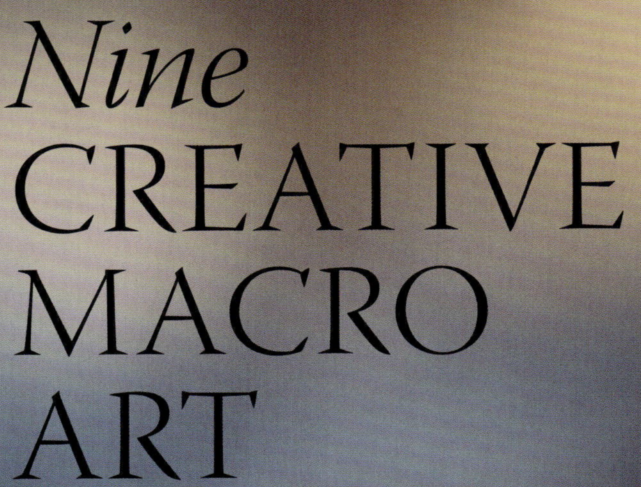

Nine
CREATIVE
MACRO
ART

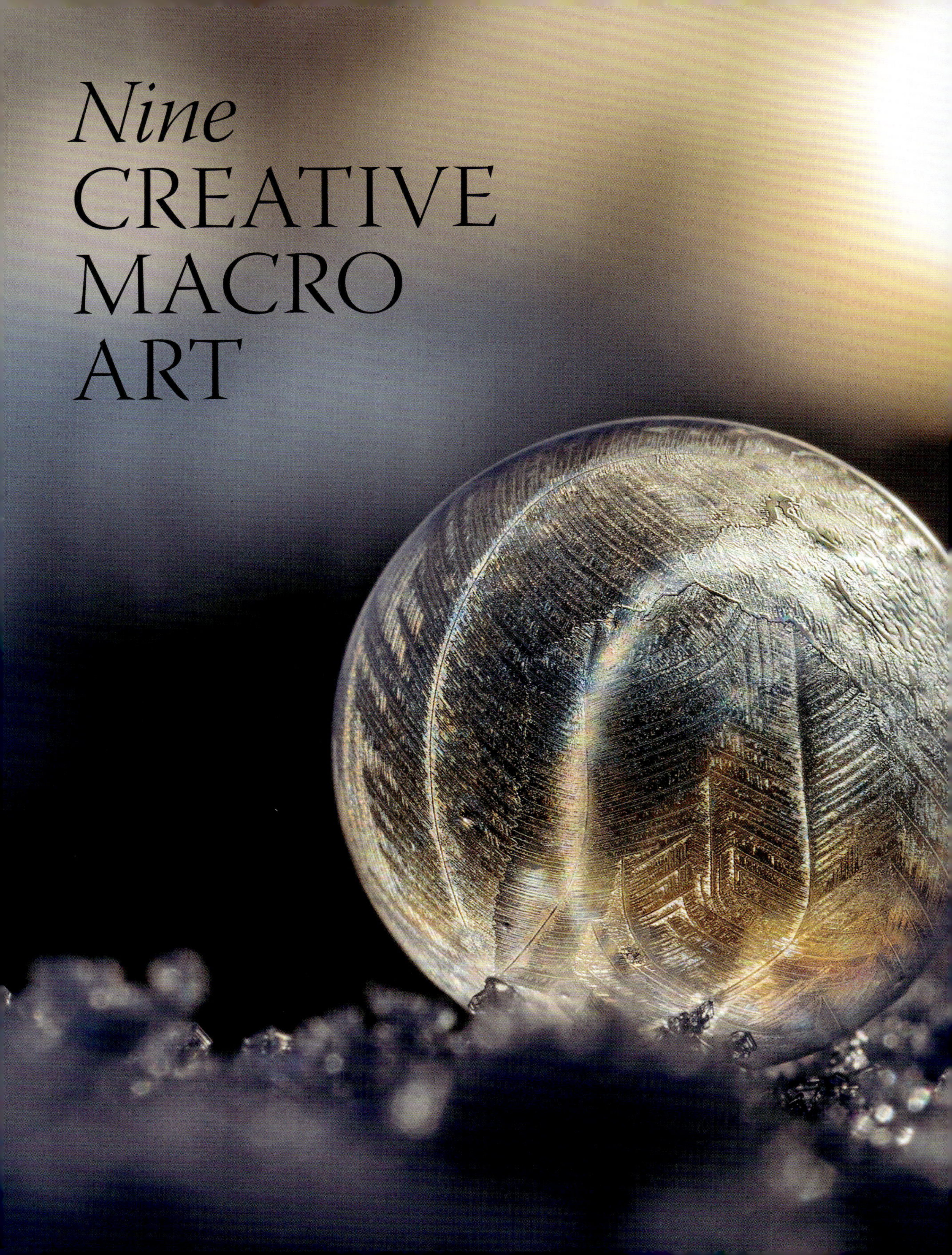

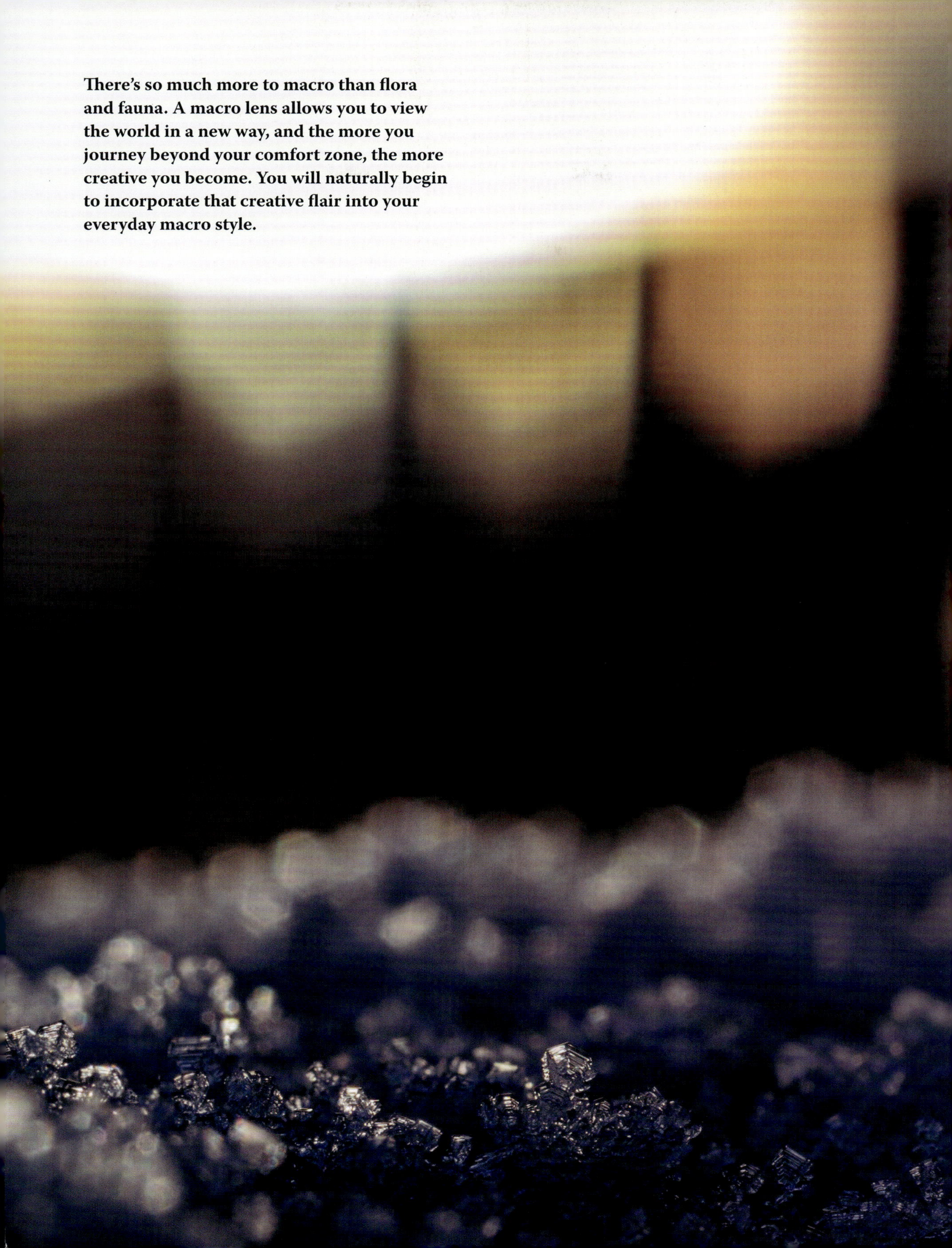

There's so much more to macro than flora
and fauna. A macro lens allows you to view
the world in a new way, and the more you
journey beyond your comfort zone, the more
creative you become. You will naturally begin
to incorporate that creative flair into your
everyday macro style.

Macro bubbles

Have you ever stood by the sink washing dishes and noticed how a spectrum of colour and patterns erupt around the bubbles before they suddenly pop? With a macro lens and simple set-up, you can capture this dazzling array of colour and turn it into beautiful art.

Equipment needed

- Camera with macro lens
- Tripod
- Flash or constant light source
- Prepared area
- A glass or mug
- Washing-up liquid
- Glycerine
- A straw for blowing bubbles
- Black card

Photographing the subject

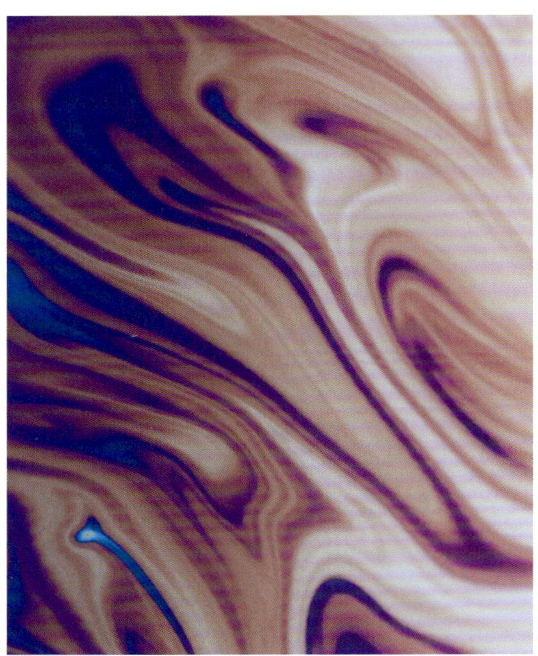

Step 1 Create your bubble mixture by mixing dish soap with some glycerine in a cup or mug. I use a ratio of 75% washing-up liquid and 25% glycerine, with about 50ml of water. Feel free to add more of either of the ingredients and play around to see what works for you. For example, if the bubbles don't last long enough you can add more glycerine.

Step 2 You are going to need to put some towels or waterproof sheeting down, so find an area with plenty of space. I use a small studio lightbox on my dining-room table, but you can use a table with a towel if you don't have a lightbox. Use black card or some other dark material as the backdrop, as this will help the colours to 'pop'.

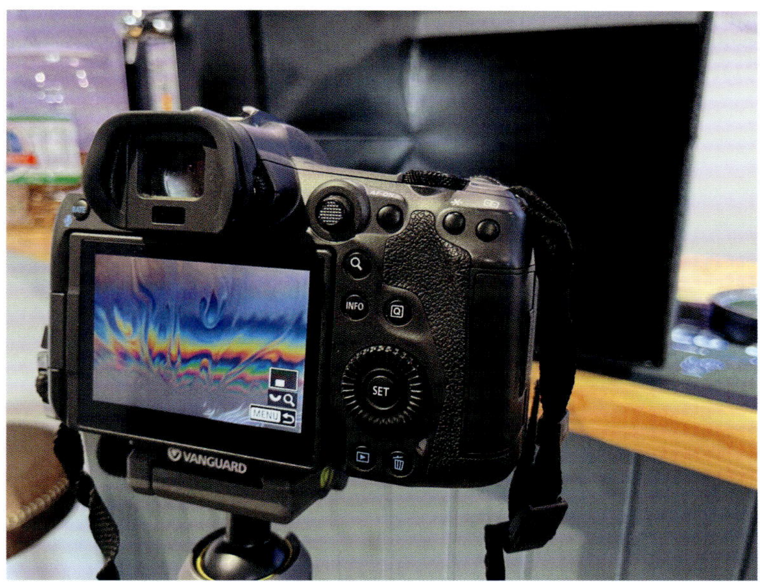

Step 3 Set up your lighting. I like to use LEDs or external flashes set at an angle away from the bubble mixture, as this captures more colour. Play around with different angles to see what works.

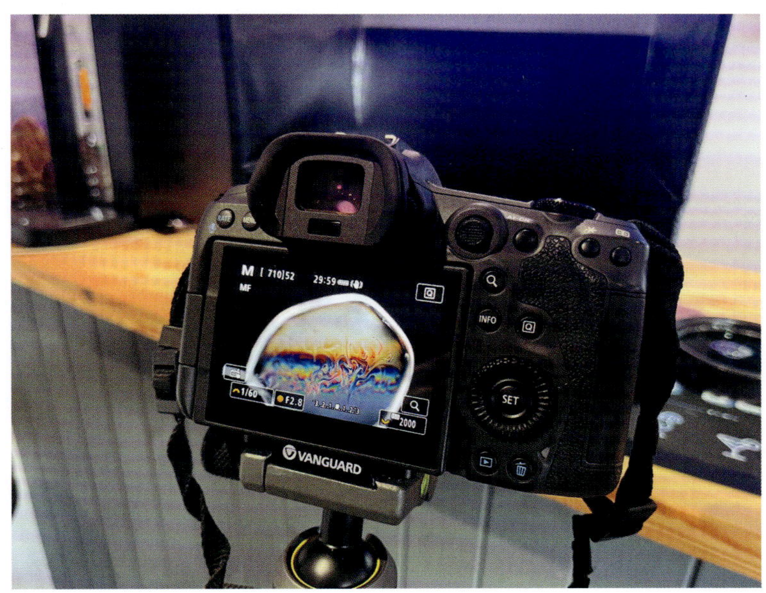

Step 4 Mount your camera on a tripod and shoot in manual mode, as this will give you more consistent results. Settings will vary, but aim for an aperture between f/10 and f/16 and keep the ISO as low as possible. A shutter speed of 1/200sec to 1/300sec is ideal (check your camera's sync speed if using flash). Due to the lighting conditions, autofocus may struggle, so try focusing manually.

Step 5 Insert the straw into the bubble mixture and blow some bubbles. Place the cup in front of your set-up, move the lighting around until you can see those vivid colours appear in the bubbles through your viewfinder and take some shots. Experiment with compositions and magnifications too.

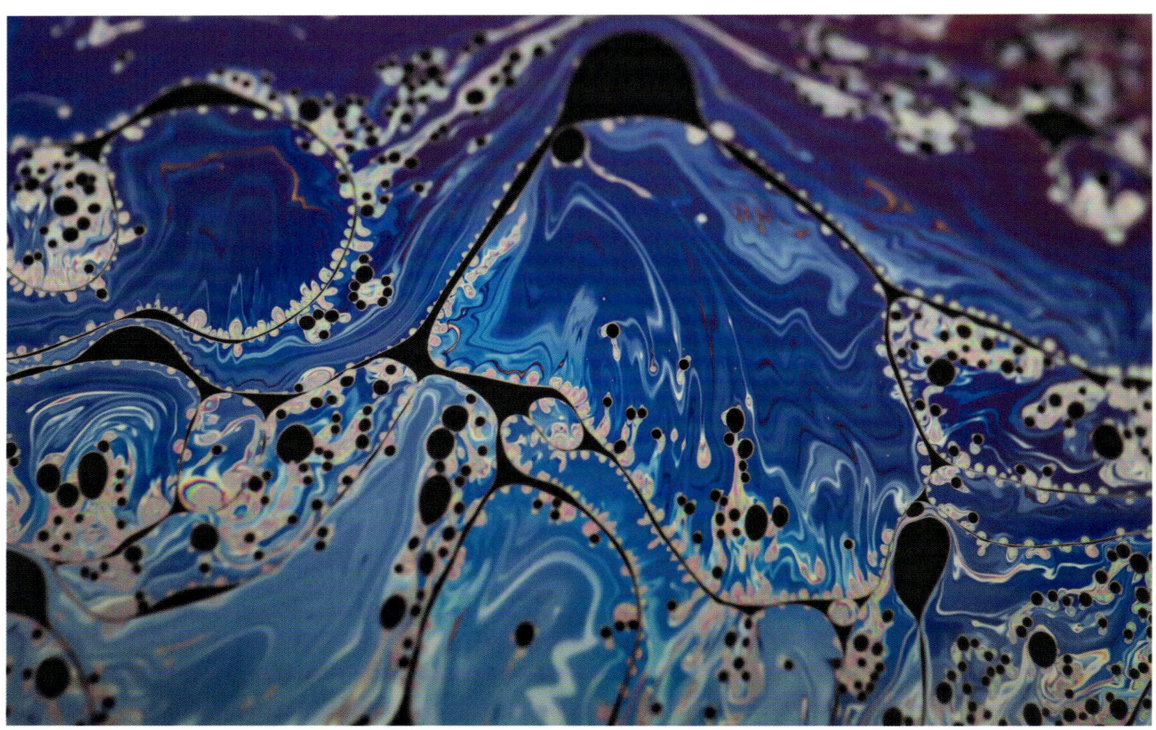

Try this

You could even create a metal hoop and dip it into the mixture, like the bubble wands you played with as a child. Remember to have fun and let your creativity flow.

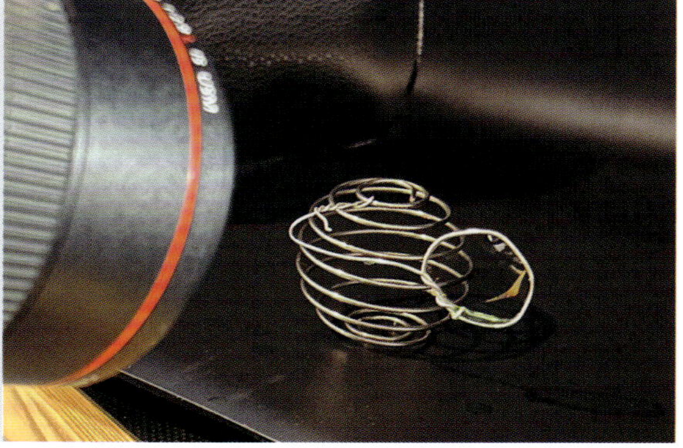

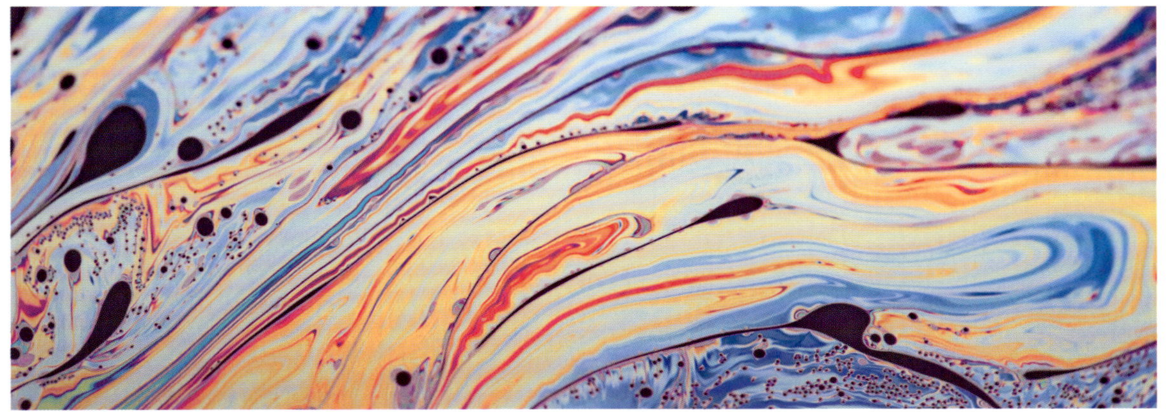

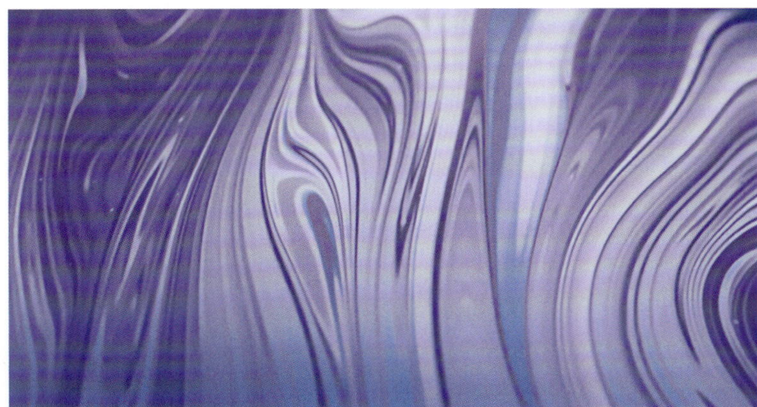

All Look for shapes and patterns when selecting your images. Try cropping in to enhance interesting abstracts.

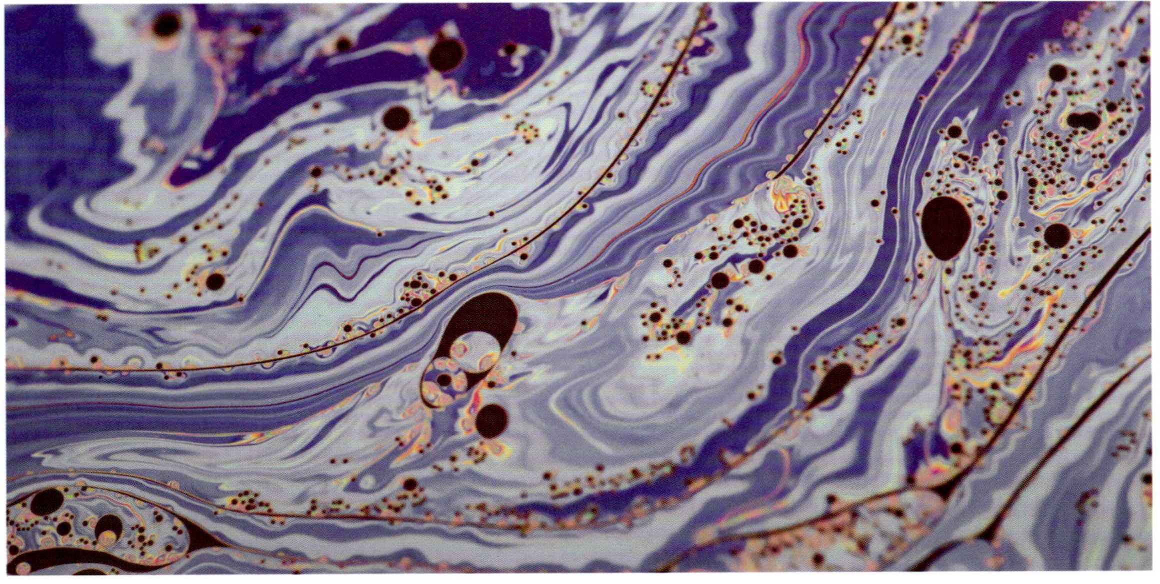

Freeze the beauty of bubbles

The fun doesn't stop there with the soap mixture: you can also use it in the winter to create frozen bubble abstracts. You will need to wait until the temperature drops to -8ºC (16.5ºF) or colder to do this. The idea is the same as shooting the bubble mixture in your home, only this time you will blow the bubble mixture on some frost or snow and watch in amazement as the bubble freezes and intricate patterns appear. Once the bubble has frozen, you have a limited amount of time to capture your images before it collapses.

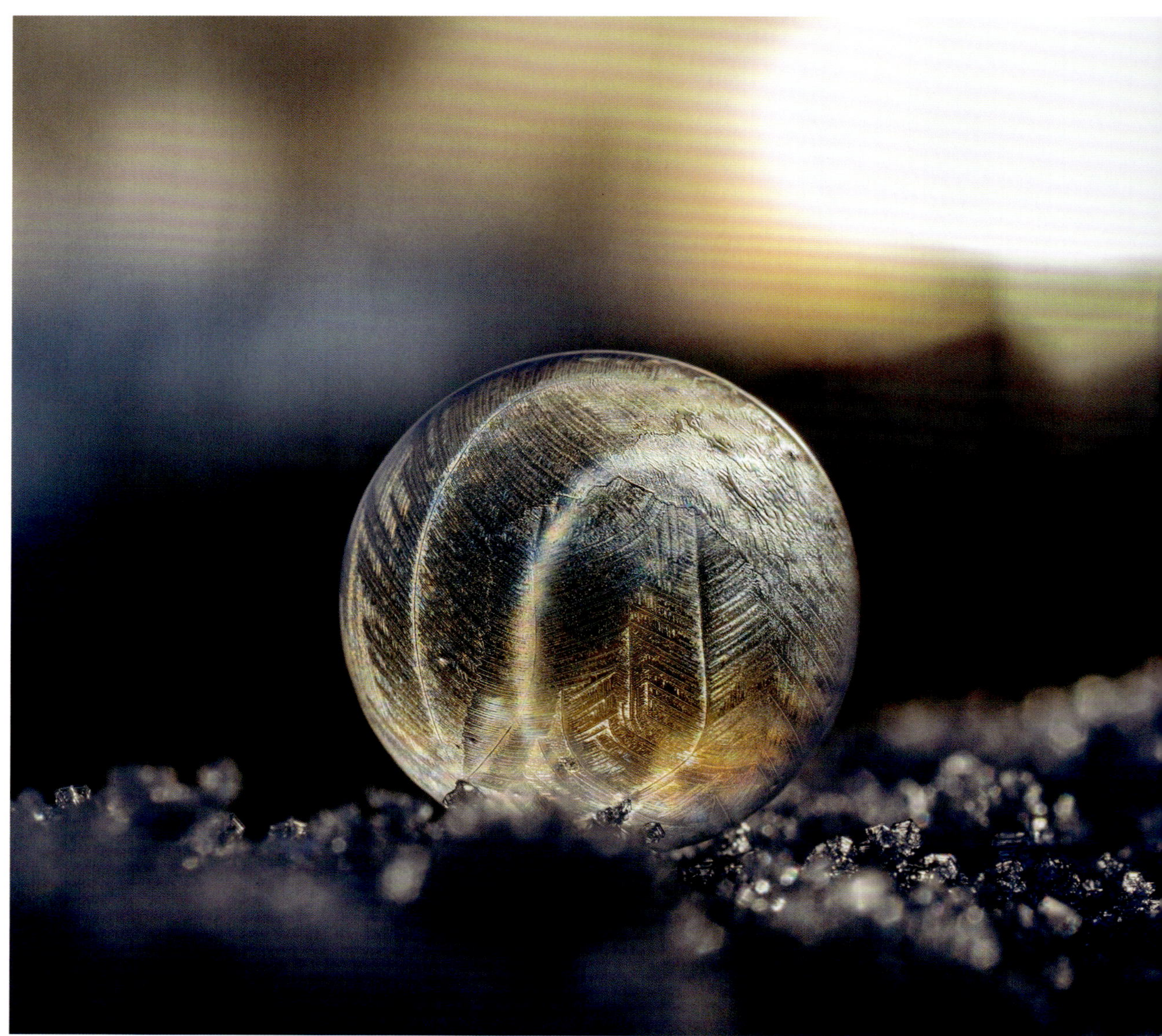

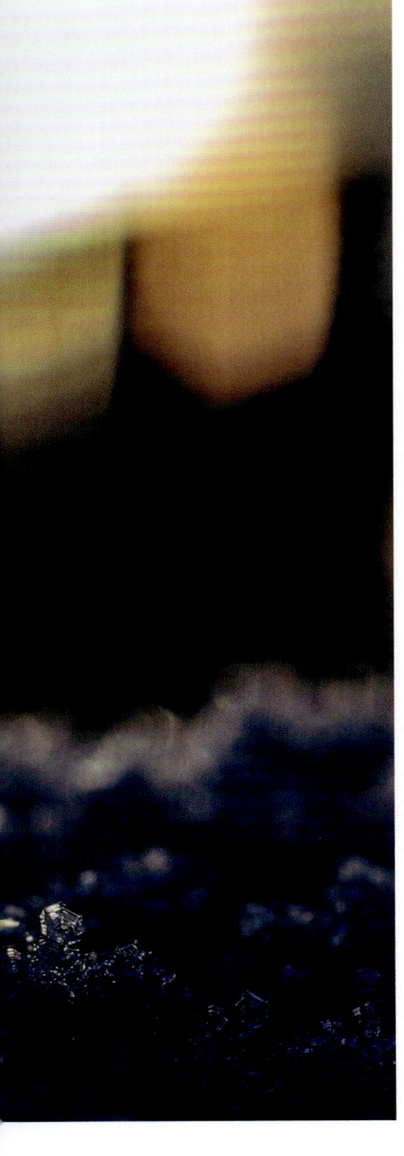

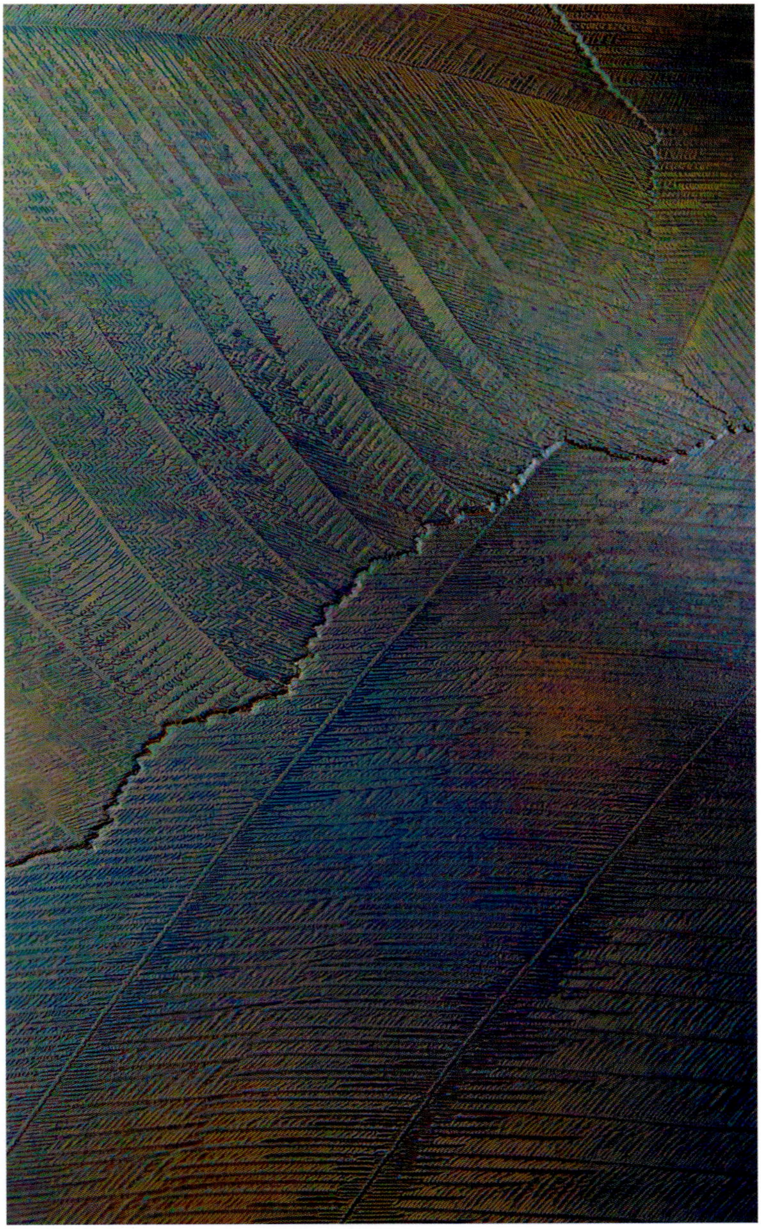

Left This frozen bubble was photographed in front of the rising sun on an early winter morning. It erupted into colour as the light refracted through the surface.

Above An increased-magnification macro stack reveals the hidden textures and details captured by the freezing temperatures.

Macro water drops

If you have a spare photo frame lying about the house, it can be used to create abstract works of art using water and a colourful material.

Step 1 Remove the cardboard mounts and any paper, so you are left with just the frame and glass.

Step 2 Place the glass onto two raised stands. I use food or drink cans, as they are the perfect height to place objects beneath.

Step 3 Place a small dish or plate below the frame with something colourful on top. This could be confectionery, coloured paper, flowers – whatever you like.

Step 4 Spray the glass with water from a misting bottle.

Step 5 Mount your camera on a tripod, angle it over the glass and begin to experiment with various viewpoints and compositions.

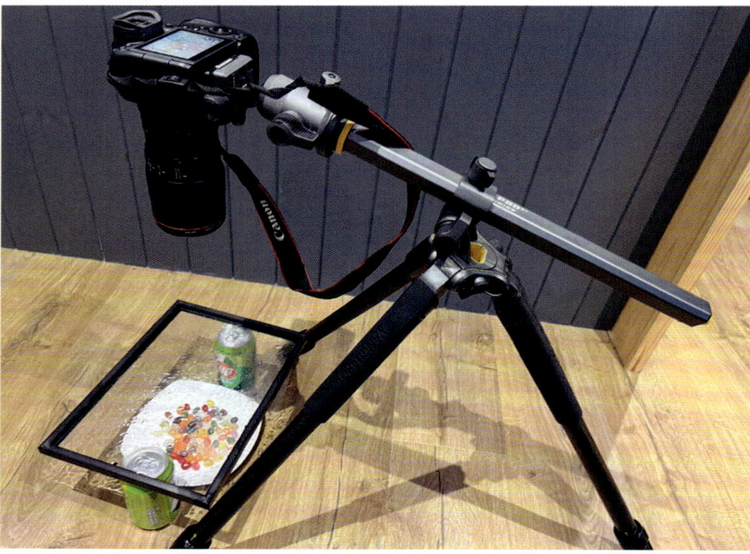

Above The camera is mounted onto a tripod and positioned directly over the frame. This can be tricky, so make sure everything is tight and secure before moving the set-up over the glass frame.

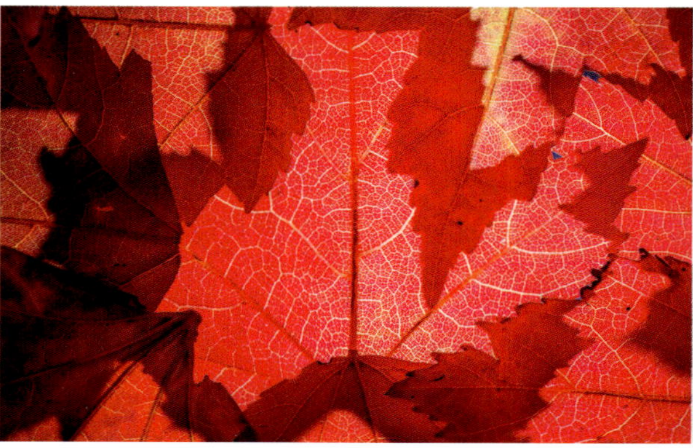

Try this

The frame and glass can also be used to photograph other subjects, such as these autumn leaves. By placing a light source below, you can reveal the hidden and intricate veins of a leaf.

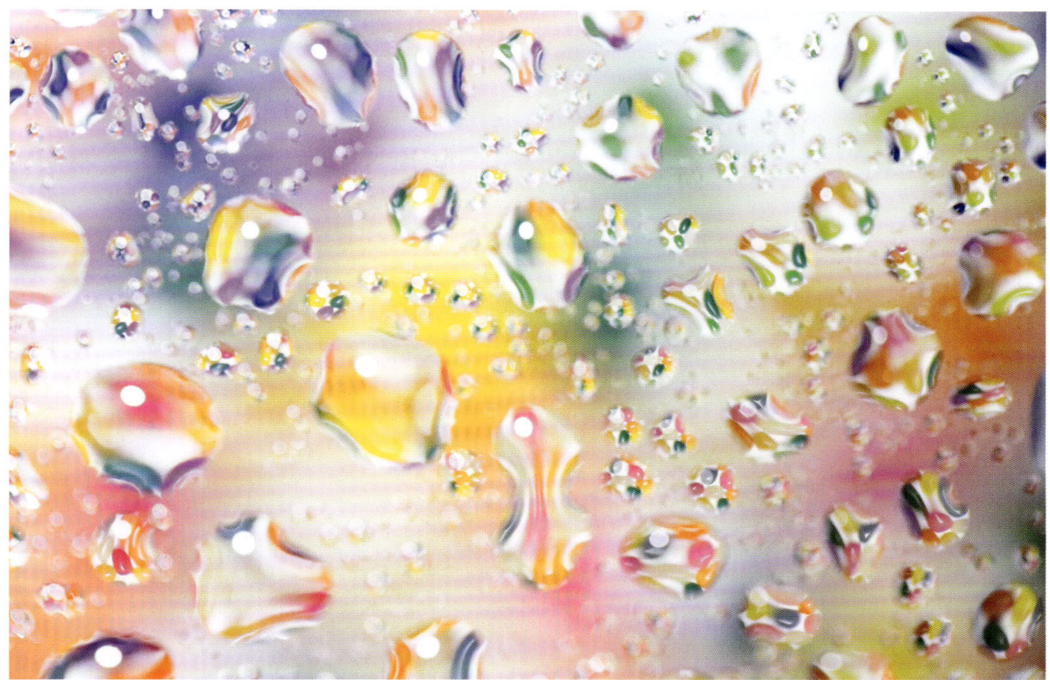

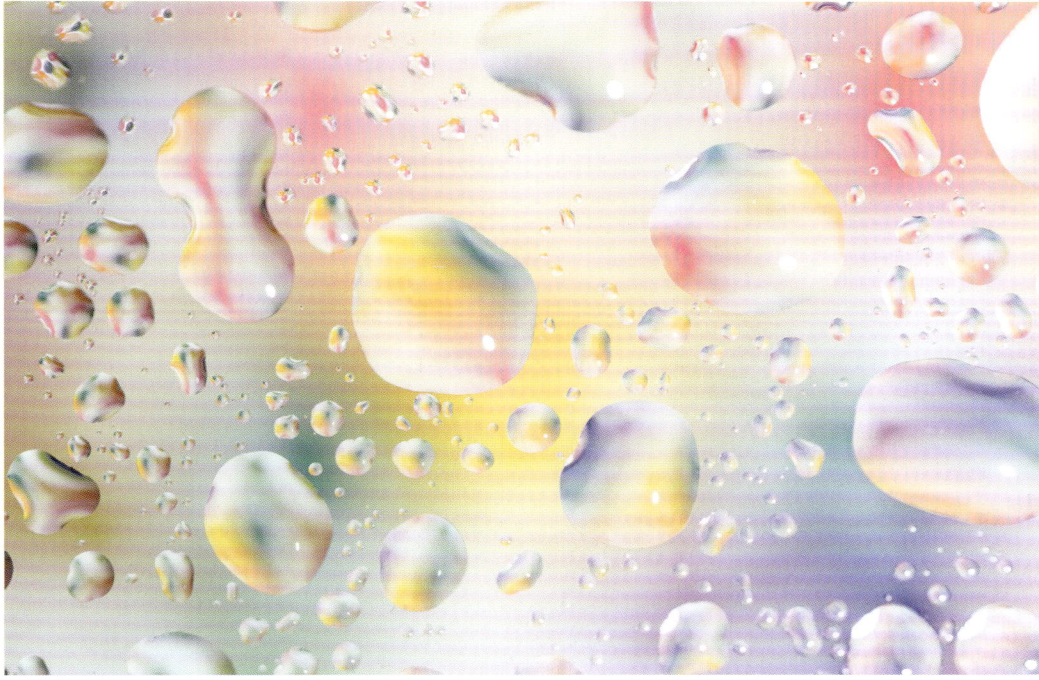

This page Try changing your point of focus. Focusing on the water droplets blurs the subjects beneath the glass but retains the colours, creating a smoother, more abstract piece.

Blend images together by making a double exposure

Most modern camera systems allow you to create artistic double exposures in camera without the need for editing software such as Photoshop.

Below and opposite are some examples of how I used double exposures to create a series of artworks called *Belle Ame (Beautiful Soul)*. In the days of film photography, 'sandwiching' two images together was tricky to do, but modern cameras have made this process seamless.

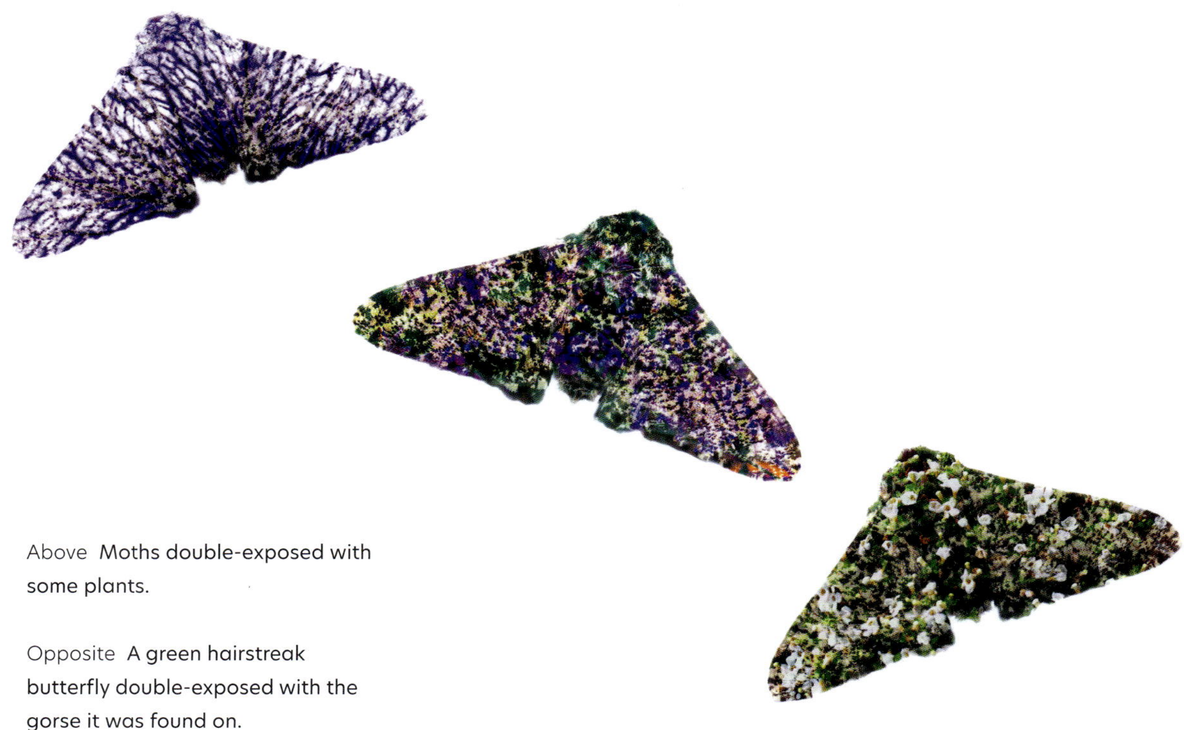

Above Moths double-exposed with some plants.

Opposite A green hairstreak butterfly double-exposed with the gorse it was found on.

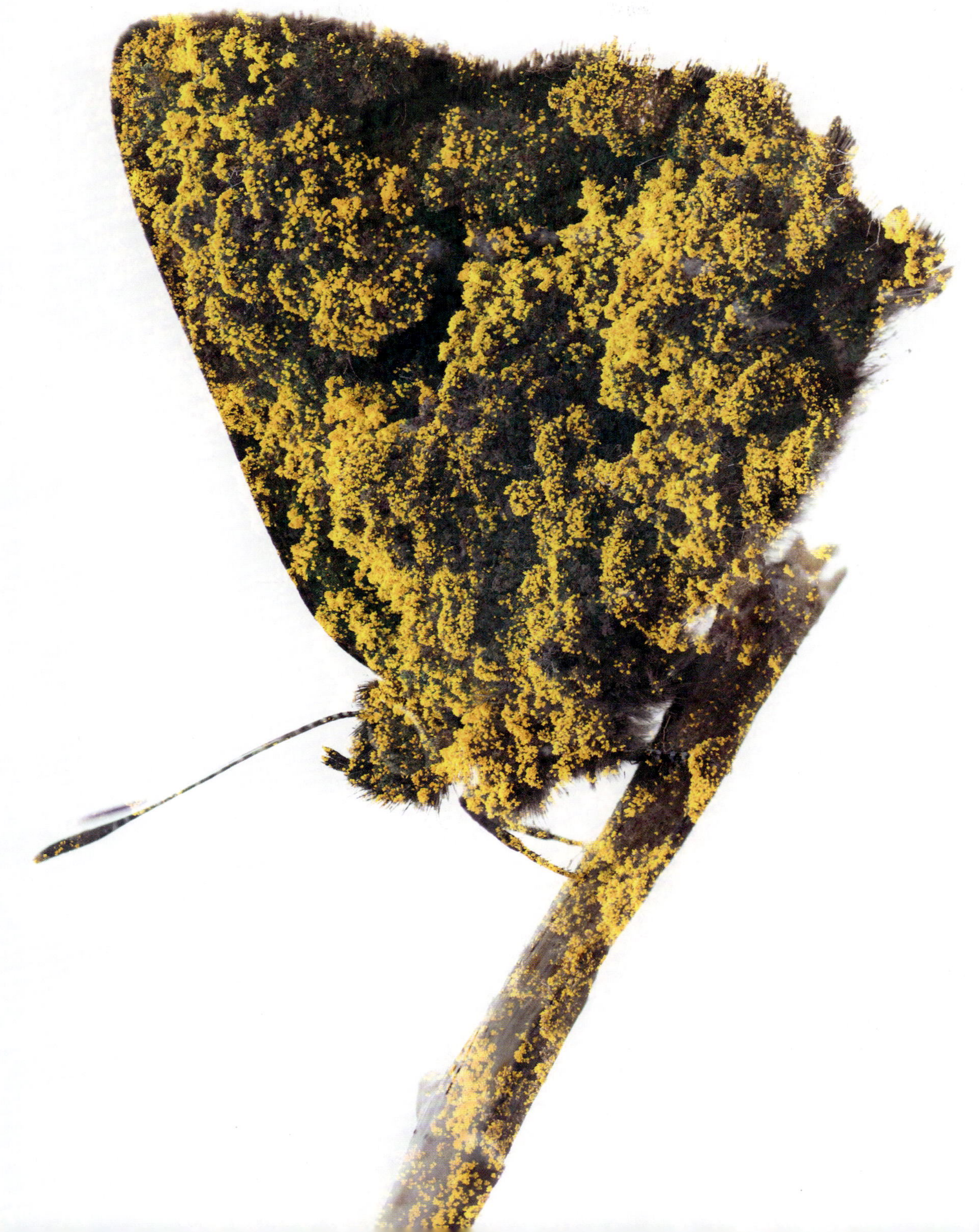

Photographing the subject

Follow these steps to create your own double-exposure photograph:

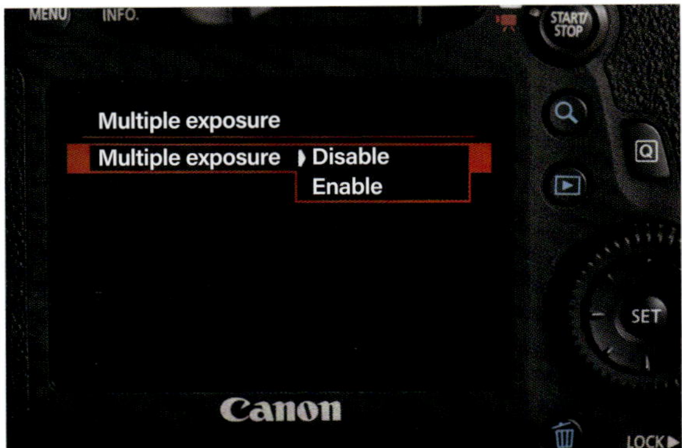

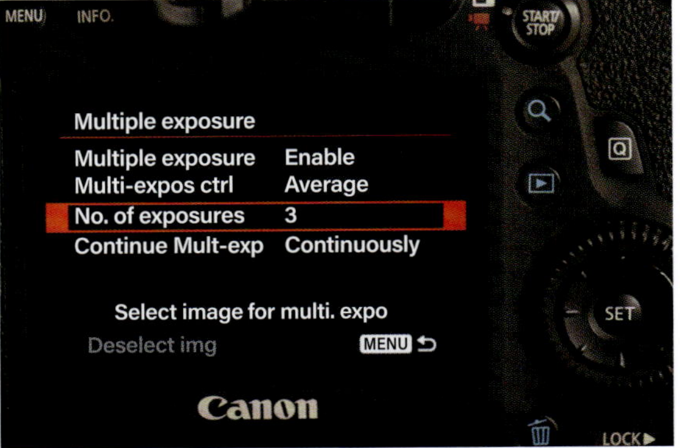

Step 1 Activate your camera's multiple-exposure mode. The exact name can vary from system to system, so check your camera's manual for specifics.

Step 2 Select the number of exposures you would like. For a double exposure you would select two, although most systems allow you to select far more.

Step 3 Take the first image, which will serve as your base. In this instance, the first image was of a woodlouse.

Step 4 Most camera systems will display your base image on the LCD or in the viewfinder with reduced opacity, so you can see how it will overlay on your second image.

Step 5 Take the second image, using your base image overlay to align it according to your artistic vision.

Step 6 Review your double exposure. Experiment with blending modes and the number of exposures until you find a style that appeals.

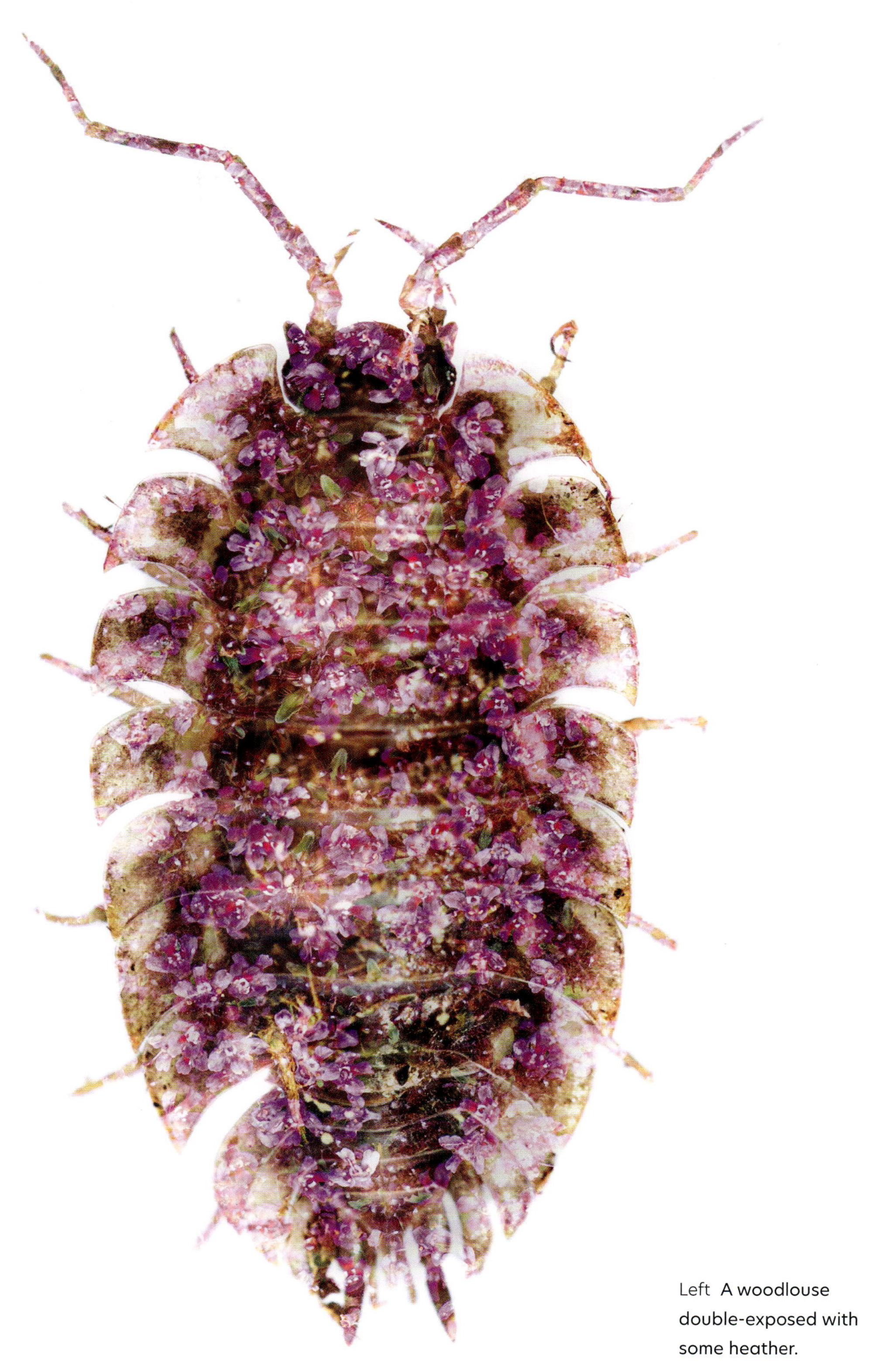

Left **A woodlouse double-exposed with some heather.**

Today's world is fast-paced, rapidly growing
and full of social and economic pressures.
We have an abundance of information at
our fingertips and 24/7 news on tap. It's an
information overload. Constant exposure
to this can lead to anxiety, stress and even
depression. Anxiety is a common human
experience, but it is important to note that in
some cases, worrying is an adaptive response
that allows us to plan for future change or
threats. However, excessive worrying caused
by information overload can be harmful to our
mental well-being, and we can become trapped
in a cycle of negativity. For me, photography
has provided a way out of that trap, and I hope
it can do the same for you.

Ten
NATURE PHOTOGRAPHY AND MINDFULNESS

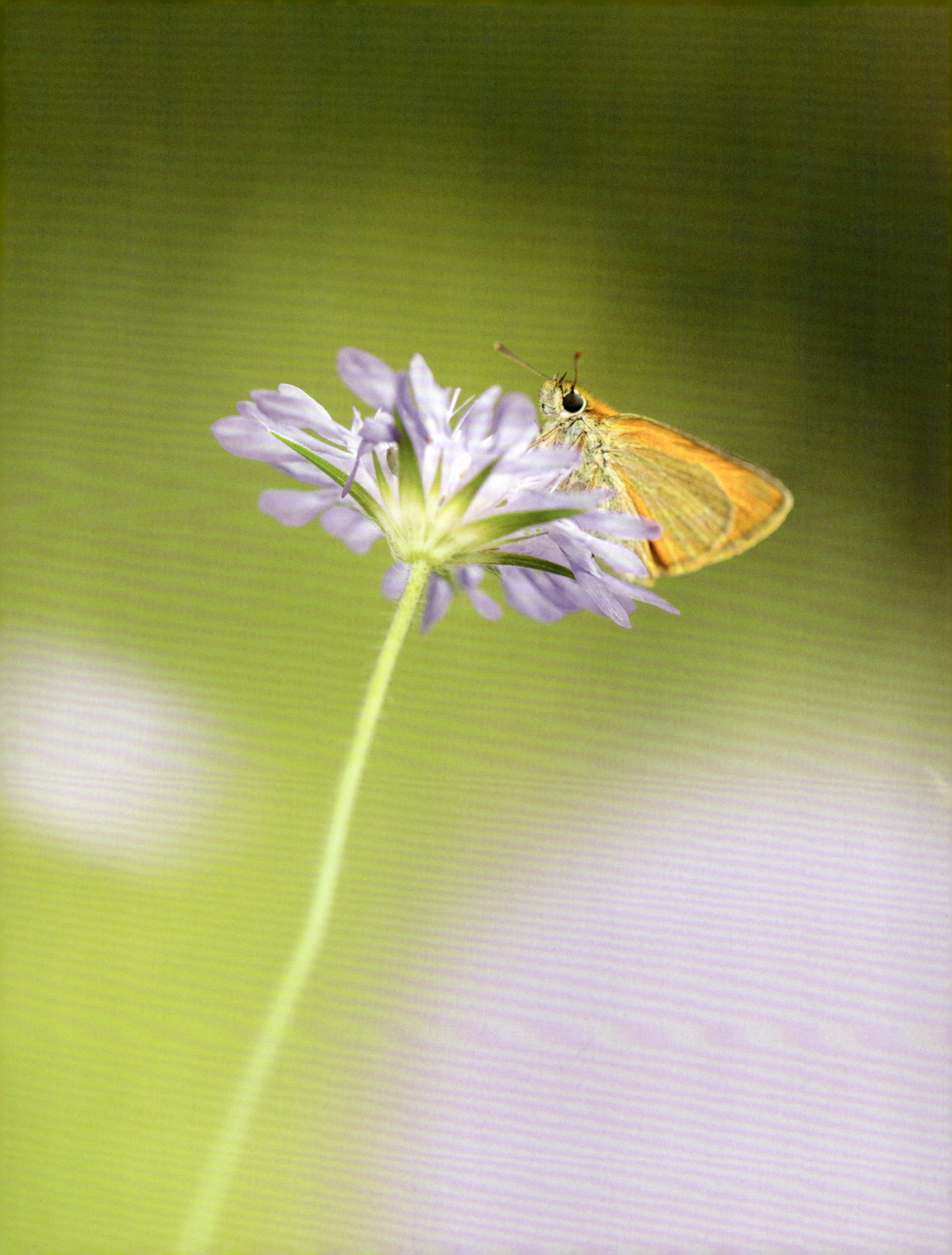

Rediscovering the natural world

In my late teens and early twenties, I struggled to make sense of the world I lived in. The ongoing pressure of trying to keep up with this rapidly evolving world and ever-changing culture left me feeling lost and questioning my identity and purpose. I was a prisoner in my own mind. I did what I had to do to get by, to fit in, to survive, but my mind was like the busy streets of New York, intrusive thoughts running back and forth like rush-hour traffic. Something had to give, and unfortunately it was my mental well-being.

Everything changed when I picked up a camera and immersed myself in nature.

The natural world can be discovered in your local woods, in the flowers in your garden, the birds feeding, the dragonflies flying, the wind, the rain, the landscape, the ecosystems – and even your body. The profound, positive impact being in nature can have on our lives, especially our mental well-being, has been well documented throughout history. How many times have you been told to 'walk it off' or 'go get some fresh air' when you've felt stressed? Our instinctive response to our mental well-being coming under threat is seemingly to 'go to nature'.

Right Often we can feel blue, but finding solace in nature can sometimes be a great antidote. This common blue butterfly was photographed against a subtle blue sky.

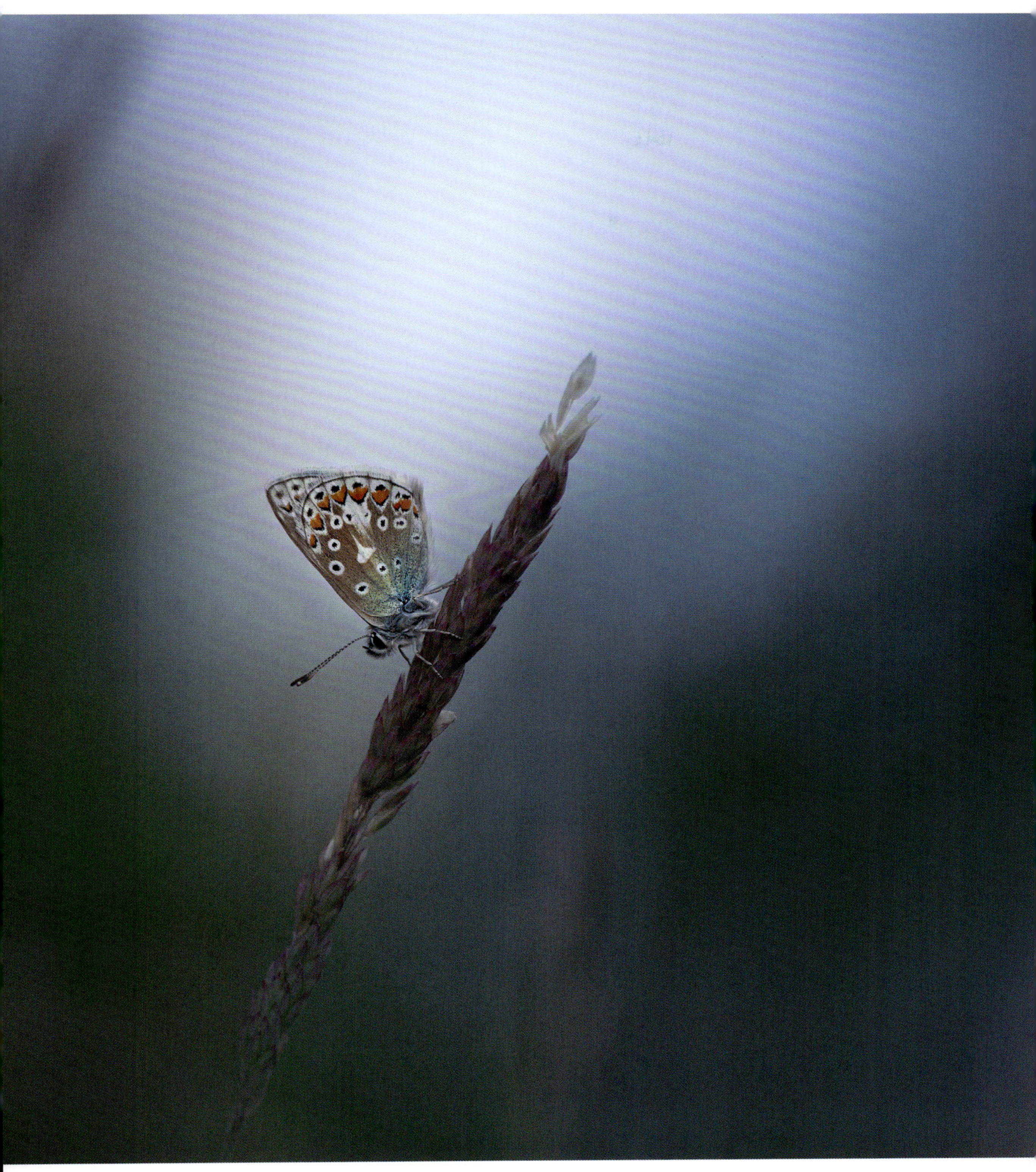

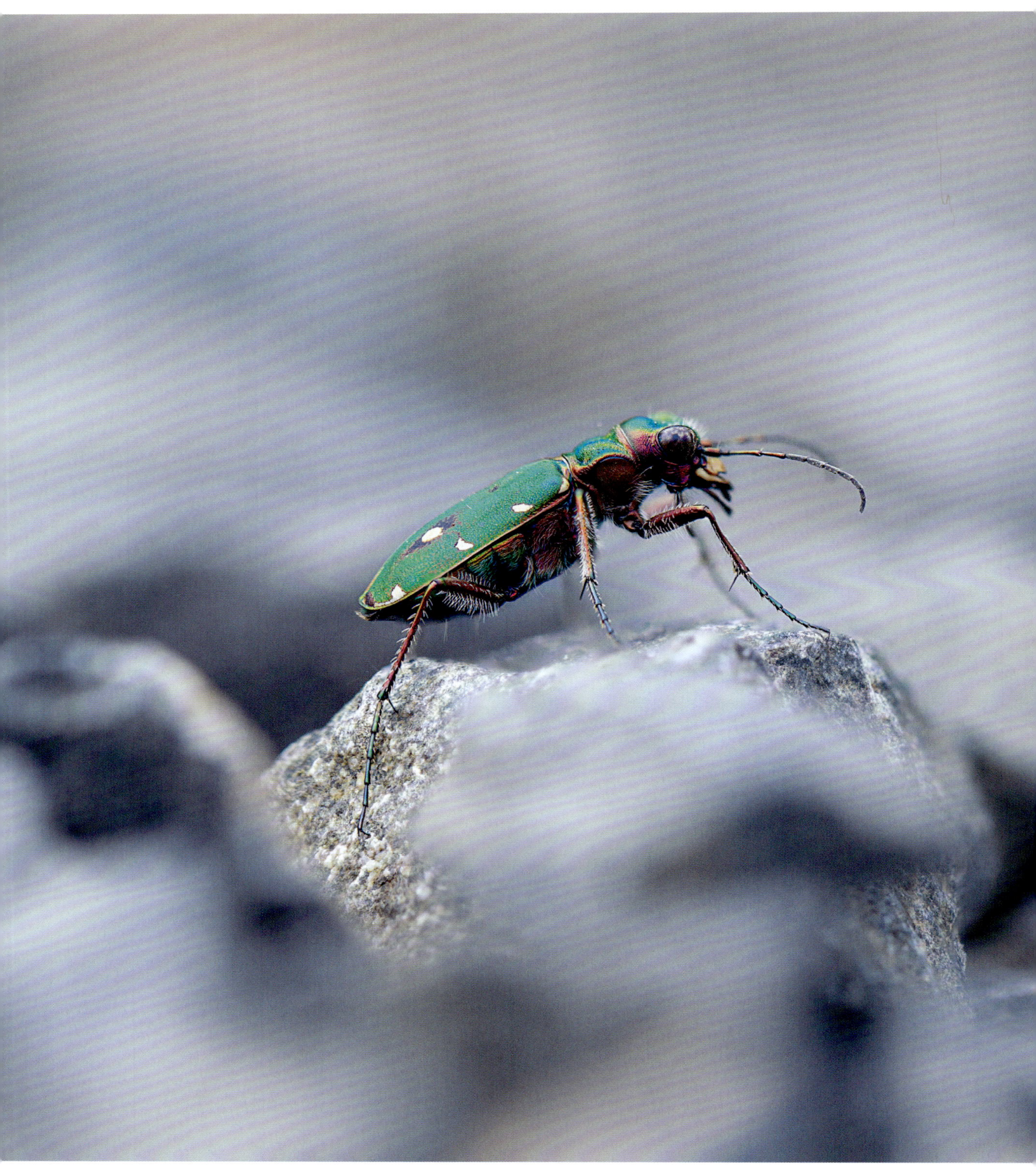

It has been proven time and time again that spending time in nature has restorative effects on our mental state. The sights, sounds and smells of the natural world can trigger relaxation responses, lowering our heart rates and decreasing stress-inducing hormones. Not only does spending time in nature improve our mental state, but it can also contribute to a healthier lifestyle and improve our physical well-being – all while strengthening our connection to the natural world.

Macro photography was the key that allowed me access to all these benefits. Something special happens when you look at the world through a macro lens; you are instantly transported to a world in which all your stresses and worries seemingly disappear. Macro photography also requires you to pay close attention to what is happening in front of your lens, so you are almost forced to forget about everything else, other than what you are trying to photograph. You are no longer focused on yesterday's arguments or tomorrow's worries. Instead, you are living in the present, focusing on the subject in front of you.

I can become lost in the world of arthropods, sometimes no longer taking photos but instead just observing these creatures go about their daily lives, unconcerned with financial constraints, politics or social media. I think we can all learn from these fantastic creatures. When you immerse yourself in nature you begin to disconnect from your busy mind and reconnect with wildlife; what you're essentially doing is practising mindfulness.

Left Tiger beetles are notoriously fast – they run around from one place to another and rarely stay still for long – but even they have to rest at some point. The macro world is a constant reminder to slow down.

Mindfulness is a skill; a state of conscious awareness focusing on the present moment. It is you being fully present in the here and now, recognizing your thoughts, your feelings, the sensations and your environment and allowing them to be. Mindfulness can be practiced in many ways: through meditation, breathing exercises and even photography.

Have you ever been worried or stressed, but suddenly a butterfly has fluttered past or a bird landed in front of you? I imagine your worries and stresses disappeared – even if just for a moment – while you watched that butterfly dance from flower to flower or that bird hop along the ground in search of food. The encounter may have been brief, but for its duration you allowed your mind a moment of calm clarity. Now imagine extending that feeling. Practising mindfulness means cultivating a deep and conscious awareness of the present moment, letting go of your worries and preoccupations. Serenity can be found in the natural world; we just have to open the door and find it.

When we combine the natural world with macro photography, we are invited to look closer, not just at the subjects in front of us but at ourselves as well. The macro lens bridges the world we see and the world we overlook; it becomes a tool for fine-tuning our conscious awareness. Each photograph is a moment in life paused; the world slows down and we narrow to that one singular focus, resulting in a profound sense of self-presence.

The more you get out there, the more mindful you become, and this can have such a positive impact on your day-to-day life.

Below A spider waits on a web, backlit by the beautiful sunlight at golden hour.

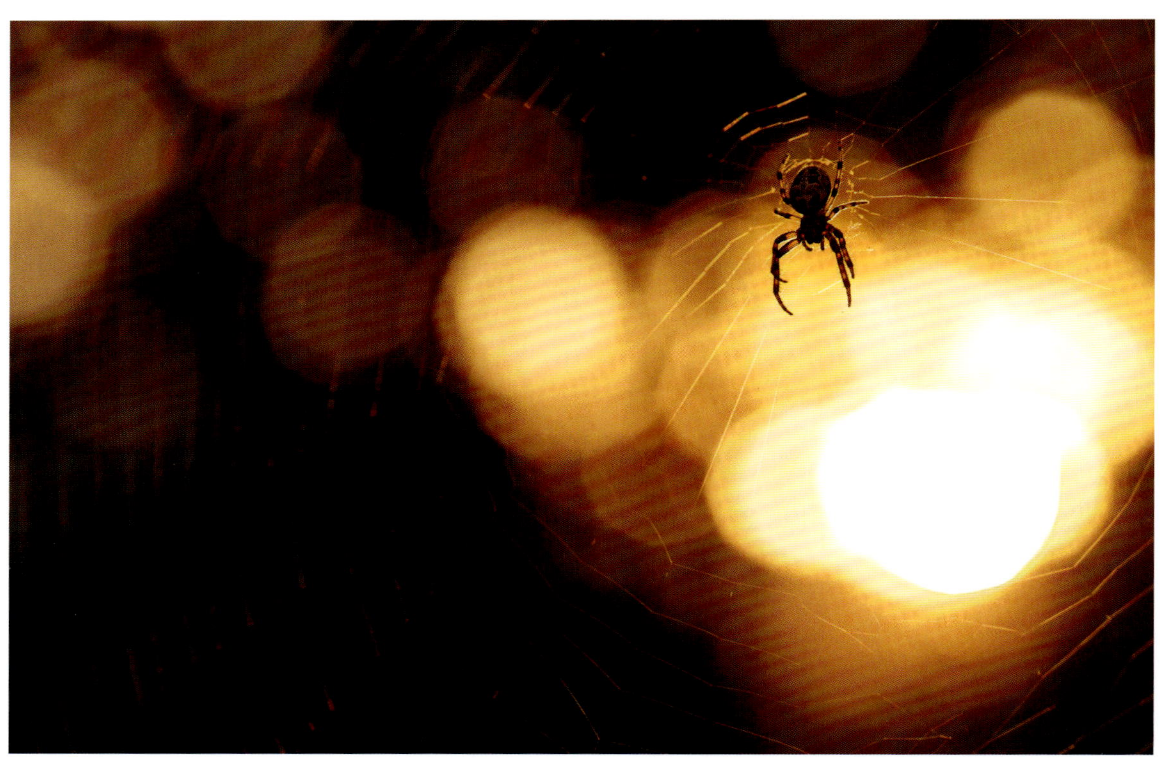

Right It's okay
to curl up and
rest sometimes
– millipedes are
great at it.

Below Ants
are great
community
builders; each
member of the
colony works
together in
harmony.

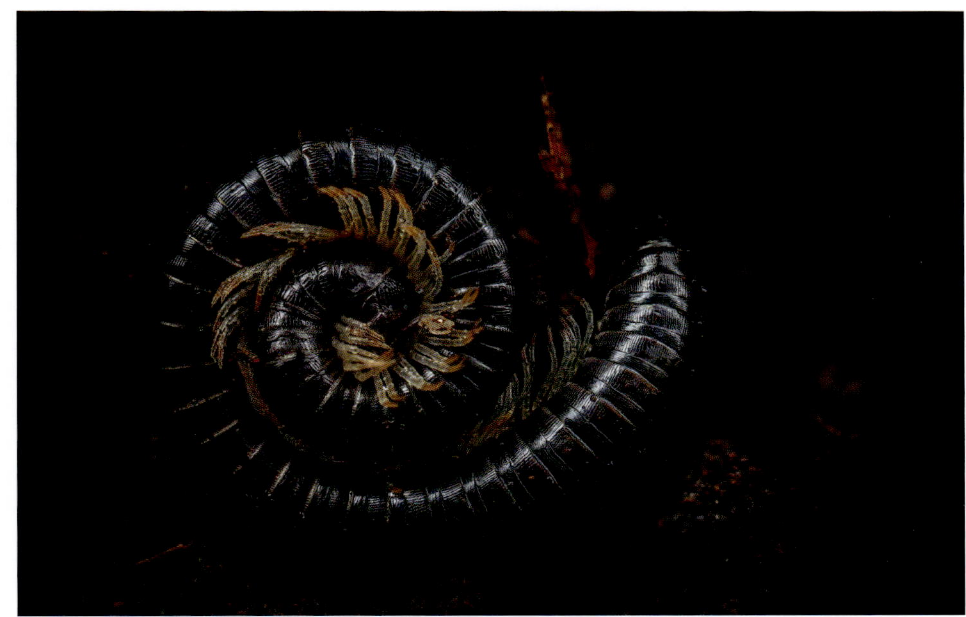

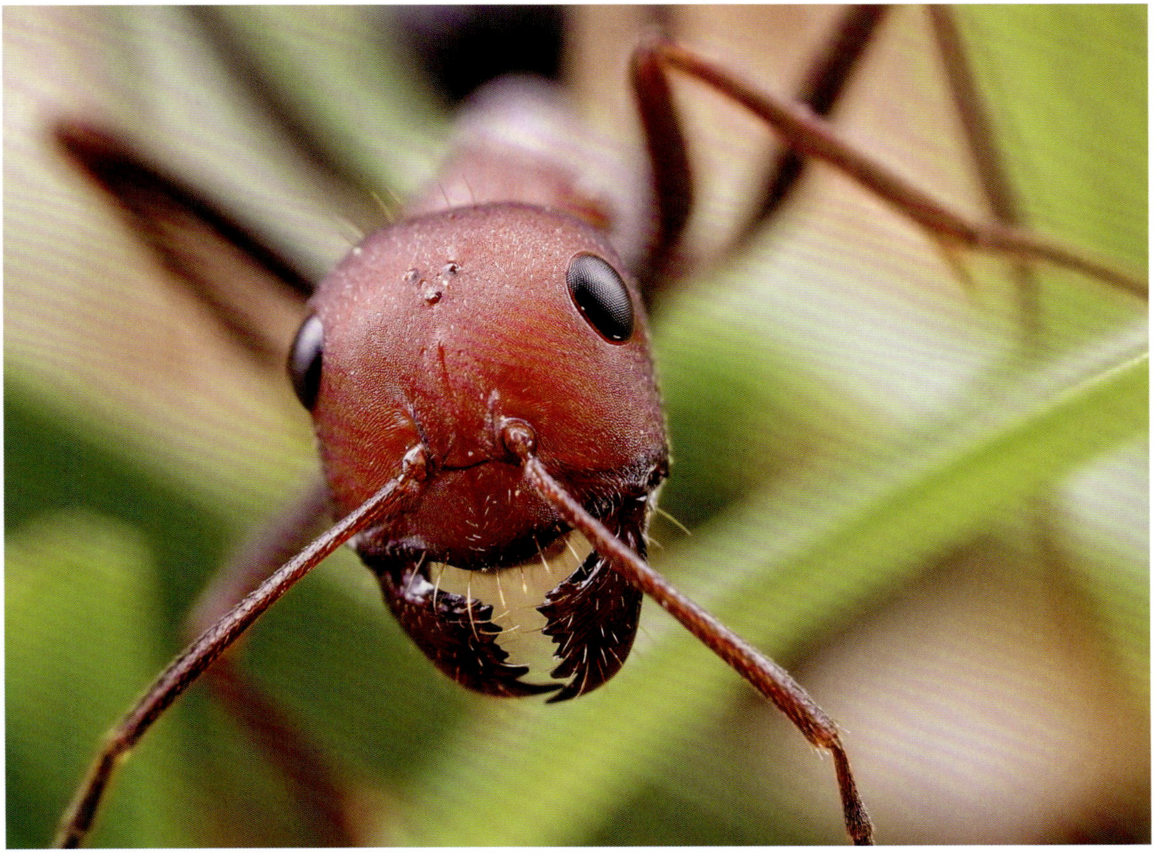

Index

Acknowledgements

I would like to express my heartfelt thanks to all the incredible people and organizations that helped me in bringing this book to life. It has been a labour of love and undoubtedly one of the most rewarding things I have ever done.

To my wife, Abigail, my partner in crime and best friend: your love and support while I locked myself away each evening typing away has been instrumental in the creation of this book.

To my awesome daughters, Jasmine and Amber: you two inspire me every day to live life to the full.

To my friend and biggest photography critic Chris Packham: thank you for your epic foreword and invaluable feedback.

A huge thanks to Richard, Rachel and the whole team at Octopus/Ilex who have worked with me over the last year to bring this project to life. The layout of the book is stunning, a work of art in itself.

To my friend Asaf, you've been my go-to ear whenever I was losing my mind from the hours and hours of typing and typing, week after week. Thanks for being there when I needed it most.

Big props to Ross Hoddinott for being a constant inspiration. Your work pushes me to think creatively and strive for compositional excellence whenever I bring the camera to me eye.

A special thanks goes to Phillip Schofield for hooking me up with my first camera many years ago. That was the key to all of this, kickstarting my passion for photography. I'll forever be grateful.

A huge thanks to Canon for producing the best macro kit on the market, which allows me to capture this hidden universe.

Thank you to Zerene Systems for letting me use their software to produce some of my case studies, a lifesaver in the editing process.

Thank you to my friend Ashleigh Whiffin and the National Museum of Scotland for granting me access to photograph some of the amazing specimens in the collection.

Thank you to Ailsa Miller for letting me hang out with her awesome pets – so many amazing creatures in one house!

And last but not least, thank you to Mother Nature herself for being the ultimate muse.

An Hachette UK Company
www.hachette.co.uk

First published in the UK in 2024 by ILEX,
an imprint of Octopus Publishing Group Ltd
Octopus Publishing Group
Carmelite House
50 Victoria Embankment
London, EC4Y 0DZ
www.octopusbooks.co.uk
www.octopusbooksusa.com

Distributed in the US by Hachette Book Group
1290 Avenue of the Americas, 4th & 5th Floors
New York, NY 10104

Distributed in Canada by Canadian Manda Group
664 Annette St, Toronto, Ontario, Canada M6S2C8

Design and layout copyright
© Octopus Publishing Group 2024
Text and illustrations copyright © Matt Doogue 2024

Publisher: Alison Starling
Commissioning Editor: Richard Collins
Managing Editor: Rachel Silverlight
Editorial Assistant: Stephanie Selçuk-Frank
Art Director: Ben Gardiner
Design: Chris Robinson
Senior Production Manager: Peter Hunt

ISBN 978-1-78157-924-4

A CIP catalogue record for this book
is available from the British Library

Printed and bound in China

10 9 8 7 6 5 4 3 2 1

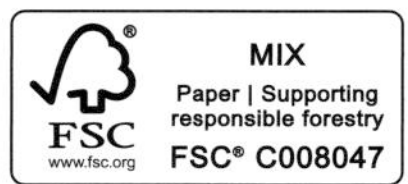